MAN DESCENDING

SELECTED STORIES BY
GUY VANDERHAEGHE

MAN DESCENDING

MACMILLAN OF CANADA / A DIVISION OF GAGE PUBLISHING LIMITED

TORONTO, CANADA

Canadian Cataloguing in Publication Data

Vanderhaeghe, Guy, date
    Man descending

ISBN 0-7715-9713-4 board
ISBN 0-7715-9766-5 pbk.

I. Title.

PS8593.A52M36   C813'.54   C82-094141-7
PR9199.3.V37M36
Originally published in hardcover 1982
by Macmillan of Canada
Paperback edition 1983, Laurentian Library No. 75

A PEPPERMINT DESIGN © RICHARD MILLER

Macmillan of Canada
A Division of Gage Publishing Limited

Manufactured in Canada by Webcom Limited

TO MARGARET
*in gratitude for her faith
and encouragement*

Some of these stories first appeared as follows:
"The Watcher" in *Canadian Fiction Magazine*
"How the Story Ends" in *Dandelion*
"What I Learned from Caesar" in *The Malahat Review*
"Drummer" in *NeWest Review*
"Cages" in *Prism international*
"The Expatriates' Party" in *Aurora: New Canadian Writing 1980*
"Dancing Bear" in *The Chelsea Journal*
"Man Descending" in *Aurora: New Canadian Writing 1978*
"Sam, Soren, and Ed" in *Journal of Canadian Fiction*

Quotation from Soren Kierkegaard's *The Diary*, translated
by G. M. Anderson, edited by P. P. Rhode, reprinted with
permission of Philosophical Library Publishers.

Quotation from "A Corner-to-Corner Correspondence" from
Russian Intellectual History, edited by Marc Raeff, reprinted
with permission of Humanities Press, Inc.

CONTENTS

YOU'RE ONLY AS GOOD AS YOUR NEXT ONE

100 Great Films,
100 Good Films, and
100 for Which
I Should Be Shot

MIKE MEDAVOY

with Josh Young

ATRIA BOOKS
New York   London   Toronto   Sydney   Singapore

ATRIA BOOKS
1230 Avenue of the Americas
New York, NY 10020

ISBN: 0-7434-0054-2
 0-7432-0055-0 (Pbk)

First Atria Books paperback printing January 2003

The Library of Congress has cataloged the Pocket Books edition as follows:

Medavoy, Mike.
   You're only as good as your next one : 100 great films, 100 good films,
   and 100 for which I should be shot / Mike Medavoy with Josh Young.
      p. cm.
       1. Medavoy, Mike. 2. Motion picture producers and directors—
   United States—Biography. I. Title: You're only as good as your next one.
   II. Young, Josh. III. Title.

PN1998.3.M398 A3 2002
384'.8'092—dc21
[B]

                                                              2001056000

10 9 8 7 6 5 4 3 2 1

ATRIA BOOKS is a trademark of Simon and Schuster, Inc.

For information regarding special discounts for bulk purchases,
please contact Simon & Schuster Special Sales at 1-800-456-6798
or business@simonandschuster.com

Printed in the U.S.A.

To my wife, Irena, who reinforces that old adage
that a great woman can give you a great life;
my sons, Brian and Nicky;
my sister, Ronnie; Irena's late mother, Margaret;
and my parents, Mike and Dora

The business of film is the business of dreams.

—*NATHANAEL WEST*

I don't think anyone should write their autobiography until after they're dead.

—*SAMUEL GOLDWYN*

Contents

INTRODUCTION *Movies Are Everybody's Second Business*

In fall 1999, entertainment attorney Peter Dekom embarrassed the hell out of me at an American Cinematheque tribute to Jodie Foster. After giving his welcoming remarks, he introduced me as his co-chairman by saying, "Mike is writing a book. For ten thousand dollars he'll keep your name out of it." Everyone laughed, but I cringed.

I've never thought much of tell-all Hollywood memoirs designed to generate gossip-column items, nor have I particularly admired the kind of self-aggrandizing books that aim to heighten the profile of the author. I love what Mark Twain said about writing autobiographies: "An autobiography is the truest of all books; for while it inevitably consists mainly of extinctions of the truth, shrinkings of the truth, partial revealments of the truth, with hardly an instant of plain straight truth, the remorseless truth *is* [emphasis my own] there, between the lines." That is why I have gone back and talked to some of the people who were there at different junctures of my career to find out the part of the truth that I might have missed along the way.

I've always felt that one of the danger signs of age is when one dwells on the past, so I don't do that; rather, I try to learn from it, which is not an easy task in the film business, because everything is constantly changing. Nevertheless, I've been counseled for years by colleagues to maintain a higher profile, to go out and tell everybody what I've done, so I will be "more valuable"—I haven't got a clue what that value is and to whom I would be more valuable.

But spurred on by a post-open-heart-surgery new outlook on life—which included giving up my passion for cigars—and the little part of me that wanted to become a history teacher, I decided to write this book to document some of the amazing changes in the movie business that I've seen firsthand over the last four decades, to debunk a few myths about how some movies got made, to give credit to some people who should have gotten it the first time around, and, selfishly, to make some sense of the journey. But rather than a compendium of my career, this is a look at the rocky road the movie business has traveled over the past four decades and how I absorbed the bumps. If anything, it was inspired by how different the process of getting a movie made and selling it to the public is today than it was thirty-six years ago.

Most filmmakers nowadays make twelve to fifteen movies in their lifetime. The most prolific actors might go before the camera in thirty films. As a studio executive, I've had a hand in more than ten times that many films. Some I had almost nothing to do with; they were acquired by executives who worked under me or over me and then released. On others I was the catalyst in bringing the idea to the studio, and I remained intimately involved in the process of translating the idea to the screen. Of the three-hundred-plus movies I've been associated with, I would say there are probably around one hundred or so really good ones, including eight Academy Award winners for Best Picture and seventeen nominations in the same category. There are another hundred or so I'd watch myself on a rainy Sunday afternoon. And then there are about a hundred for which my colleagues and I should be shot for thinking it was a good idea.

In Hollywood terms, that's a pretty good record. And there is more to come.

■

Fade in: Shanghai, 1940. I, Morris Mike Medavoy, am born to Michael and Dora Medavoy.

We lived in China until I was seven. My father fled Communism as a child, escaped Russia, and found refuge in Shanghai. But in 1947 he knew it was time to find refuge again. My mother was born in Manchuria, China, the youngest of fifteen brothers and sisters. As the Communists prepared to invade China, my father sold all our furniture and his prized 1940 Plymouth and loaded the family onto a Dutch steamer.

I knew we were in danger, too. The first movie I saw in my life was a wartime Russian propaganda film about the Nazis. The image etched in my mind was that of a woman holding two hand grenades at the battle of Stalingrad, jumping under a tank to blow it up.

Heroism is a big emotional kick, but even at six I knew I didn't want my own mother doing that.

▨

I have watched the movie business change many times over, in ways that I didn't fully realize until I sat down to reflect on how the thirty-six years have gone by. As a young agent, I carved out a niche for myself representing almost all the hot young directors of the early seventies, at a time when these guys were staging a creative revolution: Steven Spielberg, John Milius, Terry Malick, Philip Kaufman, Monte Hellman, George Lucas, Hal Ashby, and Francis Coppola. These roguish American auteurs created a cinematic style and legacy that continues to shape Hollywood to this day.

Then I moved to United Artists, where I was able to make movies with this new generation of filmmakers. UA was a company that pioneered the notion that filmmakers should have freedom from interference and an honest accounting of profits. In the four years I spent at UA, the studio won back-to-back-to-back Best Picture Oscars for *Rocky*, *One Flew Over the Cuckoo's Nest*, and *Annie Hall*, and finished number one among all studios at the box office for two of those four years. We also made Francis Coppola's controversial Vietnam film *Apocalypse Now* and put into motion Marty Scorsese's *Raging Bull*, a film that was later voted the film of the decade by a nationwide group of movie critics.

All of this happened at a time when conglomerates were buying studios to prop up their balance sheets. In the case of UA, the buyer was the insurance giant Transamerica, and the results of this purchase were so disastrous that four of my colleagues and I resigned en masse to escape corporate oppression.

When my associates and I left UA and formed Orion, we spent four years under the Warner Bros. umbrella, making us one of the first fully financed, autonomous satellite production companies to use a major studio for distribution. Today, every studio relies on two or three of these types of deals. Then we broke away from Warner and reconstituted Orion as a public company. For the next eight years, Orion championed films that the other studios rejected. Throughout the eighties, a time when movies needed to be sold on the basis of one line of high-concept advertising copy, we backed a string of thought-provoking films, including *Platoon* and *Amadeus*. We also formed a creative nucleus with talents such as Kevin Costner, Jodie Foster, Woody Allen, Gene Hackman, Sean Penn, Milos Forman, Jonathan Demme, and Susan Seidelman. We gave each member of this extended Orion family the chance to realize their unique, singular vision in films that couldn't be made at other studios.

I left Orion to become chairman of TriStar Pictures, which had just been bought by Sony, and I soon found myself at ground zero of a culture war: the Japanese were (supposedly) taking over Hollywood. A media maelstrom ensued over Sony's decision to hire the high-flying producers Peter Guber and Jon Peters to run the studio, but none of that affected me because I had TriStar to run. There I worked with whom the press commonly refer to as the biggest names in the business: Warren Beatty, Steven Spielberg, Sylvester Stallone, Tom Hanks, Dustin Hoffman, Robin Williams, Julia Roberts, Robert De Niro, Sharon Stone, Michael Douglas, Danny DeVito, Meg Ryan, and Denzel Washington. But I will always regard my greatest accomplishment at TriStar as pushing through the first mainstream film to deal with the then (and now) controversial topic of AIDS, *Philadelphia*.

After four years, a benign conflict between Peter Guber and me led to the end of my tenure at TriStar, and I set out to recapture the days of UA and Orion. I wanted once again to make thoughtful and provocative films in an orderly atmosphere, so I formed my own company, Phoenix Pictures, and raised enough financing to be the master of my own destiny. With the release of Phoenix's very first film, *The People vs. Larry Flynt*, I found myself at the center of a debate about whether this was a film about the First Amendment or the story of a pornographer. The debate jumped from the entertainment pages to the editorial pages. I also committed to back the first film that Terry Malick, my former client, had directed in two decades, a World War II story entitled *The Thin Red Line*. Even though the film was released in the same year as the hugely successful Steven Spielberg film *Saving Private Ryan, The Thin Red Line* proved that art can still be rewarded: it received seven Academy Award nominations, including one for Best Picture.

More recently, I backed the first major film about human cloning, *The 6th Day*, starring Arnold Schwarzenegger. It's the first film I've ever signed my name to as a producer—I've always felt that if you were in a position to give credit, you didn't need to take it. But things are different now, and some of my most cherished and personal projects, like "Shanghai," are yet to come.

≡

Hollywood is an egotistical world where everyone falls prey at one time or another. It's natural to want your fifteen minutes of fame in a business that produces more famous people than any other. Today, fame is like fast food: With so many outlets in today's world, more people than ever are looking to get their fifteen minutes of fame, but in most cases, it's over before they realize it. When I started in the 1960s, the media paid little attention to executives. The only thing the press cared about was movie stars. Everything changed in 1978 with the David Begelman check-forging scandal, which was Hollywood's Watergate and the subject of David McClintick's *Indecent Exposure*. Now there are at least three nightly TV shows dedicated to the business of entertainment, as well as dozens of weekly and monthly magazines. I wish I could say I was the lone executive whose ego never got the best of him, but I can't. I love what I do and I like to talk about it.

I've seen the movie business from three unique inside perspectives: I got my start in the agency business. I was a member of the team that ran United Artists and co-founded Orion Pictures, and I served as chairman of TriStar Pictures, all during a time of enormous creative turmoil in the movie business. Most recently, I've been running my own shop, which has brought me even closer to the movies I produce. As an agent, a producer, and a "greenlighter," I've worked with some of the most talented people who have ever passed through our business. The Academy Award winners and box-office champions like *One Flew Over the Cuckoo's Nest, Platoon,* and *The Silence of the Lambs* are the ones people ask me about. But some of the films that didn't win Oscars or gross $100 million have been even more rewarding, films such as *Coming Home, Raging Bull, The Great Santini, Mississippi Burning, Arthur, Philadelphia, The People vs. Larry Flynt,* and *The Thin Red Line.* These films set trends, started careers, broke barriers, and captured society.

Then there are some of those one hundred really stupid movies, made for the sole purpose of making money, films like *Without a Clue, Another You,* and *Under the Rainbow.* These movies were made by following some kind of trend—always a sure kiss of death for a studio head—rather than by trying to do something original, which is often tough but more rewarding.

In recent times, a handful of executives and filmmakers have succeeded by being able to grab the zeitgeist by the throat. That's great, and I've done it myself from time to time, but I'm always suspicious of the hot new thing. You can really get burned attempting to make films like the ones that worked last month or last year.

The best work often comes from the most original ideas: I had something to do with eight Best Picture Academy Award winners, starting with *The Sting* in 1973 and ending with *The Silence of the Lambs* in 1991. The success of these eight movies can be attributed only to William Goldman's often-quoted, partly accurate observation: "Nobody knows anything."

In the seventies, there were four Oscar winners: *The Sting,* which I helped put together as an agent, was written by a young writer out of film school who wasn't on the studio's radar screen. *One Flew Over the Cuckoo's Nest,* the first of three consecutive Oscar winners we had during the four years I was head of production at United Artists, had been rejected time and again over a thirteen-year period. The next, *Rocky,* was a labor of love written by an unknown, Sylvester Stallone, and it was done partly because the producers agreed to make it on a shoestring budget of $1.3 million and cross its profits with *New York, New York,* which we thought would be a sure hit. *Annie Hall* was the creation of Woody Allen, a virtual one-man band of a filmmaker who did his movies the way he wanted, turned them in to the studio, and then went back to his apartment to write another one. All of them were unusual fare for Best Picture.

By the eighties, my senior colleagues from United Artists and I had formed Orion Pictures. *Amadeus,* the first of four equally unlikely Best Picture Oscar winners for Orion, was a costume drama about Mozart at a time when MTV was all the rage. *Platoon* was Oliver Stone's ultra-personal film about Vietnam, based on a script that had bounced from producer to producer until it was finally put together by a man named John Daly. At the time, everyone—including me, I admit it—was skeptical and believed that movies about Vietnam had run their course. Nevertheless, at United Artists, we had two of the most powerful of the bunch: *Apocalypse Now* and *Coming Home.* But it was *Platoon* that became the standard for Vietnam films.

The final two of these eight Oscar winners came in the nineties at a time when, ironically, Orion was headed for bankruptcy. Nevertheless, *Dances With Wolves* won. More amazingly, it was a three-hour Western that was regarded as an indulgence on the part of Hollywood's newest leading man, Kevin Costner. (During production, in a reference to the notorious cash-drain *Heaven's Gate,* cynics dubbed the film "Kevin's Gate.") The eighth Best Picture, *The Silence of the Lambs,* was about a guy who ate people. The film ran the risk of being gory, so much so that Gene Hackman, who had agreed to split the cost of development with us, became squeamish and dropped out before the script was turned in. When Jonathan Demme made the film with Anthony Hopkins and Jodie Foster, it became a commercial hit, a genre-breaker, and the third film ever to win the five major Academy Awards—Best Picture, Best Director, Best Actor, Best Actress, and Best Screenplay—and it eventually led to a successful sequel, *Hannibal.*

▦

My parents' goal was for our family to settle in the United States, but they weren't able to get visas before our departure from Shanghai. Like so many other emigrants, my family and I saw America as a place where the streets were paved with opportunity and hard work. When we reached South Africa, my dad learned that our U.S. visas had been approved in Shanghai. However, there was no turning back, so my parents decided we would continue on to Chile, which accepted political refugees without much difficulty. We had to wait ten years for a second visa, during which time I grew up knowing America only through its movies.

▦

The first time a film swept the five major Academy Awards, I wasn't even born yet. It was 1934 and the film was Frank Capra's *It Happened One Night.* But the second time, I was sitting in an orchestra seat, celebrating the fact that one of the first movies I had worked on as an executive was being recognized as a landmark achievement. It was 1975 and the film was *One Flew Over the Cuckoo's Nest.* The third and only other time a five-Oscar sweep occurred was in 1991, for *The Silence of the Lambs.* I was again seated in the orchestra, but on this occasion I was seated next to disappointed executives who had worked tirelessly to promote another film I had put into production, *Bugsy.* As *The Silence of the Lambs* Oscars began piling up, I remember sitting back in my seat, finally beginning to understand—I mean really understand—the serendipity and irony of life.

Bugsy was one of the first movies I put into production at TriStar. It won the Golden Globe for Best Drama—often an Oscar bellwether—beating out *The Silence of the Lambs.* It got ten Oscar nominations, five more than *Silence.* Warren Beatty had pushed us to the brink on the marketing of *Bugsy,* to the point that a rift developed between me and Peter Guber, who was the chairman of Sony Pictures, TriStar's parent company. A win for *Bugsy* would have been vindication for me from all the ugliness that ensued after its release, but the gods of irony apparently thought it was more interesting that little *Silence* take the prizes.

The gods of irony wield a lot of power in Hollywood.

▦

*I attended an English-language school in Chile, but I spent count-
less hours in darkened rooms watching movies. Every Saturday, I
went to a small adobe theater on the town square and sat through
two, sometimes three, matinees, which gave me glimpses of the
American way of life and fueled my childlike fantasies. As a kid, I
was Robin Hood, I was Bogart, I was whoever was up there on
screen. Though I never thought of working in films, I often
dreamed about riding across the prairie with John Wayne, jumping
ship with Errol Flynn, and kissing Liz Taylor—all within the span
of a minute. At the movies I could daydream life as I wished it to be
and see how I feared it could become. Now, everywhere I go in the
world, I can turn on the television and see a film being broadcast
that I had some hand in getting made.*

▦

The movie business is probably the most irrational business in
the world.

These days, all the major studios and most of the minor ones
are owned by multibillion-dollar multimedia conglomerates such
as Viacom, News Corporation, Sony, Walt Disney, and AOL Time
Warner. When Hollywood was formed at the turn of the last century, the showmen were in charge. The studios were owner operated by the likes of Jack Warner, Adolph Zukor, Louis B. Mayer,
and Darryl Zanuck, creative people with the mentalities of river-
boat gamblers. It's startling, but without Jack Warner, there
would be no AOL Time Warner. Today, the lawyers, bankers, and
businessmen are in charge because the CEOs of the conglomerates that own the studios feel more comfortable with them, and to
some extent, this is a good thing. Given the economics of movies
these days, the studios could never survive as the small principal-
ities they were under the stewardship of the founding moguls.
But for the most part, the businessmen have done away with
much of the creativity that Hollywood was built on.

Studios are no longer incubators for movies. Their primary
function now is to provide a distribution and co-financing system
for films, leaving the making of the movies up to others. Movies
aren't seen as eleven thousand feet of celluloid with sprocket holes

on both sides and certainly not as the art form of the twentieth century; they are seen as "content." (And with the advent of digital, they won't be seen as celluloid at all.) "Content" isn't something that makes us feel but rather something that fits into the business plan of the company that owns the studio. This is true even at the company Walt Disney created: in the Walt Disney Company's annual report, movies are listed under "Creative Content."

Darryl Zanuck used to say that he put together an entire picture in ten minutes; now it can take years. As his son, Dick Zanuck, explains it, Darryl had a chart underneath a glass top on his desk. On it were the names of all the talent under contract to Fox. He would look and see which actors were available, pair them up with a director and a writer, and send everyone off to make the picture. That was the casting session. To land a major star today, first you have to beg the star to the read the script, then you have to offer to pay him or her $20 million, and then you have to plead some more and offer a Gulfstream V, a fully furnished house with worldwide satellite TV, a twenty-four-hour masseuse and—don't forget!—a cook. The fact that the stars are taking so much up front and on the back end has increased budgets and cut into the studios' profits. This has made the movie business unattractive to new investors.

Why do studios put up with solipsistic actors and their erratic behavior? Billy Wilder tells a story about working with Marilyn Monroe on *Some Like It Hot* that goes something like this: "There was an actress named Marilyn Monroe. She was always late. She never remembered her lines. She was a pain in the ass. My aunt Millie is a nice lady. If she were in pictures, she would always be on time. She would know her lines. She would be nice. Why does everyone in Hollywood want to work with Marilyn Monroe and no one wants to work with my aunt Millie? Because no one will go to the movies to watch my aunt Millie and everyone will come out to watch Marilyn Monroe."

Movies require months of preparation, filming, and post-production work, and until the process is finished you have absolutely no idea if it's going to work. Given how much films cost, this can be terrifying to the faint of heart—one of the most recent films I backed was $85 million plus another $25 million for marketing. The only formula for success in today's expensive, competitive marketplace lies somewhere between independent and interdependent. Movies need the leg up of a conglomerate, but they also need the freedom to be made by creative people.

Present-day studio owners think that the movie business doesn't make any sense, and they are probably right. They come from a much more orderly universe, whereas making movies is a recipe for chaos from start to finish. The new owners often nod in agreement and say they get it, but they don't really. They think they are dealing with people who are crazy, and they are partially right. People who make movies are passionate, often to the point of being crazy, which can be both good and bad. Some of the best movies of our time have been created by sending a madman genius to the jungle with a script, a group of actors, and a fixed amount of money, and then seeing what he comes back with. (So have some of the worst.) The entire movie business is governed by a set of rules that are absolutely irrational.

To survive as long as I have, you must learn somehow to play by those irrational rules.

So what makes a film work?

The truth is, you can never be certain because no two films are alike, which is part of the magic of moviemaking. A good film is like a symphony: it has *independent* movements working *interdependently*. Usually, it starts with the script. My rules for a good script are simple:

Do I want to turn the page to see what happens?

Do I care about the characters?

Does it strike an emotional chord?

Is it thematically interesting?

Is it unique?

The second film I worked on as a studio executive was *One Flew Over the Cuckoo's Nest*. What I liked about that brilliant script's ending was that it wasn't a compromise. Other studios had turned it down because the ending was too dark, but I liked that darkness. The scripts for *On Golden Pond* and *Driving Miss Daisy* were precisely these kinds of page-turners, but I let other factors get in the way of my criteria, and I missed out on being a part of two great films.

Often a good film idea is not the same thing as a good film. It takes a director with a vision to convert a good film idea into a good film. Choosing the right director often requires studio executives to refrain from their natural instinct, which is to pigeonhole creative people and ask them to repeat themselves. Early in my career I had lunch with the great writer Paddy Chayefsky and his producer Howard Gottfried, in the old MGM executive dining room where you could still get Louis B. Mayer's chicken soup. We were talking about directors for Paddy's script *Network*, and Howard asked me what I thought of Sidney Lumet. "Sidney Lumet to do *Network*?" I gasped. "What was the last funny movie he made?" In response, Paddy turned his bowl of chicken soup over on the table. "You're right, Paddy," I replied, "he'd be great." But I learned my lesson, and proved to myself that I had, when I fought to put Jonathan Demme on *The Silence of the Lambs*.

Casting is often the hardest part of putting a movie together. At Orion, when I suggested that Arnold Schwarzenegger be considered for a role in *The Terminator*, it was because of his force of personality. At the time, he had had a speaking part in only one feature movie, *Stay Hungry*, which we had done at UA. But I'll be the first to admit that I had no concrete evidence that he would be any good, let alone that he would create such an indelible character. To be honest, I also floated the name of O. J. Simpson for the same role. Casting is far from a science. In one situation two actors might be magic, while in a different situation they might have no chemistry at all. After Tom Hanks and Meg Ryan co-starred in the not-so-successful *Joe Versus the Volcano*, I supported putting them together again in *Sleepless in Seattle*. Even Nora Ephron, who is a first-rate writer-director, was skeptical. Not only was *Sleepless in Seattle* a huge hit, the two got back together a third time in *You've Got Mail*, also for Nora Ephron.

Putting together the elements of a film is a succession of best guesses. You have to trust your instincts. Not long ago, I had a conversation with the chairman of a major studio who said to me: "Okay, no more chick flicks—they aren't working. I don't care about dramas either—let somebody else make dramas. I'm just going to make event movies and genre pictures for teenagers." That mentality is not unique; it pervades the movie business today because teenagers go to the movies over opening weekend more often than the over-25 crowd.

Studio owners have been known to tell production people: "Make popcorn movies—that's what people want." The only definition I know of a successful movie is one that succeeds at the box office. Steven Spielberg, whose *Hook* I greenlit at TriStar, has directed and/or produced more successful popcorn movies than any filmmaker in history. He makes wide-audience movies because he connects to that inner feeling of amazement he had as a child and translates it to the screen. Trying to make popcorn movies is a recipe for failure because you spend all your time looking in the rearview mirror, pointing at what worked last time and the time before that. Today, with marketing people making or significantly influencing which films get made, this has become the norm, and it has resulted in the sameness of what we see on the big screen. The truth is that nobody knows for certain what will make a hit movie. Most of the times I've declared my intention to make a hit, I've ended up with egg on my face. I have a dictum that I try to follow if at all possible about getting people for a movie: Go directly to the talented people. If I could say that I had a talent for anything, it was a talent for knowing who was talented.

■

As a teenager growing up in Chile, I was so inspired by the music of Nat King Cole that I wanted to be a singer. Later, I even thought about becoming an actor. But as I grew older, the prospect of exposing the deepest parts of my personalities to total strangers began to seem like the equivalent of strolling naked through a shopping mall. When I finally gained a foothold in the movie business, I was so comfortable working behind the scenes that I never once second-guessed not trying to become a performer.

Everyone is a critic, and the movie business is everybody's second business.

I'll be using the men's room at the AMC Century 14 and someone will hand me a script. "You should make this script," the man will say—there hasn't been a woman in the men's room yet, but there will be—"It's a lot better than the last film you made."

How many times have you gone to a movie and said, "Geez, why did they ever make that movie?"

There are many reasons why one script gets put into production and another of equal quality sits on the shelf for years and collects dust. For starters, we're always very concerned—usually too concerned—with having a big opening weekend at the box office, usually so that we can justify our decision for greenlighting the film. The pressure for profits is enormous. I pushed for films like *Desperately Seeking Susan* and *House of Games* because I believed in the creative vision of the artists. But there is also a long list of films I'm sorry to say I put into production at both Orion and TriStar just to fill out the studio's annual release slate. Those kinds of films are often flops: *UHF* and *Heart of Dixie*. These are the kinds of films that have made the process tiring and caused me to become fed up. But invariably, I would return for another round because the good ones are magically rewarding.

People sometimes criticize my taste in movies for being too highbrow, by which they mean that I don't do the kind of movies that Jerry Bruckheimer and Joel Silver do.

Now, those guys are really good producers, and I like their films as much as the next guy. I'd love to be paid millions of dollars by the studio to make action films. *The Rock* was a wild ride and *The Matrix* was a superb film, but I'm much more drawn to films that are rooted in truth or history, like *Gladiator*. I don't look down on broad-audience films or even mindless comedies. I like them though I prefer wit to toilet humor. I've made several in both categories because I realize that I can't make films for myself; I have to make them for an audience. But as for my taste veering toward art-house fare, I hardly walk around in tweed jackets with elbow patches contemplating Fassbinder. I've been involved with many mainstream commercial hits—*Rocky, Arthur, The Addams Family,* and *Sleepless in Seattle.* I just look for stories that make me laugh or cry or feel. I look for stories that feel real to me, or at least plausible.

What I don't like about mainstream filmmaking, however, is when we are forced to make changes just to give the audience what it wants so we get what we want at the box office. Most recently this happened to me on *Urban Legends: Final Cut.* At a test screening the audience told us there wasn't enough gore in the movie. Though I'm very uneasy about this type of prefabricated violence that isn't part of a movie's story, we went back and shot another urban legend about a guy's head being chopped off. When we retested the movie, that scene was almost unanimously the audience's favorite. I'm not sure if we would have been number one at the box office on opening weekend without that additional violence. Do I understand it? Yes. Do I like it? No.

The two things most missing today in both movies and in the business of making them are subtlety and intelligence. For the most part, studios produce movies for the lowest common denominator. I try to avoid this herd mentality, but it's very hard. The margins in the movie business today are very small, and the tendency to chase the audience is always strong.

The audience may not know what it wants, but it certainly recognizes a second-rate product when it sees it. It ought to: it grew up watching second-rate stuff on television. However, these days what you get on cable television is sometimes better than what you get at the theater.

So what makes a good head of production?

Being a good head of production requires the blending of two separate instincts: art and business. A degree in office politics is also helpful. There is always a fragile choreography between the creative and the business sides of the equation. One minute you must be able to talk calmly to actors, who can sense fear better than any group of people in the world, while the next minute you have to translate what you are doing to a group of M.B.A.'s. It all comes down to combining experience and intuition, learning how to know which star will match with which filmmaker. Instinct in choosing movies relies on antecedent information, like demographics, cost analysis, and even who is owed a movie. It is the ability to take hundreds of very small considerations and unconsciously roll them into one. Instinct can't be taught, but years of experience can help you develop a feel for it. You also need to maintain a perspective on what is going on in the outside world to keep your bearings on what you think audiences will respond to on the big screen. Los Angeles and New York are only a small part of the world.

As a studio executive, you have to have confidence in your abilities, but you must also keep your natural arrogance in check. Young studio executives often have an amount of power disproportionate to their experience. I've always loved the story about the snot-nosed executive who was having a meeting with the late Fred Zinnemann, who had directed such films as *High Noon, From Here to Eternity,* and *A Man for All Seasons.* The young man asked Fred what films he had made, to which Fred replied, "You first."

It is the responsibility of a studio head to make films that earn money, but it is also true that most people in the movie business are paid too much in relation to their contribution to society, including myself. Does any entertainment CEO deserve to earn more than $100 million in a single year? Does any actor truly deserve $20 million to star in a motion picture? Does any writer deserve $250,000 to punch up some dialogue? This is not unique to the movie business; it's the American system of business. Just because someone is earning millions making movies doesn't make him better than a schoolteacher, someone who changes people's lives, though it often makes him or her more arrogant. Understanding this is essential to dealing with the egos involved in the movie business, including your own.

You also have to be prepared to have your heart broken, your mind broken, and your body broken—and then get up and fight a new day. If you have a string of movies that fail, it's easy to get thrown off your stride. This happened to me in varying degrees and at various times at United Artists, Orion, TriStar, and Phoenix. When this happens, you begin stumbling on hurdle after hurdle, and it becomes harder and harder to regain your balance. When you're not doing well, everyone thinks they know more than you do. The thing to remember is that even the best studio executive only has five good weekends at the box office a year—if he's lucky. Not the easiest way to spend three decades, but I wouldn't trade places with anyone.

Part of the battle comes from the business side. While there has always been a struggle between the bankers and the artists, this conflict has become more unhealthy today than at any period in the past. The business side often blames the creative side for being too close to agents and talent and agreeing to pay exorbitant prices, and in part, they are right. The creatives can take those relationships with them to the next job and leave the old studio stuck with the tab. But the concern for the creatives is that banker types have essentially taken control of the studios, and the only thing they have confidence in is empirical data. The danger with bottom-line thinking is that decisions based solely on business reasoning or by committees don't work. You can't shoot the deal. As the profit margins from movies have shrunk, the lines between art and commerce have become nonexistent.

But movies are art and there is no formula for art.

What drives me crazy is that people in the movie business are always looking for a formula, and that formula is usually based on what worked last week.

History has always been forgotten in Hollywood. For young people in Hollywood, history begins the day they are born.

I took the cast of *Whatever It Takes* to dinner at Mr. Chow's, a favorite film-industry restaurant, in spring 1999. The movie was Cyrano-set-in-high-school, so the principal cast members were all in their late teens and early twenties. We sat upstairs in a private room where a David Hockney pencil drawing of Billy Wilder stared down at us. "Do you know who that is?" I asked one of the film's twentysomething stars. She didn't. "That's Billy Wilder, the great director," I said. "He's made some of the best movies ever." I ticked off a very brief Wilder filmography: *The Apartment, Some Like It Hot,* and *Sunset Boulevard.* But the actress just smiled at me. "That was before I was born," she explained.

To some degree, the fault for this myopia belongs to my peers and me. I grew up revering the history of the business, but that isn't the case of young people in the business today. We're responsible for much of the sameness of movies today. The movie business has always run on a here-and-now mentality: Who's hot and who's not is all that has ever mattered.

But increasingly, in daily negotiations, fewer and fewer people care about even the recent past.

It's no longer "What have you done for me lately?"; it's "What can you do for me right now?".

≡

I am the child of survivors. My father had eight brothers and sisters and only three of them survived the famine in Russia at the turn of the century; my mother had fifteen siblings and only three survived. My mother, too, was the child of a survivor. When my grandmother arrived at the train station in Shanghai with my mother and her sister and brother after a grueling journey from Russia, she had no place to live and no money to buy food. As she stood there sobbing, a stranger walked up to her and asked what was wrong. She explained her situation. The stranger offered her the spare room in his house, and from that room my grandmother built a life for her three children. Later in my adult life, I discovered that there was in me a survival instinct that I have called upon time and again throughout my career.

If they could beat those odds, I've always felt I could beat the odds in the movie business.

≡

My Hollywood career started when a family friend wrangled a meeting for me with a man named Al Dorskind at Universal, who sent me to see the department head of the international sales division. I arrived for the interview wearing a suit and tie, ready to jump on a plane for my first overseas trip if need be. I figured I was the model candidate. After all, I spoke Spanish, English, and traces of Russian, Italian, and French. I was something of a citizen of the world with my overseas upbringing, and I had been schooled in world history and political science at UCLA.

Unfortunately, there were no jobs available in the international department.

In fact, the only job open to someone with my qualifications was in the mail room. Short of going to Schwab's and sitting at the counter drinking root beer floats until Mervyn LeRoy offered me a job as a production assistant, it looked as if the only way Morris Medavoy was going to break into the movie business was delivering mail, bicycling around the Universal back lot in 100-plus-degree heat or the pouring rain. When I started the mail room job, I did so with the indefatigable confidence that a promotion was imminent. My line of reasoning was quite simple: *Once they see how smart I am, I'll be out of here in no time.*

My rude awakening came when I realized that everyone working in the Universal mail room was just as smart as I was, if not smarter.

The $67-a-week job might have become a cliché—everyone from Michael Ovitz to Barry Diller to David Geffen got started in a Hollywood mail room—but my colleagues certainly weren't clichés: John Badham, who would direct *Saturday Night Fever;* Marc Norman, who would become the Oscar-winning screenwriter of *Shakespeare in Love;* Walter Hill, who would direct *48 Hours;* Steve Wolf, who would promote the first Beatles concert at the Hollywood Bowl and be killed shortly afterward for the ticket money it was thought he had; and Ken Handler, who was the model for the Ken doll, partly because of his looks and partly because of the fact that he was the son of one of the owners of Mattel. The one thing we all had in common was that none of us wanted to be delivering mail, so it shouldn't be terribly surprising that we weren't very good at the job.

We all had the same basic goal: to get the hell *out* of the mail room and *into* the movie business. Our agenda resulted in a great deal of incompetence, perhaps the most egregious being the accidental placement of a pack of important party invitations in the studio's international pouch to London rather than to the local post office. The party, it turned out, was being hosted by Lew

Wasserman for Joan Crawford. Though the invitations were eventually located in London, it was too late, and the party had to be arranged by a flurry of phone calls and telegrams to the invitees from Wasserman's secretaries.

Precocious and ambitious, my mail room colleagues and I were the source of many uncredited innovations at Universal. One day we all sat down and drafted a memo to the studio management proposing paid public tours of the back lot. A few months later the Universal Studios Tour was inaugurated—not that we were ever given any credit. Our particular group was so unique that it later inspired Iris Rainer Dart, who was married to Steve Wolf, to write a book entitled *The Boys in the Mail Room.* But, as anyone who started in any Hollywood mail room will tell you, the only good thing about the mail room is being able to reminisce about it once you have moved on.

I learned early on from a series of mentors four of the most important things in life: maintain your character, maintain your dignity, be loyal, and never stop learning. And I have never forgotten the apocryphal words of my grandfather on his deathbed: "You spend your whole life learning and then you die."

In this business, it's easy to confuse character with reputation. The great UCLA basketball coach John Wooden once defined character as what you *really* are, whereas reputation is what you are perceived to be. My first mentor was a man I met while we lived in Chile. Donald Decker ran a camp for eight- to twelve-year-old boys, modeled on the American YMCA camps. Being selfish wasn't tolerated, and Don's motto was "The other guy first." Through games and storytelling, Don taught us how to get along and work with other people.

Ralph Winters, a well-known casting director at Universal, hired me out of the mail room to help him cast the pilot of *Dragnet.* Jack Webb, the show's wily star, often took me out to dinner and, while downing double scotches, lectured me about the business. At the time, I knew virtually nothing about the inner workings of the industry and less about scotch. When I mentioned to Jack that I wanted to leave Universal, Jack set up a meeting with

Lew Wasserman, the legendary Hollywood powerbroker and head of MCA/Universal. Lew asked me, "So what job do you want?" "Yours," I told him. Since Wasserman wasn't going to step down for a redheaded twentysomething who had been out of the mail room for only eighteen months, I went to work as an agent for Bill Robinson, who gave me my first real break in the movie business.

Years later I was hired to be head of West Coast production at United Artists by Eric Pleskow, the company's president. Eric became more than a mentor; he became a great friend. United Artists was run by Arthur Krim and Bob Benjamin, the two men who instilled in me the importance of character and dignity. Lawyers by trade, Arthur and Bob bought the ailing United Artists in 1951 from two of its founders, Mary Pickford and Charlie Chaplin, and turned the company into one of the preeminent places to work in the movie industry. Eric, Arthur, and Bob were gentlemen filmmakers who set the standard for film executives. They started out as my mentors, and I became their partner. Together, the four of us and Bill Bernstein left UA and formed Orion Pictures.

Our group (reduced to four when Bob Benjamin died in 1981) worked together from 1974 to 1990 in one of the most unique executive partnerships in Hollywood history. Arthur was a silent giant in the film business with interests reaching into politics, arts and letters, and charitable causes. As a close adviser to President Lyndon B. Johnson, he actually lived in the White House two days a week. LBJ aide Jack Valenti, who is now head of the Motion Picture Association of America, told me that every major decision Johnson made was in consultation with Arthur Krim. Bob Benjamin was a quiet and contemplative father figure whose wit and wisdom were unmatched. Eric Pleskow, who continues to put films together as an independent producer, is a brassy and somewhat stoic Viennese immigrant whose practicality rubbed off on me. Bill Bernstein, who is now executive vice president of Paramount Pictures, has a brain like a hard drive, and he could come up with facts and figures, date and deal points at a moment's notice. We all learned from one another.

Arthur, Bob, and Eric taught me how to trust filmmakers. United Artists used a system of five basic approvals to greenlight movies: script, director, producer, budget, and principal cast. Because material was submitted through various channels, there was no particular order to the approvals. For example, if a producer brought the script in with a director on board, we would then turn our attention to cost and casting. Once the five approvals were in place, the filmmakers would go off and make the movie. As long as those elements remained, we didn't second-guess our filmmakers, but if any of those elements changed without our approval, then we reserved the right to shake down the producer and director. Never once did things become so out of hand that we fired a director. We also gave a fair accounting of profits to talent and didn't charge overhead on film budgets. In a business known for its shifty reputation, this kind of honesty and decency was unparalleled. Over the years, we stuck together through Oscar wins and box-office losses. We were always underfinanced, yet we almost pulled it off, and we left behind a long and distinguished list of movies.

I've always thought of a mentor as someone who can teach me something vital. Even after my career was well established, I found a new mentor in Gerry Schwartz, whom I met while forming Phoenix Pictures in 1994. Gerry knew very little about the movie business, but he agreed to be the primary backer of Phoenix because he wanted to expand his horizons. Because of that I, too, have expanded mine. We talk several times a week about business, culture, or family, and we often spend vacations together.

But the challenge for me remains: *How do you make interesting films that will support themselves in the marketplace?*

▬

The daily lives of the people at the upper ends of the movie business are centered on what happens inside of a large diamond-shaped section of greater Los Angeles that stretches from Culver City to Burbank and from Beverly Hills to Hollywood.

Nevertheless, particularly as I grew older, I wanted my life to be more than just the film business. I have a library full of books about history, politics, and culture, and I've read them. Movies are high profile all over the world, and as a result of my work, I've had "access," made close friends with political leaders both foreign and domestic, and sat courtside at countless sporting and musical events. Two of the highlights of my political involvement were my work as a finance co-chairman on Gary Hart's 1984 presidential campaign and my association with Bill Clinton, who invited me to spend the night in the White House a couple of times—which I did without ever having to become a soft-money donor.

In 1998, I was reminded of life outside of this glass bubble. Upon being named co-chairman of the Shanghai Film Festival, I invited my parents to make the trip with me. It was their first visit to Shanghai since we left. When we arrived at the airport, my father broke down crying. He knew this was the place that had saved not only his life but the lives of me and my mother. We had all survived World War II in occupied China.

In the four decades that my career has touched, my colleagues and I have been in the eye of several well-documented Hollywood storms. My indoctrination as a studio executive came when I flew to the Philippines to visit the set of *Apocalypse Now* and arrived to find Francis Coppola on the verge of madness, Martin Sheen recovering from a heart attack, and a film that had no end in sight. A different kind of storm occurred on another project I worked on with Francis: *The Cotton Club*, which became the subject of a murder trial. Then there were films that saw political battles accompany the release: Coretta Scott King took *Mississippi Burning* to task without seeing the film; the Guardian Angels had toilet seats covered in a bloodlike substance delivered to our offices when the gang-themed *Colors* was released; gay and lesbian rights groups picketed *Basic Instinct;* and Gloria Steinem went on a vendetta against *The People vs. Larry Flynt*.

The most personal of all the controversies came in 1992 with the tabloid scandal surrounding Woody Allen. I had brought Woody to TriStar. Months before *Husbands and Wives*, his first film with us, was going to be released, Woody became embroiled in an epic scandal. First, he revealed that he was having an affair with his longtime companion Mia Farrow's adopted adult daughter, Soon Yi Previn. Next, Mia filed charges accusing Woody of sexually molesting their young daughter Dylan. When the scandal reached its peak, I found myself sitting in Woody's screening room, listening to his side of the story, trying to get enough information to decide when and how to release the film. It was a moment I never want to repeat.

Years ago, I said to myself, "Don't peak too early. Life is, at best, a marathon."

I didn't understand then what a long career meant, but I knew I wanted to have one. Along the way I learned a couple of things:

I learned that you can rediscover yourself and make your life fuller.

I learned that the business of film is a business of manufacturing dreams. Movies are part of the world's cultural framework, and they are our nation's largest export, having recently passed plastic. We can't live without plastic, and I don't think we can live without movies either.

And I learned that a good film gives people from all walks of life that chance to sit in the same theater and share a dream. What I love most about films is that they are a telling of a story in photographic images that opens up new worlds both consciously and subconsciously. Films have left indelible images in my mind that have become part of who I am.

Even when I worked in the world of corporate competition and quarterly dividends, I always kept those dreams in the back of my mind. I've had to make compromises, I've been at the center of bad publicity, and I've been less than charitable on occasions. It's considered chic in Hollywood to be destructive and to gloat over the failures of others, and I'm a creature of Hollywood. But we all fail someday. It's easy to be cynical about Hollywood and about life imitating fantasy, but each movie brings new hope.

Good films can really change people's lives for the better, and good films can still be made.

This is the story of how we try to do just that, despite impossible odds.

1   *Making Sausage*

Until I got my first Hollywood job in the mail room of Universal Studios, I had no idea what an "agent" was, let alone that the formative years of my career would be spent agenting. Yet it was my agency days that established a network from which my entire career expanded. Working as an agent taught me how to talk to filmmakers, how to put together movies, and how to deal with strong personalities. Getting films made was like watching sausage be produced: the finished product was great but the process of putting it together was often messy.

But it's not what goes into a movie that's important; it's what comes out on the screen.

You're gonna have a hard time in this business as a Morris," Bill Robinson told me when he hired me to be an agent at his agency. "You got a middle name?"

"Mike," I told him. I was never crazy about my first name anyway. Besides, I had nothing to do with my naming.

"Mike . . . Medavoy," he repeated. "That works."

When Bill Robinson offered me a job as an agent, I was working in the Universal casting department, a job I had been given either because the studio figured I had paid my dues in the mail room, or because too much mail was getting lost. During my days at Universal, I was plagued with insecurities about whether I could actually get a real job in the movie business. Besides, Robinson's offer was also $25 a week more than I was making at Universal. The Robinson client list was composed of luminaries from old Hollywood that had fueled my imagination as a kid: Lloyd Nolan, Keenan Wynn, Van Heflin, and Barry Sullivan. Over the years, I ended up representing many of my childhood idols, including George Sanders, Wendell Corey, Jeanne Moreau, and George Cukor. These were old-timers who knew how to be treated, and they taught me how to get what they needed. But I found out that being an agent was an education into all areas of the business.

I knew from reading everyone's memos in the Universal mail room that the golden rule of Hollywood was relationships are the cornerstone of the business. One of the first things I did when I became an agent was to make a list of everybody I wanted to meet in the business. Most acquaintances are made at social functions and not by cold-calling like a telemarketer offering a free chimney sweep. However, since I didn't know anyone in power at the time, I didn't expect any of the industry's players to invite me to their parties. My sales pitch was simple: I would get them on the phone, introduce myself, and say that I just wanted to drop by and meet them. Then, after each meeting, I would send them a thank-you note and cross them off my list.

Once I called Otto Preminger, introduced myself, and asked if I could come by. When I arrived, his secretary asked me if she could take my raincoat. I assured her that wouldn't be necessary because I wouldn't be staying long. She showed me into Preminger's office, which was all white. The carpet was white. The curtains were white. Even his desk was white. The only splash of color was a glass of red wine sitting on his desk.

Preminger stood up from his desk, and I walked across the room to meet him. When I reached his desk, I extended my arm to shake his hand, and the sleeve of my raincoat caught the glass of red wine, spilling it all over his white desk. As I stood there watching the wine drip onto the white carpet, he slowly turned beet red. I half expected him to belt me. After he calmed down and blotted the wine stain with his white handkerchief, we had a pleasant meeting. As I was leaving, I remember thinking that he'd always remember me as the klutz who stained his carpet with red wine.

Years later, Preminger got even with me when he made a turkey called *Rosebud* for UA.

A year after I started working for Bill, he came into my small office and told me that he couldn't afford to pay me. We then made a handshake deal that, in lieu of a salary, I would get 50 percent of the 10 percent commission on any business I brought in. (Up to this point, I hadn't been allowed to sign clients because Bill insisted on keeping the agency small.) I immediately signed actress Diane Baker, which turned out to be a career-saver for me. She was coming off Alfred Hitchcock's *Marnie*, with Tippi Hedren and Sean Connery. I landed her the lead in a film called *Krakatoa, East of Java*, for which she was supposed to be paid $35,000. (Krakatoa is actually west of Java.)

The film went so far overbudget and beyond schedule that Diane ended up making close to $100,000—thereby raising my take to half of nearly $10,000, a hefty sum for a struggling agent. Had I not signed her, I probably would have had to get another job, which I wasn't terribly confident I could do. I had had only twelve months of experience as an agent, and very few people even knew who I was. Years later, when Diane lost her producing deal at Columbia, I gave her an office and an assistant at Orion. I was more than happy to pay back someone who had saved my career.

From an agent's point of view, however, the main problem with representing actors is that they need a new job every three months or so, while writers and directors typically spend a year on each film, sometimes longer. Actors also need more hand holding. Theirs is a profession where rejection feels (and often is) quite personal. By and large, they can also be a strange breed of artists. As Marlon Brando once said to me, "Can you imagine going to work every day and pretending to be someone else?"

I'll never forget visiting Dean Stockwell, another Robinson client, at his house and hoping that I never got that jaded about movies. (This was years before he became a reliable character actor with his work in *Paris, Texas* and *Blue Velvet*.) Movies had provided me with some of my fondest childhood memories, but they had scarred his childhood since his parents forced him to go under contract to MGM when he was nine. When I first met him, he lived in Topanga Canyon, which was still very rustic and undeveloped, and he hated working. He took five-year hiatuses from acting and made movies only for the money. I had such a pure love of movies, and I wondered what had soured him. I remembered actually wanting to be him after seeing *The Boy With Green Hair* in my youth. Now, I couldn't help but wonder how I really would have felt in his place.

▦

During the late sixties a new generation of filmmaking talent began to form. By and large, it wasn't welcomed by the studios, which were controlled by the old establishment. Jack Warner was still running Warner Bros., Darryl Zanuck was still in charge at Fox, and Adolph Zukor still tooled around Paramount in his wheelchair. Today, youth is regarded as essential and it is coveted. These days you sometimes have a better chance of getting a film made if you've never made one than if you have a track record.

But during the late sixties, a small group of young filmmakers banded together like a battering ram and banged on the gates of old Hollywood. It was very much us (the new guard) against them (the old guard). It seemed as though the same counterculture that marched on Washington, protested the Vietnam War, and hung out in the Haight-Ashbury was now making inroads in Hollywood. Under the old moguls, the town had become creatively dormant, but the young revolutionaries, influenced by European and American masters like Federico Fellini and John Ford, were waking it up and putting an edginess in filmmaking.

It was a movement I not only wanted to become a part of, but one that I wanted to help lead.

▦

As a young agent, I seized on the notion that the only way I would ever have any leverage was to sign up the young filmmakers I believed would revolutionize the business. The first person to set me on this road was a young actor represented by Bill Robinson named Tony Bill. Tony's acting credits included Bud Yorkin's *Come Blow Your Horn* alongside Frank Sinatra and a feature part in Francis Coppola's funky comedy *You're a Big Boy Now,* but his goal was to become a producer. Today, almost every actor is a producer, but back then, it was practically unheard of. Producers were guys like Ray Stark or major stars like Kirk Douglas and Burt Lancaster.

Although Tony was my age, he became something of a mentor to me because he had experience that I didn't. We often socialized together. Unlike most actors, he was more interested in discussing art and society, rather than the latest part that he didn't get. Tony constantly encouraged me to cultivate the careers of young filmmakers and to stop merely holding actors' hands. The common bond in my relationship with Tony was that we could help each other cultivate new talent. The only way he could become a working producer was to get movies made, which I could help him do, and the only way I could make a name for myself as an agent was to find new talent, which he could help me do. So Tony began introducing me to young writers and directors, and I did the same for him.

By the early seventies, I was working at Creative Management Associates (CMA) after it merged with General Artists Corporation (GAC), where I had landed after two years at Robinson, and I turned Tony on to Terrence Malick, whom I signed fresh out of the American Film Institute. I signed Terry by reading upside down— a must-learn for any young agent. I was sitting on the opposite side of Monte Hellman's desk, and there was a treatment for *Two-Lane Blacktop* on his desk, written by an AFI student named Terrence Malick. I thought it was pretty good—even upside down and even though Monte wasn't going to use it—so I called Terry and offered to be his agent. I got Tony to hire Terry to write Terry's first full-length feature film, *Deadhead Miles*. Tony convinced Alan Arkin to play the lead and the film got made—poorly. It was directed by Tony's partner, first-timer Vernon Zimmerman, and upon completion, it was deemed unreleasable by Paramount.

When Tony came across a talented younger writer out of UCLA film school named David Ward, he, in turn, asked me to help him "put together" two of Ward's scripts. Tony's company, American Biplane, had an overall deal with Warners to distribute its films, but first, Tony needed to raise money to buy the rights to the scripts. The first script was *Steelyard Blues*, which David Ward had written for his master's thesis at USC film school; the second was *The Sting*, which existed only as a pitch on tape.

When David first told Tony the story he had in mind for *The Sting*, Tony told him not to write anything. He simply pulled out his tape recorder and had Ward retell the story. Tony then went around playing the five-minute tape for anyone interested in investing seed money to get the script written. At one point, Tony asked me if I wanted to put up the money for *The Sting* and produce it with him. Unfortunately, I was too scared to leave a paying job, so I told Tony I was more comfortable representing the project as an agent—a decision that cost me several million dollars and an Academy Award.

▬

My campaign to be the go-to agent for the next generation of Hollywood filmmakers got a boost when I read an article in *Time* magazine about a talented group of aspiring young filmmakers emerging from college film schools. At the time, film schools were virtually ignored by the mainstream of the film business. Majoring in film studies was for people who couldn't find anything better to do after high school, or who went to college to avoid the draft for the Vietnam War and didn't want anything too challenging. Universities didn't take these programs too seriously. USC's film school was located in an old stable, and UCLA taught its film students in dilapidated World War II Quonset huts. But where others saw slackers, I saw filmmakers in the rough, and I knew that if I could control some of their careers, I would become an important factor in the business.

I immediately pulled out the phone book and began calling the students listed in the article to ask them if they wanted an agent. Right away, I signed a USC student named John Milius, who had collaborated on a short film made of pencil drawings with a bookish kid named George Lucas, who also became my client. Milius was something of a badboy mad genius in a teenager's body, but he was a good and fast writer with original ideas.

Soon I added Steven Spielberg, also straight out of film school, based on a 16-millimeter experimental film. Another of my promising clients was a director named Monte Hellman, who made *Two-Lane Blacktop*, one of my favorite road movies of the seventies. Carole Eastman, maybe the best of my writers, started out as an actress, became friends with Jack Nicholson, and then teamed up with Bob Rafelson to write *Five Easy Pieces*. I ended up selling her script for *The Fortune* for the staggering sum of $350,000 (1970s dollars) to Warren Beatty for him to co-star with Nicholson and with Mike Nichols to direct. Regrettably, she never found a workable ending for the film, and neither could the sure-handed Mike Nichols.

I tried to make myself something of a magnet for independent-minded filmmakers with edgy sensibilities, and my client list continued to grow throughout my years in agenting. At CMA, I signed the offbeat Henry Jaglom. I shared George Lucas as a client with another agent, and I represented Francis Coppola (along with CMA head Freddie Fields) when the deal was made for him to work on *The Godfather*. Later, at International Famous Agency (IFA), I added Hal Ashby, Phil Kaufman, Bob Aldrich, and veteran director George Cukor. At one point, I shared Michael Crichton with Lynn Nesbit, who was based in the New York office.

I had two requirements for my clients: that they be talented and that they be passionate about their work. Most shared a rebellious attitude toward films with conventional stories and a proclivity for European filmmakers like Antonioni and Truffaut, whom I had become close to professionally as well. Above all, these writers and directors regarded the medium of film as a religion. Nonconformity was the order of the day, which made everyone very interesting to be around. You never knew where the next crazy idea was coming from. As an agent who sold these ideas that shocked the establishment, I prided myself on being an innovator in my own part of the profession. The older clients, particularly Bob Aldrich, taught me how to keep studios honest with regard to directors' contracts. Aldrich, whose career I revived by getting him *The Longest Yard*, had a detailed list of controls he needed, and this became my template for the younger directors I represented.

The deck was stacked against change, causing the young filmmakers to act more like brothers than competitors. There was an overwhelming feeling that they were all in it together. Francis Coppola, who was the first film school graduate to make it big, was the big brother to the group. He established himself as demigod to the young set by coming out of UCLA film school in

1963, actually directing a feature film, *You're a Big Boy Now*, and then signing a deal with Warner Bros. for his company, American Zoetrope, to develop projects with young filmmakers. It was under that deal that I sold him Milius's script for *Apocalypse Now* for $15,000, plus another $10,000 if the movie got made.

Zoetrope was a haven for young filmmakers, and Francis functioned as their leader. Among the filmmaking banditos who ran with Francis were John Milius, Carroll Ballard, film editor Walter Murch, and George Lucas. Zoetrope was like a commune, where they all freely exchanged ideas and protected one another to the point that they even shared profits on one another's films. The most famous example turned out to be when Lucas gave Milius one point (or 1 percent of the net profits) in *Star Wars* in exchange for Lucas taking one point in *Big Wednesday*, which bombed. John Milius has earned roughly $1.5 million from that deal over time.

Francis, however, was always the first among equals. When one of the guys declared that since Zoetrope was a Marxist-Leninist organization, everyone should be allowed to ride in Francis's limo, Francis casually replied, "Some of us are more equal than others."

I handled my clients differently than most agents—and radically different from the way agents work today. My two main mantras were: *Make the deal work if the film is worth doing*, and *Get the movie made*. When I made Milius's first writing deal, a term deal at Universal, I asked him how much money he needed to live on for a year. He told me $15,000, so I rounded up and got him $20,000 plus a brand-new shotgun that was part and parcel of every Milius deal. Milius was a strict constructionist when it came to the Second Amendment: he wanted guns to field a militia in the event it became necessary to overthrow the government. At the time, there were executives making $20,000 a year, so this was a decent amount of money. In fact, when John told his father about it, his dad cautioned him not to take the job, theorizing that it must be dirty money because his son had never written a script that had been made into a movie.

What Milius and the other young writers needed was to get their work produced. The only way these guys would gain any credibility or power with the studios, and therefore make any real money, was if their work made it to the screen. I told them to ignore the big-splash announcements in the trades about some unknown writer getting $50,000 for a script because often those guys were never heard from again. I didn't want clients who felt like lottery winners when I got them a job; I wanted filmmakers who wanted to build careers.

I was a solid agent, but negotiating the fine points of a deal wasn't my strong suit, and it usually bored me. I found the deal, introduced the people, and then helped package the movie to get it made. If I thought we could get the movie made faster, I'd make almost any deal the studio wanted. The two guys who were best in negotiating when I was at CMA were Jerry Steiner and a twenty-two-year-old go-getter named Jeff Berg, who had an instinct for the kill that I never had. Jeff was the pet of CMA head Freddie Fields, the superagent of his day, and his talent for pushing through deals that studios weren't even sure they wanted to make took him far in the business; in fact, he is now the chairman of ICM, which is what CMA became after it merged with IFA.

There was a slight arrogance to the way I operated, which was not a trait that is conducive to working as a Hollywood agent. At the time, it was one of the only ways to mask my shyness. This attitude both helped and hurt me, and it ultimately even led me to abandon Steven Spielberg as a client.

≡

One afternoon Spielberg was sitting in my office, his small frame barely taking up any space in the chair, his words accented by a nasal twang. At the time, he was under contract at Universal, making episodic TV and TV movies for very little money. Universal was a schlockhouse in the feature film department at the time—the studio's idea of art was its upcoming film *Airport*—and I had recently pulled another client, Phil Kaufman, out of a contract there. I wanted to get Spielberg out, too. I was convinced that if Spielberg stayed at Universal, his career would amount to nothing.

"Look," I told Steven, "if you ever want to do an interesting movie, you're not going to do it there. All they're doing is movies like *Airport*. If you stay there, your career will be doomed."

"They gave me my start," he protested. "Sid Sheinberg is my friend." Sheinberg had signed Spielberg on the basis of a short film, *Amblin'*, and Steven regarded him as a mentor. "I can't leave there; I have many friends there. Besides, I need the money."

"You're crazy," I insisted. "Your career is doomed, and I can't represent anyone whose career is going to be over before it gets started." I was playing my trump card, trying to force my point and gambling on the outcome.

"Mike, I can't do it," he muttered.

"Okay," I declared. "I can't represent you, and I'm giving you to someone else in the agency."

His voice became filled with anger. "No, wait . . . you can't do that. How would you like that done to you?"

"I'm absolutely going to do it. As a matter of fact, just to prove it to you, I want you to get up and walk down the hall with me. I'm going to introduce you to your new agent right now."

Steven looked shell-shocked. Without saying a word, he got up and followed me to Dick Sheperd's office. Dick was the head of CMA's talent department. "Dick," I said, "I want you to meet your new client. He is a very talented director. He wants to remain at Universal, and you are very friendly with the Universal guys. You may be able to do something for his career there that I can't."

I turned and walked back to my office, leaving Steven Spielberg standing in the doorway, staring at Dick Sheperd. As arrogant as I was, I expected Steven to be back in my office within minutes, pleading with me to get him out of his deal with Universal, but he never came back.

History obviously proved me wrong—to put it mildly.

Steven ended up making his home at Universal. His first feature film there was *Duel*, but over time he delivered them *Jaws*, *E.T.*, *Jurassic Park*, and *Schindler's List*. His career didn't end by staying at Universal.

Looking back, I'm just glad this wasn't the defining point of my career, but rather another part of my learning curve. Maybe I wasn't as smart as I thought I was. This was the lesson that taught me that arrogance is one of the deadliest sins in Hollywood. I learned to be humble the hard way. Ironically, years later

Spielberg said in an interview that he should have left Universal early on because it might have caused him to make more interesting films at a younger age.

I guess everything turned out fine for both of us. We even worked together on a film, *Hook*.

■

Today, studios have become more content to act as banks, distributors, and copyright holders for films. They often abdicate the responsibility of picking and choosing the elements for those films to agents. But when I was an agent in the late sixties and early seventies, I had to be creative with my packages to get the studios to notice them. It was the only way I could really be involved in what made it to the screen.

Freddie Fields and David Begelman, the co-heads of CMA, taught me that being a good agent is usually synonymous with being a good packager. They taught me that agenting wasn't about selling actors, writers, and directors individually; it was about putting the pieces together and handing them to the studio so that all the executives had to do was nod their heads yes. While I packaged some duds, like Steelyard Blues, *four of my favorite movies to this day are packages I had a hand in:* The Getaway, The Sting, Young Frankenstein, *and* Jaws.

Learning how to package would prove to be critical when I became a studio executive. The three simple rules of packaging are: Writers get directors; directors get actors; and the right combination of all three gets the money.

■

There were several ways to put together a package. Typically, it started with the source material, such as a book like *The Getaway* by Jim Thompson, the manuscript for which came from a most unlikely place: a dingy, one-bedroom apartment in a run-down area of Hollywood. Thompson was a washed-up writer who was living on the brink of poverty, and the book existed only in photocopied form. Tony Bill tracked down the writer and introduced me to him. At the time, Thompson was an underground writer, with almost no following. But on the basis of some sweaty, whiskey-stained pages that told the story of an ex-con getting out of jail and going for one last score, I agreed to sign Thompson as a client. His dark vision of the world, where much of what went on between characters was unspoken yet understood, fit right in to the types of films I wanted to be involved with.

The only way I could get a studio to pay attention to *The Getaway* was to attract the interest of a star. The perfect guy was Steve McQueen, then the biggest star in the business, so I made a deal with producer David Foster to option Thompson's book and the rights to the script. Foster had become friends with McQueen while working as his publicist, and it was exactly the kind of role that McQueen wanted, one that Bogart might have played, in which the character straddles good and bad. Jim took a shot at the first draft of the script, but no one was happy with the result, so Walter Hill was hired to revise it. Hill updated the setting from the forties to present-day Texas and changed the ending.

Getting the film made was the usual series of advances and setbacks. First, the film needed a director. Peter Bogdanovich, a very hot director at the time, agreed to come aboard, which made Paramount take an interest in backing the film. No sooner did we have Bogdanovich than we lost him to Warners, where he went to write and direct *What's Up, Doc?* According to Paramount production chief Robert Evans, Bogdanovich quit because Evans insisted that his wife, Ali MacGraw, play the lead. McQueen then called Sam Peckinpah, who had directed his last film, *Junior Bonner.* Stella Stevens was considered for the female lead, but she was unavailable. In the meantime, David Foster was sued by actor Jack Palance, who was upset that Peckinpah had dropped him after he thought he had the part. By the time Palance dropped his suit—he didn't have a signed contract—Paramount put the film in turnaround despite the fact that Ali MacGraw was committed, which is the film industry equivalent of Siberia.

Working with Foster and my colleagues at CMA, we set the picture up at First Artists with the following deal: The CMA-created actors' production company agreed to take over the film for a fee, and McQueen cut his price to 22.5 percent of the net plus a share of First Artists' gross. Based on these machinations, a distribution deal was struck with National General.

Finally, the package was complete and the movie could be made.

The Getaway had an important lasting impact on Hollywood and on my life. The movie created a Jim Thompson renaissance that continues to this day. Based on his newfound fame, he was able to make a European publishing deal for his books. His old novels were dusted off, resulting in a couple of films—*After Dark, My Sweet*, which was directed by James Foley, and *The Grifters*, directed by Stephen Frears. The man who had been lost and forgotten became not only a working writer but a cult figure. It's unfortunate that it climaxed after his death.

My job often was to keep the damn thing from falling apart.

The Sting was one of the most complicated packages I ever worked on, largely because the film was put together at one studio with a director and a primary cast but landed at another studio with a different director and cast. Because of the dynamic personalities involved, there was a land mine at every turn.

The three producers, Tony Bill and Michael and Julia Phillips, made a series of rookie mistakes. First, they promised screenwriter David Ward that *The Sting* would be his directorial debut, despite the fact that the film was an expensive 1930s period piece. One Friday afternoon when I was out of town, the three of them went to see Dan Melnick, the head of production at MGM, and made some sort of vague deal. Besides Ward directing, they also attached Peter Boyle to play the part of Henry Gondorff, the washed-up gambler.

This created a situation fraught with peril. For starters, we had submitted the project to Dick Zanuck and David Brown, who had been supportive of a previous Bill-Phillips project, *Steelyard Blues*. Dick and David were setting up a production company at Universal, where a film like *The Sting* could become a high-profile project. In the back of Dick's mind, it would also be a reteaming of director George Roy Hill and stars Paul Newman and Robert Redford from *Butch Cassidy and the Sundance Kid*, which he had greenlighted at Fox.

Early Monday morning, Tony, Michael, Julia, and I gathered in a conference room at IFA to meet with Dick Zanuck and Rudy

Petersdorf, the head of business affairs at Universal. Dick started the meeting by locking the door and declaring that he wasn't leaving without a deal. In the end, it was agreed that the film would be made at Universal, not MGM; Tony, Michael, and Julia would be the film's producers and get the lion's share of the profits; and Dick and David would be credited as "presenters" of the film.

After everyone shook hands on the deal, I told them there was one last order of business before we left. I had to call MGM chairman Jim Aubrey and inform him of what had transpired—not a pleasant task. With the smell of stale sandwiches and cigarettes in the air, I took a deep breath and dialed. When Aubrey came on the line, I told him that what I was going to say would be hard for him to accept. After berating my clients and me, he curtly informed me that I was henceforth banned from the MGM lot.

I learned that day that any agent worth his salt must be willing and able to take a bullet for his clients. However, it is rare that a client will take the sword for his agent, which is one of the reasons I finally left the agency business.

Somehow, Tony, Michael, and Julia all ended up annoyed at me. Once George Roy Hill came aboard the picture, they were relegated to the sidelines. Hill was an experienced, authoritarian director who was going to make the movie he wanted to make, so there was really no need for the three of them. In fact, Hill allowed only one of them on the set at a time.

I've always felt that I saved their film. None of them had ever produced a successful film, so it was unlikely that Universal would give them much power on a Hill-Newman-Redford film. At the end of the day, they struck gold when the film became a monster hit. For developing the script and going along with the deal, they ended up making millions of dollars.

They also won the Academy Award for Best Picture.

▦

Controlling the elements of a package is even tougher than keeping them together. On *Jaws,* it proved to be impossible.

I was working with Lynn Nesbit, a literary agent in IFA's New York office, to sell the movie rights to Peter Benchley's novel

Jaws. We both sensed we had a hot property, so I sent it to Dick Zanuck and Lynn sent it to David Brown in New York simultaneously. After the success of *The Sting*, they were two of the hottest guys in town. I explained to Dick that there was a lot of interest in the book and told him that a condition of Zanuck-Brown buying the rights would be that they hire a director we represented to make the film. From a list of five names, he picked Dick Richards, whose only produced film was *The Culpepper Cattle Company*, produced by his then-partner Jerry Bruckheimer.

As soon as Zanuck and Brown read the book, they wanted to buy it. Before I closed the deal, I insisted that the two of them have a creative meeting with Peter Benchley and Dick Richards to make sure that everyone was on the same page. Zanuck agreed and the four made plans to meet at the "21" Club in New York.

Over lunch, the deal nearly fell apart.

I happened to be in London when the phone rang in the middle of the night. It was Dick Zanuck calling to relate what a disaster the lunch had been. Dick Richards sat down at the table and began telling Benchley, Zanuck, and Brown how he saw the movie: "The picture opens. We're in a quiet fishing village. People are going about their business. The camera pans out over the water and suddenly, swooping out of nowhere is the giant whale."

Whale?! Zanuck quickly corrected Richards. It was a *shark*. Richards continued his pitch, again calling the beast a whale. Benchley, who was downing one martini after another, became quite upset. As Zanuck kept pressing Richards to call the man-eating fish a shark, Benchley went from frosty to downright livid.

From three thousand miles away, Zanuck implored me to let him get rid of Richards. He was paying $175,000 for the book, a nice price in those days, along with 5 of his 50 net-profit points in the film. While I wanted the package to have as many IFA clients as possible, I realized our first loyalty was to Peter Benchley. Besides, only one other studio had bid on the book, so we didn't have a lot of options. Zanuck also volunteered to call Dick Richards and soften the blow. I agreed to let him off the hook on the director. He could set up the picture and choose a director who wanted to make a film about a killer shark.

The film was one of the first blockbuster-event films that Steven Spielberg directed. Dick Richards went on to do *Rafferty and the Gold Dust Twins*, a soon-forgotten film.

▬

The package I am proudest of as an agent was something of a whim.

I was sitting at my desk one day when funnyman Marty Feldman walked into my office. What a face, I thought. His cheeks were sagging to his knees and his eyes were bulging out of his head. I had already agreed to represent Marty, and now I needed to find him a movie. Five minutes later, another client, Peter Boyle, lumbered in. "The two stooges," I said to them. "All we need is a third stooge and we've got a movie."

I picked up the phone and called Gene Wilder, who had been talking about writing a film.

I put Gene on the speakerphone, introduced him to Marty and Peter, and told him that if he wrote a treatment for the three of them, I would set it up at a studio. Ever the client who needed to be pushed and pulled at the same time, Gene hemmed and hawed and said that he only had something for himself to star in. I told him to write it for all three guys. He said he would try.

A few weeks later, the treatment for *Young Frankenstein* arrived. Doing a satire of all the Frankenstein movies with the physical comedy that Gene, Peter, and Marty brought to it was one of the funniest ideas I've ever come across. I gave the treatment to producer Mike Gruskoff, who hadn't worked in a while. He immediately thought to pair Gene with Mel Brooks. They had done *The Producers* together and were finishing *Blazing Saddles*. Mel agreed to do it, so I was able to set it up at Columbia with my friend Peter Guber, the studio's head of production.

The deal was for Gene to write a script based on the treatment and then for Columbia to finance the film with the package of Mel directing and Gene co-starring with Peter and Marty. But when the script was finished, the film was budgeted at $2.3 million. Leo Jaffe, who was then chairman of Columbia and part of the town's old guard, would only commit $2 million to the film, and he wasn't crazy about Mel's idea to shoot the film in black and white, so he let the picture go. That night, the script went to Alan Ladd, Jr., a friend of Gruskoff's who had just started at Fox. I made the deal the next day. Dropping the film cost Columbia at least $50 million.

This is a business of missed opportunities.

▬

Hollywood is often a place where no one disagrees with talent. An agent will always get a lot further by agreeing with his clients. But the longer I spent as an agent, the less I was able to do that, so I decided to move into making movies.

▬

As rewarding as handling talent was, it was often a tiresome job. Take Gene Wilder, for example: an absolute comic genius who could make a slapstick masterpiece out of anything he touched. But Gene also had wild mood swings. When I first approached Gene about bringing him to IFA, he told me he wanted to be loyal to his New York agent, Lily Veidt. This seemed honorable on his part, so I was more than willing to be fair and split the commissions with her. Nevertheless, Gene kept threatening to walk out on us for no apparent reason. (This wasn't as bad as the suicide note that George Sanders left: "I'm bored.")

Even directors could be tough to deal with. I remember getting a call one day from Steven Spielberg's lawyer, Mike Emery, before I fired Steven as a client. Emery, to whom I had introduced Steven, complained that his client was unhappy with the job I was doing. I immediately called Steven and asked him exactly why he was unhappy. Instead of telling me what was wrong, Steven got pissed off at his lawyer for telling me that. Then Emery got upset at me for telling Steven what he said. This juggling of human emotions took up much of my day and, as I saw it, had little to do with getting movies made.

Colleagues were often treated as disposable—and worse. When Freddie Fields and David Begelman retired veteran agent Marty Baum from CMA, they gave him a Cartier Tank watch. One day, I went with Marty to get the watch adjusted. It turned out to be a $280 Japanese knockoff—one that didn't even tell time.

But what most wore me down as an agent was constantly having to ask for favors and jobs on behalf of my clients. Though this changed in the eighties when the balance of power shifted to the agent, being an agent in the seventies meant that you had to ask everyone for everything, from morning until night. Because of growing up the way I did, it was not in my nature to ask others for help. I've always liked to make my own way through life. Maybe it was pride. Every deal was about getting more money or more control for the client than he or she had had the time before.

Some deals are just not worth it.

When I was at CMA, I represented producer Chuck Barris, who had bought the rights to the book *Or I'll Dress You in Mourning*, the story of the Spanish bullfighter El Cordobes. In order to make the film, he needed the matador's permission, and that proved much harder to get than we thought. For two years, Chuck pursued Cordobes by phone and mail. Finally, he agreed to meet with Chuck, so the two of us flew to Mexico City, where we sat in a steamy hotel room for two days waiting for his call. Just as we were ready to call it quits, the summons came: we were to meet him at his hotel at 5:30 P.M.

When we arrived, the hotel was surrounded by fans screaming Cordobes's name. We were taken to an underground garage to meet the famous bullfighter and then whisked off to a local watering hole, which was a place where the party never stopped. The combination of bottomless glasses of wine and a rowdy mariachi band had people dancing on their tables. After two hours of this and too much wine, Chuck told me to press the issue. I climbed onto our table, where Cordobes was dancing as if the bulls were chasing him, and I asked if Chuck could have the rights to his story.

"Tell him to meet me in Costa Rica next week and we'll talk," Cordobes said to me in Spanish, as he shimmied across the tabletop.

I leaned down and gave Chuck the news.

"Tell him to go fuck himself," Chuck said, smiling at the great bullfighter.

Continuing to stomp my feet to the sound of the Spanish music, I moved close to Cordobes's ear, cupped my hands, and said, "Mr. Barris would like some time to consider your offer. A long time."

An agent has to keep the arena open even when he knows that the bullfight is over.

▦

Sometimes it was dangerous. On one film a nameless producer was hopelessly slow in paying my clients. Halfway through the movie, he hadn't paid anything. Fed up, I called him and exerted pressure. "Unless I get this money today by three o'clock," I told him curtly, "everybody is going to walk off." At precisely five minutes to three the guy walked into my office, carrying a black bag filled with $500,000 in cash, looking as if he was packing. He gave me a stern look and asked if I wanted to count the money. Slightly shocked, I muttered, "I'll take your word for it."

▦

Often, doing my best job as an agent created conflicts with my friends and made me out to be something of a heavy. When I gave *The Getaway* to David Foster to produce because he had access to Steve McQueen, Tony Bill was mad at me. Tony felt that this was an act of betrayal, since he had introduced me to Jim Thompson. At the time, I felt that I needed to get Thompson some money (which Tony didn't have) and find a producer who could get the movie made (which Foster could do quicker).

Looking back, I realize that I was caught up in the agent's life and I was wrong not to include Tony as a producer, but what I regret most is not talking it through with Tony at the time. It is always awkward to represent all the parties in a deal, and agents should admit that more often than they do.

An agent's responsibility ends the moment he makes the sale. I was much more passionate about movies than deals. The more packages I put together, the more I wanted to be on the other side making the decisions. This is why agencies became such a fertile training ground for studio executives. Certainly, there was no better place to learn the business.

Over the years, there had been opportunities for me to leave the agency business, but I wasn't ready. David Foster had asked me to produce *The Getaway* with him, and Tony Bill had asked me to do the same with *The Sting*. Both times I felt that it was too big of a risk to take. I wanted to be on more solid ground when I left the cocoon of agenting. I wasn't far enough along in my career to cover up a misstep, and besides, I had a family to support.

While those films turned out to be successes, that all happened before I learned that nothing is a sure thing.

The Lunatics in the Asylum

In 1919, when Charlie Chaplin, Mary Pickford, D.W. Griffith, and Douglas Fairbanks founded United Artists, Metro Pictures executive Richard Rowland remarked: "The lunatics have taken charge of the asylum."

Shortly after the 1973 Christmas holidays, when the rest of the Hollywood community was still in Aspen or Hawaii, I picked up a call from Eric Pleskow, who had recently been named president of United Artists. He explained that he was coming to Los Angeles from New York late in the week for his monthly round of meetings, and he wanted to talk business. I had never met Eric, and I did very little, if any, business with United Artists. While the company had a great past, it had become old and staid and was out of the loop. Many people in town were predicting Eric's demise. But my job as the head of the talent division at IFA was to represent my clients, so I made plans to meet Eric at the Polo Lounge for drinks.

Eric was easy to pick out among the regular crowd of agents and producers at the Beverly Hills Hotel. Wearing large, plastic-framed glasses and dressed in a very simple, solid-colored suit, he looked like a character from an Austrian art film. He was a smart, taciturn Viennese with a wicked wit and a dry sense of humor, and I immediately found out that Eric was no one's fool. I was Hollywood and he was old world, but there was an immediate kinship between us. Eric had grown up in Austria and emigrated to America in his teens. English was his second language, as it was mine. We shared a worldview that extended beyond the movie business, and I found myself disarmed by his candor and, most of all, his sense of humor.

Eric knew he needed to do something to bring UA into the present, and his agenda for our meeting was straightforward: he wanted to make a deal for Raquel Welch to star in UA's movies, and he wanted to meet novelist Michael Crichton. Raquel was charming and sexy, and as her agent, I was happy to oblige, as I was with Crichton. Still, as we moved deeper into conversation, I couldn't help but think that if Eric, as the president of United Artists, was focusing his attention on Raquel Welch, they were in worse trouble than everyone imagined. If the head of UA was flying across the country to land a lead actress of midlevel status, I couldn't imagine what his staff was working on. I explained to Eric that he needed to be making movies with the young, passionate filmmakers whom I represented. These guys, I told him, were the future of the business. They are who he should be meeting with.

Eric obviously agreed with me. A week later he called again, this time to offer me the job of United Artists's West Coast head of production.

I told Eric I was interested, but I asked for a few days to mull it over and discuss it with my boss and friend, Marvin Josephson, who owned and ran IFA. I flew to New York and had lunch with Marvin. When I told him that I had an offer to run UA's West Coast office and was inclined to accept, he began working me with the soft sell. The future of the business was with the agents, he told me. Ever the agent, he promised to "make me rich" if I stayed at IFA. Money was (and still is) always the first concern for most agents. I told him that he'd had his opportunity to do that and missed it. As I saw it, I was making *him* rich.

The Sting and *Jaws* alone—two projects that I had packaged—were going to make the agency somewhere between $15 million and $20 million; I was earning $75,000 a year. But Marvin was serious. Little did I know, he was working on a deal to buy CMA and merge the two to form International Creative Management.

Had I stayed, I might have made a small fortune in the merger.

But it wasn't about money. Status at that time was held by the buyers, not the sellers. Studios were the buyers, the choosers who listened to hundreds and hundreds of pitches from agents, selected the one or two they liked, and discarded the others. Agents were the sellers, the beggars who were constantly peddling and repackaging rejected ideas to anyone who would listen even if the agents themselves didn't believe in the projects. Being an agent was wearing on me, and representing individuals had become very mechanical. It had gotten to the point that when I picked up the phone, I often knew exactly what the executive or the client on the other end of the line was going to say. I'd respond and then move on to the next deal. I had done all I knew how to as an agent, and now I wanted to move closer to the actual making of movies. Change is good if you don't feel challenged, especially at age thirty-three.

▤

In the entertainment industry, people change jobs faster than they change cars, clothes, girlfriends, sometimes even underwear. I had no idea that saying yes to Eric Pleskow's offer would commit me for the next sixteen years to one of the most unique executive partnerships in twentieth-century Hollywood. Nor did I know it would turn out to be the single most important decision of my professional life. Eric's bosses were Arthur Krim and Bob Benjamin, two men whose guidance would save me from a typical Hollywood career.

▤

From the time I first heard their names, Arthur Krim and Bob Benjamin were always mentioned in the same breath, as if they were one entity. In fact, they were perfect complements to each other. They thought alike and often arrived independently at the same conclusion. Arthur was the heart of United Artists and Bob was the soul. Together they were the brains. They shot straight, ran a hard bargain, and put their character above all else. There were no good-cop-bad-cop Hollywood games, where one would come in and play the heavy while the other soft-pedaled. They had backed such classic films as *The Apartment, West Side Story,*

The Manchurian Candidate, Tom Jones, Marty and *Midnight Cowboy*, as well as the James Bond and Pink Panther films and the spaghetti Westerns—in all, roughly 25 percent of the American Film Institute's 100 Best Films. They were also caring people whose vision of life encompassed far more than just making movies. Arthur and Bob lived in a world that was infinitely more important than the movie business, and this ultimately made them better at making movies.

By going into business with them, I began to realize dreams far beyond those I had imagined in 1956 as a sixteen-year-old looking out the airplane window at the lights of Los Angeles as my flight from Chile was on final approach. Hollywood is a dream factory, and for each dream that comes true, a million nightmares are created. For anyone in the movies business, regardless of his or her job, the dreams are the pictures you work on. The nightmares are what you go through to get them made. I learned from Arthur Krim and Bob Benjamin that the true beauty of this business, the one thing that gets you up each day and keeps you alive, is that each film is a new business full of promise and fraught with peril, and that whatever happens, the only knowledge comes from years of daily struggles. The end result is a memory that may alter you forever.

▬

Most people in Hollywood are so swept up in finding the next big script, or the next hit movie, jockeying for the important job at the hot agency, or pushing on all fronts for the sought-after part, that they miss the more interesting opportunities out there. There are actors whose careers have been defined by taking what were perceived as middle-of-the-road parts but turned out to be Oscarwinning, star-making turns. Hollywood lore is also full of stories of actors whose third choice of projects made their careers, like Humphrey Bogart in The Maltese Falcon. *Studio executives have become legendary for picking up a little movie like* Home Alone *and watching it become one of the highest-grossing films in history. Sometimes the best movie is the one playing next to the one that is sold out. While everyone is fighting for a table at the Zeitgeist Café, check out the food in the little dive across the street.*

Or how my fledgling executive career was saved by a film that no one else would touch.

▤

I had something to prove at United Artists, and there was plenty of room to prove it. When I moved into my office at what was then the Goldwyn Studios on May 1, 1974, the West Coast operation was practically dormant. You could feel the stellar history of United Artists hanging from the walls, a daily reminder of what once was: two-foot-by-three-foot pictures of John Wayne, Bette Davis, Spencer Tracy, Marlene Dietrich, Gloria Swanson, Woody Allen, and the Beatles, all starring in past UA movies. Yet you could feel the cobwebs left behind from the fifties and sixties.

The other major studios had their own back lots and office buildings, but UA rented a suite of offices, small and dreary. Even the furniture looked as if it was from the days when Chaplin, Pickford, Griffith, and Fairbanks ran the place. I'm not allergic to antiques or anything like that, but the couches looked like they hadn't been recovered since Joseph Schenck stopped by to hash out his employment contract with Mary Pickford. I moved into Mary Pickford's old office, which had, I'm reasonably certain, the same flowered easy chairs and the tawny-hued couches that she left behind.

The optimism of the California sunshine that led Hollywood's founding fathers to settle on the West Coast wasn't shining through the windows of the UA offices.

As successful as the company had once been, it was very much part of the old Hollywood establishment at a time when a new one was emerging. If UA even made it onto the radar screen, it was easily the place of last resort for young filmmakers to take their projects, and the disparity between the two worlds couldn't have been greater. No one there was quite sure who Steven Spielberg, George Lucas, Marty Scorsese, and Hal Ashby were. Francis Coppola had already made a name for himself with *The Godfather,* but even that didn't mean much to UA. One of the actors lists I received in my first few days on the job listed the young leading man who had starred in *Easy Rider* as "Joseph Nicholson." The company needed to be coaxed into the present, and my job would be to support the higher-ups in New York in this modernizing process.

The dated sensibility that afflicted UA could be explained partly by the fact that all the decisions were made in New York and there was no real presence in Los Angeles. The L.A. office had been run by David Chasman, Herb Jaffe, and Mort Engelberg. The scripts from the usual suppliers were delivered to them, and they forwarded them to New York with their recommendation for approval or rejection, and then passed along the decision. Eric Pleskow likened the operation to the famous Hollywood cemetery Forest Lawn: "UA doesn't bother anyone in Hollywood, that way they don't bother us." This had worked in the late sixties because most of UA's films originated in New York and Europe, but with the new creative boom in American film that was taking hold, it was a formula for slow death. The office in Hollywood needed to take some action.

The first thing I did was to seek out a creative second in command: Marcia Nasatir, a low-key literary agent with true taste in material, a rarity. Marcia was working for the venerable literary agent Evarts Ziegler, representing high-brow writers such as Lorenzo Semple, Jr. (*Papillon*), Robert Towne (*Chinatown*), and Irving Ravetch and Harriet Frank, Jr. (*Hud*). While she was technically becoming story editor, the traditional job for a woman at a studio, she made it clear that the only way she'd move to UA was if she were made a vice president. I supported her, appealed to New York for a decision, and Arthur and Eric quickly agreed. Eric told me that Arthur's strong-willed wife, Mathilde Krim, the future founder of the American Foundation for AIDS Research (AMFAR), told him to not even entertain the thought of not giving Marcia the title. With that, Marcia became one of the first female vice presidents of a Hollywood studio.

To fill out this minimalist operation, I hired as story editors and office assistants Tom Parry, a Harvard-educated young man who had more than just book smarts, and Mark Canton, a hard worker who constantly needed to be validated. Helping them were a group of freelance readers that now comprises a creative who's who of Hollywood: Edward Zwick, Marshall Herskovitz, Walter Parkes, Lawrence Lasker, Lucy Fisher, and Jon Avnet. The rest of the office staff consisted of Lee Katz, the head of physical production; Bob Geary, our West Coast lawyer; a small publicity division headed by Lloyd Leipzig; and a woman named Florence Carpenter, who ran the office.

▦

Two weeks after I started at UA, I was sitting in my office, cursing the dreary surroundings of the Goldwyn lot, just hoping that the whole place would burn to the ground. Minutes later, I looked out the window and saw that a soundstage was going up in flames and taking the lot where my car was parked with it. My wish had been granted—but I had forgotten about my car. While cinders flew everywhere, I raced out of my office to move my car because I didn't want to be late to the Beverly Hills Hotel, where I was meeting Eric and Dino De Laurentiis, burning my head in the process. When I arrived at the hotel and stepped out of the car to greet Eric, the seam of my pants split, leaving my boxers exposed to the small crowd at the valet parking stand. Eric insisted on walking behind me—literally covering my butt. It wasn't the last time we would cover for each other over the years.

▦

Exactly six months after I took the job, I had gone to New York with Marcia for a series of meetings with Arthur, Bob, Eric, and Bill Bernstein, who was head of business affairs. "Where are the movies?" Arthur Krim barked at me across his desk. "What are you doing out there in Hollywood? You haven't started a single movie yet. We're going to have to shut down our distribution apparatus and start laying people off unless you find some films to make." Arthur was like a father to his employees, and he clearly didn't want to do that. While he would over time become both a father figure and a close friend to me, I was feeling a little queasy about the prospect that the great United Artists would have to close its doors unless I could find movies to make.

Just days after I had started the job, the company had held a big press gathering at the Beverly Hills Hotel to introduce me as UA's new man in Hollywood. Eric and I announced that UA would release twenty-three to twenty-five movies a year in 1974.

For 1975, we were on pace for about eight, none of which I had initiated. It was a hard realization: *Finding movies to make was a lot more difficult than selling them.* I was learning that it's easy to be gun-shy because you can't lose if you say no. I also wanted my first movie to be perfect.

UA's cupboards were bare. The Mirisch brothers, who had supplied an incredible sixty-seven movies in eighteen years, were out of the picture; Harold Mirisch had died and Walter Mirisch had moved to Universal. But besides the annual UA tent poles like the Bond and Woody Allen films, the release slate was unimpressive: a film starring John Wayne, who had, to put it politely, passed his peak, and an Otto Preminger film that just disappeared from theaters. Norman Jewison had a deal with UA, but he wasn't sure what he wanted to do next.

The phones weren't exactly ringing off the hook either. During my first few weeks I often picked up the receiver to make sure that there was a dial tone. In the agency business, I'd clock at least sixty and as many as one hundred calls per day. At UA, I was getting maybe twenty. About forty scripts arrived soon after I had moved in—all of which had been passed on by every studio in town. The producers had dusted them off and rebound them with fresh script covers to make them look as though they were still dripping with ink from the screenwriters' battered Underwood typewriters. But the occasional coffee-cup stain on the inside pages was a dead giveaway that I wasn't the first person to read this script.

As the new studio executive on the block, I was the mark for every producer in town, and every rejected script in town wound up on my desk.

I realized how little I knew about the production side of movies. As an agent, I would put together a package and sell it. But the packages you sell are not necessarily the ones you buy. The burden of assembling the other elements and getting the movie into production fell on the studio. Now I was one of the guys who was accepting responsibility for what a movie cost, when and how it would be made, and whether or not the company could make any money on it. As an agent, I was more concerned with my clients' fees than the overall budget of the movie.

At UA, I would have to concern myself with the movie from the day we bought the script until the day it left the theaters. Marcia was a former agent herself, and she had never seen a film past the deal stage either. On top of everything, I had a one-year contract and no easy way back into the agency business. I had given up all my clients when I came to work for UA.

So I left Arthur's New York office in a daze. Marcia was equally drained. As we walked the thirty-some-odd blocks back to the Carlyle Hotel, I kept thinking that within the year I would be out of this job. If the first six months were any indication, certainly I was headed for failure as a studio executive. Fortunately, fear turned out to be a great motivator, and my immigrant's survival drive took over.

■

As an agent I had learned that when you are in trouble, the easiest and fastest way to make a sale is to use the relationships you have, rather than try to make new ones. So I decided to find something I liked that was available and just make it. The project was a script based on a book that had become a play, called *One Flew Over the Cuckoo's Nest*. At the time, everyone in town believed that whoever picked up this project was nuttier than some of the characters, but it was exactly the kind of groundbreaking film that UA would become known for over the next four years.

I first read the script as an agent. Kirk Douglas, who controlled the rights, was looking for representation as an actor, so Marvin Josephson sent me over to his house to try to sign him. When I arrived, Kirk opened the door and escorted me into his study. For an hour or so we talked about art, architecture, and politics—everything except film or his representation. Finally, I moved to business and asked him what he thought about signing with me. He furrowed his brow. Clearly, he had already sized me up and made his decision. All that was left was for him to deliver the news. "Mike," he began, "you're not going to be an agent for very long, so I'm going to sign with Stan Kamen at the William Morris office. You're going to move on and then I'll be left without an agent." However, he went on to explain that he liked me, so as a consolation prize he was giving me a project to represent:

One Flew Over the Cuckoo's Nest. Feeling as though I had accomplished something, I thanked him and left.

What I soon learned was that he had spent a decade at the height of his powers trying to get the project made.

Kirk's relationship with *Cuckoo's Nest* began in 1963 when he played the lead crazy, Randle Patrick McMurphy, in the Broadway production. He optioned the film rights to Ken Kesey's cult novel, on which the play was based, to be a starring film vehicle for himself. After a decade of rejection, Kirk brought in his son Michael to help find the financing. Michael was best known at the time for his work on the TV series *The Streets of San Francisco* and wanted to follow in his father's footsteps and forge a dual career as an actor-producer. I had no luck finding a home for *Cuckoo's Nest* in the twelve months that I tried, but before leaving the agency business to come to UA, I advised Kirk and Michael to make a deal with record producer Saul Zaentz, who wanted to back the film. Saul was a doer who had made his money in the record business and had a line of film financing.

I always thought that the script was very literate, but I never envisioned the kind of humor the film ultimately had. Originally, Hal Ashby, a client of mine, was going to direct, but by the time the project found its way to me at UA, Hal had been replaced by Milos Forman. Kirk had talked to Milos ten years before Hal became involved, but the copy of the book that Kirk sent to Milos in Czechoslovakia was either lost or confiscated. Milos had directed only one English-language film, but his work was known to many executives and agents in Hollywood. I had seen *The Firemen's Ball* at the San Francisco Film Festival and met Milos there, and the film had me laughing on the floor. It's centered on a small town retirement party for the local fire chief. As the ball unfolds, all the gifts are stolen and ultimately, the fire chief's house burns down. Both *The Firemen's Ball* and one of Milos's earlier films, *The Loves of a Blonde*, had been nominated for Academy Awards for Best Foreign Language Film.

I was convinced that Milos could bring out the humor of the loony bin in *Cuckoo's Nest*.

Saul had decided to back the film himself and cover the budget with foreign and domestic distribution deals. As the film was about to go into production at the Oregon State Hospital, Saul was still shopping for a domestic distributor. The project had taken so long to get financed that Kirk was now too old to play McMurphy. Michael had recruited his friend Jack Nicholson to do it. After an extensive search for a lead actress, during which Anne Bancroft, Geraldine Page, Ellen Burstyn, Colleen Dewhurst, and Angela Lansbury all said no, Milos had cast the gifted Louise Fletcher as Nurse Ratched. Still, the only nibble Saul had for domestic distribution was at 20th Century Fox— which agreed to finance the entire film if the ending was changed to allow Nicholson's McMurphy to live.

Hollywood loves happy endings—*Think sequel!*—but this was silly. The entire emotional architecture of the story was predicated on McMurphy's being silenced and killed in the end by the hospital, so having him live wasn't a realistic option. I thought it was an emotional moment, and people go to movies because they want to get engaged emotionally. A character you care about dying onscreen is a moment that stays with you, especially if it's a principal character. Even though UA drove a hard bargain financially, we didn't tinker creatively.

We liked the script; the only issue was money.

I recommended to Arthur and Bob that we invest half of the $6 million for all rights. Like everyone else in the business, UA had turned down the offer to fully finance the film. When Arthur and Bob weren't crazy about something, they'd simply move the goal post and make me extract a better deal. If I told them I needed $3 million, they'd say yes to $2.5 million. This often sent me back to producers, asking them to defer part or all of their fees—as I began to call it, "Let me have an arm . . . and a leg, too. . . . How about an ear?" Negotiations with Saul, which Bill Bernstein handled, were tough and nearly fell apart several times. Eric finally interceded and got the deal done. Eventually, UA ended up with all rights for $3 million—a good deal for UA given the market conditions and a good deal for Saul given the fact that his film was like a leper in Hollywood. At the time, television was beginning to pay a lot of money for the rights to broadcast films, and in the case of *Cuckoo's Nest*, this amount covered most of our risk. Even if the film flopped, we knew that the television rights were worth at least $1.5 million, due to Nicholson's popularity. Lesson number one for a studio executive: *Protect the downside risk because everything is a long shot.*

When the film was finished, we all flew to San Francisco for a screening. I couldn't believe my eyes. Milos had balanced the moments of hilarity and tragedy perfectly. With its complex portrayal of an individual's struggle against an oppressive institution, the film was moving and poignant, but never pandering. It would be presumptuous to say I knew I was watching an American classic, but I was certain the film was something special, and I thought it would win the Academy Award. For many reasons, *Cuckoo's Nest* remains the favorite of all the films I've been involved with in my career. After all, it was the firstborn.

Cuckoo's Nest opened to good but not great reviews. However, word of mouth carried the film at the box office where it earned more than $180 million. The high point of the experience came on March 29, 1976, when the film won the five major Academy Awards: Best Picture, Best Director, Best Adapted Screenplay (Lawrence Hauben and Bo Goldman), Best Actor (Jack Nicholson), and Best Actress (Louise Fletcher). Milos Forman thanked everyone at UA—singling out Arthur, Bob, Eric, and me by name—for our part in helping bring the film to fruition. It was the first time I was thanked at the Academy Awards, and I felt like the happiest person in Hollywood.

The film gave Arthur, Bob, and Eric confidence in my ability to pick successful projects, and they soon promoted me to head of worldwide production. The film also started relationships with Milos and Saul that resulted in a handful of films for us over the years, including *Amadeus,* which won eight Oscars, including Best Picture. I went into business again with Milos on *The People vs. Larry Flynt,* and we are now working on a new project, *Bad News,* an adaptation of a Donald Westlake novel.

■

United Artists was never a movie studio in the strictest sense of the term. There was no back-lot operation, no soundstages, no editing facilities, and no giant tank where a high-seas boat chase could be simulated. Soon after I started, UA moved its L.A. base from the dank rented offices on the Goldwyn lot to the Irving Thalberg Building on the MGM lot. This at least made the company feel more like a major player. But UA wasn't a company of buildings; it was a state of mind, where filmmakers created and executives assisted them.

▬

It was harder for filmmakers to get a yes out of United Artists, but it meant more because the filmmakers were not only left to their creativity but were also financial partners with the company. As long as they stayed within budget, filmmakers had total control over what they put on the screen. With *Cuckoo's Nest,* we also proved that our marketing department could pack the theaters for a film with challenging subject matter. A primary reason United Artists became the place to work for filmmakers was Arthur's theory, which Eric often related to me: "Nobody ever went out of business by giving away profits."

When Krim and Benjamin arrived at UA in 1951, profits were equally divided between the filmmakers and the studio after UA earned back its distribution fee. UA always gave artists an honest accounting on films, even though the reputation of the Hollywood studios was that they *never* gave talent an honest count. Other studios charged an overhead fee to the budget of each film, which made it difficult to even make a profit. When I arrived at UA, Universal and Paramount charged a whopping 25 percent of a film's budget for overhead; Columbia 15 percent; and Warner Bros. 12.5 percent. This made it easier for us to make deals with talent, because they had a fighting chance at the back end. As UA slowly turned into the preeminent place to work, the overhead fee charged by other studios began to shrink.

United Artists earned most of its money from distribution fees, which ranged from 30 percent domestically to as high as 40 percent in some foreign markets. While this was the only inviolate business policy when I arrived at UA, it was forced to change over time. UA also did not insist on guarantees from theater owners like other studios until we picked up *A Bridge Too Far* in 1977. The business became so competitive that studios were backed into a corner and forced to adopt a number of unfavorable business practices that would eventually make it almost impossible for them to earn any money. The lawyers and agents representing the talent felt that in a competitive environment studios were not entitled to make large profits on the backs of their clients, and there was nothing studios could do about this. The important filmmakers and stars were concentrated in the hands of a few lawyers and agents, and so the studios capitulated and began to hope that one or two home runs would salvage an entire year. This practice has all but spelled the end of what was once a lucrative business that built the libraries that have given movie companies their lasting value.

Since UA relied on our distribution fees and profits to cover our operating costs, we had to be smaller and more frugal than the other studios. Places like Universal and Warner Bros. had hundreds of people working in buildings spread across acres and acres on their back lots and in high rises throughout the world. If you were a top executive there and you landed in a foreign country, they'd have a guy waiting for you at the baggage claim with a wad of cash and a car stocked with cigars and champagne. By the midseventies, Warner Bros. had so many jets, limousines, and helicopters to ferry around their executives that the company had its own transportation captain. At UA, we lived a more frugal existence: we flew commercial, carried our own bags, and were happy when the car service showed up at all.

The independent spirit that characterized UA from its founding fit perfectly with the freewheeling approach of the auteurs who were reviving America film in the seventies. A basic philosophy took shape in the four years I was at UA, and it was one we would use after we left UA and formed Orion: We were interested in the entire package that would become the movie, not just a single element. All the elements had to fit tightly together like a puzzle.

■

United Artists became a director-driven company in an actor-driven business. As the seventies unfolded and revealed itself as the decade of the American director, this turned out to be a cutting-edge strategy that played to my strength, which was handling writers and directors. At the time, it was something of a novel idea to give so much power to a director. *Typically, on big films, the studio shad-owed the director and let him know who was boss. Francis Cop-pola went through the entire* Godfather *shoot fearing he was about to be fired by Paramount production chief Robert Evans.*

UA didn't operate that way. Once we decided to back a director, we lived or died by that decision.

The directors we worked with at UA had bold artistic visions and very different temperaments: Bob Rafelson, who had a four-picture deal with us, had a godlike attitude. He felt that because he had done films such as *Five Easy Pieces* and *The King of Mar-vin Gardens* he was to be taken seriously—or else. He completed one film for us, *Stay Hungry,* the story of a rich guy (played by Jeff Bridges) who falls for a working-class girl (Sally Field) he meets at a bodybuilder's gym he's trying to sell. The most signifi-cant aspect of the film was that a bodybuilder named Arnold Schwarzenegger had his first feature-film speaking part in it.

Rafelson gained a reputation as an abrasive know-it-all who thought nothing of lecturing Ingmar Bergman's sure-handed cin-ematographer Sven Nykvist on lighting. He hurt himself by adopting that attitude. He's very smart and talented—and his early films had a sense of realism that resembles a good novel—but I don't think he ever did as great a movie as *Five Easy Pieces.*

Equally as tough a guy was Sam Peckinpah. One of the first pictures I worked on at United Artists was Sam's film *The Killer Elite.* Sam had just come off the film *Bring Me the Head of Alfredo Garcia*—or as one Hollywood type screamed out at a screening, "Bring me the head of Eric Pleskow!"

After I read *Killer Elite,* I went to Sam's office. He was sitting behind his desk, throwing knives at a dartboard hanging near the entrance of his office. At the time, he was also drinking a lot. With the combination of the knives and the booze, I decided to keep the meeting social and write him a letter about the script.

When I returned to the office, I wrote: "Dear Sam. Don't make changes to the script. We are happy enough with it as it is. Mike Medavoy." A few weeks later, I received his reply, a long, lugubrious note outlining all the changes he could make pursuant to the Directors Guild contract. He had taken my encouragement as an order, and I felt like a buffoon being dressed down in writing by the great Sam Peckinpah. It turned out that he had a pretty decent sense of humor. After the film was released, he sent me a T-shirt, the front of which was my note to him and on the back was his letter to me. That T-shirt drew quizzical looks when I wore it, but it remains one of my favorite souvenirs of the relationship between filmmaker and production executive.

We were so trusting of directors that we offered—over a bowl of matzo ball soup at the MGM commissary—to buy the finished film of *Taxi Driver* from Columbia sight unseen. Columbia president David Begelman hated the film and demanded that Martin Scorsese denature the film's climactic scene. Not surprisingly, Marty didn't want to change a frame. When I heard from Michael Phillips, the film's producer, that Marty was looking for a new distributor, I set up a lunch with Eric, Marty, and me. Eric and I had read the script, but we hadn't seen the film.

Marty explained his dilemma in his passionate, rat-tat-tat delivery, and Eric told him that if he had the contractual right to buy back the film, he had a deal. Marty murmured something about the blood and violence assuring the film would receive an X rating, but Eric said that didn't matter. He explained that UA had a successful track record with mainstream X-rated films like *Last Tango in Paris* and *Midnight Cowboy,* the first and only film with an X to win the Best Picture Oscar. When we made the offer, Marty Scorsese was known only for *Boxcar Bertha* and *Mean Streets,* two small films that played to a downtown audience; it wasn't until after *Taxi Driver* that Marty became a star director.

Back in my office, Eric told me that Arthur would probably kill him if he knew that we were trying to buy a finished film without seeing a frame, but he added that he felt good about making the offer. Though Eric sometimes seemed dispassionate and had a managerial approach to things, he was an inspiration to me when he wore his passion for artistic freedom on his sleeve. I was surprised almost to the point of being shocked at Eric's magnanimous gesture, but it was a perfect lesson in UA's philosophy of not tinkering with a director's work. Strictly speaking, because the film was finished, the five basic approvals—

script, director, producer, budget, principal cast—had all been met, so why not buy it?

Unfortunately, Begelman refused to sell.

For better or worse, I learned to believe in the directors we hired. As an agent, I was fascinated by directors, but as a studio executive, I came to respect exactly what the director did on a film. The French new-wave filmmakers, dubbed the "Nouvelle Vague," were the first to declare that the director, rather than the writer, was the author of the film. I came to agree— but with a few caveats: Movies are dramatic expressions of sound and light, and their styles are set by the *collaboration* of writer, director, actor, production designer, composer, and technicians. The writer starts the process, then hands it off. Ultimately, the director is responsible for every single frame of the movie, and everything must conform to his or her vision. If the director fails to shoot an image that supports or enhances the words, there won't be any magic, and the film simply won't work.

▬

In a Newsweek *story published in February 1978, Tony Bill summed up the Hollywood hierarchy: "The creative impetus is with the producers, the practical power is with the directors, but the ultimate power is with the stars." This made things tricky for UA because we didn't have the relationships with the stars that Universal, Warner Bros., or Columbia had. Our relationships were with the filmmakers.*

▬

During the four years I was at UA, directors had to build their ambitiously themed films around name-brand actors, or make them for a price without stars. On some films, final cut was actually in the hands of the actors—Steve McQueen had final cut on *The Getaway,* which was directed by Sam Peckinpah, and Barbra Streisand had the final say on Irvin Kershner's *Up the Sandbox.* But UA operated differently when it came to actors.

Arthur and Bob were hardly star-struck—they would never pay millions of dollars to a star so they could be seen with them at a premiere. Only with great reluctance would they pay a star a million dollars to topline a potential hit film. Therefore, it was rare for us to have big-name stars in our movies. When we did go after them, we often couldn't make their deals. When Richard Dreyfuss turned down the lead in *Bound for Glory* over money, the lesser-known David Carradine got the job. After winning his Oscar for *Cuckoo's Nest*, Jack Nicholson was too expensive for *Coming Home*, so Bruce Dern was cast.

Having represented actors of all generations, I was aware of their peculiarities. My job as an agent was to support the odd request and rationalize the actor's behavior. Seeing it from the studio's point of view, I began to realize just how strange some actors could be. I remember Dan Rissner, UA's head of European production, showing up and telling stories about Peter Sellers on the shoot of *The Pink Panther Strikes Again*. For starters, Sellers had a love-hate relationship with director Blake Edwards. However, the dial was stuck on hate to the point that the two refused to eat in the same restaurant together. Everything had to be equal, from their salaries ($1.25 million each) to the size of the letters on their dressing room signs. Once, Sellers called Dan Rissner in the middle of the night, woke him from a deep sleep, and said that Sellers's mother told him to quit the film and go to Hawaii. The next morning when Dan was more coherent, he called Sellers back and said that he had talked to his own mother and she said that if Sellers left the picture that Dan should have his legs broken.

Here's the dark part of the story: Sellers's mother had been dead for years.

As actors' prices started ticking upward, I was the first and only senior studio executive in all of Hollywood to speak out in the press. The others were probably just scared that the stars wouldn't work with them—or were smart enough to keep their mouths shut. When Steve McQueen's price hit $3 million in 1977, I questioned publicly if anyone was worth that much. I was trying to look at the big picture of what might happen to the business if film budgets became so top heavy above the line that everyone else was suffocated, or that all salaries would increase and price certain films out of the market. Escalating actors' salaries was the biggest factor in driving up the cost of making movies. The average cost of making a movie in 1977, for example, was $5.3 million, representing a 178 percent increase in four years and pushing the break-even point from 2.5 times a film's cost to 4 times' cost. Agents and lawyers, however, felt that these star prices were well deserved because the studios relied on them to carry the films in the marketplace. Besides, the more the actors made, the more the agents got paid.

The elite $3 million club at the time also included Paul Newman and Robert Redford. However, like runaway inflation, the numbers kept climbing. In 1978 Marlon Brando got $2.5 million for twelve days of work on *Superman*. My favorite comment came a few years later when Dustin Hoffman's agent advised me to pay Hoffman's asking price of $2.5 million for the film *Gorky Park*. "Why?" I asked. "Because next year it's going to be more," the agent responded. We didn't hire Dustin, but the agent was right.

The day Paul Newman told me that he wanted to make a greater contribution to society was one of my worst days at UA.

After working for two years cultivating a relationship with Newman's then-partner, producer-director George Englund, I finally broke through and made an overall deal with Newman's company. While I explained we couldn't pay him the big bucks of other studios, I tried to take a page from the UA playbook in the fifties: The company would sign stars like Kirk Douglas, Burt Lancaster, Frank Sinatra, and others, and let them produce their own movies. For Newman, the attraction was that ultimately he could make more money and have more control. Plus there was an added benefit: he could direct.

Newman was by far the most important actor UA had a deal with. He was white hot in 1974, thanks to *The Sting*, which had just won the Oscar for Best Picture and was hauling in the cash. Getting him in a movie was a must, so when the deal was concluded, I visited Newman at his house in Connecticut to discuss his next project for UA. Personally, I had a loose connection with him—I had packaged the writer-producer side of *The Sting*—which I thought would be a good starting point for our discussion.

But there was a blizzard the day of my trip to Connecticut, so I arrived all bundled up. Larger than life, Newman greeted me at the door, shirtless, with an ice cold beer in his hand. "Have a brew," he said. "You'll feel better." Of course, he said, he remembered my role in putting together *The Sting*, but after the small talk ended, the big star broke the bad news to the desperate, neophyte studio executive: Not only did he not have a film in mind, Newman told me that he was quitting acting altogether to pursue something far more important to the world as a whole. He was going to study to become a marine biologist. So after a two-year negotiation, we had a production deal with a closet biologist.

It was a fitting irony that the only film we got out of Newman in the two years was the flop *Buffalo Bill and the Indians*. We would have been better off if he would have become a marine biologist.

At that time, stars were more important to booking movies than to opening them. Having stars in one or two upcoming films gave you the muscle to book your entire slate of pictures for that year. If theater owners knew you had a film with Brando, Nicholson, Newman, Streisand, or Redford, then you could book three films around it and get better financial terms for all four films. Because of this, we weren't immune to picking up a star-powered project for leverage. A high-profile project also sends a message to the Hollywood creative community that we would back an expensive film if all the elements were right. It forced producers and agents to give us a look at every project they had, rather than exclude us because their budget might be too high.

What was true then about stars remains true today: There are pictures with stars that work and just as many that don't, and no star can save a bad picture. It's the picture; the whole picture needs to work. An agent always gets a 10 percent commission, so highly paid actors can make your business flourish, but for a studio executive, the opposite is true. Learning a lesson like that in the first two years of a thirty-six-year career was, to put a fine point on it, priceless.

Very few UA films fell into the big-star category, the most obvious being *The Missouri Breaks*, which we agreed to finance in 1975. At a time when the average film cost about $3.5 million, the budget on *The Missouri Breaks* was a hefty $7.8 million. (The final tally crested at $8.5 million, due to a laborious editing process that had thirteen people working on the film for four months.) The talent seemed to justify the price: Arthur Penn was directing Marlon Brando and Jack Nicholson from a script by novelist Tom McGuane and Robert Towne. Nearly everyone involved had recently won an Oscar: Penn for *Bonnie and Clyde,* Brando for *The Godfather,* and Towne for *Chinatown.* The producers were Bob Sherman, who brought Penn to the project when Bob Rafelson was wavering, and Elliott Kastner, who owned the material and had interested Brando. What was clear to me but not to my colleagues in New York was that the script was mediocre and it was not a commercial movie. Brando and Nicholson, who were neighbors, were at a stage in their careers when they could afford to gravitate toward offbeat material. Our rationale, however, was that this kind of film sent a signal to the creative community that we could package the big ones, so we backed the film.

As it turned out, the ongoing saga of who would end up with the stars' profit points in the movie was a who's-on-first routine that ended up being more entertaining than the film itself. It started when producer Elliott Kastner was slow in signing off on the last point-and-a-third of Brando's back end. Marlon was earning $1.25 million for five weeks' work, plus 11.3 percent of the gross. In retaliation, Marlon was softly mumbling his lines and phoning in his performance until Kastner would resolve his problems. Darryl Zanuck or Hal Wallis would've probably fired Brando, but since the movie needed Brando more than he needed it (or it needed Kastner)—Nicholson after all was only in the movie because Brando was—Kastner got on the first plane to go on-location to Montana and give the mumbling Marlon his agreed-upon profit participation. Then, when Nicholson saw the finished film, he complained to Kastner that he didn't like it. In an effort to give Nicholson his comeuppance, Kastner offered to buy Nicholson's points for $1 million. Nicholson gladly agreed, but Kastner never paid and Nicholson ended up suing him for the money. They ended up settling, with Nicholson keeping his points.

You would think that Brando and Nicholson would be enough insurance to bring people to the theaters. Then again, you'd be wrong—as we were.

When *The Missouri Breaks* opened to lackluster business, I learned never to trust a star to open a film that doesn't work. Ultimately, because of new technologies and avenues of distribution, the film has grossed $21.6 million and has paid $2.6 million out in profit participation, but even today, you don't make movies to earn a meek profit twenty-five years later.

Over time, I found that sometimes it's better to make a picture with an actor who has just had a failure if you have the gut feeling that the actor is right for the part. Deals in Hollywood are aligned with previous results, so often you don't have to pay a star as much if his or her last film flopped.

Nobody has a winner every time in this business. That's why a good executive learns to cast stars in the right part and not just for the benefit of having a recognizable name on the marquee. Casting stars for the sake of having a star is executive comfort food.

▬

In a tradition that dated back to the days of Selznick, Disney, and Zanuck, producers had a special place at United Artists. Arthur and Bob had an immense amount of respect for producers, and I quickly learned that they were to be treated like family members.

My additions to this family were the two men who produced a series of films that includes New York, New York; Rocky; *and* Raging Bull.

▬

Because UA didn't shadow the director during the shoot, we put a tremendous amount of faith in producers. Today, producer credits are given out like lollipops in a pediatrician's office—to managers, wives, girlfriends, lawyers, and development executives. They are the ego badge of the business. But at UA, our producers actually *produced* movies. The embodiment of a hands-on producer was the Italian triumvirate of Alberto Grimaldi, the stylish producer of the spaghetti Westerns; the outgoing Albert "Cubby" Broccoli, who, along with Harry Saltzman, produced the Bond films; and the prolific Dino De Laurentiis. We could always rely on these guys to supply UA with films—and find a proper Italian meal in any city. I added two producers to UA's list of distinguished producers by spearheading a deal that brought the producing team of Robert Chartoff and Irwin Winkler to United Artists.

Bob and Irwin were successful producers because they were good packagers and extremely committed to the material they wanted to produce. Bob and Irwin had particularly strong relationships with agents, and they moved very quickly. Besides the above-the-line elements (script, director, cast), they also knew how to get good below-the-line people (cameramen, grips, gaffers).

However, they had a spotty track record at the box office. While they got movies made, none of their films had been unqualified big hits. They had produced eleven films over a four-year period, maybe four of which were profitable. They had produced three fairly forgettable films for UA: *Leo the Last, The Mechanic*, and *Busting*. While they were an obvious choice for UA at the time because of their output, they were still a small gamble.

Over steak and salads at Chez Jay, a dumpy little place in Santa Monica with sawdust on the floors, Bob and I talked about Chartoff-Winkler coming to UA on an overall deal. "Look," I told Bob, "you guys have come close so many times you've got to hit pay dirt sooner or later."

On April 23, 1975, we signed Chartoff-Winkler to a four-year deal for a minimum of twelve films. It was the first exclusive deal I had a hand in and UA's biggest since the Mirisch brothers left. The deal called for us to pay the producing team's overhead and guaranteed fees that were applicable against the ones they charged for the films that were made. The first picture under the deal was to be a sweeping musical budgeted at $3.5 million called *New York, New York*. This was as close to an event film as we ever did at UA, and on paper it looked sure to be one of the company's biggest hits ever.

I had been a big fan of early musicals, so I had been looking for a classic musical story to do. The old RKO and MGM musicals had always transported my imagination to a world of charmed lives. I loved almost any kind of music in movies because the music in movies underlines your emotions. There was a universal magic watching Gene Kelly or Fred Astaire singing and dancing, and I felt that magic had been missing from the movies in the seventies. *New York, New York* seemed better than I had ever hoped for: A love story set in the forties, *New York, New York* would have Liza Minnelli singing and dancing alongside Robert De Niro, who had just come off his sensational performance in *The Godfather II*. Martin Scorsese, himself a New Yorker, was hired to direct. It appeared that Chartoff and Winkler had brought us the ideal package.

When *New York, New York* went into production in the spring of 1976, the budget jumped from $3.5 million to $6.3 million. No matter, we thought this was the one. As the dailies came in, everyone at UA, from New York to L.A., was *sure* we had a hit. One day, I personally escorted Transamerica chairman Jack Beckett on a tour of the sets on the MGM lot and screened some of the footage for him so he could see for himself what a masterpiece we had in the making. He was so dazzled that he wrote me a personal note when he returned to San Francisco that echoed all of our sentiments.

We were all convinced it was going to be an Oscar-winning commercial hit.

We were wrong.

■

While *New York, New York* was shooting, I read the script for another Chartoff-Winkler project, *Rocky*. They had given me the script for a flight home from New York to L.A. (The smartest producers and agents always send scripts to executives when they hear the words "airplane trip," because they know it's the one time in an executive's life when the phone isn't ringing.) *Rocky* was a page-turner. Though it was a boxing picture and the hero lost the fight, the story had an authenticity that made it stand out. Bob explained to me that the unknown actor who had written the script had to play the lead.

Rocky had come in to Bob and Irwin because of their gentle touch with talent. It all started when their head of script development, Gene Kirkwood, insisted that Bob watch part of *The Lords of Flatbush* to see if they had any parts for this young actor named Sylvester Stallone. Reluctantly, Bob agreed to watch a half-hour of the film, but it was so enchanting that he ended up sitting through the whole thing. Though Bob and Irwin didn't have any parts for Stallone, Bob wanted to meet him.

Stallone turned out to be charming and forthright. During the meeting, Stallone told Bob and Irwin that he was trying his hand at screenwriting and asked if they would read *Paradise Alley*, a script he had written about three brothers living in Hell's Kitchen in the forties. Bob and Irwin politely agreed. After reading the script, Bob decided it was good enough to option and develop, so they invited Stallone back in for a second meeting.

Stallone appeared at their offices, with his head down and voice almost trembling. Addressing Bob as Mr. Chartoff, Stallone apologized for not being straight with them about *Paradise Alley*. He explained that he had shown the script around for years and nobody wanted it, but last month, he had let a producer option it for $500 so he could pay his rent. He had given it to them just to show that he was more than your average struggling actor. Bob made it easy for Stallone and told him not to worry. They liked him and something else would come along. Relieved, Stallone said he had another idea for a movie, about a boxer, and promised to write the script quickly and bring it back to Bob and Irwin.

Arthur, Bob, and Eric liked the *Rocky* script, but they weren't sure about making the movie. The budget was $1.29 million, which was small, but money was money, and it was risky without a no-name actor in the lead. There were also prints and advertising to add on. The first thing they suggested was casting James Caan as Rocky, but that was immediately rejected by Bob and Irwin. Not only were they morally and contractually committed to Stallone, they were fervent in their belief in him. Since we had hired them to bring in packaged projects, we wanted to give them every chance, so I arranged a screening of *The Lords of Flatbush* for the New York office so they could see Stallone on screen.

Arthur was pleased with Stallone's acting—except that he thought Perry King, the blond Californian who co-starred in *The Lords of Flatbush*, was Stallone. Having read *Rocky* with all its references to the "Italian Stallion," Arthur turned to Eric during the screening and wondered how an Italian could be blond and blue-eyed. Eric casually responded, "In northern Italy there are a lot of blond, blue-eyed Italians."

Based on Stallone's (née Perry King's) performance as one of the four street toughs, Arthur agreed to proceed with negotiations on *Rocky*. He insisted that the film be made for $1.25 million and that Bob and Irwin sign a personal guarantee against overages, which they did. This was uncommon, but the film was seen as risky on all levels. Arthur also insisted we get some insurance by crossing the profits of the sure-fire winner *New York, New York* with this commercially dicey boxing picture. Bob and Irwin were dying to make the film so they agreed. Bill Bernstein dotted the *i*'s and crossed the *t*'s on the crossing deal.

In effect, if *New York, New York* was a hit and *Rocky* wasn't, the losses from Rocky would come out of Chartoff-Winkler's share of the profits. The reverse also applied as we soon saw.

This idea of crossing profits was a micromodel of the studios' philosophy that the hits pay for the misses. Surprisingly, crossing isn't widely used today, though it should be. This would allow studios and producers who were regular suppliers to take more risks by leveraging a chancy, offbeat drama against a summer action film. At the time, it turned out to be the kind of smart business thinking that Arthur was known for throughout his career.

The irony, of course, was that instead of *New York, New York* paying for *Rocky*, we ended up getting back most of the money we put into *New York, New York* out of Chartoff-Winkler's *Rocky* profits: *New York, New York* was a bomb while *Rocky* was a blockbuster. *New York, New York* ended up costing $8.4 million to make, which was $2.1 million over budget, and it grossed less than $14 million, roughly half of which was returned to UA. *Rocky*, which cost $1.3 million and grossed more than $115 million in the United States, alone, landed fifth on the all-time domestic-box-office list in 1976.

It also spawned four sequels, which collectively grossed more than a billion dollars.

We learned several more lessons from *New York, New York,* but the main one for me was: *The dailies don't tell the whole story.* Sam Goldwyn once declared that if everyone liked the dailies, the picture would be a stinker. I would spin that a slightly different way: *If the dailies look good, the finished film may be great, but it may also be a clunker.* (Many years later, on *Hudson Hawk,* a movie I inherited from the previous regime at TriStar, I learned the corollary to this theory: *Bad dailies mean a bad movie.*) In the case of *New York, New York,* everyone was predisposed to be dazzled by the dailies because we had Marty Scorsese directing Liza Minnelli and Robert De Niro in a lush period setting. Unconsciously, the *New York, New York* experience was probably why I stopped watching the dailies in their entirety over the years once I was sure the film wasn't a disaster in the making. From that point on, whenever someone tells me the dailies look great, I smile, knowing that even if their film is a hit this time, someday they'll learn their lesson about dailies. This is even truer of comedies. If they are honest, most directors will tell you that they don't know if the film will work or not—even when they have finished assembling the dailies into a rough cut of the film.

There were a handful of eternal optimists who thought people would like *New York, New York* after they saw the finished film, but we knew there was a problem. After an advance industry screening in L.A. at the Thalberg Screening Room on the MGM lot, Eric and I were terribly disappointed. The film didn't work. Walking across the room to talk to Marty, we were cut off by Sam Fuller, an old director client and a friend of Marty's, who was chewing on his cigar. In a raspy voice that sounded as though he was talking through his nose, the director of *Shark!* and *Dead Pigeon on Beethoven Street* sternly advised Marty, "Don't change a frame, my boy. You have a winner!"

Eric turned to me and said facetiously, "How much money does he have invested in this picture?"

▬

Closed preview screenings in Hollywood attended by friends, family, and assorted hangers-on rarely give you an honest reaction to a film. In truth, industry screenings might be the ultimate hypocrisy in a business that can be very hypocritical. The audience is usually composed mostly of the filmmaker's genuine friends, who applaud and laugh at all the right moments. They want the studio executives in the audience to hear what a great film it is so the studio will support their friend's film with marketing dollars. The studio executives tend to be a group of people who either inherited the film from a previous regime or don't want anything to do with what they think is a potential turkey, so they walk out and praise the film in Hollywood double-speak. Typically, they can be heard telling the producer and director things like, "You did it again!" or "What a picture!"—neither of which says what it really means. Those executives also know they might need that producer or director in the future. So in the end, everyone runs from a failure and tries to walk alongside a success.

In early 2000, I was watching Sylvester Stallone's newest film, *Driven*, when I heard a line that he had written for his character. I thought it summed up the *Rocky* experience perfectly: "If you have the passion and the will, you can do it."

By any standard, *Rocky* was a true labor of love by everyone involved, every step of the way. Bob and Irwin's first two criteria for everyone who worked on the film were that they had to work cheaply and efficiently. John Avildsen was hired to direct because he had a proven knack for getting the most out of every dollar. He had directed *Joe* on a $300,000 budget and made it look like a $2 million film. Bill Conti was paid about $18,000 for his score, perhaps the most memorable film score of the decade. To this day, the music is a symbol of athletic triumph around the world. Almost every sporting event blasts the inspirational theme song "Gonna Fly Now." It has become a symbol of the triumph of the human spirit and the courage to take that once-in-a-lifetime chance. Like it did for others associated with the film, *Rocky* made Conti's reputation, and he has gone on to earn millions from the four sequels and his subsequent work.

Avildsen finished shooting in just twenty-five days and brought the movie in at only $100,479 over the original budget of $1,220,011, which was very impressive for a film shot on location in a major city like Philadelphia. The first time we saw *Rocky*, we all agreed it was pretty good. But it didn't have the final fight scene in it—the one scene that delivers on the promise of the entire movie. Upon seeing the movie, Arthur proclaimed that it would do $7 million. To emphasize the love affair and downplay the boxing in hopes of making the film a "date movie," Gabe Sumner and Freddie Goldberg, who ran our marketing department, created a poster showing Rocky, wearing his boxing shorts, and his girlfriend (played by Talia Shire) walking hand in hand with their backs to the camera. The tag line: HIS WHOLE LIFE WAS A MILLION-TO-ONE SHOT.

Originally, we wanted to release *Rocky* in February and not give it a qualifying run for the previous year's Oscars. (To be eligible for the Academy Awards, a film must run theatrically for at least two days in either New York or L.A. before the end of the calendar year, so it's typical for studios to open films the last week of December and then either close them and reopen them or slowly roll them out in January.) We had another film that seemed sure to win some awards, *Bound for Glory*, based on the life of folk singer Woody Guthrie. The film starred David Carradine and was directed by Hal Ashby, whose forte was emotional material. On *Bound for Glory*, he went behind the lyrics of Guthrie's songs to capture his life.

Chartoff, Winkler, and Gabe Sumner were convinced that we had magic in a bottle with *Rocky*, so we decided to hold an industry screening at the Cary Grant Theater on the MGM lot. The audience literally got up and cheered during the new final fight scene. "Hit him Rocky!" they screamed. Even for a friends-and-family screening, this was extraordinary, so we decided to try the film out on the public.

The first preview screening was held at the Baronet Theater on Broadway in New York. Again, the audience went wild. From the moment the screening let out, Stallone was a star. The transformation was almost instant. He stood in the lobby wearing a $20 suit, and people walked up to him and just wanted to touch him. They were calling him "Rock" and talking to him as though he were really the street fighter from Philadelphia who had just gone the distance with the heavyweight champion of the world.

This marked the end of the humble guy with the Swiss education I met before we okayed *Rocky*. Not since *Giant* splashed James Dean on the scene had a new star sparked such excitement.

Rocky's release strategy was small and delicate, and the promotion relied heavily on Stallone. We didn't want people to think it was the Rocky Marciano or Rocky Graziano story. If there was ever such a thing as a word-of-mouth strategy, this was it. We booked the film in smaller theaters that would promise open-ended play dates to allow one person to tell another. Since television advertising was cost-prohibitive relative to the budget, we sent Stallone to as many small towns as possible to give personal interviews to the local newspapers and radio stations. We encouraged him to emphasize the central message: *This is a personal film, I'm the little guy, and you know how those big, bad Hollywood studios are—so I need your help.*

Stallone ended up repeating this promotional mantra so many times that he began to believe that we were the evil corporate robber barons. He forgot that we were the friends of the artists who had agreed to let him star in his own script despite its dubious commercial potential. We gave him his shot when no one else would.

At one point during the promotional tour, Stallone's manager called me from Chicago and asked for a $150,000 advance from his client's share of the inevitable profits. He said Stallone wanted to buy a house when he got back to L.A. I stalled him by telling him I didn't have the authority to write a check that big without the okay of Eric and Arthur. But by the time Stallone returned, the film was doing so well that he had forgotten all about the $150,000. Now, he was thinking mansion, which was easily within his reach.

It wasn't long before Stallone's share of the first *Rocky* brought him $4 million. For their faith in the material and the cast, Chartoff and Winkler soon became multimillionaires as well.

Not only did Stallone's future change with the film's success, but his past was changed, too. By the time we started promoting Stallone for the Oscar, he had been force-fed so many stories from Bob and Irwin about how he stood up to the studios when they wanted to cast a star and buy him off that he now believed them. He laid out a somewhat fictitious rags-to-riches story in a *New York* magazine story, "He Could Be a Contender," and he told *Time* magazine that he had battled against the producers who wanted to cast Jimmy Caan or Burt Reynolds.

Burt Reynolds? As Rocky?

To this day, Stallone apparently still believes he went a few rounds with the studios over casting and won. In a *Newsweek* commemorative issue in May 1999, he wrote that we offered him as much as $360,000 for the script (which, he explains, would be the equivalent of $2 million today) if he would drop out. The myth has become reality.

In our star-driven culture, Stallone gets to write history the way he chooses.

When I read the story, I knew the "we" wasn't United Artists, so I double-checked with Bob Chartoff to see if Stallone might have been talking about another studio. "All rubbish," Chartoff said, after reading a faxed copy of the article. "No one ever offered him anything to drop out."

Lana Turner wasn't discovered at Schwab's either, but it still makes for good Hollywood lore.

≡

When the nominations for the 1976 Oscars were released, three of the five Best Picture nominees were UA releases. Rocky *and* Network *(our co-production with MGM) collected ten nominations each, and* Bound for Glory *earned six nominations, though Hal Ashby, to my amazement, was not nominated as Best Director. In all, UA's releases received thirty-one nominations, a deeply satisfying embarrassment of riches. Theoretically, we could have had four of the five Best Picture nominees, but we turned down* All the President's Men.

Bad move but, still, we had three of five.

▬

All the President's Men was submitted in both book and script form. At the time, we felt that after the country had been so saturated with the media coverage of the national nightmare that no one would want to watch a two-hour movie about two reporters following the money. After we passed for the second time, Warner Bros. quickly snapped it up.

I still regret having made that decision. The lesson was obvious: *Sometimes trying to read how people will feel about politically charged material obstructs your view of potentially good entertainment.* Nevertheless, I repeated the error many years later when I passed on *Good Morning, Vietnam.* I had been an army disc jockey in Korea and Panama, and the script was nothing like I had remembered my service days.

Careers are made by ones you *make,* not the ones that get away. On March 28, 1977 (the night the Oscars were presented for the 1976 movie year), *Rocky* won the Academy Award for Best Picture, our second in a row after *Cuckoo's Nest.* John Avildsen won Best Director and the editors also won. Stallone, who was nominated for both Best Actor and Best Screenplay, didn't win a statue himself, but Bob and Irwin pulled him on stage when they accepted their Best Picture statues. The image of Stallone standing on stage, wearing a tux with a wide, seventies-style shirt collar folded over his lapel, basking in praise from the audience was the culmination of his transformation into an almost mythical figure, from Sunset Boulevard to Main Street.

Winning our second consecutive Best Picture Oscar was an incredible triumph for everyone at United Artists. No one would have predicted we would make it a hat trick with *Annie Hall* the following year.

Then again, who would have predicted that none of us would be at United Artists a year later either?

3   *The Madman in the Jungle*

*Vietnam is one of the most difficult issues the
United States and, therefore, Hollywood has confronted since I began my career. The complicated
issues of this conflict were as hard for Hollywood to
reconcile as they were for the rest of the country.
Novelists like Norman Mailer and musicians like
the Rolling Stones tailored their art to the times. It
seemed inevitable that filmmakers would rush to
make Vietnam movies, but not one single important
film about Vietnam came out while the war was
being fought.*

The conventional wisdom in Hollywood in the early seventies
was that people didn't want to see Vietnam-themed movies. During World War II, Hollywood was making propaganda movies
designed to sell our cause, and because of that, studios managed
to export our culture and influence other cultures. The American
Film Institute's current catalog of movies lists nearly four hundred World War II films made during the 1940s alone. The exact
opposite occurred during the Vietnam War, and Hollywood executives shied away from Vietnam-themed movies.

As always, Hollywood's thinking was based on box office: The
ever-popular John Wayne made *The Green Berets* in 1968, but the
only memorable part of the film was its patriotic theme song.
One of the few films made in response to what was happening in
Vietnam was the documentary *Hearts and Minds*, which won the
Academy Award for Best Documentary about a month before the
official end of the war in 1975. People wanted to see more of the

escapist fare that had been cleaning up at the box office—*Rocky, Jaws, Star Wars, The Other Side of Midnight*—because television was putting them as close to the war as they wanted to be, so much so that Lyndon Johnson himself declared that when he lost Walter Cronkite, he lost the war. Besides, the conflicting emotions were being explored in music, which is always faster to respond to social issues than film.

But suddenly, after 1975, things changed, and there was a flood of Vietnam-themed movies. By the end of 1977, there were no less than seven in various stages of ready, including *The Deer Hunter*. UA alone had two Vietnam movies in production, with Karel Reisz's audacious adaptation of Robert Stone's *Dog Soldiers* (eventually and stupidly retitled *Who'll Stop the Rain?* by the next regime) in the can and ready for release. It featured Nick Nolte as a temperamental Vietnam veteran who teams up with a cynical journalist played by Michael Moriarty to smuggle a large amount of heroin into California. It was *almost* beginning to look as though Hollywood was feeling pangs of guilt.

Initially, like many Americans, I felt that the Vietnam War was in the national interest of stemming the tide of Communism. Once our troops were in-country, I fully supported the U.S. effort. My own family had escaped Communism, causing me to buy into President John F. Kennedy's domino theory. But once I began seeing those images of body bags on national television, I was as outraged as anyone. When the realization that this war was being fought on the same principles as the Korean War hit me—we weren't there to win a war, we were there to fight a war of containment—my views changed.

However, I never proselytized my personal beliefs, and neither did the rest of UA's senior management. We made decisions based on scripts, filmmakers, and actors, not on some universal political statement that should be made. When the issue of doing a Vietnam-themed movie with Jane Fonda came up, and we began to put together *Coming Home*, I gave considerable thought to what had happened to her after she won the 1971 Best Actress Oscar for *Klute*.

I had been Jane's agent when she was pictured on the cover of *Newsweek* sitting on a North Vietnamese antiaircraft gun under the headline HANOI JANE. She first became a client of mine when I moved to IFA to head up the motion picture department, where I shared her with her longtime agent Dick Clayton, who also represented Burt Reynolds and at one time had handled James Dean. By this time, Jane was regarded by many people in and out of the business as the poster child activist for all that was wrong with Hollywood actors using their influence to send political messages, and I saw firsthand how her career paid dearly for it. But at the time she was so passionate about her feelings that she didn't care. More than one studio head told me that she was now almost universally hated and that they couldn't book a movie if she was in it. The damage done to her career by her position on Vietnam was considerable. After expressing herself so publicly, Jane couldn't get a job. It wasn't that Hollywood was mad at her; after all, the liberals have always far outnumbered conservatives in the entertainment industry. It was that the theater owners didn't want political demonstrations at their theaters—and they booked the movies. And it was that some of the moviegoing public was repulsed by her views—and they bought the tickets.

I never intruded in Jane's private life. As far as I was concerned, Jane could protest anything she wanted. Some agents like to take on the role of confessor, life adviser, or best friend, but I think that sets both sides up for disaster. While I was representing her, I remember getting a call one day from a man who told me that he was in a phone booth and that he had Jane's secret FBI files. After a long pause, the man asked me if I would meet him in a phone booth across from Schwab's (of all places), and get the files. "Let me give you a clearer picture of the situation," I told him. "I'm her agent. A-G-E-N-T. I get her acting parts. If you've got a script with a firm cash offer then call me. But for any personal matters, let me give you her lawyer's number and you can call him." Thankfully, I never heard from him again.

Since I had been so close to Jane's situation, the decision of whether or not to support making *Coming Home* was somewhat personal for me. I came to the conclusion that she was probably right to do what she did for reasons that had nothing to do with her as an actress. The people closest to her all agreed with her actions at the time, and maybe her career should not have been her first consideration—maybe she was right to insist that her beliefs should be more important to her. Having seen such an accomplished actress near her low, I was glad to participate in her comeback, but I didn't push for *Coming Home* as a political redux for her. I pushed for it because it was a good project. In the end, I was more worried about the film's politics than about Jane's. In the first scene, when a veteran talks about his moral obligation to fight in Vietnam, he is ridiculed by his fellow veterans, the message being that the war is wrong and that there are no heroes. I wasn't sure how audiences would respond, and we all knew we were taking a chance.

Coming Home was a project that took years to come together. In 1973, while I was still Jane's agent, she and her producing partner, Bruce Gilbert, commissioned Nancy Dowd to write a script about two women whose consciousness was elevated by men fighting in Vietnam. Dowd's script, "Buffalo Ghosts," was then rewritten by the acclaimed screenwriter Waldo Salt, who had won the Oscar for *Midnight Cowboy*. British director John Schlesinger was signed to direct *Coming Home*, but he became uncomfortable with the subject matter. Hal Ashby, himself a critic of the Vietnam War, was then hired. When Salt became sick, Ashby turned the script over to Robert Jones, his film editor and trusted friend.

The finished film sparked a visceral reaction from Gabe Sumner, our head of marketing, and his team. He had come to L.A. to see the film and to begin planning the marketing and publicity campaign. After seeing the movie, he was irate, calling the film "anti-American" and me "irresponsible" for being its champion. Dismayed and depressed, I phoned Eric and relayed Gabe's assessment. "Send him home," Eric said. "I'll take care of him in New York. Their job is to sell the film. I don't care if they like it." That was the end of that discussion. The film gave what I thought was an honest portrait of two Vietnam veterans and showed the impact that the war was having on the wives of the vets. The film's plot of a wife (played by Jane Fonda) of a proud Marine captain (Bruce Dern) who learns to live and to love through her relationship with a bitter paraplegic (Jon Voight) destroyed by the war employed a cruel irony that many people were unprepared for.

Coming Home was accepted into competition at the 1978 Cannes Film Festival, which helped give it a publicity boost. Cannes turned out to be the beginning of many awards for the film, including several accolades for its acting. Many Hollywood insiders thought that United Artists might win its fourth consecutive Academy Award for Best Picture, after *Cuckoo's Nest*, *Rocky*, and *Annie Hall*. *Coming Home* ended up winning Best Original Screenplay, and Voight and Fonda both won acting Oscars, but *The Deer Hunter* won Best Picture. For Jane, winning her second Best Actress Oscar was laced with political significance. For me, her Oscar completed a professional circle.

▬

There was no collective conscience in the creative community that rose up and decided it was time to make a statement about Vietnam. Trends don't start that way. What happens is that someone of critical or commercial stature breaks the mold and people fall in line behind him. That's why there always seems to be a group of movies on a subject that has been around for years or even decades. There are very few secrets in Hollywood, everybody seems to know everybody else's business—or at least they think they do.

The sudden burst of Vietnam movies at that time was no different than when Robert Redford decided to do a rodeo movie, and presto, there were two others ready to go. The Deer Hunter was one of those made-to-order Vietnam films. The film's American soldier stationed in Vietnam who ends up playing Russian roulette for a living became a metaphor for the U.S. involvement in Vietnam, but that, in fact, was not screenwriter Quinn Redeker's intention. That part of the story was conceived by Redeker while he was playing with his kids in his kitchen. He set it in Vietnam because it was the world crisis of the moment and he was looking for dramatic tension, not to make a statement about the war.

▬

The first director to make a major Vietnam movie was Francis Ford Coppola, who was coming off his first two Academy Award–winning *Godfather* films. Francis opened the floodgates in the spring of 1975 when he decided to direct *Apocalypse Now*. Interestingly, Francis was not a war protester, or even an artist who wanted to make a point about the Vietnam War. Once he decided to make *Apocalypse Now*, Francis immersed himself in Vietnam the same way most filmmakers do when they are tackling a new subject. He was a filmmaker looking for a grand-scale project—or as Willard says at the beginning of *Apocalypse Now*, "I was looking for a mission for my sins."

Francis Coppola found one in *Apocalypse Now*.

Apocalypse Now was a script by John Milius that had been in limbo since I sold it during my agency days. John had written the script in 1968 as an allegory to Joseph Conrad's existential novel *Heart of Darkness*. When he started the script, John decided not to adapt Conrad's novel per se. Rather, he wanted to apply *Heart of Darkness* to Vietnam, and he wanted to do it the way he remembered the novel the first time he read it at age seventeen— as a dream. To maintain this dreamlike sensibility, he purposely didn't reread the novel, which is amazing considering how faithful he was to Conrad's vision. I sold the script to Francis's company, American Zoetrope, which had a deal at Warner Bros. at the time.

Zoetrope paid John $15,000 for *Apocalypse Now*, with another $10,000 due when (and if) the film was made. In those days, option fees came with unlimited rewrites, and John ended up doing eleven drafts of *Apocalypse Now* over the next eight years. (One summer, John rented a beach house in Malibu and trailed Steve McQueen around, tailoring the script for McQueen to play Captain Willard. This was during McQueen's martial arts period, so John frequently had to suit up in armor and fight. "This'll make a man out of you," McQueen would tell John, as McQueen's instructor kicked the shit out of him. One day when Milius showed up at McQueen's house the actor wasn't home. It turned out that the night before McQueen was driving home with his wife, Ali MacGraw, and had driven off the road into the ditch. Unhurt and too tired to go for help, they curled up and went to sleep in the car.)

Originally, one of Francis's Zoetrope disciples, George Lucas, was going to direct *Apocalypse Now* as a documentary-style, 16-millimeter film with a budget of about $6 million. George sent his producer, Gary Kurtz, to the Philippines to scout locations. But ultimately Francis became impatient with George, who was spending too much time puttering around with what Francis believed was a silly science fiction project entitled *Star Wars*. In a let's-separate-the-men-from-the-boys gesture, Francis decided to do *Apocalypse Now* himself.

Over dinner, Francis and I discussed the project and how UA could become involved. He explained that he had decided to direct it himself because it was a fairly easy story to tell. It didn't require the heavy lifting of a third *Godfather*, which he would need to write. He would simply go to the Philippines to shoot a nice little war movie. He wanted $12 million from UA to make the film, roughly twice as much as George Lucas had said he needed. The extra money was for a top-notch cast. After the two *Godfather* films, Francis was certain that anyone would work for him, and he planned to get McQueen, Newman, or someone of that caliber, and then raise the rest of the money through advance sales of foreign rights, which would allow him to control production. He wanted UA to invest part of the budget in exchange for the domestic rights, but he wanted to own the film.

The first sign of trouble was that no big star was willing to spend six months in the Philippines, which made it tougher to raise money than Francis thought. After Francis secured several foreign sales commitments, Eric and I went to San Francisco to finalize a deal for the domestic rights. Francis had just moved his offices into the new Zoetrope building, just across the street from the Transamerica Tower. He loved the idea of being the little guy in the shadow of the conglomerate that was going to finance his most ambitious movie to date. If anyone could shake the ground on the subject of Vietnam, it was Francis Ford Coppola. Shortly after Coppola started, we announced a release date of April 7, 1977, Francis's birthday. Francis's favorite number is seven, and he always claimed it was particularly lucky for him.

A few weeks after Francis set out for the Philippines, Fox gave George Lucas the greenlight on *Star Wars* for $8.5 million.

■

By the time I was dispatched to the set of *Apocalypse Now*, the film was in real trouble. Francis Coppola started shooting his Vietnam epic in the Philippines on March 26, 1976. Three weeks after filming commenced, troubles began. Coppola fired Harvey Keitel and replaced him with Martin Sheen, necessitating that all of Keitel's finished scenes be reshot. Then in late May, less than two months into production, a monsoon hit and wiped out one of the locations. Francis, already weeks behind and millions over budget, was forced to shut down and to return home to San Francisco.

During this time, Francis had appealed to UA for another $3 million to cover mounting overages. He was given the loan, provided that he secure it personally if the film didn't return $40 million to UA. Much has been written about how UA made Francis put up his house or his vineyard as collateral, but it never happened. Transamerica was pushing for us to put a lien on his properties, but we wouldn't do it. What director would want to work with a company that took a man's house away? Eventually, Francis signed his own personal guarantees for the film, but if it had failed, he would have been bankrupt and there would have been no way for UA to collect our money.

In July, Francis and the cast reconvened in the Philippines to finish the film. In September Marlon Brando refused to show up until Francis escrowed $1 million of his salary. In retrospect, who could blame Marlon for wanting his money up front on a film that was running out of money? But according to Francis, Marlon showed up unprepared: he hadn't read either the script or Conrad's *Heart of Darkness*, and he was so overweight that Francis had to shoot him only from the neck up. (Marlon disagrees with this account.)

We were constantly sending people to the Philippines for progress reports on our investment. Although it was our policy not to meddle, Francis violated our approval rules several times over. Other directors, like William Friedkin, wrote me notes, expressing concern for Francis and the studio. Finally, Transamerica's Jim Harvey, who oversaw UA, insisted that Eric take action, a serious development underscored by the fact that Jim Harvey and Coppola were friends. My duty, as head of production, was to talk to Francis. Fred Roos went with me to the Philippines. Fred was a sure-eyed casting director (now best known for putting Harrison Ford in *American Graffiti*) who had become one of Francis's producers. In fact, it was Fred who had suggested the Philippines; he had produced two films there in the sixties starring Jack Nicholson and then turned Francis on to the location. So while the trip was a hop, skip, and a jump for him, it was a journey to the Magi for me.

To reach the location, we flew from Los Angeles to Tokyo, grabbed six hours of sleep in a hotel, then got on a plane to Manila. I was concerned about the film, but I also had an eerie personal feeling about the trip: I hadn't been to Manila since 1947, when my family and I had stopped there on our way from Shanghai to Chile. My faint memories of Manila were of bombed-out buildings, an almost leveled city, and a hotel where we had spent the night before continuing on to Chile. Now I was flying there under very different circumstances, with a very different predicament.

I wrestled with what to say to Francis. Our biggest problem was that Francis was shooting without any hint of an ending in sight. No one, including Francis, knew how the film was going to end. But realistically, there was little I could do. We weren't going to put Francis in a straitjacket and have someone else take over the movie. It wasn't our style to replace a director, but we also couldn't fire Francis because he was putting up some of the money through foreign presales. He was also the reason we were doing the film in the first place.

I expected trouble, but what I was greeted with was near tragedy.

The first thing I saw after clearing customs at the Manila airport was a production assistant with huge sign towering over hundreds of people waiting for passengers: MEDAVOY URGENT. I was happy to see him because I figured he could grease the wheels for us through customs and carry our bags, but the flustered production assistant holding the sign explained to me that we were getting into a car and going straight to the hospital. Martin Sheen had suffered a heart attack. Though the P.A. didn't have any details on Sheen's condition, as Fred and I headed for Manila, I braced myself for the worst.

Marty was lying in bed with tubes running out of every orifice of his body, his wife kneeling at the foot of the bed, sobbing hysterically. My heart sank. My first thought was that I didn't want Marty to die because he was a wonderful person. Then practicality hit: I wasn't sure how much of his part had been shot, whether Marty was finished, whether Francis needed him, whether the movie could be finished without him. It occurred to me that it might be a bad practical joke that everyone was playing on the visiting studio head.

But as soon as Marty's wife, Janet, saw me, I understood how badly things had turned. She was angry that Francis had been making her husband work in that blistering heat. "Francis doesn't care about anyone!" she yelled. In the corner, a priest stood patiently, waiting, I thought, to deliver the last rites. Marty wasn't moving or talking; he was just sucking air.

Finally, the doctor arrived and briefed me on Marty's condition. I was relieved to hear he wasn't dying, but his prognosis suggested that the film might be dead: it would take Marty six months to recover, and his family wanted him to do it on Malibu beach. "Maybe he can come back, maybe not," the doctor shrugged. I left the hospital wondering what other disasters lay in wait for me.

After a short helicopter ride across Manila Bay, I found Francis at his compound at Palsanjan. The grounds were fit for a king, with several houses covered in mosquito netting and a series of pools with waterfalls pouring into them, each more beautiful than the last. I walked into the main house carrying my two overnight bags, sweating from the heat and the anxiety over the phone call I would have to make to my superiors in New York about Martin Sheen's heart attack. Then I spotted Francis. He was lying shirtless in the middle of the living room floor with a beard virtually covering his face, clutching his wife, Elie's, ankles. He looked like a wounded bear, begging for his life to be spared.

Apparently, Elie had found out that Francis was having an

That headline made me feel like Monroe Stahr in F. Scott
Fitzgerald's *The Love of the Last Tycoon* but I was surprised they
picked my photo to be on the cover. The story looked at the seven
young studio heads of production and how we were helping push
through a creative revolution in the late seventies—five of us,
including me, had worked under seventies superagent Freddie
Fields at CMA. (COPYRIGHT © *THE NEW YORK TIMES*, INC.)

Morris Mike Medavoy at age six, living in Shanghai. The following year my family would move us to Chile just before the Communists invaded China. I don't know who cut my hair, but if I ever find him . . . (COLLECTION OF THE AUTHOR)

Living in Chile for nine years, I learned about America through its movies, which is probably why I was able to do my best James Dean pose only days after I arrived in the U.S. at age sixteen. (COLLECTION OF THE AUTHOR)

Mike Medavoy, executive vice president of worldwide production for Orion Pictures, looking about as formal as we ever did at Orion. The inner thoughts of a head of production at this moment: Hurry up with the picture, because my phone is ringing. (COLLECTION OF THE AUTHOR)

Inscription reads: "Oh, Mike Medavoy, oh, oh, Christ. Donald." Every fledgling agent needs one or two movie stars as clients upon which to build his reputation. Donald Sutherland (seen here in *Kelly's Heroes*) was that man for me, because he became a real commodity after I signed him. (COLLECTION OF THE AUTHOR)

Some of the crazies from *One Flew Over the Cuckoo's Nest:* Jack Nicholson in the stocking cap and Danny DeVito leaning over the table on his right. Much of Hollywood thought my colleagues and I at United Artists were even nuttier than this group for backing the film. (COURTESY OF THE SAUL ZAENTZ COMPANY)

Chatting with director Milos Forman, who would save my executive career with *One Flew Over the Cuckoo's Nest* shortly after I started at United Artists in 1974. We went on to work together on three more films, *Amadeus, Valmont,* and *The People vs. Larry Flynt,* and we've got still a couple more to go. (COLLECTION OF THE AUTHOR)

What a mug! Peter Boyle as *Young Frankenstein*. I packaged the film with three of my clients—Peter, Marty Feldman, and Gene Wilder, who wrote the script. The pitch: the Three Stooges do Frankenstein.

Rocky was promoted as a love story, because conventional wisdom held that people didn't like boxing pictures, but thanks to stunning performances by Sylvester Stallone and Talia Shire, *Rocky* shattered those preconceived notions.

The walls of the conference room at Phoenix Pictures are lined with pictures of all the stars and film-makers I have worked with in my career. Robert Redford is razzing me a little with the inscription, asking for his own wall. He didn't get it, though he deserved it.
(COLLECTION OF THE AUTHOR)

Not your average story conference. On the set of *New York, New York* with director Marty Scorsese and Liza Minnelli in full makeup. Working on *New York, New York* was a dream come true for me as a young studio executive at United Artists, because I loved musicals. Unfortunately, audiences didn't like this one as much as I did.
(COLLECTION OF THE AUTHOR)

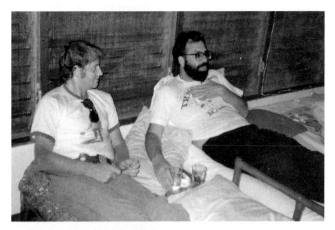

On my visit to the troubled shoot of *Apocalypse Now* in
the Philippines, Francis Coppola lays out his plan for
finishing the movie, which was that he had no plan.
(COLLECTION OF THE AUTHOR)

We became known as the UA Five on the day we resigned from
United Artists in 1978, but to me these four are known as the guys to
whom I owe my career. From left to right: Eric Pleskow, me, Arthur
Krim, Bob Benjamin, and Bill Bernstein. In one of the most unique
Hollywood executive partnerships ever, we stuck together for sixteen
years, first at UA and then at Orion. (COLLECTION OF THE AUTHOR)

Pictured with Hollywood's best friend, Oscar. Betting on horses will get you more wins quicker than trying to back Oscar winners, but my partners and I managed to come up with seven Best Picture winners at United Artists and Orion. (STEVE BANKS © 2002. ALL RIGHTS RESERVED)

affair with his assistant. Francis arose from his supine position and ambled over to me. "Mike, why don't you find your room and get comfortable," Francis said. "We'll talk at dinner."

≡

I was lucky to get out of the jungle alive. The first morning I was there, I was flown in via helicopter by Francis's pilot who had so angered the Philippine Air Force, I later heard, that they were trying to shoot him down.

There was little I could do about the delays. My entire trip to the Philippines was more to show Francis that we cared about him and our investment and to see if there was a reasonable chance that he would finish any time soon. I'm sure none of this phased him. He had practically turned into Kurtz. From the three days I spent trying to talk to him, I was certain he was slowly losing his mind. Often, he spoke to me in the tongues of the natives he was living with. In the few seemingly lucid moments he had, Francis told me that he didn't know how he felt about the war or, for that matter, the film. His main problem was that he couldn't figure out how to end the darn thing.

"Maybe it should just be a perpetual work in progress," he told me, which isn't the kind of thing a studio executive ever wants to hear. "I don't know if I want to finish it this year. I might want to finish it next year." There was a long pause that seemed longer. "Or maybe I should just start improvising and seeing where it goes." I thought, he can't be serious, can he?

Even when Francis finally finished shooting (with a fully recovered Martin Sheen), he still wasn't sure how the film should end. He shot four endings and tested them all at various stages of release. In fact, the DVD version released some twenty years later has two different endings on it.

Francis had planned to make the film for $16.2 million in 155 days. He wound up shooting for 238 days and spending some $30 million. When he was finished with his first cut of the film, we all gathered at his house in San Francisco. I took the Western Airlines shuttle up from Los Angeles and met Arthur, Eric, and Bob, who had flown in from New York. The screening was scheduled for 1 P.M., but we sat in the living room of his Victorian house, admiring the ornate moldings until he arrived with the print at 6 P.M. He walked into the room ranting and raving about how hard it was in America to make an important film about an important subject with the press railing about his overages and saying nothing about this overblown movie about an ape (referring to *King Kong*). Arthur quietly turned to me and said, "I think he really has gone mad."

In 2001, when Francis rereleased the film as *Apocalypse Now Redux,* he was still battling the apes—*Planet of the Apes* came out the weekend before and broke the all-time nonholiday opening weekend record. He'll never get rid of those damn, dirty apes.

The cut he screened for us was four and a half hours and didn't end until 11 P.M., which was 2 A.M. for Arthur, Bob, and Eric, who had come from New York. This lunacy and arrogance shown to Arthur and Bob, two men in their seventies, was very strange. Still, it was hard to ignore that while the film was flawed, it had many touches of brilliance. When *Life* magazine asked me for an assessment of the film, I declared, "Francis is either going to soar like an eagle or drop like a rock."

This line was actually furnished to me by Francis, who took a certain amount of glee in the situation. He was right about both.

■

Francis's behavior on Apocalypse Now *brings to mind the classic Herman J. Mankiewicz line uttered when Orson Welles walked by him during the filming of* Citizen Kane: *"There but for the grace of God goes God."*

Francis has since said that we didn't "like" the film, which is absolutely not true. We saw the film for what it was: a flawed masterpiece and the greatest test of the philosophy of artistic freedom that we gave filmmakers at United Artists.

We sent a creative man to the jungle with a pile of money and when he went crazy trying to realize his artistic vision, we bailed him out of a huge jam by continuing to fund the movie, despite the fact that he had made mincemeat of our five-approval system.

In the end, Francis had nothing to complain about because he got exactly what he wanted: a chance to make the film the way he wanted, without any financial boundaries and with full creative

control. To this day, he owns the film, which allowed him to add
fifty-three minutes in 2001 and to rerelease it through Miramax.
Alas, he found the ending . . . twenty-four years later.

▬

In *Coming Home,* Jon Voight's character, Luke Martin, pierces
the big-screen war myth: "You remember all the films and you're
gonna think about the glory of other wars," he says. "I'm telling
you, it ain't like it is in the movies. That's all I want to tell you." In
the seventies, filmmakers started to wonder if the old war movies
that made going to war seem like volunteers were entering a
Hemingway novel might have encouraged young men to take up
arms and fight in Vietnam. Those romantic war films certainly
didn't dissuade anyone.

But if the World War II films created the myth that combat
had a manly glamour to it, the Vietnam-themed movies of the
seventies, like *Coming Home, The Deer Hunter,* and *Apocalypse
Now,* deconstructed that myth. These films were made by directors who were responding to how they felt about the Vietnam
War personally, not politically. As they often do, movies were
reflecting society. Like millions of other Americans, these filmmakers were resisting, questioning, and condemning the war,
and they felt strongly that it was their responsibility as artists to
create these films. But principled as they were, they were still
filmmakers working in the Hollywood dream machine.

This changed when Oliver Stone made *Platoon,* a film we distributed at Orion in 1986. While the seventies Vietnam-themed
films attempted to tap into the emotions of some of the 2.7 million American soldiers, *Platoon* was a personal statement based
on Stone's own experience in Vietnam, and it showed Vietnam as
it really was. The first of Stone's Vietnam trilogy, *Platoon* was followed by *Born on the Fourth of July* and *Heaven and Earth.* The
first two films upped the cinematic ante and cleared the way for
other highly personal cinematic statements, such as *Three Seasons,* a film made by Vietnamese-born Tony Bui, which calmly
enters the lives of the working class in postwar Ho Chi Minh City.

The conflicting emotions about Vietnam have been altered
by these films, particularly in young people who didn't experi-

ence the war firsthand. Seeing the brutality of combat and how the lives of those at home were affected in films like *Platoon* and *Coming Home* has not altered history, but it has changed the prism through which we see history. This evolving group of Vietnam-themed films helped build the Vietnam Veterans Memorial on the National Mall in Washington, D.C.—on the very site where the war was so forcefully protested—and make it one of the country's most emotionally stirring monuments. Arguably, these films have even contributed to the ability of former Vietnam P.O.W. John McCain to make a serious run at the presidency. The heroes are now those who fought for their principles, whether here or in the war, whether they survived or gave their lives.

As a studio executive involved in these seminal Vietnam films, I have come to the absolute realization that films can have a great social impact. Movies are the literature of this generation, and the Vietnam chapter is particularly powerful. While the past is now being understood through movies, it is also being shaped by movies. And so there is often an awesome responsibility in choosing which films are made and which are not. While a studio executive may not know the smell of napalm in the morning the way he knows the smell of fresh-baked croissants at the Four Seasons, our actions can have consequences far greater than we think.

4   *Gypsies, Tramps, and Auteurs*

The seventies gave us so many forgettable fads—like disco, bell bottoms, and the Ford Pinto—that looking back, it's hard to imagine how important the films of the decade of bad taste were: The Godfather *films,* The French Connection, The Exorcist, The Sting, One Flew Over the Cuckoo's Nest, The Last Picture Show, Star Wars, Chinatown, Taxi Driver; *and* Apocalypse Now. *Some of the fundamental changes that occurred in the industry during the seventies created a legacy that continues to shape Hollywood to this day: the television networks saved the movie studios from going out of business; the roguish American auteur was born; and the popcorn blockbuster—complete with sound track, action figures, and Big Mac tie-ins—showed the film studios where the* real *money was.*

By the dawn of the seventies, the three TV networks—ABC, NBC, and CBS—began paying top dollar for feature films, which fundamentally changed the way studios made money. The escalation began in 1966 when ABC paid an eye-popping $2 million for the broadcast rights to *The Bridge on the River Kwai.* By 1968 the average price paid for a movie was $800,000, and the numbers kept rising. In 1975 one of the networks offered to pay at least $1.5 million, sight unseen, for *Cuckoo's Nest,* based on Jack Nicholson's name alone, a factor that contributed to our going ahead with the film. The networks were also buying from the studio's libraries: in 1976 ABC paid $5 million for *Gone With the*

Wind. At one point, ABC offered Francis Coppola $10 million for the television rights to *Apocalypse Now.* (Unfortunately, Francis asked for $12 million and by the time he got around to lowering his price, he couldn't even get $4 million.)

The networks were paying such high prices because they had the viewers and the advertisers in their hip pockets. As CBS founder William Paley once said, "We are not in the programming business; we are in the advertising business." Sitcoms like *All in the Family, Three's Company, Happy Days,* and *The Mary Tyler Moore Show,* and one-hour dramas like *Charlie's Angels, The Love Boat, The Waltons,* and *Dallas,* had audiences glued to their living-room couches in record numbers. Flush with cash, the networks began buying more feature films and paying higher prices than ever before. In 1977 *The ABC Sunday Night Movie* became a top-10 program in the Nielsen weekly ratings, thanks to films like *Butch Cassidy and the Sundance Kid, Patton,* and *The Way We Were.*

At the same time, the studios received an unexpected gift from the Federal Communications Commission—the financial interest and syndication rules, or the "fin-syn" rules. In 1970, the FCC undid the television networks' monopolistic practices, much the way it had gone after the film studios in the fifties (the FCC discovered that the old consent decree had targeted only exhibition and not distribution, so little had really changed: the studios still controlled film distribution). This time, when the FCC targeted television, it went after the production and the distribution of shows. Fin-syn dictated that the three television networks—ABC, CBS, and NBC—could not have a financial interest in any programming produced by outside producers; could not sell any programs abroad produced by third parties; and could not sell (or syndicate) their programs to independent stations in the United States. These rules paved the way for the movie studios and independent producers to make a fortune producing shows and selling the reruns in syndication. (The rules have since been rescinded.)

Still, television and film in the seventies remained two different media for actors. You could use TV as a launching pad to a film career, but you were either a movie star or a TV star. Clint

Eastwood got his start on *Rawhide,* but once the spaghetti Westerns put his name on the big screen, he never returned to
episodic TV. The same was true of Steve McQueen, who made a
clean break from TV's *Wanted: Dead or Alive* to leading-man film
roles. It was considered déclassé to go back, and actors didn't go
back unless their careers were dying. There was a clear pecking
order for stardom in Hollywood from top to bottom: film star, TV
actor, rock 'n' roll singer. Today actors are allowed to move back
and forth at their whim. Tim Allen goes from doing his hit series
Home Improvement to doing the voice of Buzz Lightyear in the
animated *Toy Story* to doing the sci-fi comedy *Galaxy Quest.* It's
not uncommon for movie actors to look for well-conceived TV
roles when movie scripts aren't to their liking, as Martin Sheen
did by accepting the lead on *The West Wing.*

Television has become an even more important part of the
movie business since the advent of cable and pay television. Not
only do cable networks like HBO and TNT provide more outlets
for movies, they have also become producers of films. As the
major studios began churning out safer and more predictable
films in the nineties, cable and pay television became a primary
creative outlet for top filmmakers to make more challenging and
innovative films. HBO was the first to make feature-length films
with film actors, and Showtime quickly followed suit. Now TNT
is making quality films with top-notch feature filmmakers like
Phil Alden Robinson, who directed *Field of Dreams.* For actors
and directors alike, going to HBO or TNT with a project these
days is often a necessity if you want to tell a smaller, gritty, or
more personal story. Mike Nichols, for example, made *Wit* at
HBO with Emma Thompson in the lead role. The built-in audience these networks have enables them to take more chances on
audacious projects.

The greatest irony is that while the networks saved the movie
studios, the movie studios now virtually control television: Walt
Disney owns ABC, Viacom (the parent company of Paramount)
owns CBS, and AOL Time Warner owns HBO, TNT, and TBS,
among other cable networks.

By the time the fin-syn rules were finally relaxed in the
nineties, the ultimate benefactors were the studios.

≡

The label of "auteur" was applied to the several directors of cutting-edge films in the seventies: Francis Coppola, William Friedkin, Martin Scorsese, Hal Ashby, Bob Rafelson, George Lucas, Steven Spielberg, Brian De Palma, and Terrence Malick. Not since the thirties, when America saw the likes of Frank Capra, George Stevens, Ernst Lubitsch, John Ford, Howard Hawks, Alfred Hitchcock, and William Wyler all making movies, did such a group of talented filmmakers come together at the height of their powers.

The disenchantment with government that stemmed from Vietnam and Watergate, the assassinations of Martin Luther King and Robert Kennedy, and the rising tide of violence in America created a cynicism that was fundamental to the work of these directors, just as the Depression and World War II had informed the work of earlier artists. The seventies auteurs took risks with the storytelling process; they broke down the traditional approach to film narrative, told their stories from the anti-hero's perspective, and delved into darker themes, such as drug abuse, sexual license, and the pathologies of violence. They made movies about their own ethnic cultures and shot them in a style influenced by cinema verité that would have left American directors of the thirties and forties slack-jawed. Television also had a stylistic impact, apparent in the profusion of closeups and tight shots to create emotional urgency.

▩

The influence of drugs on these young American filmmakers has been sensationalized over time to the point that the seventies are now regarded as the drug-induced decade of moviemaking. There is some truth to this because, after all, movies reflect society. I rarely drank and I avoided drugs, primarily because of a fear of getting hooked, so my memory is pretty clear on this period.

This Hollywood drug subculture of the film industry was a major theme in Julia Phillips's best-selling autobiography, *You'll Never Eat Lunch in This Town Again.* Julia wrote openly and frequently about everything, from smoking pot to freebasing cocaine, and she mentioned just about everyone who joined her. In Julia's case, the drugs in her life helped destroy a very successful producing career. Julia shattered the glass ceiling by becoming the first woman to win an Academy Award for Best Picture, for *The Sting* (which she earned together with Tony Bill and her husband, Michael). But Julia's demons got the best of her, and she ended up deep in debt and virtually out of the business by 1980. Her book, which emphasized the side of Hollywood she lived in, seems to have been written in large part to explain to herself how she ended up where she did. It would be naive to think she didn't expect to make money from the book, which may explain why she took so many cheap shots at so many high-profile people. In Julia's mind, she was being honest and truthful, but at what cost?

Journalist Peter Biskind's 1998 book *Easy Riders, Raging Bulls: How the Sex–Drugs–and–Rock 'N' Roll Generation Saved Hollywood* was received as the definitive portrait of the nature of the auteur generation and its sources of inspiration, and it underscored the film world's drug culture that Julia wrote about. When Biskind came to interview me in May 1995, he wanted to know about "influences" on the filmmakers I represented as an agent and worked with at United Artists. For an hour, I told him about what I thought were the *real* influences of the time: the European directors of the sixties and the American directors of the thirties and forties. Biskind ultimately presented my view in the preamble to his book, but merely as a footnote to what he felt was the more important source of inspiration: drugs. But I maintain that the impact of a group of European directors was felt in almost every frame of the films that have come to define the New Golden Age of American cinema. The American directors might have been movie brats, but they weren't movie druggies.

The artistic catalysts for the young American directors were the films of French new wave filmmakers Jean-Luc Godard, François Truffaut, and Eric Rohmer; the British directors Lindsay Anderson, Karel Reisz, and Tony Richardson; the Italian classical movement led by Frederico Fellini and Michelangelo Antonioni; and Japan's Akira Kurosawa. Films like *Blow Up* and *Saturday Night and Sunday Morning* were studied by these young American directors. Coppola, Scorsese, Ballard, De Palma, Milius, and Lucas all went to film school, and Malick came through the AFI program. Woody Allen, of course, was a close observer and passionate admirer of the work of Ingmar Bergman.

Stylistically, the American directors were adopting the film-making techniques of their European antecedents. Scorsese and Friedkin used Godard's technique of combining documentary with personal essay in their films, and Antonioni's haunting images of deterioration could be seen in Malick's work. Film-making became a form of personal catharsis for these directors as it was with Fellini. Editing became less linear and more play-ful—which led, over the years, to the MTV-style filmmaking seen in today's young film directors like Spike Jonze (*Being John Malkovich*) and David O. Russell (*Three Kings*). The seventies auteurs also began to infuse popular music and cultural refer-ences into their films, which has now become de rigeur for film-makers like Quentin Tarantino (*Pulp Fiction*) and Paul Thomas Anderson (*Magnolia*).

For these reasons, I felt that the credence *Easy Riders, Raging Bulls* gave to the idea of drugs as the primary force in moviemak-ing during the seventies diminished the achievements of those films. One of the book's central themes is how drugs helped define the entire generation. At times, it seems like Biskind forces drugs into the creative process to make his subplot of a whacked-out Hollywood hold up. At the same time, he admits that these were some of the greatest films of the past fifty years. John Milius's theory is that Biskind created a vision of the party he wanted to have happen. Well, I was there, Milius was there, and drugs didn't dominate the movie scene.

Sex maybe, but not drugs.

I'm not denying that there was hard partying in Hollywood in the seventies, but I maintain that it was no different than the twenties, the thirties, the forties, the fifties, the sixties, the eight-ies, and the nineties. There has just been more discussion of the partying in the seventies. There was recreational pot smoking, and there were small amounts of movie budgets that were eaten up by drugs. But, as Dick Zanuck deadpanned in *Newsweek* at the time, "Everybody knows certain people are on drugs but that doesn't make them unreliable."

The only experience I ever had with drugs was when I found myself unknowingly eating some wonderful brownies at a dinner party at a producer's house. Driving along Sunset on the way home, I started laughing so hard that I nearly had convulsions. I pulled over to the side of the road until the laughing stopped. It didn't occur to me until a week later that hash was baked into the brownies. A few years later, thinking about those brownies, it occurred to me that maybe I was missing something all along.

As far as the filmmakers we worked with, Hal Ashby was a fairly heavy pot smoker, and I'm sure there were other things going on on the set of *Bound for Glory*. I was always mystified at how, despite the fact that Hal had started his career as a film editor and served as his own principal editor, he shot miles of film. He came in thirty-nine days behind schedule, which pushed the film's budget from $4.4 million to $7.6 million. Worse, he couldn't get the film down to less than two and a half hours in the editing room. Yet we knew he was talented so we hired him to make *Coming Home* when John Schlesinger fell out because, in Dick Zanuck's phrase, Hal was "creatively reliable."

Much has also been written about drugs on the set of *New York, New York*, but I didn't hear about it until after the movie was out of theaters. We always tried not to act too overly parental toward filmmakers. Besides, I was more concerned with how we could have been so wrong about the film after watching the dailies that we declared it one of the jewels of our slate. We didn't even have drugs to blame it on.

▨

The seventies embody a profound contradiction: the decade that gave the movie industry the American auteur also gave it the broad-audience event film.

▨

Blockbuster films may have taken on a larger importance in the seventies, but they certainly did not originate then. There had always been big, bold, blockbuster-style films: the thirties had Cecil B. De Mille's *Cleopatra*, the forties had David O. Selznick's production of *Since You Went Away*, the fifties had De Mille's *The Greatest Show on Earth*, and the sixties had David Lean's *Lawrence of Arabia*. This was the beginning of the American auteur's biggest contribution to film worldwide: the broad-audience film. What happened in the seventies was that studios discovered just how much money they could make from a movie that captured the attention of all the age groups. Films like *Jaws, Star Wars,* and *Close Encounters of the Third Kind* made studios realize that there was an *unlimited* amount of money to be made on event films. This mentality set the business on an even more dangerous feast-or-famine course than ever before. The new rule was: *Make your money as fast as possible because there will be a new film out next week.*

Instead of films rolling out slowly, studios began releasing them on hundreds of screens at the same time. In 1970, 300 screens was a wide release; today it's more than 3,000. Big movies were more expensive than ever, and getting their money back as quickly as possible became the primary aim of the studios. That began in 1975 with *Jaws*. Sensing that it had lightning in a bottle, Universal opened the film in 460 theaters on Memorial Day weekend, the largest number ever for a film's opening day. The studio also blitzed the public airwaves with ads in the three days leading up to the opening. Paramount had started this with smaller wide releases for the *Godfather* films, but Universal took it to another level with *Jaws*. In order to make such a large opening work, the studios had to create word of mouth through advertising rather than waiting until the movie opened and hoping people talked about it to their friends.

Wide-audience films like *Smokey and the Bandit* and *Star Wars* started effectively saturating prime-time television shows with ads. Costs were going up and studios needed to find audiences quickly. In the summer of 1977, the seven major studios released films costing a combined $180 million, a huge jump from previous summers. Fox had *Star Wars* budgeted at $8.5 million; Columbia had Peter Guber's production of *The Deep* at $10 million; Universal and Paramount were partnered on Billy Friedkin's *Sorcerer* at $21 million; and we had *New York, New York* at UA, which ended up at $8.4 million.

While the business was moving in this direction, UA tried to steer away from the wide release as a business practice. Most of our films continued to be "platform" releases, which were designed to build on good reviews and word of mouth. We started in a core group of first-run theaters, anywhere from one each in New York and L.A. to twenty or thirty in major cities across the country. Then we added screens as the film gained momentum. UA became a master at this technique of rolling out a film slowly, which allowed us to protect our spending on marketing rather than finding out we had overspent by releasing widely a film that nobody wanted to see.

Surprisingly, in the period during which this blockbuster mentality took hold, UA won the box-office battle for two years running. By focusing on a diverse slate of films, UA grossed $229 million in 1976 and $318 million in 1977, an all-time industry record at the time. Today there are studios that release film after film to claim bragging rights to the number one spot in market share at the end of the year. It's possible for one studio to outgross another simply by releasing thirty films to the other studio's fifteen, but that doesn't take into account how much you spend to get that market share. At UA, we were not only outgrossing the other majors, we were *underspending* them.

In reality, box-office rankings don't give any clue as to profitability, but now that the media closely scrutinizes the movie business on a daily and weekly basis, the studios are under intense pressure to maintain the *appearance* that they are making hits. Besides the box office, studios also discovered the numerous merchandising opportunities that blockbusters offered. Over the next two decades, this phenomenon would give studios other sources of revenue to recoup their costs and increase their profits, and event films soon became the centerpieces of a cottage industry that encompassed sound track albums, action figures and other toys, candy, fast food, and just about any other consumer product you could imagine. *Saturday Night Fever* producer Robert Stigwood, for example, reportedly earned $20 million from album sales alone. This trend continues today. Sales of sound track albums have become a revenue-driver in the music business to the point that now as many as five of the top ten selling albums can be feature-film sound tracks. The cross-promotional appeal has resulted in blockbuster films with platinum sound tracks, like *The Bodyguard*, which starred Whitney Houston as a singer and featured her music. In fact, there are now films that begin with music rather than a script and are remembered more for the sound track than for their extraordinary action sequences or love scenes. Warner Bros. now has an entire division devoted to coming up with films with musical-themed ideas.

Star Wars was the merchandising juggernaut that showed the economic reach of a blockbuster. George Lucas insisted on 40 percent of the box-office profits on *Star Wars* and the rights to own all sequels, but his biggest coup was having the merchandise rights revert to him after one year. Until the midseventies, toy licensing from films amounted to pocket change, but *Star Wars* changed that forever. All those Darth Vader plastic figures and glowing light sabers returned more money than the movie itself—and *Star Wars* was the highest-grossing movie ever in its initial release, long before name-brand consumer products were used to promote a movie and vice versa. When M&M's candies passed on a product placement tie-in with *E.T.*, Universal and Steven Spielberg used Reese's Pieces. The deal put the peanut butter candy drops on the map.

Star Wars was only the beginning: in the eighties, *Batman* grossed $250 million domestically, but more significantly it spawned a multibillion-dollar merchandising business. Ancillary revenue became reason enough for the studio to make expensive *Batman* sequels, for which the box office was never expected to be the primary source of revenue.

■

UA helped pioneer the auteur spirit by giving directors control of their movies as long as our five approvals were met—producer, director, script, cast, and budget. We never really made costly, all-or-nothing event movies. And while the industry functioned largely on a two-season basis in the late seventies, we never chose films like that at UA. We decided what would be the best season to release a particular movie, as opposed to tailoring a movie to a particular season. There were no committee meetings at which we talked about finding a "summer film" for a broad audience or an "Oscar film" for an adult audience at Christmas-time. Our idea was to find interesting films that we thought would be commercial. Of course it helped that we could rely on franchises like the Bond and Pink Panther movies as our Christmas and summer cornerstones, which meant that we could afford to take some chances on so-called auteur films.

David Picker, who served as head of production at UA and later at MGM and Paramount, was part of this legacy. However, he once made a frustrating comment that has stuck in the pantheon of Hollywood clichés. He said that if he would have reversed all his decisions—in other words, had not made the pictures he did and had made the ones he didn't—the results would have been exactly the same. He said it facetiously, and it's not true. Not only does it almost imply that a monkey can pick the movies, it neglects the many layers of decisions that go into greenlighting a film and ignores the central characteristics of what makes a good studio executive: instinct and experience. You have to trust your instinct, which is not to say that you're always going to be right. In fact, every studio executive is dead wrong at one time or another. Going on instinct led me to support *Rocky*, but it also led me to reject *The China Syndrome*, which I felt was too much of a message film. Boy was I wrong. In my defense, however, I wasn't able to predict the nuclear catastrophe of Three Mile Island, which occurred almost on the day of its release.

Instinct is partly learned, but experience must come one day at a time.

Trying to make decisions by any sort of scientific method often catches up with you and bites you in the ass because art is not science, but that's how Universal let *Star Wars* slip away. George Lucas's *American Graffiti* cost $760,000 and returned film rentals of $52 million to Universal. (It remained the most profitable movie in terms of cost to gross until *The Blair Witch Project* in 1999.) Nevertheless, Universal passed on Lucas's next film, *Star Wars*. Lucas thought that Universal would let him shoot the phone book after making them all that money, but the studio's box-office charts said that science fiction movies were poison at the ticket counter. Boy was Universal wrong.

Interestingly, after Lucas made the deal with Fox but before *Star Wars* started shooting, I heard that Fox was weakening on its commitment to doing *Star Wars*. I called Eric and told him that George had given me the script and it could be a huge movie. If we had the chance, I told Eric that we should pick it up if it went into turnaround. Unfortunately for us, Alan Ladd, Jr., was able to convince the Fox board of directors to go forward with the film. The day the film opened, I remember driving by the theaters and seeing lines around the block at every theater. Passing on *Star Wars* cost United Artists and Universal a few billion dollars each. It's yet another lesson that dispels conventional wisdom: *You're not as good as your last film, you're only as good as your next one, which makes it almost impossible to figure out which films will be hits.*

So which had the most lasting impact, the auteur films or the event films? The jury is still out, but the event films of the seventies are still more popular than the seminal auteur films. When Francis Ford Coppola's recut, enhanced version of *Apocalypse Now* was released in 2001 by Miramax, it pulled in less than $5 million, despite a barrage of press articles attesting to its brilliance. When *Star Wars* was rereleased in the spring of 1997, it brought in another $130 million at the box office.

▬

John Milius always likens what has happened to the auteur directors and the event-film directors of the seventies to combat. Each time the platoon of directors advanced, a few guys on the front line got killed off, like Hal Ashby. Terry Malick, who made Badlands *and* Days of Heaven, *got "wounded" and was M.I.A. for twenty years. The rest of the guys, like Coppola, De Palma, and Scorsese, somehow keep making it over the barbed wire. They're still fighting in the creative trenches of Hollywood, while Steven Spielberg and George Lucas go speeding past in their tanks.*

Over time, Spielberg and Lucas have been able to walk between the rain drops, while the rest of their peers spent the next two decades fighting through storms. It's all the more ironic that Coppola, once deemed the visionary, has achieved his greatest business success not forming his dream movie studio, but as a wine merchant with his Neibaum-Coppola vineyard.

When Gore Vidal wrote that "every time a friend succeeds, I die a little," he could have been talking about a phenomenon that took

hold in the seventies: the so-called Hollywood Boys' Club that exists
to this day. We're still dying a little each time someone else succeeds.

■

The culture of the auteur generation and the rise of the blockbuster combined to focus the media's attention increasingly on
those who ran the business of Hollywood. Prior to the seventies,
the happenings of producers and executives who weren't married
to movie stars were chronicled in small forums like Army
Archerd's column in *Variety*, but by the late seventies, you could
turn on ABC's *Good Morning America* and find Rona Barrett talking about producer Julia Phillips being arrested for a DUI or the
various twists and turns of Robert Evans's life. The spotlight previously reserved for stars, directors, and studio moguls like
Mayer, Zanuck, and Zukor began shining on younger executives.

This trend started in the late sixties and early seventies when
a new breed of young, charismatic executives began running the
production divisions of the studios. The first of the group was
Richard Zanuck, who at age twenty-seven took over the studio's
day-to-day control from his father, the legendary Darryl Zanuck.
Shortly after Dick took the reins, John Gregory Dunne followed
him around and wrote a detailed book entitled *The Studio*, about
the daily machinations of his job.

Compact, tightly wound Dick Zanuck was the most insulated
of the young executives. Even to those of us who were top agents
at IFA, he was virtually inaccessible. Dick pretty much ignored
the world beyond the gates of the Fox lot. More than any other
young executive, he focused his attention on the details of
moviemaking and gave his input on virtually everything. He ran
the place in a very autocratic, old-style manner, much like his
father had done. All communication with him went through his
right-hand man, David Brown, who later became his producing
partner in a rich deal at Universal. I didn't get to know Dick well
until I helped put together *The Sting* in 1972. Once he became an
independent producer, his door was always open to agents.

Several young executives relished the attention. Peter Guber
became head of production at Columbia in 1971 and survived
the Herbert Allen–led takeover until Columbia president David

Begelman pushed him out of the executive suite and into a producer's deal in 1975. At Paramount, freewheeling Robert Evans, as Paramount's head of production, reported to studio chairman Frank Yablans. Evans was a former actor with a theatrical manner and a devil-may-care attitude. He had the highest social profile of all the executives, due in large part to his marriage to Ali MacGraw and his friendships with Jack Nicholson and Warren Beatty. Although I was never invited, he hosted a seemingly endless string of parties at his house in Beverly Hills. I dealt mostly with his second-in-command in the production department, Peter Bart. On Evans's watch, Paramount soared with films such as *The Godfather, The Longest Yard,* and *Love Story.*

But for me, being in the public eye was a major adjustment. I was in my midthirties and had no formal training in the ways of the world press. These days, many executives have their own publicists; at the time, however, there were no studio flacks watching over or cultivating the images of the executives. As an agent, I had used arrogance—or the appearance of arrogance—to cover up my deep shyness and insecurities. Now, as a studio executive, I had to be careful not to come off as a Hollywood asshole with the press. Early on, I decided the best way was to tell the truth and speak my mind. Some people in the business respected this, though not everyone wanted to hear candid answers. Invariably, I would end up pissing someone off. But praise is rare when you have a public profile, and I learned not to take things personally, not to expect praise, and not to need it.

By far my biggest press coup came one Sunday in August 1977, when I found myself featured on the cover of the *New York Times Magazine* in an article titled "The New Tycoons of Hollywood." The story focused on the production heads of the various studios, including Columbia's David Begelman; Fox's Alan Ladd, Jr.; Paramount's Michael Eisner; and Universal's Ned Tanen. Letters of congratulations poured in—some of them even genuine. As flattering as it was to be on the cover, I was even more satisfied with the article's content, which I took as an acknowledgment of the changing of the guard that I had seen start back in the midsixties. Significantly, six of the seven of us featured were former agents, and five of us had worked under Freddie Fields at

CMA. Since the dawn of Michael Ovitz as the industry's prototypical *über*-agent, you don't read much about Freddie, but he was the one who taught us how to talk to filmmakers, how to put together talent with similar interests, and how to create interesting and saleable movie projects.

Even though the so-called young tycoons all had bosses—Eric was mine, Alan Hirschfield was Begelman's, Lew Wasserman was Tanen's, and so on—we had a big impact on what movies the seven studios made and, in turn, what the 100 million moviegoing Americans and another 100 million people throughout the rest of the world saw on the big screen. In the early days of the movie business, the founding pioneers ruled their studios like dictators—Harry Cohn at Columbia, Jack Warner at Warner Bros., Spyros Skouras at Fox, Adolph Zukor at Paramount, Louis B. Mayer at MGM. They not only controlled the talent, they owned the theaters. By 1977 the power had shifted to us, younger executives who had relationships with filmmakers our own age. We were finding the projects that our bosses chose from, and our sensibilities were much more in tune with both the filmmakers and the audiences.

This transfer of power from the Lew Wassermans of the business to us created a new boys' club. Over the course of the next twenty years, the game of executive musical chairs would reach near-comical proportions, with some guys coming back to run the same studio two or three times in their career. Once you got in the executive club, if you kept your nose clean, you were almost certain to be offered a senior executive job by a number of studios. Nothing is in perpetuity, but club membership can last a long time.

Running a studio is not for the faint of heart. Trying to corral the endless egos of lawyers, agents, actors, directors, and producers, and to make movies that people want to see—and that make money—is something very few people can do well, especially for a sustained period of time. This is one explanation for why people keep reappearing in the same job at different studios. The other, more cynical explanation is that friends take care of friends in the movie business even if they aren't the best ones for the jobs. Eventually, though, every old guard is replaced by a new one.

The relationship between executives at rival studios is an interesting sociological phenomenon unique to Hollywood. To some degree, every studio head is hoping his counterpart fails, at least some of the time. The prevailing belief is that there is only room for a limited amount of success.

■

A certain nostalgia for the movies and the ways of the seventies took hold in the nineties, due to the fact that the seventies decade was the reference point for a new generation of executives, agents, and filmmakers whose knowledge of film doesn't go back much further than *One Flew Over the Cuckoo's Nest* and *Star Wars.* Having come of age in the decade of junk bonds and Reaganonomics, and having been raised on a diet of overblown action films, dumbed-down comedies for kids, and the mewling Brat Pack coming-of-age movies, the filmmakers, executives, and agents of the nineties were naturally drawn to the gritty, less contrived, and more personal films of the seventies, a time when art and commerce were not mutually exclusive and films like *The Godfather* could be of the highest quality *and* be commercially successful at the same time. By the midnineties, the seventies were being hailed as the heyday of American cinema, and the period itself became the backdrop for movies like *Boogie Nights, The People vs. Larry Flynt,* and *Pulp Fiction.*

Every year more people ask me why we can't make bold, entertaining movies like we did in the seventies. I tell them that at that time I wondered why we couldn't make bold, entertaining movies like they did in the forties. Also, every film has its own Zeitgeist. Films with subject matter that worked in the seventies might not work today. Recently, Sydney Pollack said to me that he thought the years from 1967 to 1979 were probably the best period in American film history. You always tend to look backward with admiration, because you're always too close to the present to evaluate the here and now. It's too soon to say whether *Saving Private Ryan* or *The Thin Red Line* will become definitive films about World War II. Maybe we *are* making great movies now—maybe *Three Kings, Being John Malkovich,* and *Traffic* will be landmark, turn-of-the-century films. Time will tell, but right now they look pretty good.

5 *When Accountants Run Studios . . .*

---

*United Artists symbolized creative freedom in Holly-
wood with a financial upside. By sharing profits
honestly, we made multimillionaires out of Alberto
Grimaldi, the Mirisch brothers, Norman Jewison,
Bob Chartoff, Irwin Winkler, Bond producers Albert
"Cubby" Broccoli and Harry Saltzman, Jerry Hellman (who produced* Midnight Cowboy *and* Coming Home), *and Saul Zaentz. To audiences around
the world, the appearance of UA's logo on the screen
meant that quality entertainment followed. Since
1951 United Artists changed the way movies were
made, pushed the limits of the medium, and delivered 108 Academy Awards, the Bond pictures, and
both the* Rocky *and* Pink Panther *series.*

*But to Transamerica, the behemoth insurance
giant that controlled UA, we were simply a division
that fell under the subheading "Leisure Services" on
the annual report.*

I was sitting at my desk in the United Artists suite of offices in
the Thalberg Building in January 1978 when Eric Pleskow called
and told me the news: Arthur Krim, Bob Benjamin, and he were
leaving UA. When I hung up the phone, I gathered a few papers
and headed home to pack a bag for a trip to New York to determine my own future. In addition to the historical significance of
Arthur Krim and Bob Benjamin leaving United Artists after

twenty-seven years, my own career now hung in the balance. As I dashed down the hallway of the UA offices, I paused at the two framed pictures at the end of the corridor: one was of Mary Pickford, sitting at her desk in 1919, surrounded by Charlie Chaplin, Douglas Fairbanks, Jr., and D. W. Griffith; the other was of Arthur and Bob surrounded by their associates in 1951. Who would guide United Artists through the third phase of its history? And, more important, who was left that cared about the company?

Being in Los Angeles, I was isolated from the corporate side of the business, but I was always aware of the fault line running from the Transamerica Tower in San Francisco to 729 Seventh Avenue in Manhattan. The longstanding dispute had centered on Arthur wanting Jack Beckett to spin off United Artists and Jack's refusing. Eric always said that Beckett loved seeing the tag line "A Transamerica Company" below the United Artists logo so much that he would never part with UA. The more I learned about the Transamerica–United Artists relationship, the more I was sure it couldn't last. The personalities of both companies were shaped by the men who ran them, which made conflict inevitable: Jack Beckett was a tall man physically and a rigid corporate man. Arthur Krim was the opposite, a brilliant polymath who became a world-renowned expert in African and Middle Eastern affairs and who worked as a negotiator on the SALT treaties. Beckett seemed jealous of many things about Krim, not the least of which was the fact that every time he wanted something done in Washington, he had to call Krim.

The growing unrest between the Transamerica executives and our New York colleagues crested in the first week of January 1978. A Transamerica executive ordered Eric to gather the medical records of all UA department heads and to send them to San Francisco. Eric refused on the grounds of confidentiality. Besides, as he so aptly put it, "I don't want to know if any of my guys has a social disease." That afternoon, Eric, Arthur, and Bob were having lunch in Eric's office, discussing the problems. When Arthur remarked that something had to be done, Eric stood up, walked over to his desk, and called Jim Harvey in San Francisco. When Harvey picked up the call, Eric informed him that he was resigning. Eric hung up, turned to Arthur, and said, "Something is done—me."

Arthur persuaded Eric not to follow through with his resignation, but it was clear that the beginning of the end was in sight. The next battle in the war came when an article was published in *Fortune* magazine detailing the difference in philosophies between UA and TA. Appropriately titled "United Artists' Script Calls for Divorce," the article detailed how Krim and Beckett were at loggerheads over the direction of UA. Krim explained why a UA spin-off was necessary and beneficial to both companies. Beckett's response: "If the people at United Artists don't like [the way Transamerica oversees them], they can quit and go off on their own"—nothing less than a public declaration of war.

The real issue was that Beckett and Jim Harvey wanted Arthur to retire. (By this point, Bob served as only a consultant.) They felt he was too old for the business, and, besides, they reasoned, if the company could be run with charts and numbers, why listen to "the grousing of an entrepreneur," as Beckett complained to *Fortune*. Transamerica was a company that employed thousands of people to study when the average person would get sick or die and then price insurance accordingly. The Transamerica business plan called for each division to return 16 percent on investment each quarter; the unspoken Wall Street requirement was at least 15 percent, with less than 12 percent putting you in the danger zone. The problem with anyone demanding these results is that expecting predictability of any kind in the motion picture business is like waiting for rain in the Sahara Desert: it rains—sometimes—but not often enough. Regardless, Transamerica wanted their movie company to function like their car rental business. But United Artists wasn't Budget Make-A-Movie; it was a company with a human voice and a soul.

Beckett summoned Arthur and Bob to San Francisco, saying he wanted to discuss the grievances aired in the *Fortune* article, but Arthur and Bob didn't go. They were certain he was going to fire them, and they were too proud to be fired by anyone, let alone an insurance salesman. They had rescued United Artists from certain death in 1951 and transformed it into a company

without peer in the movie business. Instead, they decided to tell
Beckett they were finished with Transamerica. On Friday, January 13, 1978, in a show of unity, Arthur and Bob accepted Eric's
resignation and tendered their own.

I had no choice but to do the same.

*Everyone from Cubby Broccoli to the president of the United States
knew that with Arthur Krim and Bob Benjamin, their word was
their bond. You had a handshake, you had a deal—simple—which
was unheard of in the movie business then, and pretty much still is.
The four years I spent at United Artists determined the kind of person I would become in the movie business and how others would
regard me. I learned at UA that your character and your dignity are
all that matter. Everything else is just cocktail party conversation.*

Arthur Krim, Bob Benjamin, and Eric Pleskow were as smart,
honest, and decent, if not more so, than anyone else in the movie
business. They weren't slick like so many Hollywood characters.
They even ate lunch in the same restaurant every day: Vesuvios, a
restaurant with a reputation for its mob clientele—every seat
back was against a wall and the cook had a heavy hand with the
garlic, which made for interesting afternoon meetings with
everyone talking at their feet. They conducted their business
with the same integrity, they maintained one set of books, and
they cared about the people who worked for them. Their version
of life was bigger than just the movie business; their vision
inspired me. I always had outside interests, but when you're
absorbed in carving out a place for yourself in movieland, it's
easy to be simpleminded. Being around Arthur especially had
helped me see a world beyond movies.

Arthur, Bob, and Eric were always willing to share credit,
and they taught me how important that was. Hollywood is a jungle where everyone fights to survive and get ahead, and it's easy
to fall under that spell. Most people take credit for any success
they can while begrudgingly giving it to others. In our most
unique of all Hollywood partnerships, taking credit was never an

issue. Everything was done under the auspices of the company, and our reputations lived and died as a group. Every decision went through Arthur, but he never once took a unilateral bow for a success—a rare concept in the movie business. Arthur could be domineering and depressing; Eric could be shortsighted and obsequious to Arthur; Bob could be too soft. But compared to every other dysfunctional, self-centered executive in Hollywood, they were giants in every regard.

All of this was on my mind as I walked through a rainstorm from our offices to the Transamerica corporate apartment at 200 Central Park South for what was to be one of the defining meetings of my career. Upon receiving the three resignations, Jack Beckett and Jim Harvey flew to New York to assess the damage, just like insurance agents rushing to the scene of a disaster. They asked to meet with me on Monday at noon. I spoke to Arthur, who told me that he didn't know what the three of them would do next, simply that they weren't going to continue to work for Transamerica. "What works for rental car companies doesn't work for movie companies," Arthur said. Eric's feeling was that he had come to this country with nothing and he could go back to Europe and start over. In truth, the financial loss for him was staggering. By leaving one year before he was fully vested, Eric forfeited millions of dollars in pension-fund rights.

When I walked into the corporate apartment at noon, Harvey was meeting with Bill Bernstein, who headed up business affairs. Even though we had been scheduled an hour apart, Bill was still here. Awkwardly, I stood there, while Harvey invited me to join the conversation and filled me in. They had offered Bill a job as co-president of the company, working alongside me and reporting to Harvey. They had even presented him with a spreadsheet detailing how much he would earn over a ten-year period. The plan was for Bill to be in New York tending to the business side while I supervised the movies from Los Angeles. I couldn't help looking around the apartment and thinking, what a luxurious corporate pied-à-terre overlooking Central Park. I was often in New York, always bouncing around from one hotel to another. Why hadn't I ever been invited to stay here?

After a few minutes of listening to Harvey outline the new UA without Arthur, Bob, and Eric, I politely cut him off. Bill was either thinking about the offer and waiting for me, or Harvey had detained him in hopes that I would go along. "I don't know about Bill," I said, "but I'm leaving. I came to UA because of Arthur, Bob, and Eric. We've had a tremendous amount of success together. If we wind up splitting up and not finding another place to make movies, then I'll find something else to do with my life." Bill seconded my motion and the meeting was over.

United Artists was also over—at least the United Artists the film industry had come to love and respect.

The story of the resignations spread in the media over the next few weeks, and reporters for some reason made an issue out of my Mercedes company car, writing about how it was an affront to Transamerica's executive policies. The *New York Times* regurgitated this industry gossip and called my Mercedes the "flash point" for the resignations. The story was both absurd and inaccurate. It was ludicrous to think that Arthur, Bob, Eric, and Bill would sacrifice their twenty-seven-year-long careers at UA over my company car, and for the record, I had leased the Mercedes two years before the tension between TA and UA reached its boiling point. The *Times* also failed to realize the obvious: None of the other senior executives at UA had to worry about the car policy because they lived in New York and took car services. But to be fair to both the *Times* and the gossips, Transamerica did in fact complain about the car. In early 1976 when I first leased the Mercedes, I received a memo from Alan Wilson, who worked in our business-affairs office, relaying that the Transamerica auto-fleet office had conducted a study that found that operating a Mercedes 450 SL costs forty-four cents per mile versus twenty-two cents a mile for a Cadillac Seville or a Lincoln Mark IV.

In the four years I was at UA, the box-office take increased from $70 million to $380 million. If the Transamerica bean counters had charted that, they would have found a 543 percent increase—perhaps that would have justified the extra twenty-two cents a mile to and from lunch.

Whatever the UA Five (as we became known in the industry) did next was going to be major news in the film business. United

Artists was the premier movie company in the world in every regard, and our recent results, both commercially and critically, equaled and probably surpassed any studio in the history of the movie business. When the final 1977 box-office numbers were compiled, our films had grossed an all-time industry record. We had won two consecutive Best Picture Oscars and were only months away from getting our third. *Apocalypse Now, Coming Home,* and *Raging Bull* were all in various stages of production. Most important, we had the implicit and explicit support of Hollywood's creative braintrust. Days after our resignations were announced, the creative community came out in force behind the UA Five: a letter of support signed by sixty-three filmmakers, running alphabetically from Robert Altman to Fred Zinnemann and including Francis Coppola, Billy Friedkin, Saul Zaentz, Blake Edwards, and Marty Scorsese, was published in *Variety*. That was the kind of support that the Krim-Benjamin philosophy engendered.

▄

Heaven's Gate: *When accountants make movies.*

▄

Within days of our departure, Beckett appointed Andy Albeck president of the company. Eric Pleskow predicted that Albeck would get the job because he was perfectly suited to work for an insurance company. Albeck was basically a numbers cruncher who had no hands-on movie experience, although he had come to UA to be Eric's assistant. After that, his various duties included supervising the sale of three UA radio stations and later overseeing the operations of the company's international unit. In his new position, he would report to UA's new chairman, Jim Harvey, who assumed Arthur Krim's position.

There's nothing wrong with a conglomerate trying to make money in the movie business. Long before the talkies, the movie business attracted companies whose core business wasn't entertainment simply because there was money to be made in a glamorous, high-profile environment. Coca-Cola never claimed to want to change the artistic course of cinema when it owned Columbia Pictures; it wanted to make money. But there is something of an art to the process of choosing movies and supervising talent with a benevolent show of muscle that brings out the best in your talent pool.

Transamerica learned that when Michael Cimino's notorious opus *Heaven's Gate* virtually sank the studio.

Andy Albeck gave *Heaven's Gate* the greenlight at $11.5 million—and Michael Cimino delivered the film at $44 million. Cimino's abuse of the studio's trust caught the eye of every other studio in town. The movie was hardly an *Apocalypse Now.* Cimino may have had a grand vision for the film, but it was a financial indulgence no studio could afford, especially given the finished product. He wasn't pushing the envelope—he was emptying it. Steven Bach, a production executive under Albeck, later detailed the situation in his excellent book *Final Cut*, which explored and attempted to explain the decision-making process that led the studio to place its entire livelihood in the hands of a director who could charitably be called a megalomaniac.

As sad as it made us to watch United Artists crumble under the weight of one film, we felt that our point was being proven. While *Heaven's Gate* was bad luck, it was also bad management. The Albeck-run UA had a dangerous movie-by-committee philosophy; when coupled with Albeck's inexperience, this philosophy was a sure recipe for disaster. Instead of making decisions based on informed instinct, films were run through "economic models" to gauge their box-office potential. Shortly after we left, UA tried to the tell the town they were still in business by paying a then-record $2.5 million for Gay Talese's novel *Thy Neighbor's Wife* and announcing that they would make *two* films based on it. Needless to say, neither ever got off the ground. Transamerica was grasping at straws and living in the vacuum created by our departure, and something like *Heaven's Gate* was probably inevitable.

Nevertheless, the financial services company wasn't about to let another Hollywood creative type loose with millions of dollars of its money. In 1981 Transamerica sold United Artists to MGM for $350 million, a great irony since UA distributed MGM's films. MGM's majority owner, Kirk Kerkorian, folded UA into MGM and rechristened the company MGM/UA. In one financial transaction the United Artists that I knew ceased to exist. Other than being a nostalgia-killer, Kerkorian's strategy of combining the companies turned out to be a financial blunder. Since UA's foreign distribution was not separated from MGM's in the deal, the company that held the foreign distribution rights to MGM's films got all the UA pictures. To save money, the UA foreign distribution arm that the Krim-Benjamin management team had built to a seventy-five-country apparatus, which was generally regarded as the best in the business, was totally dismantled.

By the mideighties, the remains of United Artists became part of an elaborate shell game between Kerkorian and cable TV entrepreneur Ted Turner. When MGM piled up large losses in the early eighties, Kerkorian sold MGM/UA to Turner for $1.6 billion and then, as part of the deal, repurchased the MGM and UA logos for $480 million, which he raised through a public stock offering. Basically, Turner ended up with the television rights to the MGM and UA libraries, and Kerkorian got the logos. Both of them got rich on the deal: Turner used the library to build his cable channels TNT and TBS, and Kerkorian simply started raising money all over again using the prominent names.

When Arthur Krim, Bob Benjamin, Eric Pleskow, Bill Bernstein, and I were running United Artists, the company's name still meant something. By the time the accountants and businessmen were through with it, it didn't really stand for anything.

MGM/UA has since bounced through the arms of Italian financier Giancarlo Parretti, who was later indicted for financial misdeeds while owning the company, then into the hands of the Credit Lyonnais bank, which seized the studio from Parretti when he defaulted on his loans, and ultimately back into Kerkorian's empire. In the past couple of years, I've gotten to know Kirk, and he's a brilliant businessman. He was roundly criticized for selling the MGM/UA piece by piece, so he bought it back and put his faith in the value of the library, which has made him a pile of money.

In 1999 MGM decided to change the direction of the UA label. Instead of having two production entities trying to do basically the same thing, MGM is now the mainstream division and UA is the specialty division, à la Miramax, Fine Line, or Fox

Searchlight. MGM shifted the last remaining UA franchises, Bond and Pink Panther, to its distribution label. In fall 1999, United Artists contemplated making *Rocky VI*, also under the MGM label. The idea for the film was to make it a return to the roots of the original film in both story and cost. The studio's proposal to Sylvester Stallone, Bob Chartoff, and Irwin Winkler was that the film be made for $15 million and everyone take no money up front and a piece of the back end—an idea the three never seriously considered. Legally, UA can't do the film without Chartoff and Winkler and as a practical matter, no one can do it without Stallone.

Their plan ran counter to the old UA philosophy of "If we win, you win." Never mind the merits of making another *Rocky*, filmmakers have every right to be rewarded richly for delivering a wildly profitable franchise. *Rocky VI* will never happen unless both sides alter their positions.

Perhaps out of nostalgia, it soon seemed as if everyone wanted to rekindle the old UA flame. Throughout 1999, Francis Coppola worked on a plan to become chairman of UA and to buy back the studio from Kerkorian over three to five years. It never came to fruition. Francis has long wanted to recapture the glory of the Krim era at United Artists. While the deal for him to take over UA was never consummated, he did make a production deal for a series of films that his company produces, some of which he will direct. Miramax's Harvey Weinstein, who was apparently briefly unhappy with his arrangement with Disney, also held talks with MGM/UA vice-chairman Chris McGurk to leave Miramax and take over UA. Those talks also fell apart.

Harvey Weinstein has often told me that he wanted to model Miramax on United Artists. The problem with doing that is that UA made money despite the fact that its business model was always secondary to how it treated people and filmmakers. While Harvey puts his name on nearly every movie that Miramax makes, Arthur, Bob, Eric, and I never once took a producer, executive producer, or any other kind of credit on a film, and we never interfered with a filmmaker's vision. We didn't take credit; we *gave* credit.

▦

The story of United Artists under Arthur Krim and Bob Benjamin shows how different the movie business is from any other business. Joseph Kennedy famously observed that in the movie business "the assets put on their hats at night and go home." What happened to United Artists after the five of us walked out shows that the personality of the people running a movie company really *is* the company. Here was a company that reached extraordinary heights of creative and financial success in several decades, only to essentially be killed by the conglomerate culture of corporate America. Of the American Film Institute's 100 top movies ever made, Arthur had a hand in seventeen; together with my partners, I had a hand in ten of them.

The United Artists story can serve as an allegory for what happened to the entire entertainment industry. A handful of companies have taken control of all the various movie studios, publishing imprints, cable networks, and music labels, and the human touch is being lost. When the movie business was born at the turn of the last century, the founders of the companies owned and ran them like family businesses.

Today there is no such proprietary interest. The magic of making movies is slowly being turned into a factory line for making "product" that will feed emerging technologies. The movie companies themselves have become one of the smallest parts of that food chain.

The saddest part of all this is that we have come to accept the factory line as an inevitability.

6 *You Can't Shoot the Deal*

Ma Maison was the power lunch spot of the moment in 1978, and in mid-January the place was buzzing with speculation about where the UA Five would set up shop. The agents, lawyers, executives, actors, and assorted other Hollywood types who dined out on daily gossip on the restaurant's Astroturf-covered patio could be heard talking about the various entreaties, proposals, and offers we had from Allied Artists, MGM, Columbia, Paramount, and Warner Bros. Rarely had the availability of a group of executives sent such shock waves through the Hollywood creative and executive community. Newsweek declared that it was "as if George Foster, Tom Seaver, Pete Rose, Joe Morgan, and Johnny Bench quit the Cincinnati Reds to offer themselves around the league as a pennant-producing package."

The magazine added that my loss "could be particularly hard on UA: Hollywood puts him almost in the legendary class of Irving Thalberg." As flattering as the Thalberg comparison was, it sounded more like something my father would tell our guests at Thanksgiving dinner.

Two weeks after we left Transamerica, we all met at Arthur Krim's townhouse in New York at 33 East 69th Street, a place steeped in history: presidents and foreign leaders had stayed there, and it was where John F. Kennedy first met Marilyn Monroe.

In fact, if you look closely at the first photograph taken of JFK and Marilyn, Arthur Krim can be seen standing discreetly in the background.

The prospect of a new beginning was in the air, and it was downright scary. I had been a studio executive for only four years and already I felt as if I was starting over. While it never occurred to me to stay at UA without Arthur, Bob, and Eric, I was a bit frightened to be starting a new life because I had no financial cushion, but the overriding feeling was that we were going to create a company that would be different from all the others in Hollywood.

We decided almost immediately to work for ourselves rather than manage an existing studio like Columbia and report to the executives of another corporate parent company. At the time, Columbia was looking for someone of high integrity to fill the shoes of studio chairman David Begelman, who had been caught embezzling money from the studio. Arthur rightly felt that even if we were willing to spend time cleaning up the David Begelman mess at Columbia, we would never have the latitude to restructure that studio our way as long as Herbert Allen and Ray Stark were involved, despite the fact that Columbia head Alan Hirschfield had reassured Arthur that Allen was hands-off and Stark would stick to producing movies. (Later I found out that Allen didn't want us there anyway.)

We needed a name. People in Hollywood agonize over the names of their companies and their logos. Louis B. Mayer's staff spent days debating how many times the MGM lion should roar; Mayer decided that only two short blasts followed by a final growl would send the right message. We decided that our new venture would be named the Orion Pictures Company, after the five-star constellation that lights up the wintry skies and a swirl of stars in the night's darkness would be our logo. (Alas, *Newsweek* later pointed out a small mistake: Orion was an eight-star constellation.)

The basic goal of Orion would be to duplicate United Artists by creating a home where filmmakers could realize their visions without interference from executives. The best way to achieve this was to start a new company that could finance movies, though none of us fully realized how difficult this would be to execute or how much money it would take. Since building a distribution system from scratch was prohibitively expensive, we concluded that we needed to attach ourselves to a first-class distribution apparatus. Arthur and Bob Benjamin had done this in the fifties when they took over UA, but the rules had changed dramatically and the cost had risen significantly.

Without much debate, we agreed that the best offer was Steve Ross's invitation to distribute our films through Warner Bros. There had also been a brief discussion about having us run Warners as part of the management team, but this seemed far too cumbersome. Besides, Arthur, Bob, and Eric would never move to Los Angeles. Steve wanted to follow the same business template he used in the music business: Warner's music division had separate labels—Warner Bros./Reprise, Atlantic, Elektra, and Asylum—and each company had its own management and put out its own product through the same distribution channels. Since Warner had experience in dealing with these autonomous units in music, Ross felt that it would work equally well for film, and we agreed. Orion would be the first of Warner's satellite film companies.

At the time, the Warner's movie division was run by Ted Ashley, Frank Wells, and John Calley, who had built a very successful company. I saw it as a great opportunity to be working with them. Ashley, a former talent agent, had stepped down as chairman in 1975 but had recently returned. Wells, the studio's president, oversaw the business end of things, and Calley, a thoughtful person with a reputation as a friend of the filmmaker, was in charge of production. Throughout the seventies, Warner had a string of commercial and critical successes that put it in the league of United Artists in the eyes of the creative community, including *A Clockwork Orange, Dirty Harry, Klute, The Exorcist, Dog Day Afternoon,* and *All the President's Men.*

But more than anything, it was the charisma and abilities of Steve Ross that sold the five of us on the idea.

■

The Orion-Warner model worked like this: Orion Pictures Company, which was the five of us, formed a 50-50 joint-venture partnership with Warner Bros. called Orion Ventures, Inc. Through a consortium of banks led by the First National Bank of Boston, we arranged a $100 million line of credit to finance films, which Warner Bros. guaranteed, but we had complete autonomy over the number and type of films we made. Warner Bros. would then market and distribute the films, though even in this area we were contractually given the "broadest autonomy and control over distribution and advertising," to quote our contract.

Eric insisted that the five of us all be equal partners in Orion, meaning that we each earned equal salaries of $500,000 each for the first year, with bumps for subsequent years. While this wasn't bad, considering I started at UA four years earlier making $90,000 a year, it was a fraction of what Warner's film chiefs Bob Daly and Terry Semel and other studio heads would soon be earning. We also had no stock options. The big payout would come only if our movies were successful.

The titles at Orion were similar to the ones we held at United Artists: Arthur was chairman; Bob, co-chairman; Eric, president; Bill, executive vice president of business affairs; and I was executive vice president of worldwide production. Decisions were made collectively, though, in a practical sense, Arthur always had the final word. The geography was the same as well: the others were based in New York, at Warner's New York headquarters in Rockefeller Center, and I worked out of a bungalow on the Warner's lot in Burbank.

The deal between Orion and Warner Bros. was announced in February 1978, three weeks after we left United Artists, and it was trumpeted as unprecedented. Based solely on our reputations and track record, we had been given access to $100 million to make whatever movies we pleased. At the time, it was a fortune; today it's the cost of one movie. The new company's only assets were seven-year employment contracts with the five of us, our Rolodexes, our reputations, and what was thought to be our Midas touch. We didn't own any scripts or have a single filmmaker under contract. It was one of the first deals of its kind for a group of executives, and it was hardly the last.

Warner Bros. (and other studios) repeated the Orion model many times since then, with varied success. Shortly after we made our deal with Warner, the Ladd Company joined the Warner's fold when Alan Ladd, Jr., and two other executives, Jay Kanter and Gareth Wigan, fell out with Fox chairman Dennis Stanfill and struck out on their own. In the nineties, Warner made similar arrangements with Arnon Milchan's company, Mel Gibson's Icon Productions, and Steve Reuther's Bel-Air Entertainment. Phoenix Pictures, which I co-founded seventeen years later, would have a similar arrangement with Sony Pictures.

The core philosophy of these deals is for the studios to get more movies to distribute with less risk. In Orion's case, Warner got all of that and more.

▬

In the first phase of Orion, we moved quickly to establish our profile as a major player by signing several actors to production deals. We made a deal with John Travolta just after Saturday Night Fever *and bought the book* Prince of the City *for him (though Treat Williams ended up in the lead). But by far, the most interesting signing was with Jon Peters, a producer living with an actor.*

Jon was a likeable huckster who had a disheveled beard and favored a tough-guy look: cowboy boots and jeans. Though he was a short-tempered fast-talker, I liked his enthusiasm and hard work. There was a certain charm to his madness, and I always chuckled when people told me that he referred to me as "a red-headed mad man." Me mad? My only madness was that I made a deal with him.

▬

A short attention span and a vigor for the sizzle proved to be Jon Peters's greatest asset throughout the eighties, a time when a movie needed to scream MUST SEE in its marketing campaigns to cut through all the clutter. Jon was often a nice antidote to a slow day—you never knew what the guy was going to say or do next. We made our producing deal with him at Orion primarily to get us instant access to his then-girlfriend, Barbra Streisand, with whom I wanted to do a film.

Though I knew Barbra well and had a friendship with her, Peters was both living with her and functioning as the doorkeeper to her career. After famously getting his start as a hairdresser (and later claiming that Warren Beatty's character in *Shampoo* was modeled on his life), Peters had gone from being Barbra's hairdresser on *For Pete's Sake* to being a producer on two of her films: *A Star is Born* and *The Main Event*. Peters's deal with Orion called for Barbra to act in one of three films, but even without his ties to Barbra, I suspected Peters might be able to harness all his energy into finding a project for us. He seemed to have some kind of forcefield around him that sucked movie ideas and movie people in. Peters's head of development was Mark Canton, our former assistant and story editor at UA. Bob Sherman, one of our vice presidents of production, helped Canton get the job.

Soon after we made the producing deal with Peters, he showed up at my office with two comedy writers in tow, Harold Ramis and Doug Kenney. They pitched me on doing a comedy about the Skokie Nazi March, with Peters producing, Ramis directing, and Kenney scripting.

I thought it was one of the worst ideas I'd ever heard—tasteless, offensive, and not very funny.

Nevertheless, I told them to come back to me with their next idea.

Two weeks later, Ramis and Kenney were back, this time without Peters. They pitched me on a comedy set in a *nouveau riche* country club that seemed like the ultimate spring-break movie. If ever there was a place that needed to be ridiculed and satirized, it was the country club. The title was perfect, too: *Caddyshack*. Since Peters introduced me to them, I figured one good favor deserved another, so I put him on the film as producer, which happened also to help me justify some of the overhead cost of his production deal.

You could probably chart Peters's entire career through people giving him things to work on, rather than film projects that he originated.

While *Caddyshack* ultimately became a hit whose lines are often quoted in *Sports Illustrated*'s golf stories, little did I know that these guys were going off to do all kinds of crazy things while making this movie in Florida. Reports came back about drugs on the set and constant partying. Undoubtedly, some of the recreation money was siphoned from the budget. Whether or not it was drugs, Doug Kenney was unstable. A few months before the release of the film, Kenney and I nearly came to blows over the poster, which he hated. I didn't have control over the poster and even if I did, it wasn't important enough to have a fistfight over. He didn't feel the same way so he jumped me outside of our bungalow and we literally ended up in a wrestling match on the sidewalk. A year or two later, he ended up driving off a mountain in Hawaii and dying. Excess kills faster than success.

Eventually, Jon Peters did what we had hired him to do and brought in a project with Barbra attached. Although we had been hoping for something closer to *A Star Is Born*, we agreed to develop *Yentl*, based on the Isaac Bashevis Singer story. Barbra was to play a young Jewish girl who masquerades as a boy in Eastern Europe in the early 1900s. Eric and Arthur felt it was not a commercial project, but I thought if we could do it for a modest budget, it was the kind of film that would do okay and make us proud creatively. At one point, Barbra had thought of not doing it as a musical, then she said that if it were to be a musical, she didn't want to sing. Eventually, she decided both to co-write some songs and perform them as well. After I heard the music over the phone, I was certain that the best way to tell the story was with song. I convinced Arthur and Eric to listen to her so they could understand how moving the story was. After listening to Barbra's song ideas for *Yentl*, Eric called me and said he, too, wanted to move forward, provided that we could contain the budget, which was then pegged at $12 million.

A half-hour later, Jon Peters's possessive and volatile behavior torpedoed the project at Orion. Shortly after I spoke to Eric, Peters called Eric and reamed him for meeting Barbra outside his presence—the meeting I had set up directly with Barbra without telling Peters. Eric listened politely to Peters's tirade, then called me and told me to dump the project.

"We're not going to work with this guy on anything else," Eric said calmly. When I called Peters and gave him the news, he started yelling at me, telling me how he could set this film up at any studio. "The whole town wants it!" he bellowed. Well, I told him, go ahead, because Orion doesn't.

Peters ended up setting it up at MGM, but Barbra gave up a lot to make the deal work. Had Peters not gone ballistic on Eric,

Barbra would have had more money to make the movie and a larger share of the profits.

The crowning irony is that by the time the film was released, Barbra and Jon had broken up.

■

By bringing Peters on to *Caddyshack*, I had inadvertently helped form one of the most notorious, high-flying boys' clubs ever in Hollywood: the axis of Jon Peters, Peter Guber, and Mark Canton. Even more ironic was the prominent role this would play in my own professional life: when Guber and Peters became co-chairmen of Columbia Pictures Entertainment, they wanted to bring Canton into the company and force me out of my job as chairman of TriStar Pictures, a Columbia subsidiary. In other words, I helped to load the gun that later executed me in public. But, then again, guys like that might have found each other anyway.

The chain of events started when my friend Peter Guber left his job as head of production at Columbia and formed his own film production company, called Peter Guber's FilmWorks. Guber quickly made a name for himself as a producer by convincing Columbia chairman David Begelman to pay $1 million for the rights to Peter Benchley's *The Deep*. He did this after Dick Zanuck and David Brown had already passed on it. The deal was the kind of eye-catching event that would become Guber's stock-in-trade as a producer. Before *The Deep* was released (and largely on its box-office promise), Guber merged FilmWorks with his good friend Neil Bogart's Casablanca Records, a disco label that had the Village People, Donna Summer, and KISS.

The new company, christened Casablanca Records and Film-Works, made *Midnight Express*, which Guber had optioned with $10,000 of his own money and brought with him to Casablanca. *Midnight Express*, which was based on the true story of Billy Hayes being jailed in a Turkish prison, was written by Oliver Stone, produced by David Puttnam, and directed by Alan Parker. Guber took more than his share of credit for *Midnight Express;* Parker claims he never saw Guber during the making of the film. This would also be true of Barry Levinson's *Rain Man*.

When disco began to die, Casablanca was absorbed into PolyGram, Guber became 50 percent owner and head of Poly-Gram Pictures, and Jon Peters—post-Orion—showed up looking for a home. Peters partnered with Guber and Neil Bogart in a production company named Boardwalk, after the most expensive property on the Monopoly board. Not long after its formation, Guber and Peters dissolved Boardwalk in May 1980 and dumped Bogart. Guber then cut Peters into his 50 percent stake of PolyGram Pictures—in exchange for a stake in Peters's profits from *Caddyshack,* which was a runaway hit.

So by putting Peters on *Caddyshack* as a producer, I provided Peters with the asset he needed to bring to the table to form a partnership with Guber. While Guber had the portfolio and Peters had the derring-do attitude that would carry the partnership, nobody could figure out why Guber needed Peters. I asked Guber more than once, but he never gave me a satisfactory answer. Later, after working for Guber at Sony Pictures, I discovered the glue that made their partnership work: Peters was confrontational and aggressive while Guber was nonconfrontational and passive-aggressive.

Under Guber and Peters, PolyGram released six flops in a row, including forgotten films like *King of the Mountain* and *The Pursuit of D. B. Cooper.* By January 1982, in a little over two years, PolyGram had reportedly poured more than $80 million into its film adventure in America with little to show for it. Predictably, the German company pulled the plug. This wasn't a big deal for Guber and Peters. They decamped for Bungalow 66 at Warner Bros.—where Mark Canton had become a production executive—and took the rights to *Batman* with them.

Eventually, Guber and Peters convinced Warner's chairman Bob Daly and its president Terry Semel to promote Canton to head of production—or so they claimed. Guber and Peters virtually had Canton in their back pocket, and he supported them at every turn over the years. They returned the favor to Canton years later by making Canton the head of Columbia Pictures—partly at my expense and largely to my public humiliation.

I came to admire Jon's brio and scoff at his boast, but one of the things I like about him is the fact that he always gives me credit for helping him learn to be a producer.

Whether or not he's just blowing sunshine up my trousers is another question. It's just Hollywood.

≡

We had been at Warner Bros. only six months when the question of who had authority over whom came up. Eric was always very tough on the Warner's guys when it came to marketing and distribution, because he had spent years building UA's distribution apparatus. Even though our contract with Warner Bros. stated that we had autonomy over how a film would be released, we never really had control over the selling of our films to theater owners or to the public. Despite having our own marketing team to work on advertising and publicity campaigns, we still had to release the films through the Warner's marketing department, which was not accountable to us.

After all, it was their money.

≡

"If I screw up one of your movies, can you fire me?"

That was the question posed by the head of marketing at Warner Bros. as Eric and I sat across from him, bewildered.

It was a time when the movie business was entering the era in which marketing could make or break a movie. Regardless of whether we could fire anyone at Warner, the question set the tone for how our pictures were distributed over the next three and a half years. Implicit in the question (which was really more of a statement) was that since we didn't have any authority over him, then so what if our films didn't do well? I shot back, "Forget about getting fired. If you screw up one of our movies, we are going to kill you." I was kidding, of course, and based on some of the results, it was obvious that he didn't take me too seriously either.

The increasing importance of distribution and marketing to the moviemaking process by 1980 made our position all the more tenuous, which was troubling because we had started Orion to become the masters of our own fate. Fewer films were being produced, and the sales push behind each film was becoming more concentrated. By 1979, the market share of the top ten films had tripled. In response, studios began looking for home runs, rather than being satisfied with doubles and triples. The way to accomplish that was to sell your movie aggressively and book it in as many theaters as possible. Executing the platform release and babying a film city by city, which drove the success of some of our UA films like *Rocky, Carrie,* and *Annie Hall,* became more difficult and a lot more expensive.

The first movie put into production at Orion, *A Little Romance,* was one that should have carried a "handle with care" label when we delivered it to the marketing department. Directed by George Roy Hill, best known for *Butch Cassidy and the Sundance Kid* and *The Sting, A Little Romance* was a movie nobody wanted to make, but we felt it was a great opportunity to start a new relationship. *A Little Romance* was a sweet story about adolescent love in Paris. Laurence Olivier played the sage to the young lovers, one of whom was Diane Lane making her film debut. "Too soft" was the word on the street, and while that might have been true, I regarded it as a little gem that would translate to future generations. The film received a smattering of accolades: Allan Burns's screenplay was nominated for an Academy Award, as was the musical score. The film didn't make or lose any money in its initial release, though with all the recent ancillary markets, I would venture to say that it has returned some profit. *A Little Romance,* which opened on April 25, 1979, cost $4 million—and grossed $4 million in the United States. Bill Bernstein sent each of us a framed copy of the first five dollars collected at the box office in New York. To this day, it hangs on my office wall.

Since we had little control of the marketing and distribution of our films at Warner, we were weakened all the more. There were a number of casualties, but the saddest was *The Great Santini,* based on Pat Conroy's highly personal novel.

We had left *The Great Santini* (and for that matter all of our other projects) behind at United Artists, but the Albeck regime didn't like it. The film centers on a World War II fighter pilot (nicknamed "the Great Santini") who tries to bully his son into following in his footsteps. When the producer, Charlie Pratt, told me that UA was putting Lou Carlino's script into turnaround, we picked it up. The script was ready to shoot, so it immediately went out to several actors. We were trying to do the film inexpensively, so an A-list star like Paul Newman was too expensive. We went with Robert Duvall, whose father was a navy officer. Blythe Danner was cast as his wife and Michael O'Keefe was the son. Half of the $4 million budget came from the Bing Crosby Organization and Taft Broadcasting, and I convinced Orion to put up the other half.

The film featured a tour de force performance from Duvall, and the character he played was a complex hardass. In one momentous and telling scene, as his wife and daughters watch, Santini (Duvall) is beaten by one point in a pick-up basketball game by his son (O'Keefe). When the family congratulates the son, Santini protests that a win must be by two points. When the mother protests that that isn't the rule, Santini throws the basketball at her, and she rushes into the house. After Santini berates his daughters and makes each of them cry, his son refuses to continue the game. As the son walks away, Santini throws the basketball at his head and calls out to his son, "You're my favorite daughter, my sweetest little girl." The son finally turns on his father in a rage and shouts, "This little girl just whipped you good, Colonel." This kind of daring story and filmmaking had been our hallmark at United Artists, but it proved too tough to sell to the public in our current situation.

When the film was finished, Gabe Sumner and the Warner's marketing staff sat down to formulate a release strategy. Lou Carlino had directed a quality movie, they said, but it was going to be a tough sell. Robert Duvall wasn't a marquee name. He was known as a character actor for his work in *The Godfather* and *Apocalypse Now*. Neither Duvall nor the rugged subject matter lent itself to a fast-paced, thirty-second television spot. The film was previewed to high marks in Dallas, but the audience scores only measured how the film was playing, not its marketability. This concept often gets lost on studios. The marketing braintrust decided on what would be the equivalent of an out-of-town test run for a Broadway play.

In August 1979, the film had its gala premiere, complete with a Marine band and full color guard in Beaufort, North Carolina, where the film had been shot. To take advantage of the local publicity from the premiere, the film opened the following day in North and South Carolina, but no one showed up. Worse, no one on our end was sure what to do next. The film wasn't a master-piece, but it was a lot better than most films showing at the time. Frankly, without some sort of national release covered by the media, the film was doomed.

Our first thought was that maybe it was the title. After all, *The Great Santini* seemed to imply some sort of high-wire, death-defying circus act. The marketing guys decided to test the film with a new title—in fact, with three new titles. In January 1980, the film was rereleased in three Peorias (proverbial and actual); in Fort Wayne, Indiana, as *Sons and Heroes;* in Rockford, Illinois, as *Reaching Out;* and in the actual Peoria, Illinois, as *The Ace.* It played best in Peoria, so *The Ace* became the new title.

A month later, *The Ace* was released in Cincinnati, where it tanked. During April and May, it opened and quickly closed up and down the California coast, in San Diego, Sacramento, Stock-ton, and Modesto. Orion's investment was now $2 million in the fim itself and another $800,000-plus in distribution costs such as prints and advertising. Eric and Arthur decided to pull the film from theaters and sell the ancillary rights to recoup some of Orion's money. The cable rights went to HBO, and the airline rights also were sold off. But Charlie Pratt refused to give up.

Pratt went out and raised just enough money to open the film in New York under its original title, and we agreed to match it. We were embarrassed by the press reports that we had blown the release of an excellent film, so the only thing we could do to save face across the board was to try again. Some people in our New York office wanted to put the whole thing six feet under and move on. *The Great Santini* opened to rave reviews in New York. Vincent Canby of the *New York Times* applauded the film and hailed Duvall as perhaps the best American film actor. The film started doing steady business, but two weeks after the theatrical release, *The Great Santini* debuted on HBO and people stopped buying tickets.

The Great Santini was dead.

Though I left the marketing decisions to the marketing team, in all likelihood the picture should have been released more traditionally, opening in New York and then slowly platforming to other markets. But this required more money for marketing, more confidence in the picture, and more guts. Despite the fact that *Santini* ended up with much-deserved Academy Award nominations for Duvall for Best Actor and for O'Keefe for Best Supporting Actor, the film deserved a better fate. It was one of the better movies we made under the Orion-Warner deal and easily one of the top third in quality of the three-hundred-plus films I've been involved with as a studio executive.

▬

Not long after we started Orion, *Annie Hall* was nominated for five Academy Awards, including Best Picture. Before we had released our first movie at Orion, *Annie Hall* won four Oscars, including Best Picture, Best Director for Woody Allen, and Best Actress for Diane Keaton. *Annie Hall* was released when we were still at United Artists, but the Academy Awards for the films released in the preceding calendar year are given in late March of the following year. Not only was this the third consecutive Best Picture for our United Artists group, but *Annie Hall* won over *Star Wars*, *Julia*, *The Turning Point*, and *The Goodbye Girl*, which was somewhat of a shock to the business. It was the first comedy since *The Apartment* in 1960 to win Best Picture.

Woody Allen had wanted the title of *Annie Hall* to be "Anhedonia." His co-writer, Marshall Brickman, said it should be titled "It Had to Be Jew."

Brickman, of course, was joking, but Woody was serious.

When Arthur heard the title, he threatened to jump out of the window onto Fifth Avenue. Eric had to look the word up in the dictionary ("anhedonia: the inability to feel pleasure"). The film told the story of the relationship between Alvy Singer, a nebbishy comedian, and his neurotic girlfriend, Annie Hall.

Woody refused to allow *Annie Hall* to be sold as an Oscar nominee in the New York or Los Angeles press. Studios routinely blast these ads after the Academy Award nominations are released in mid-February. To Woody, the only necessary marketing was a double page ad in the Sunday *New York Times* one week before the film opened. He felt that reviews brought people to the theater, not something as crass as marketing. Woody created his own trailers and designed his own ads. He did very little publicity, and when he did, it was not the kind of kissy-kissy stuff marketing people expected. In fact, he did virtually the opposite. In a pre-Oscar interview with NBC's Gene Shalit, Woody said he wasn't interested in "an inanimate statue of a little bald man."

Besides, Woody had a previous engagement on Oscar night: he was playing clarinet with his band at Michael's Pub, his Monday-night ritual. Studio executives never find that kind of tranquility.

Movie by Committee

High concept.
    A movie in a sentence.
    A quick television spot with a simple message.
    For people with short attention spans.
    But at Orion we continued to back Woody Allen.
We wanted films to be made by filmmakers and not by committee, which was a risky strategy entering the eighties.

Cineastes now point to the seventies ending with two seminal film events: the colossal failure of *Heaven's Gate* in late 1980 and Robert Redford's mainstream drama *Ordinary People* beating out Marty Scorsese's *Raging Bull* (a film we had greenlit before leaving UA) for the Best Picture Oscar at the 1980 Academy Awards on March 31, 1981. The profligacy of *Heaven's Gate* helped close the door on the notion that directors could be given an open checkbook and told to come back with art, and the victory of *Ordinary People* showed that Hollywood was cooling to the gritty auteur films. The energy and enthusiasm of many of the filmmakers who came of age in the seventies abated as the tastes of audiences changed in the eighties. Audiences' tastes change as rapidly as the Zeitgeist, and studio selectors must adjust to those changes or perish.

But something far more important was happening, something that had a profound effect on the outcome of Orion's relationship with Warner Bros. and forever shaped the way that films would be made.

On the other side of the Hollywood Hills from my office on the Warner's back lot, in the heart of Hollywood on Melrose

Avenue, Paramount was changing the movie business forever. Paramount became a breeding ground for executives who went on to run other studios—and are still running them—using the same formula: gather a committee of executives around a table and make movies that can be summed up in one line.

Paramount was headed up by a group of executives whose background had been in television. The thirty-four-year-old chairman was Barry Diller, a studious, smart, and hard-nosed negotiator who came to Paramount in 1974 from ABC, where he had helped pioneer the movie of the week and the miniseries with *Rich Man, Poor Man* and *Roots*. Barry had hired David Picker as his president at Paramount, but the two men's styles clashed horribly. Barry was hands-on creatively; David, hands-off in the UA tradition. This friction led Barry to hire Michael Eisner, also thiry-four, from ABC to be his president of production. Just as he did after leaving UA, Picker moved from the executive offices to a production deal, an exit strategy that has since become standard.

Diller's lineup was like an all-star team: Eisner was a hard worker who craved being at the center of the action and was perfectly comfortable there. The flashy Don Simpson was vice president of production. Simpson was brash, outgoing, and seemed to love everything about Hollywood. The studio's creative executive on the rise was Jeffrey Katzenberg, whose first job in the business was as my New York–based assistant at IFA. Katzenberg was an aggressive and nakedly ambitious go-getter who could walk into a party and meet everyone there in the first fifteen minutes. Together, this group could have conducted a tutorial in how to run a studio that made box-office hits.

Under this management team, Paramount largely moved away from the dramatic epics they made in the early seventies when Robert Evans was in charge, such as the *Godfather* films and *Love Story*. Diller did make one epic, Warren Beatty's *Reds*, but he managed to lay off most of the budget on a British tax shelter. Instead, Paramount perfected what is known as the "high-concept movie" and rode a popular wave with it well into the eighties, with films like *Airplane!*, *48 Hours*, *Flashdance*, *Beverly Hills Cop,* and *Footloose*.

Basically, a high-concept movie is one that can be explained in a sentence: *"A black cop from Detroit goes to Beverly Hills to find his partner's killer."* Then the premise has to invite chaos: *At one point the city cop gets the Beverly Hills police off his back by placing a banana peel in the tailpipe of their patrol car.* Typically, these films are so-called fish-out-of-water stories. They also tend to be derivative of television product: fast-moving stories with smash cuts from scene to scene and hip sound tracks. They are the polar opposite of the kinds of films we made at United Artists. High-concept films generally require bigger budgets, stars to sell them, and a slick marketing campaign. The fact that we were having marketing problems in our arrangement with Warner Bros. compounded our problems, but, in truth, we were also out of step.

We were no longer leading the pack, we were trying to follow it. The growing impact of MTV was also being felt. *Miami Vice*, which became one of the most popular TV series in the eighties, played like an hour-long MTV video, the ultimate mix of high-concept premise and MTV panache. MTV influenced the way films were marketed (through music videos) and edited (with quick cuts). In fact, our head of marketing at Orion, Charles Glenn, used MTV to sell *Amadeus* to younger audiences. Charles came up with the premise that Mozart was the original rock rebel. Charles made a music video of Elton John, Diana Ross, and The Who intercut with clips of the film and got it aired on MTV. The message: Without this Mozart dude, there would be no pop, rock, jazz, or soul.

In a time of near 20 percent interest rates and a nagging recession, audiences couldn't get enough of escapist entertainment. Beginning in the late seventies, television programming began enjoying a commercial renaissance with shows like *Charlie's Angels*, *Mork & Mindy*, and *The Love Boat*. *Three's Company* landed on the cover of *Newsweek*, which wondered if network programs were becoming too racy and violating the public airwave privilege. Television was having a stronger effect on our culture than ever before. In the midseventies, the television set was on for an average of seven hours a day in the American household. People turned to it for news, entertainment, sports, and even religion. In fact, watching TV was something of a religion unto itself.

It was Paramount that brought television to the movies: They moved *Star Trek* over to the big screen, and they took John Travolta, who had come out of *Welcome Back, Kotter,* and created a cottage industry out of him. His three back-to-back hits—*Saturday Night Fever* in 1977, *Grease* in 1978, and *Urban Cowboy* in 1980— earned the studio millions. Realizing that their style made for good business, I tried unsuccessfully to convince my partners to buy *Grease,* which I had represented as an agent earlier in my career.

Diller and Eisner had come out of television, and they understood how to sell films on television. If it could be pitched in a sentence, it could be sold in a sentence. High-concept movies like *Beverly Hills Cop* lent themselves to being sold on television because the story was easy to explain. Even though television buys were expensive, it was the quickest, easiest way to reach a wide audience. From 1976 to 1980, there was a staggering 600 percent increase in studios' television advertising spending.

In other words, the sizzle started to become more important than the steak.

Diller's Paramount regime was also the beginning of the movie-by-committee syndrome that pervades Hollywood today. Diller and his lieutenants began setting the agenda at the script stage. Previously, it was left to the director and the screenwriter to work out what the movie would say and how it would be said, and then run it by the studio for input. But at Paramount, the executives would get involved with the first draft of the script, typing up voluminous notes for the filmmakers. Next, they would hold story meetings so the executives and filmmakers could float their ideas, many of which were undoubtedly in conflict with one another. It was then left up to the filmmakers to cut and paste it all together. Soon, the joke going around Hollywood was that "Paramount is the place that gives you a green light and then dares you to make the movie."

The executives who engineered this system at Paramount spread it like cancer across Hollywood over the course of the eighties and nineties until it became the accepted way to develop, make, and market a film. Diller moved to 20th Century Fox, where he oversaw film and television and launched the Fox Network, and he now owns USA Networks and USA Films, a consolidation of film companies including PolyGram Films, October Films, and Gramercy Pictures. Eisner went to Disney and became CEO of the entire Walt Disney empire. Katzenberg followed Eisner and ran Disney's film division and eventually left to partner with Steven Spielberg and David Geffen in DreamWorks. Ricardo Mestres, David Kirkpatrick, and Bill Mechanic all went to Disney with Eisner: Mestres ran Disney's Hollywood Pictures division, Kirkpatrick ran Disney's Touchstone unit, and Mechanic worked in business affairs before jumping to Fox, where he rose to chairman of the studio. Larry Mark followed Diller to Fox to head up production. Dawn Steel moved on to Columbia Pictures, where she became president of production.

Interestingly, Dawn Steel replaced David Puttnam, who had come to Columbia after producing *Chariots of Fire*. Puttnam, with what appeared to be arrogance, promised a retreat from high-concept, star-driven movies and ended up being run out of town after picking fights with some of the town's bigger players like Ray Stark and Michael Ovitz when his films were mostly duds. The town wasn't big enough for that many egos.

The more success Paramount had with high-concept movies during this time, the more other studios followed their lead. The top films from 1979 to 1983 outside of the Paramount lineup were *E.T.: The Extra-Terrestrial, Superman,* and the two *Star Wars* sequels, *The Empire Strikes Back* and *Return of the Jedi*. At Orion, we finally capitulated and made a few films that tried to follow this trend, but we made them for the sole purpose of making money, so they invariably failed; *Under the Rainbow,* with all those little people chasing Chevy Chase and Carrie Fisher around in circles, is easily one of the worst movies I've ever been involved with. We also tried to rebottle the magic of Peter Sellers from the Pink Panther series in *The Fiendish Plot of Dr. Fu Manchu,* but there was nothing funny about the result. *Fu Manchu* was one of those films that we should've taken a bullet for doing. I knew it would flop when I read the script, but we fooled ourselves into thinking that Peter Sellers could make it work.

No one could have made *The Fiendish Plot of Dr. Fu Manchu* work.

■

Companies like Paramount, Universal, Warner, and Columbia flourished because they were willing to spend big money making and marketing these kinds of movies, while Orion simply didn't have the deep pockets to keep up. Still, I felt that failing to invest in at least a few high-profile packages a year made us less competitive. This argument over spending on bigger films would become a recurring theme in our partnership in the ensuing years and a source of frustration for me. Arthur and Eric did not like to spend money developing material. Our total budget for development was $5 million, while at the major studios it was eight to ten times that much. But one of the reasons Hollywood existed was that the men who founded the studios were gamblers. Universal founder Carl Laemmle gambled on horses, cards, and roulette, and he gambled his livelihood on film after film. Samuel Goldwyn would often put up his house as collateral. We probably could've used some of that derring-do at Orion.

Arthur didn't agree with me. He felt that having the reputation of a company with an honest and fair accounting practice alone would give UA (and Orion) a competitive edge over those who hid some of the profits, and to a certain extent this was true. But we also had to keep up with the times and adapt to other changes in the business. There were generational and demographic shifts in audiences, and sometimes an executive just has to admit that he's gotten too old to know the audience firsthand. Homer described a wise man as one who sees what's in front of him and what's behind him. The opportunity to learn the business from one of the giants of the business was a precious experience, but ultimately, I had to accept that even Arthur had flaws and could lose contact with the business.

The turning point on the kinds of movies we wouldn't make really started when we were offered *Raiders of the Lost Ark*. The film was based on a terrific script by Larry Kasdan (from a story by

George Lucas and Phil Kaufman), and I strongly recommended it to Arthur and Eric, but it was immediately clear that they wouldn't back me. George Lucas, who was producing, and Steven Spielberg, who was directing, were asking for an unprecedented deal that called for large fees and a back-end deal that kicked in long before the studio would earn its money back. After Arthur reviewed the deal, he said that we were in no position to make this film, and though I felt demoralized, I certainly couldn't argue with that. In fact, the deal was so extraordinarily rich that Universal and Warner Bros. passed on the project, and only Paramount, basking in its recent successes, was willing to make the movie. We had also come close to doing *The Big Chill,* but we had become gunshy about films that didn't fit the new mold, even though turning it down ran counter to our instincts. It's always easier to take chances if you are doing well.

Shortly after this episode, Arthur sent a memo to all of us declaring that the motion picture business was in serious trouble. "Looking at the MPAA's [Motion Picture Association of America] average cost of making and marketing movies has made this a losing business," he wrote. "This business is on the verge of bankruptcy." He made the point that if you added in overhead and interest, companies without extensive libraries were in serious trouble. Arthur had seen the business at so many different junctures that his brief survey of the motion picture business landscape in the early eighties began to lay the groundwork for the future of Orion.

To survive, we would need to distribute our own films and to create our own library.

▦

Between April 1979 and December 1981, Orion put out twenty-three films through Warner Bros., about a third of which were profitable. Four more films we made were released in the following twenty-four months. For a company that was built from scratch, we were doing better than most start-ups—though probably not as well as most people had expected us to perform.

What we didn't realize in the beginning was that we were never going to personally make a large amount from our deal with Warner Bros.—and it seems that they were realizing the same about us.

From the first day I drove onto the Warners lot, I thought it was a great deal for us financially and creatively. Despite the icy patches, I remained optimistic. Steve Ross had made a lot of money for a lot of people, and I figured if we could bat at least .333 at the box office—which was better than most studios—we'd be fine. If we did better, then logically we'd get rich.

Right?

It turned out that box-office returns often made little difference to our bottom line because of the hefty distribution fee Warner Bros. was charging us. For North American theatrical, the fee was 30 percent; in England it was 35 percent; and throughout Europe it was 40 percent. This was on top of Warner's out-of-pocket expenses for such things as striking prints, buying advertising, and the time their field personnel spent on our films. These expenses came off the top, and if a film bombed and didn't recover these hard costs, then we had to reimburse Warner. So it wasn't long before we discovered that unless we churned out hit after hit, we would constantly feel squeezed financially. That 30 percent fee was enough to kill a horse because it meant that thirty cents of every dollar we collected went to Warner. In the event of a big hit, there were incentives paid to us that reduced the fee, but they weren't high enough to make a difference.

What made the situation worse was that there was a period of time during which we had actually tapped out our $100 million credit line—which bore a 20 percent interest rate from the bank—and Warner had to reach into its pockets and fund our production. Though there was money due from theater owners, we were technically out of money. This made the Warner's brass doubly angry because we were tapping into their production fund, but they weren't getting the immediate benefits. They thought they had made a bad deal with us, but in fact, it was we who made the bad deal and we would ultimately pay for it dearly. Warner, on the other hand, would come out just fine.

Our best year was 1981, but it was also the year we realized that the arrangement wasn't going to work out. We had a trio of hits, with *Excalibur, Arthur,* and *Sharky's Machine. Arthur* cost $7 million and grossed $90 million, making it the fourth-highest grossing movie of the year. After the theater owners took their cut, *Arthur* returned nearly $45 million, but by the time Warner subtracted the cost of prints and advertising and its distribution fee, the net return to us was about $23 million. It was like winning the lottery, cashing the check, and then discovering you have a hole in one of your pockets.

A combination of the high distribution fees and our inability to continually deliver hits forced us to live hand to mouth. Since Arthur was forever trying to protect the downside, Orion started to sell off rights in certain territories for pictures on which we felt Warner couldn't maximize the return. We sold *Excalibur* to a German distributor for $2 million—and they ended up making $11 million on the film. Finally, we made a deal with HBO, which had a virtual monopoly on pay cable, to pull some cash out of the films before they were finished. Steve Ross hated the deal because Warner owned a piece of the Movie Channel, which was a distant third in pay cable behind HBO and Showtime. In a particularly testy meeting with Steve that we all attended, Arthur argued that the Movie Channel couldn't pay what HBO could. Steve countered that we were giving away our upside. This was the first of several disagreements that eventually led to an unpleasant parting of ways with Warner.

It was often said of Steve Ross that he had the ability to see around corners. His business life seemed to bear that out. In the case of the Orion deal, it took a few years, but Warner eventually got rich off the movies we made.

▬

The battle of Woody Allen. Oy vey.

▬

Woody probably wouldn't want to be a metaphor in Orion's story, but that's how it turned out. Even though we had complete autonomy over the films we made, Frank Wells, the president of Warner, made it clear that he wanted us to sever our ties with Woody Allen. While we were interested in watching Woody's career as an artist evolve, Warner was interested in a bar graph of his box-office results.

Wells didn't like the fact that Woody's films weren't consistent moneymakers. His reasoning was that a thinly financed company like Orion shouldn't make movies that we *knew* might not make money. To us, it was first about making good movies and then letting the money follow. We had always seen movies as an art form married to a business; they saw it as a business saddled with an art form. That worked for their operation, but what made us different and distinct from all the other studios was that the talent we surrounded ourselves with throughout our careers was first about filmmaking and second about commerce.

We believed that good movies would ultimately make money, and with all the new technologies, that has proven to be true. Not unlike Monroe Stahr in F. Scott Fitzgerald's *The Last Tycoon,* we had very few problems losing a little money once in a while if a film won us some goodwill with the creative community and helped cement our relationship with a filmmaker we believed in.

The relationship between United Artists and Woody was one of the creative cornerstones of the company. Woody had written and acted in his first film, *What's New, Pussycat?,* for United Artists in 1965 and directed *Bananas* for the company in 1971. His first deal with UA called for him to make three $2 million movies, and like clockwork, he delivered a film a year.

Woody respected Arthur's life outside of the film business, one composed of politics and charitable and cultural pursuits. When Woody was editing *Annie Hall,* he went to Arthur and told him that he would like to make a drama different from anything he had ever done. He added that he wouldn't star in the film either. Arthur was no dummy. He realized that the film that became *Interiors* was going to lose money. Nevertheless, Arthur's response was: "You've earned it."

Ultimately, Woody was a very low risk financially. His films were inexpensive and he always delivered on time and on budget. On the balance sheet, Woody was a break-even proposition in the long run. We never made a lot, but we never lost a lot. Money aside, a film company's life blood is finding entertaining stories told in a unique voice, which is exactly what Woody brought us. He also represented a distinctive New Yorker, and Arthur and Eric had a predilection for New York over Los Angeles, in both their personal and professional lives.

We had made a name for ourselves by never tinkering with a filmmaker's vision, and our relationship with Woody was the ultimate example of this. We were completely hands-off in every way. David Picker brought Woody to UA in 1969 before I arrived, and Arthur took over the supervision of his films after Picker left. I had very little, if anything, to do with Woody other than serving as a cheerleader for his work in Hollywood. Woody's films were handled exclusively out of New York in a very laissez-faire manner, and Woody wanted it this way. The five-step approval process of script, director, producer, budget, and principal cast was considerably relaxed for Woody. His managers, Charlie Joffe and Jack Rollins, served as his executive producers and ran interference between Woody and the rest of the world. Basically, when he was ready to start a movie, Woody's producers would submit a one- or two-page summary of the plot, agree on a budget, and then go off and make the movie. When the film was finished, he would screen it for us and we would release it.

Artistically, though, Woody went through different phases, and these phases were encouraged by the long-term approach UA had toward his career. We had always believed that a film studio existed primarily to support filmmakers. If there was a darker film that didn't seem commercial in the least, perhaps it was an artistic building block to his next romantic comedy. Looking at a filmmaker's career in these terms was almost unheard of at that time, and in today's business, it is inconceivable.

I always saw Woody as a modern-day Chaplin. He had a Bergman period with *Annie Hall* and *Interiors* and a Fellini period with *Stardust Memories,* which seemed to have been modeled on *$8^{1}/_{2}$*. For me, it was fascinating to watch Woody evolve as an artist, though strangely he has never regarded himself as one. He's probably the least pretentious auteur director I've ever met. He always says that he's a guy who makes movies, some good, some bad, and then kicks back in front of the TV with a beer to watch the Knicks. The real artists of his generation, he says, are Scorsese and Coppola.

I respectfully disagree with him on this point; I think he is every bit the artist as the others.

By the time Woody finished his commitment to United Artists, it was 1980. He had just completed his on-screen self-analytical period, which was critically acclaimed inside and outside of Hollywood but not terribly profitable as a whole. *Annie Hall*, released in 1977, had won Academy Awards for Best Picture, Best Director, and Best Screenplay in a year that *Star Wars* was nominated for Best Picture, George Lucas for Best Director, and Steven Spielberg for Best Director for *Close Encounters of the Third Kind*. *Interiors, Manhattan,* and *Stardust Memories* had received a combined total of seven Oscar nominations. However, the combined box office of these films equaled their cost, a business scenario that Warner was not interested in.

Warner Bros. was guaranteeing our loan and any downside came out of the executives' profit pool. Therefore, they regarded Woody Allen as a bad deal: his films didn't make money. In December 1980, against Warner's wishes, we signed Woody to a three-picture deal, two of which he agreed to star in. The deal with Woody signaled an end to the presumption of cordial relations between Warner and us.

The Orion-Warner deal went on to earn Warner a fortune in ancillary revenues after we left, but in what seems like poetic justice, the two movies Woody made on their watch never made them a dime. His first film was supposed to be *Zelig*, a documentary spoof about the life of Leonard Zelig, whose chameleon-like condition allows him to walk in and out of any historical situation. The combination of a looming Directors Guild strike and the technical demands of inserting the Zelig character into historical footage pushed *Zelig*'s start date back. Instead, Allen began filming the less technically complicated *A Midsummer Night's Sex Comedy*, an homage to Shakespeare with allusions to Chekhov and Renoir. Diane Keaton was busy promoting *Reds* and preparing to star in Alan Parker's *Shoot the Moon*, so Allen cast his girlfriend, Mia Farrow, in the lead in both movies and shot them back to back.

Woody Allen went on to make nine more movies for Orion over the next nine years. Some of them made money, some of them lost money. Some of them were critically acclaimed and/or recognized by the Academy, some of them weren't. In hindsight, the only obvious commercial gesture he made came after the cool reception of *Zelig*. Instead of trying to mix comedy and drama in the same film, he began alternating between comedies and dramas.

From the long view, the relationship with Woody was much more valuable for Orion than the one with Warner. In the end, as long as you are not losing money, you need someone like Woody Allen to help define your company as an artistic haven and to gain the respect of other filmmakers to get to the bigger, more commercial movies.

If I needed to choose, I'd have taken Woody over Warner Bros.

■

By the time we started arguing with Warner over Woody Allen, there was probably nothing that could have salvaged the partnership. It was clear that we would have to strike out on our own. By the end of 1981, it was becoming increasingly apparent that Warner felt that they weren't making enough money from Orion and that we were too disruptive to their organization. For our part, we felt handcuffed because we didn't have full control of our own company, and we weren't getting any added benefits from being under the Warner's umbrella.

Our hope was to get projects already in development at Warner, but the only time that happened was when Warner tried to get us to pick up *Caligula*, an X-rated film based on the life of the mad sex fiend Roman emperor of the same name, which starred Malcolm McDowell and Helen Mirren. Ted Ashley and Frank Wells thought that our credibility and class might be able to take the sting off the film (à la *Last Tango in Paris*), so Eric and I flew to London to see the film. Written by Gore Vidal (who later tried to take his name off it) and partially financed by Bob Guccione of *Penthouse* magazine fame, the film was a sexually explicit piece of trash. Eric and I sat slack-jawed and jet-lagged in the screening room watching decapitations, necrophilia, rape, bestiality—you name it. After four hours of this Roman feast of debauchery, the producer knew we didn't like it. All he could mumble was, "Didn't you love the art direction?" You bet we did, but that was about all we liked.

In 1980, Bob Benjamin had died, leaving only four partners. The loss of Bob changed the way Arthur looked at the Warner's situation. He decided to move faster than he might have had Bob been alive to consult with, so in early 1982, Arthur, Eric, Bill, and I met in New York to discuss how to recast Orion as an independent film company, one with its own marketing and distribution system. Both Steve Ross and Bob Daly, the studio's new chairman, approached me about staying at Warner as head of production. But before there was any extensive conversation on this subject, I told both of them that I couldn't. I was flattered, but I had come in with Arthur, Bob, Eric, and Bill. The day I turned down Jack Beckett's offer at United Artists, I decided that these were my partners and friends, for better or for worse, and certainly for richer or for poorer. Loyalty is in very short supply in Hollywood, but it had become a cornerstone to my life. In hindsight, I probably would've made a lot of money if I had stayed, given the trajectory of the Warner's stock over the past eighteen years and the mergers with Time, Inc. and America Online. But the truth is, I never seriously thought of a career without my partners.

To become the true masters of our own destiny, we needed independent financing with no strings attached, and we needed our own distribution and marketing apparatus, as well as a library of films to throw off a revenue stream that would allow us to ride out the inevitable cold streaks at the box office. We began looking for a company with an existing library to buy and for financing to pay for it. There were three choices: Filmways, Embassy, and Allied Artists. Arthur felt that Allied Artists was too small and ruled it out immediately. Since Embassy was mostly a television company, we chose Filmways, which was a public company. The idea would be to buy Filmways for the library and the distribution system, and attach the Orion name to it.

Filmways was founded by producer Marty Ransahoff and John Calley (both of whom were no longer involved by 1982), and it had merged with the legendary B-picture company called AIP, owned by Sam Arkoff and Jim Nicholson. This company had found a niche catering to teen audiences by making movies with new talent at low cost. Filmways had a skeletal domestic distribution system (which was better than none) and a library of about 650 feature films and 300 television shows, though the titles weren't worth much. Mostly they were movies with cars and chicks with titles like *Beach Blanket Bingo* and *Black Mama, White Mama*. John Milius had written his first movie for AIP, *The Devil's Eight*. It was a take-off on the dirty dozen, but AIP didn't have enough money for a full dozen.

When we showed up at Filmways's doorstep, the company was about thirty days from filing for bankruptcy, so what we needed was a rescue package. To raise the money, Arthur turned to his friend Lionel Pincus, whose New York–based investment banking firm, Warburg Pincus, set about raising funding for Orion. The bankers cobbled together $26 million in cash (the amount needed to buy Filmways), and we borrowed another $52 million from the First Bank of Boston and Chemical Bank, of which $28 million was immediately used to pay off Filmways's past-due debts and to keep the company out of bankruptcy. Some of the money came from a deal with HBO, which got nearly 10 percent of the stock for an equity investment that also gave them cable TV rights to our films. When the deal was done, Warburg Pincus controlled roughly 53 percent of the stock and each of the four partners owned 4 percent of the warrants, exercisable over five years.

In February 1982, we formally took over Filmways and rechristened it Orion Pictures Corporation. We also quickly discovered the most devastating and lasting flaw in our Warner deal: Warner would end up owning the copyright on all the films we had produced. Since the deal was made before the home-video boom, before there were cable channels like TNT and TBS, and before foreign television started buying up every movie in sight, we're talking about a percent of a few billion dollars.

If you look at the Orion-Warner deal in hindsight, it was a phenomenal coup for Warner. Despite the fact that they had to cover us during the time we tapped out our line of credit, they have since cleaned up in the ancillary markets on the films we left behind. When the video boom hit, we were long gone from Warner, and they made a fortune off our movies. *10* has probably earned more on videotape than it cost to produce several times over, and, as Dudley Moore's character Arthur himself might say, the profits from *Arthur* don't exactly suck either.

At what price, freedom? We were starting with roughly $50 million—half the money that was available to us at the beginning of our deal with Warner Bros. Of course, having taken control of Filmways, we did own all rights, title, and interest, including sequels and remakes, to the five Annette Funicello–Frankie Avalon *Beach Party* movies. That wouldn't get us anywhere in the high-concept era.

8   *Trade Ads and Champagne*

Ramping up a new studio hadn't been done since United Artists was formed in 1919, and it has been done only once since Orion, when DreamWorks was formed in 1994. We knew it would be the challenge of a lifetime, and we thought we could do it.

The blockbuster business became the main business of Hollywood in the early eighties. The industry had gotten its first taste of monster hits with *Jaws* and *Star Wars* in the seventies. Then, in the summer of 1982, Steven Spielberg's fable *E.T.: The Extra-Terrestrial* shattered all box-office records, grossing nearly $400 million in the United States alone and showing that there was no limit to how much money could be made on a monster hit. The basic rule of thumb of the times was that every studio had to find two biggies for summer and one for the Christmas-holiday period, those being the two seasons that attracted the most people to the movies. If one or both of those films hit, it didn't matter what happened the rest of the year. Trying to create blockbusters was, however, risky business. More and more audiences seemed to be going to movies in droves in the first forty-eight hours or not at all. If your film didn't have a big opening, it was basically dead.

What most moviegoers didn't realize was that one huge film could have a disproportionate effect on the market value of the company that released it. A hit film could move the stock price of a major company overnight. MGM/UA's market capitalization shot up $125 million surrounding the release of *Rocky III*; Universal's parent, MCA, increased $275 million in value during the

125

first month of the release of *E.T.: The Extra-Terrestrial*, and Disney's value gained more than $180 million in the two weeks preceding the release of *Tron* in anticipation of a hit—though when the movie bombed the company's stock fell right back. This phenomenon put more pressure on studio executives to find mass entertainment, raising the bar for the amount of money studios would spend on movies and their releases.

As a company, Orion was held to the same standard as other studios—our stock price would also soar with a hit—except we didn't have the money to play the blockbuster game. We simply couldn't afford to make a $25 million film in 1982. Orion not only needed to use its old UA relationships, we needed to find new filmmakers and to try to keep up with the times. We needed to test the boundaries of what made traditional hits. To a degree, we did all of these things.

We had barely moved in to our new offices in Century City when Gene Tunick, our head of distribution, walked into my office and told me about a twenty-minute promotional reel of footage for Sylvester Stallone's new film, *First Blood*. The project had originally been developed by executives at Warner Bros. for Steve McQueen. When that deal fell apart, independent producers Mario Kassar and Andy Vajna stepped in. Their company, Carolco, financed films through foreign presales and complicated tax shelters set up overseas. It was one of the first companies to tap into the Credit Lyonnais branch in Rotterdam, where banker Frans Afman began loaning money to film producers against the presales of foreign rights. Based on Stallone's overseas appeal, Carolco was able to raise half of the financing by getting contracts with foreign distributors and then taking these to the bank and using them as collateral to borrow the cash to fund production. Relying on Stallone carried a small risk for the foreign distributors, but it was much riskier for us in the U.S., which was underscored by the fact that no one else wanted the flm.

Stallone's drawing power had waned. His two *Rocky* sequels made money from the built-in audience, but his attempts to play another kind of character in *Victory* and *Nighthawks* were less than successful. None of Stallone's non-*Rocky* films had ever grossed more than $23 million in the United States. Nevertheless, we were blown away by the *First Blood* footage and decided to ignore the numbers. In the film, Stallone plays a Green Beret named John Rambo whose nightmares of Vietnam come back to haunt him when he is wrongfully arrested. Rambo escapes into the wilderness and uses his survival skills to battle his pursuers in the rugged, mountainous terrain. We were all in agreement on distributing the film, so we bought the domestic rights for $8 million—a lot of money if you have access to only $50 million and haven't seen the entire film.

First Blood was released in October 1982, and it was exactly the kind of box-office winner we needed to establish the new Orion. The film rang up $45 million domestically and made us look as if we had a Midas touch. Even though we hadn't produced the film, we were the ones who saw its potential.

First Blood made everyone bullish on the new Orion. The stock, still registered as Filmways, went from a low of $3^3/_8$ a share to $13^1/_2$ in the eleven months after we took over the company, a run up attributable almost entirely to the success of *First Blood*. By May 1983, the stock hit $25 in anticipation of things to come, which was like a huge carrot at the end of a stick for the four of us, since we each had warrants that vested only over time: if we kept the stock up with a string of hits, our options would be worth millions, but a few missteps and they wouldn't be worth anything.

How apocryphal.

In what was to become a recurring theme for Orion, our first success ultimately turned out to be our first failure. For some reason, which I've never fully understood, we didn't secure the sequel rights to *First Blood* and the Rambo character. After we agreed to buy a movie, Bill Bernstein would step in and negotiate the finer points of the deal. He was in charge of all the company's negotiations, and his meticulousness was usually unparalleled. Later, when we realized that we didn't own these valuable rights, I asked Bill why, and he explained that we hadn't financed the film—we had only bought the domestic rights—so those rights weren't available to us. In retrospect, we should have received those rights as part of the distribution agreement. After all, no one was beating down Carolco's doors to pick up this film. If we had had those rights, the Rambo movies would have become a tent-pole franchise for Orion, but 20-20 hindsight is worth less in the movie business than in life.

■

It is as true today as it was then: Franchises and sequels are the major engines driving a studio's release slate. These have replaced the Westerns of the thirties and forties as staples in a studio's lineup. They can lift a studio out of a rough patch at the box office, start a hot streak, or give the studio room to take risks. In our case at UA, the reliable revenue from the Bond and Pink Panther films allowed us to take chances on challenging material, which is one of the reasons we were able to make so many cutting-edge movies. To this day, the Bond franchise continues to support MGM/UA, which is even trying to revamp the Pink Panther series. The Rambo series could have been to us what *Star Trek* was to Paramount, something that covered up our mistakes. If you have a *Star Trek* every other Christmas, you can take a chance on a picture called *Forrest Gump*, which nobody wanted, or on a small drama by a TV producer, like *Terms of Endearment.*

Even if we could have afforded to buy the sequel and character rights, by the time we reached that point, Mario Kassar and Andy Vajna wouldn't have sold them to us. They were upset that we didn't spend enough money on advertising in the United States and Canada. They felt a bigger marketing push would've resulted in a bigger hit, and they were probably right. I didn't know it at the time, but skimping on marketing would become the norm at Orion. We simply couldn't afford to spend the kind of money that Paramount, Columbia, Fox, or Universal did to launch a potential mass-audience hit. Consequently, it was tougher to generate the kind of breakout, $100 million hits that the business demanded from studios in the eighties. This also prevented Orion from reaping the large rewards from home video and foreign rights that accompanied hits in the United States.

Mario and Andy believed all along that they had gold, and time proved them right: *Rambo: First Blood Part II* went on to help launch TriStar Pictures as a public company in 1985, and the Rambo name became part of the American vernacular. In numerous dictionaries it is defined as a macho man who displays violence or aggression. At one point during the Cold War, the media spoke of President Ronald Reagan as "Ronbo," a reference to his penchant for flexing America's military muscles.

Rambo III, made in 1988, was the most expensive film to date, costing some $58 million. It, too, was a hit. Besides positioning TriStar as a major studio, the Rambo films made money and gave TriStar's library a substantial asset that Orion desperately could've used. This type of missed opportunity would become a pattern at Orion.

▤

In the mideighties, films increasingly became about making creative financing deals: foreign presales, domestic presale guarantees, and the role of foreign banks like Credit Lyonnais lending money against foreign distribution contracts created a new source of financing. Modeled on many that producer Dino De Laurentiis had done, the deal that Carolco put together on First Blood *became the new model for a producer's deal.*

Two of our greatest successes were also financed this way: The Terminator *and* Platoon.

▤

The Terminator was exactly the kind of film Orion would have to take a chance on to compete with the majors. The film was the brainchild of producer Gale Anne Hurd and writer-director James Cameron. Both had come from the Roger Corman school of filmmaking, so they were used to working with a smaller budget and getting the most out of every dime. Because they didn't yet have a track record, the film wasn't too expensive. Jim and Gale had set *The Terminator* in the present to keep the budget down. The basic story line, which came from a dream Cameron had, was that a cyborg from the future returns to present-day earth to kill the woman who will give birth to a child destined to become the enemy of the machines. The cyborg hitman is pursued by another futuristic character who comes to save the woman and ends up falling in love with her.

Cameron had a facile imagination and a gift for telling a story humorously and lacing it with mythic elements. He had spent his early days working as an art director on John Carpenter's films like *Escape from New York*, so his writing had a very visual dimension. For *The Terminator*, he and Gale started with a forty-eight-page, single-spaced treatment that detailed every scene. Jim then sketched the entire movie on an oversized art pad to show exactly what the production design would look like. When the treatment was done, they showed it along with the drawings to John Daly and Derek Gibson at Hemdale Film Corporation, who agreed to pay Jim to write the script. By the time I received it, *The Terminator* was a smart action thriller that was almost in shootable form, but it was also the kind of film that would be difficult to talk Arthur and Eric into going along with.

Eric's sensibility about films was more sophisticated, perhaps a result of the years he spent working at United Artists in Europe. He never liked *The Terminator* script all that much because it wasn't high art, but he knew we had to make all kinds of movies at Orion in order to compete—not every film could be Bertolucci or Forman. But in addition to a smartly written thriller, *The Terminator* was a good deal from a financial standpoint, and Eric knew that.

The budget was $6.4 million all in. ("All in" is studio parlance for a budget that includes the entire production budget, plus a 10 percent overbudget contingency, and a fee for a completion bond to ensure the film is finished in the event it does go over budget.) Ernst Goldschmidt, our head of foreign sales, agreed that it had strong foreign potential, so we prebought the foreign rights for one-third of the budget and agreed to distribute the film domestically. Under the terms of the deal, Gale, as producer, retained a 50 percent stake in the film, and Hemdale, as financier, retained 50 percent. Orion also received a right of first refusal to distribute the sequel, if one materialized.

Casting was critical, so we started batting around ideas for the two lead roles, the Terminator and the role of his enemy,

Reese. Jim and Gale's first idea was for Lance Henriksen to play the Terminator and for Michael Biehn to play Reese. However, for marketing purposes, we needed a more commercial name in one of the two roles. I suggested both O. J. Simpson, who wanted to become a leading man, and Arnold Schwarzenegger, who was coming off *Conan the Barbarian*. It sounds corny now, but this was 1983, when O. J. Simpson was the great ex-running back doing Hertz commercials. This was long before he had been charged with murdering his ex-wife, Nicole, and Ronald Goldman. He was still a hero in most people's eyes.

Landing Arnold to play the Terminator took a few rounds of phone calls to his agent, Lou Pitt, from everyone involved. I called Lou first and explained to him that though the Terminator wasn't technically the lead, it was the title role of the film. After I sent the script to Arnold, he called me.

"Which part do you want me to play?" Arnold asked me in his thick accent.

"The Terminator," I told him. "That's what the movie's called."

"You mean, you want me to play the heavy?" he asked suspiciously.

"Arnold," I said, "do you know how Richard Widmark made his career? He threw a woman down the steps in his first film, *Kiss of Death.*"

I felt Arnold could add something to the movie in either role, though the cyborg part had very few lines. I left it up to Jim Cameron to decide. At my prompting, he and Gale had lunch with Arnold, and Jim instantly fixated on him as the Terminator. Until Arnold came along and interpreted the role, the Terminator seemed like an indestructible piece of metal with a one-track mind. What Arnold brought to it was a force of personality that made the Terminator one of the most memorable characters in modern film history.

◼

The experience of *The Terminator* turned out to be one of highs and lows, with no middle ground. Jim Cameron showed he was an extraordinary talent. He and Gale began dating during post-production and ended up marrying, and it was just as turbulent for Orion and ultimately for me, too. Gale and Jim were young, talented, and eager to make a name for themselves in the creative community, and they worked extraordinarily hard on the film. There were plenty of twists and turns in the road and a couple of detours that soured them on Orion forever—and rightfully so.

Initially, there was some resistance within the company, especially in the marketing department, to screen *The Terminator* for critics, because they saw the film as an audience film and not a critics' pick, which is ironic considering that the film was lauded by critics and made *Time* magazine's list of the ten best films in 1984. Though the advance media screening problems were easily worked out, the situation caused Gale and Jim a great deal of anxiety. They felt that Orion had no intention of supporting their film. When the film was finished, we tested it at a shopping mall in the San Fernando Valley. The film caused a near-riot among the largely teenage audience, which was demonstrably blown away by the gripping action sequences. Cameron, however, was in a state of despair after the screening because he saw the film more as a tender love story than a testosterone action film, much as he always saw *Titanic* as a love story and not a spectacle. Despite the fact that the film played well, Cameron accused Orion of recruiting the wrong audience.

Cameron was partly right about how much Orion would (or could) spend on promoting the film. Even after the film had tested so well with what was then the biggest single audience demographic, Eric was lukewarm about putting much money into marketing. The marketing department was basically allotted enough money for a first-weekend push and then it would be wait and see. Even when the film did $5 million over the opening weekend, Eric still didn't want to increase spending. He reasoned that we didn't have to because the film had found an audience and word of mouth would take over. Distraught, Gale and Jim appealed to John Daly at Hemdale and he, in turn, went to his investors for additional money to pay for second-week television ads. *The Terminator* continued to gross in the $5 million range over each of the next six weeks.

Given the quality of the film, its final number of $38 million was about a quarter of its potential. For that film today, twice $38 million would be the opening weekend.

Shortly after the film was released, Jim and Gale went to New York to meet with Eric and Bill. This is long before they were rich, and they flew across country at their own expense, hoping to be offered another movie or a first-look production deal. To celebrate *The Terminator*'s success, the four of them went to lunch at La Côte Basque. According to Gale, when she and Jim tried to order a bottle of vintage champagne, Eric protested that it was too expensive. Gale then mentioned that it would be nice if Orion took out a congratulatory ad in the trades applauding the box-office numbers. At the time, Gale was trying to get Fox to commit to Jim as the director of *Aliens*, and she felt that anything that contributed to the perception that *The Terminator* was a hit would only help her cause with Fox. Eric rejected the idea, saying that the film should speak for itself. Although congratulatory trade ads for established filmmakers are akin to sending them a case of Evian, they are a big deal for up-and-comers trying to make an impression in Hollywood. Gale and Jim felt that they had worked incredibly hard for very little money, and while the film was making money for Orion, they were being treated as if they were unequal to other filmmakers and unimportant to Orion.

The whole situation made me feel as though I was sitting in the middle seat on an airplane between a couple who were arguing with each other. On one hand, I had to deal with my hard-nosed financial colleagues, to whom I was obviously very loyal, while on the other hand, I had to worry about the wants and desires of the creative talent, who I needed to make movies. There were no clear lines of right and wrong, just shades of people's personalities showing through, although Jim and Gale probably had the upper hand in this dispute. Though Orion didn't have a lot of money to spend on television buys, a full-page trade ad cost about $5,000 and a nice bottle of champagne about $200, and both were within our reach. The most troubling part was that I was in L.A. hearing the complaints face-to-face, while Eric, Arthur, and Bill were in New York, mostly isolated from that situation. Since I was in L.A., everyone expected me to fix problems like this, but the reality was that I couldn't: I was only one of four votes. Depending on how our films were doing, I was less influential at times. Furthermore, the geography of Orion further compromised my ability to resolve situations like this. I was in L.A., with responsibility for overseeing the development and production of movies, but, in what turned out to be a major mistake, the marketing department had been moved from L.A. to New York. This cross-country push-pull between me and my partners, which was difficult to start with, worsened over the next six years, ultimately ending my business relationship with them.

A few weeks after the disastrous New York lunch, I tried to smooth things out by setting up a dinner with Gale, Jim, and Bill Bernstein, who was in town, but by then the damage had become irreversible. Gale and Jim were furious, mostly at Eric, and nothing was going to change their minds. So while the Terminator would make good on his famous promise—"I'll be back"— since Gale controlled half of the rights, the Terminator wasn't coming back to Orion.

By the time Jim and Gale were ready to do the sequel in the late eighties, the air was so thick with irony, we couldn't have seen the Terminator if he was standing next to us. Repairing the relationship with them had become only one of the many problems Orion faced in getting the *Terminator* sequel. A cash-strapped Hemdale had been forced by Credit Lyonnais to sell its 50 percent right, title, and interest in the *Terminator* sequel to Carolco for $10 million. Based on the two Rambo sequels, Credit Lyonnais apparently felt that Carolco's Kassar and Vajna were better equipped to do the *Terminator* sequel. Contractually, they had to offer it to Orion, but they priced it high enough that Arthur and Eric passed. I felt this was a big mistake. There was no way Kassar and Vajna were going to work with Orion on the film unless they had to because they still harbored a grudge against us for not spending enough to market the first *Rambo* film. What came around, went around—and kept right on going in this case. Trade ads and champagne probably cost Orion nearly a half billion dollars, while ironically, I got to supervise the release of *Terminator 2: Judgment Day* at TriStar.

For me, the behind-the-scenes saga of the first *Terminator* film cast a shadow that continued into the late nineties. The lingering effects of how Gale felt she was treated at Orion affected my relationship with her. I finally broke the ice in 1998 and asked her to produce the film *Dick*, a Watergate spoof, for Phoenix Pictures. But that same year Jim Cameron publicly rewrote the casting history of *The Terminator* and made me look like a buffoon.

We were both speaking at a dinner honoring Arnold Schwarzenegger. The ballroom was packed with agents, lawyers, actors, managers, producers, and directors whom I have worked with my entire career. When it was my turn to speak, I stood up and talked about the three films that I had been involved with Arnold on: *Stay Hungry* at UA, *The Terminator* at Orion, and *Terminator 2* at TriStar. I told a story about Bob Rafelson coming to see me while he was casting *Stay Hungry* and telling me that Arnold Schwarzenegger was going to be a big star. "Bob," I said, "I've known you were crazy for years and now I'm sure of it. This guy has an Austrian accent and he doesn't look anything like a traditional movie star. Get out of my office." The crowd laughed at the recollection.

Then Cameron took the stage.

Cameron told the two thousand people how I had insisted O. J. Simpson play the Terminator and that he had fought to get Arnold cast. Given that O. J. was now known as the guy charged with butchering his ex-wife, this sounded hilarious. It was particularly embarrassing because a lot of the people in the audience believed him. He probably believed it himself. It was particularly unfair to me because it wasn't true. But what could I do? Seize the microphone and correct the self-proclaimed "King of the World"? Several thoughts immediately raced through my head: For starters, he was wrong. In fact, I was the one who suggested Arnold—I had my eye on him since *Stay Hungry*. The fact of the matter was that Cameron's only credit at the time was *Piranha II: The Spawning*, a track record that didn't give him the right to dictate casting. Since nobody else wanted to finance *The Terminator*, we could have vetoed anyone he wanted in the movie and that would have been the end of it.

Feeling hurt by Cameron's speech led me to write a letter to Arnold to set the record straight. In the letter, I wrote that I expected Jim Cameron to say something like that because he can't be happy unless he is in a fight with someone. I wanted Arnold to know the facts as I remembered them. Arnold had become close friends with Cameron from the two *Terminator* films and *True Lies*, which they made together. When Arnold read the letter, he was upset with me, and both he and his wife, Maria Shriver, called me to express their sentiments. Arnold thought Cameron's schtick was funny and that it was said as a joke, so I should just move on. I disagreed with him, but I told him I would drop the matter. By the time he asked me to produce *The 6th Day* with him, it was clear it was a tempest only in my tea cup.

As for Cameron, if he wants credit for the casting of Arnold, he can have it. He made a great film. But he needs to remember that history is not only a great teacher, it also kills all of its students.

▥

Oliver Stone is a filmmaker who likes to shake everyone up until the truth falls out, and that's what he did to Hollywood in getting Platoon *made.*

▥

The script for *Platoon* kept appearing and reappearing, but got made only when Hemdale got involved and provided the financing. Oliver Stone first wrote the script in 1976. Although he wanted to direct it, the grim and realistic script became something of a writing sample that began getting him work all over town. Based on the *Platoon* script, producer David Puttman hired Stone to write *Midnight Express*, which won Stone the Academy Award for Best Adapted Screenplay.

We first saw the *Platoon* script in 1977. At the time, Martin Bregman, who was to produce the Stone-written *Scarface*, was attached to produce it. The script was visceral and articulated a clear vision of how disillusionment undid our soldiers in Vietnam, but I felt that I had done enough Vietnam pictures for one lifetime at UA, so I passed. Everyone else in town passed, too.

Oliver hadn't yet directed a film either, so there was no way to know if he could bring it off. Instead, we gave Stone his directing break on the less ambitious *The Hand,* a psychological horror film that was far from an easy experience.

Next, Dino De Laurentiis promised to back *Platoon* if Stone wrote a script for him called *Year of the Dragon,* which Michael Cimino directed. Dino went shopping for domestic distributors for *Platoon* and resubmitted it to us in 1984. We passed again, because *The Hand* had come in over budget and behind schedule. But we also thought that since five years had passed, the film's release would be even further away from the Vietnam films of the seventies. America was in a jingoistic mood, so the bar seemed even higher. The rest of the studios passed as well, and De Laurentiis soon gave up on the project.

Enter Hemdale, which, by this time, had a distribution deal with Orion. Oliver had extracted a similar promise from John Daly that Dino had made, only Hemdale came through in the end. The company made a two-picture deal with Oliver for *Salvador* and *Platoon. Salvador,* which came first, told the horrific story of rogue photojournalist Richard Boyle's adventure in war-torn El Salvador. Hemdale submitted *Salvador* to us in both the script and finished film stages, but we passed both times. The film was well done, but the ending was particularly brutal and not commercial. I saw part of the film during its early stage and stupidly walked out to take a phone call. When no one else picked up the film, Hemdale eventually released it themselves. I realize now I was wrong about *Salvador;* we should have picked it up.

Of course, I don't remember whom I left the screening to talk to.

While Oliver was filming *Salvador* in Mexico, Daly hired a foreign sales agent named Arnold Kopelson and sent him to gather some footage to take to the Cannes Film Festival. While in Mexico, Kopelson struck up a relationship with Oliver's line producer, Gerald Green, and the two hatched a plan to produce *Platoon.* Kopelson also brought in another foreign sales agent and packager of movies named Pierre David, who, in turn, reapproached Daly with a slightly different package. Suddenly, this orphaned project now had people jockeying to be involved. Daly agreed to back the film with Kopelson as the producer and then reapproached Orion.

Platoon came back to us in 1985 for the third time, but now Hemdale had essentially agreed to finance the film, and they wanted us to distribute and invest in it. Ernst Goldschmidt, the head of our foreign division, thought *Platoon* was a terrific project and wanted to buy the foreign rights. *Platoon* was ready to shoot with a budget of $5.4 million. Ernst wanted to pay $2.5 million for the foreign rights. We all agreed that to keep our risk as low as possible, we would allow Ernst to buy the film—but only if he could get worldwide theatrical rights for the $2.5 million. Hemdale, which retained all other ancillary rights, agreed. At this low level of risk, we felt reasonably certain that the movie wouldn't lose money. Fixing the amount we paid would also protect us if Stone went over budget, as he had on *The Hand.*

After Oliver returned from the filming in the Philippines (where *Apocalypse Now* was also shot) and assembled a first cut, I went with other Orion executives to a screening at Culver Studios. I couldn't believe my eyes. As good as the script was, the film was better. For the first time in my life, with all the Vietnam-themed films I had worked on and seen, I really felt as though I was in the combat zone at ground zero. Although I had been in the army, I didn't go to Vietnam, but this was exactly how I imagined it when I was on maneuvers. The film was a harrowing account that captured what really happened in Vietnam through a poignant first-person perspective, as Stone had earned a bronze star and a Purple Heart for his service in the 25th Infantry Unit.

Platoon turned the entire war upside down: the enemy was on the other side of the firing line but it was also within. Stone made the line of good versus evil more porous than we had seen in previous war films. When we first saw the character of Chris (played by Charlie Sheen) kill his superior, a bastard of a human being named Barnes (Tom Berenger), we were speechless. Nobody at Orion expected to see what they saw, and none of us had a single creative comment about the film. The film was then screened in New York for Arthur, who thought it was good but questioned its commerciality.

After we picked it up, only one scene was changed.

Platoon was barely on the Hollywood radar screen in the month leading up to its release. Oliver was well known around town, but he was hardly a star director, even though he had won an Oscar for his script for *Midnight Express* and praise for his script for *Scarface*. *Salvador* had recently played to some acclaim in its small release, but Oliver was hardly mainstream. All that changed when we released *Platoon* in a few theaters on December 19, 1986. The film was everything all at once: a critical success, a financial hit in the making, a hot button for debate and protest, and a work of cinematic art. No matter what you thought of it, you couldn't ignore it.

At the time, Reaganism was hitting its stride, and the United States was unquestionably embracing the expansion of our military to win the Cold War and make the world safe from oppression. Even my father was on board. We were arming the Contras in Nicaragua and El Salvador, and we were ready to intervene in situations like Grenada. *Top Gun* had cleaned up at the box office that year by capitalizing on this nationalistic fervor, and Bruce Springsteen's "Born in the U.S.A." was misinterpreted as a prowar anthem. In the sequel to *First Blood*, John Rambo was going to win the war that we couldn't win. *Platoon* was a corrective to the mythology of our military pathos that was so integral to the Reagan ether. As powerful films often do, *Platoon* opened old wounds and forced us, in this case, to look back at Vietnam. It shined a critical light on this new American military strategy and made us wonder if there could be another Vietnam.

Orion rolled the film out slowly, expanding to seventy-four theaters in mid-January. While we all agreed the film was great, Arthur felt that it might not be commercial, hence the slow release pattern. Charles Glenn, our head of publicity and marketing, designed a marketing campaign around the strong reviews and interviews with Stone recounting his personal experience, and it was one of the few perfectly executed campaigns Orion ever launched. In fact, the campaign itself won a Clio, the Oscar of advertising.

The building blocks were Vincent Canby's *New York Times* review, which called the film "a singular achievement" and "a

major piece of work," and *Time* magazine's January 27 cover
story titled "Vietnam As It Really Was." The film then won Best
Picture, Best Director, and Best Supporting Actor for Tom
Berenger at the Golden Globes. Using the Golden Globes, which
are awarded by a loose group of foreign journalists, as a publicity tool was just coming into vogue. I don't think anyone, including myself, stopped to realize that we were demeaning the Academy Awards by positioning the Globes as some sort of harbinger
of the Oscars. Over the next fifteen years, the wink and a nod
that accompanied the Golden Globes slowly disappeared as they
grew into the second most important awards in Hollywood.

███

We were criticized for not releasing *Platoon* wider after the initial reviews, but the results made the campaign we ran a main-
stay in Hollywood, one that was repeated with much success on
Crouching Tiger, Hidden Dragon in 2000–2001. The review-based
marketing campaign like the one used for *Platoon* has been
copied many times, though it has become less and less effective
because critics have become far less important to the marketing
process. Back in 1971, *The New Yorker*'s Pauline Kael could
anoint a picture like *Last Tango in Paris* to greatness simply with
a review. But by the end of the eighties, there were so many
movie critics that their impact had become watered down as
their opinions piled up. Every small town has its own movie
critic, and there are reviewers out there working for dubious-
sounding organizations who will say something great about any
piece of junk just to see their names on the ads.

The only exception is the smaller art-house film, like those
released by the studios' classics divisions. The audience for these
films is smaller, and they tend to rely on critics from their city's
major newspapers, largely because they skew toward older audiences. For a foreign film, a favorable review in the *New York
Times* can double the film's opening-weekend gross. There is a
considerable difference between $100,000 and $200,000 in first-
weekend box-office receipts.

Today, with the exception of a limited-release art film, the
whole process of using critical acclaim is nothing but a cheap

marketing tool that doesn't work. In fact, around the release of *Apocalypse Now* at United Artists, we had commissioned a study about the impact of reviews on box-office performance. The only ones that had any impact were those from television reviewers, and that impact was practically nonexistent. On opening weekend, a sunny Friday afternoon with little competition will help you a lot more than two thumbs way up.

Nevertheless, studios still constantly use both the credible critics and the blurbmeisters' quotes on their ads, though not with any regard for which is more important. If only someone would mock the process in the film industry with the same aplomb of the legendary theater producer David Merrick. In 1966, when Merrick was certain the seven major New York theater critics were going to savage his new musical *Subways Are For Sleeping*, he went to the New York City phone book and found seven men with the same first and last names as those of the critics. He then invited the men to a private performance of the musical, and coaxed from them lines like "The greatest musical ever made." He produced a full-page newspaper ad with their platitudes—and their names—in bold letters. In 2001, Sony's advertising department went further, making up a critic, but few people seemed to care.

▬

When the Academy Award nominations for 1986 were announced live on television at 5:30 A.M. for the first time since 1955, I sat bleary-eyed on the edge of my bed and listened with delight as *Platoon* was nominated for eight Academy Awards, including Best Picture. Another Orion release, Woody Allen's *Hannah and Her Sisters*, garnered seven nominations, and Dennis Hopper was nominated for Best Supporting Actor in *Hoosiers*, another film brought in by Hemdale.

In all, Orion had fifteen nominations.

By the time I got to the office, a huge cake was sitting in the conference room. On Oscar night, *Platoon* took home four Oscars, including Best Picture and Best Director for Oliver Stone. *Hannah* won three Oscars: Woody for Best Original Screenplay, and those for Best Supporting Actor and Supporting

Actress (Michael Caine and Dianne Weist). Having a film that no one wanted and the director that Warner Bros. didn't want end up victorious on Oscar night sweetened the feeling.

Strangely though, along with the success of *Platoon* came the end of our relationship with Hemdale. Both Hemdale and Orion had done well financially from the relationship. Besides *The Terminator*, *Platoon*, and *Hoosiers*, Hemdale had also co-financed *The Falcon and the Snowman*, John Schlesinger's harrowing film based on the true story of two friends (played by Sean Penn and Timothy Hutton) who nearly sold American intelligence secrets to the KGB, and *At Close Range*, a father-and-son drama starring Penn and Christopher Walken. What happened was that both sides wanted to amend the relationship in ways that were incompatible: Orion wanted to put up a bigger share of the budget and receive a bigger share of ownership in ancillary rights such as video and television, but Hemdale felt that such an arrangement would make them too beholden to Orion. It was an amicable split, but it ultimately hurt both companies.

Hemdale's next picture after *Platoon* was Bernardo Bertolucci's *The Last Emperor*, which producer Jeremy Thomas put together and Columbia distributed in the U.S. While the film didn't do well domestically, it won nine Academy Awards, including Best Picture. From there, however, Hemdale went slowly downhill. The company began distributing all of its own films, but the increasing competition for talent to make the movies and screens to exhibit them caused Hemdale to shrink its ambitions. Hemdale financed and released a series of pictures, including *River's Edge*, *The Boost*, and *Criminal Law*, but it never had another breakaway hit. When the company got into financial trouble, Credit Lyonnais eventually forced it to sell its library to pay off its loans. The company no longer exists today, though Daly, who has since started a new company to make films for the Internet, has made it a point to keep control of the Hemdale name.

But *Platoon* lives on, not only as a remarkable contribution to American film history but also as a reminder that Vietnam is a state of mind that is not over—and never will be.

9　Finding the Beef

The old movie moguls always said they wanted to use their status in Hollywood to meet the most interesting and important people in the world. I can understand that. The profession enables you to do that, and in the ensuing years I went on to meet many of these very people. I was allowed to enter the world I read about and studied at UCLA as a student of history and political science.

Over the years, I would go to the opening of the Los Angeles Symphony every year, follow new artists in Los Angeles and New York, and have UCLA history professors lecture to small groups at my house. It was a way for me to feel a part of the world at large. So working for Gary Hart's presidential campaign seemed like a natural progression for my continuing education in government and politics outside the movie business.

If you permit it, the movie business can be your life 24 hours a day, 7 days a week, 365 days a year. By late 1983, the movie business was suffocating me.

Along with my colleagues in New York, I had worked tirelessly to launch the new Orion. I put together the slate of movies for 1983 and 1984, found projects to put in the development pipeline, and began the process of cultivating new filmmakers. Besides feeling trapped by the daily routine of logging phone calls from agents, having lunches with directors and producers, and attending necessary business-social events, I was growing tired of spending half of my day arguing with my partners, and I'm sure they were getting tired of me complaining about being marooned in sunny L.A.

I needed to step outside the business and expand my horizons to maintain my sanity. The so-called Reagan revolution was in full bloom, and trickle-down Reaganomics was taking hold, but I felt that the country needed new and younger leadership. It was time to pass the baton—not unlike how I felt about the movie business in 1967.

I had met Gary Hart through Robert Redford during Gary's victorious Senate campaign in 1980. I felt that he was someone who had thought through the issues and could articulate his positions with passion, intellect, and charisma. The one idea in particular that interested me and inspired me to become involved in his presidential campaign was volunteerism. The plan was to create a domestic volunteer corps to supplement corporate America and to get people involved in their country in a hands-on way. It drew on John F. Kennedy's Peace Corps program and, in many ways, it was a forerunner to President Clinton's Americorps program.

When Gary called me in the fall of 1983 and asked me to be a financial co-chairman for his presidential campaign, I tried to tell him I wasn't the guy he was looking for. "I'm flattered, but I don't think you can get the kind of money you need from me and my kind of contacts. You should go to someone like Lew Wasserman," who was the dean of Democratic fundraising.

Gary cut me off. "Mike, those people aren't going to help me," he said. "I need to form a brand-new group of people across the board. This is about the next generation. The only way I'm going to win is by tapping into a younger group of Americans of all ethnic backgrounds both at the polls and in my core group of supporters."

He then introduced me to a young and idealistic lawyer named John Emerson and asked if I thought Emerson would be the right guy to run his entire California campaign. I had a few informal meetings with John and passed along my favorable view of him to Gary. Soon, John was on board and he, Gary, and I were on our way to Maryland to meet with Senator Ernest Tydings, one of the patriarchs of the Democratic Party. It was there that Gary declared that he would run for president and asked all of us to join his inner circle.

◼

My political involvement dated back to my days at UCLA when my college roommate, Richard Maullin, was working for Congressman George Brown's campaign. Richard got me involved in canvassing voters in the Latino community in East Los Angeles, where I could use my Spanish. During my days at United Artists, I often contributed financially to campaigns like Jerry Brown for Governor. Years later, Jerry was the first person to offer me a job in government: about two hours before he had to give up the governor's office, he called me and asked if I wanted to be on the Board of Directors of the Museum of Science and Industry and the Coliseum Commission, where the 1984 Olympics opening ceremony was held.

Why not, I thought; I'm always up for new experiences with people outside of the movie business, and maybe I can even do something for my community.

I ended up serving a full four-year term, during which I voted for the building of the Aerospace Museum in Exposition Park and helped choose the gifted Frank Gehry as the architect to build it.

My being around Arthur Krim and Bob Benjamin and hearing about their extensive contributions to the Democratic Party and the interesting people they had met along the way had undoubtedly encouraged me to become more involved with politics on a national level. Ironically, however, when I told Arthur that I was going to become Hart's finance co-chairman, he tried to dissuade me. He recalled that he had gone to the White House to help Lyndon Johnson at a time when United Artists was running smoothly, and that he had returned at the first sign of trouble. He admired my desire, but he reminded me that somebody had to mind the store in L.A. "You have to wait to do this later in life," he advised me. "We need your undivided attention at Orion."

Arthur was speaking from experience, but I wasn't going to be dissuaded. Besides, I wasn't taking a leave of absence. I would still be in the office more often than not. I also rationalized that flying around the country with the Hart for President campaign would help me as a movie executive. People who live in the insular world of Hollywood never get to meet the rest of America, which makes it hard for them to make films with any sense of honesty about that America. I thought that by going on the campaign trail, I would learn what people in New Hampshire or New Orleans were thinking. Well, this is about as silly as a big movie star thinking he can walk anonymously through Kansas City and study people for a movie part without them recognizing him. Presidential candidates are like rock stars. When their jet lands, there are people to greet them on the tarmac, babies to kiss, autographs to sign, and then they are whisked away in their limousine to the next event. Their every move is recorded, analyzed, and then broadcast on the evening news. The whole thing took on a circus atmosphere. Kissing strange babies in small towns as a way to become the leader of the free world will always be bizarre to me.

Somehow, I never had much intimate dialogue with the locals about their moviegoing habits, though I did witness Gary alienate a sizeable block of primary delegates. Having just flown in from New Jersey, Gary was standing on the terrace of a mansion in Bel Air on a starry night, addressing a group of friends, donors, and press. "Standing here tonight reminds me of where I was last week," he began. "While my wife was out here," he said, pointing to posh Bel Air, "I was in the acid pits of New Jersey." After dinner that night, Gary said to me that he had just blown the election with that remark. It was the lead in all the papers the next morning, and it probably did cost him New Jersey, a populous state that could have thrown the Democratic nomination his way.

■

I officially began helping the Hart for President campaign raise money in Hollywood in late 1983 at an event on the 20th Century Fox lot that I co-hosted with Fox owner Marvin Davis. Over the next year, I made a few campaign stops with Gary and found myself drawn to the life of a national campaign. There was always a sense of beating down the bushes, talking about the direction of the country, and feeling that, in some small way, we could help change the world. I had become interested in subjects as varied as defense, education, infrastructure, the economy, tax issues, and the environment, just to be able to talk intelligently with people in and around the campaign. Although there was very little that I could contribute to Gary's platform, I gave him one line to his stump speeches that always got applause: "If you think that the cost of education is too expensive, you should consider the price of ignorance."

By early 1984, I was spending a considerable amount of time raising money for Hart for President. After Gary finished a surprise second in the Iowa caucus, I went to New Hampshire and watched him upset former vice president Walter Mondale in the primary. Hollywood always loves a winner, any winner, which is no different than Washington or anywhere else for that matter. The day I got back from New Hampshire, I must have logged a hundred calls. Money was pouring into my office and half of Hollywood was calling to see when the next President of the United States would be in L.A. so they could meet him. *Fortune* magazine labeled me Gary's "main man in Hollywood," and I held at least a dozen fund-raisers at my home and invited actors like Robert Redford, Goldie Hawn, and Barbra Streisand, and producers like Sherry Lansing and Thom Mount. Most of the guests attended for reasons of curiosity, but there is always a pervasive idealism in Hollywood about the possibilities of a more progressive leadership and a permanent hope for a better country, though people disagree on how and with whom they can get there.

There have always been obvious similarities between Hollywood and Washington. The concentration of power in both places is in the hands of a select few, and the leaders in both worlds tend to have high media profiles. Dating back to the early twenties, movie stars and political stars always attracted one another. If there is any quid pro quo to this fairly cozy relationship, it's that some movie stars want access to politicians so that they can be heard (these days generally on environmental, health care, abortion, and gay rights issues), while politicians want money. I completely understand this arrangement, though I have never supported a candidate because I wanted something in return. In politics as in Hollywood, it's always better to buy your own lunch, or do favors for people rather than ask for them. The world may not work that way, but I always feel better handling things that way.

The problem with doing politics as an amateur is the same as that of an amateur operating in any other profession: You are apt to be wrong, leaving others to deal with the consequences. In politics, the consequences can be serious, and amateurs are often admitted based on their wallets. Money is the key to political involvement for these amateurs, and this is why campaign finance reform is such a good idea.

My working on the Hart campaign increased my profile inside and outside of Hollywood. People in Washington running for other offices began to look to me to introduce them to movie stars and to help them tap into the Hollywood money. The difficulties of raising money became clear one night when the sheriff showed up at Marvin Davis's house in the middle of a glitzy fundraiser to seize the checks for the campaign's unpaid bills. At one point in the campaign, there was also talk (both in gossip circles and in the Hollywood trade papers) that if Hart became president, I would receive a cabinet post. To me, becoming a cabinet member was something I never dreamed would happen. I didn't want it, and it certainly wasn't the reason for my involvement. I was just trying to help someone I believed in.

Of course, Gary Hart didn't win the nomination in 1984. Walter Mondale did, and he went on to lose in one of the largest landslides in election history. For a while, I thought Gary was going to pull it off and be the Democratic nominee. Looking back, I learned two startling similarities between selling a politician and marketing a movie: Short and simple messages rule the process, and never talk down to your audience. The damage with this, as media critic Neil Postman so convincingly argues in his book *Amusing Ourselves to Death*, is that "a person who has seen one million television commercials might well believe that all political problems have fast solutions through simple measures—or ought to." In Gary's case, it was even more extreme.

Mondale tagged Gary with the line "Where's the beef?" and it dogged him everywhere he went. The line was akin to a slogan for a high-concept movie. Ironically, Mondale hadn't even seen the Wendy's commercial; the line was suggested to him by Robert Beckel, Mondale's campaign manager.

While I don't regret one minute of the time I spent working for Gary, I do regret that I caused my colleagues in New York and my staff some frustration. I made interesting friends in political circles like Gray Davis, now governor of California, and the then political consultant John Emerson, as well as Senator Christopher Dodd and then Senator William Cohen, with whom I remain close. Arthur and Eric were right to blame me for not paying full attention to Orion, and they would have been justified in asking me to leave. They could easily have said, "If you don't want to be in the movie business, then get out. We're not paying you to work in Democratic politics." My inattentiveness cost Orion dearly: over one stretch, from 1983 to 1985, fifteen of the eighteen films we released grossed less than $10 million at the domestic box office. While the rut wasn't totally my fault, I was willing to accept a large part of the blame. In 1984, I withdrew from political fundraising.

The fallout from my colleagues over the 1984 campaign is one reason I didn't get involved in Gary's 1988 presidential campaign. When Gary announced in 1986 that he was leaving the Senate after two terms to mount a full-blown presidential campaign, he asked me to return as finance chairman, but I demurred. Though I agreed to be a prominent supporter and friend, I felt that I owed my partners my all.

When the "Monkey Business" scandal erupted and ruined Gary's bid for the White House, I felt sad and depressed for him, but I was not as devastated as those who had devoted two years to his presidential efforts. Looking back, I think Gary might have survived had circumstances been different. Bill Clinton did. But Gary was a loner in Congress, and his overly cerebral nature alienated some people. By contrast, Clinton had a gaggle of friends defending him.

Gary's challenge to the press to follow him proved to be the end of his political career. He has a brilliant mind but has not been able to fully contribute to the country he loves, which is a tragedy.

One thing I learned from working with Gary was that in politics you really are alone. Aides and handlers will watch your back to a degree, but at the end of the day, it comes down to you and you alone. A similarly individualistic approach prevails in Hollywood. Many people often feel that it's them against the system, and if they could just change the system, everything would be fine. But more than anything, I came to realize that I was fortunate to have partners who would defend me—even when I didn't deserve it. Loyalty works both ways.

Morally, spiritually, and ethically, I was obligated to return with my heart and soul to the venture we had started. Usually in Hollywood, people are waiting in the wings to step in when you falter, which is why so many executives have such a paranoid sensibility.

My partners were clearly different.

Orion's Constellation

By the late eighties, Orion established a reputation for itself as a studio that made signature films, films made by directors who colored outside the lines and made bold artistic statements. Orion's films were expected to tell interesting and offbeat stories that transported the audience some place they hadn't been and showed them something they hadn't seen on the screen before, which is what made them unique. We created story- and character-driven movies that still stand out from the mostly banal studio product for which the eighties have become known.

In short, we tried to further the creative revolution of the seventies. Time has recorded that we were fairly effective in doing just that.

Over the course of the eighties, the content and subject matter of studio films became flimsy and thin compared to that of the seventies, and the generational shift that began in the seventies was completed. Teenagers became the biggest moviegoing audience and never gave up that throne, with the result being that commercialism ran rampant. Studios cashed in on high-concept films like *Top Gun, The Karate Kid,* and *Ghostbusters,* while John Hughes began turning out inventive coming-of-age films that connected with the new teenage audiences. His teen trilogy—*Sixteen Candles, The Breakfast Club,* and *Pretty in Pink*—landed Molly Ringwald on the cover of *Time* magazine and spawned a whole new subgenre of films aimed at the teen audience.

Comedies became formulaic as the landscape became dominated by Disney after Michael Eisner and Jeffery Katzenberg arrived from Paramount. There were many films starring television leads and movie actors on the rebound, such as *Down and Out in Beverly Hills, Outrageous Fortune,* and *Three Men and a Baby.* Even macho action films began to turn cartoonish and buffoonish, resulting in films like *Tango and Cash* and *Commando.*

For the most part, we at Orion steered clear of these trends. We financed and released films that tended to be distinct, even daring at times, but by and large, these films didn't do as well as we hoped.

It became clear that the influences on the group of filmmakers who were products of the eighties were different from the forces that shaped the auteurs of the seventies. The country was emerging from an economic recession, and people were beginning to feel good about themselves. The so-called Reagan revolution was giving the country a simplistic sense of national pride. The Cold War was in full swing, and the world was divided into good (the United States) and evil (the Communists). In the seventies, both audiences and filmmakers alike seemed willing to explore ourselves and our values, and to examine our consciousness; in the eighties, people wanted popcorn films, which were films with no discernible intelligence attached to them.

The filmmakers of the seventies had been inspired by foreign directors and were more attuned to the political and social upheavals of their day, but the new generation was influenced largely by television and had a new sense of confidence and an injection of jingoistic arrogance. Overall, this hurt the quality of movies by making them simpler: films needed to be more simplistic in order to be sold on television, and audiences were becoming more accustomed to the quick-cutting MTV style.

Again, Orion didn't generally do films like this. When we did do films aimed at younger audiences, they generally failed, because following a trend did not come naturally to us, or simply because we just weren't in touch with that audience. Instead, we tried to focus on directors who wanted to tell unusual stories that hadn't been told before.

To support our core group of directors, I tried to create a culture in the halls of Orion different from the structured, corporate approach of most of the other studios. Like United Artists, Orion had no back lot, no soundstages, and no editing rooms. Rather than move onto an independent lot like Raleigh Studios, we stayed in the old Filmways offices in Century City and rented more space on other floors as the company expanded. While this wasn't anywhere near as glamorous as working out of a bungalow nestled among lush greenery on the Warner's back lot just down the path from Clint Eastwood's offices, or as awesome as being in the famous black tower from which Lew Wasserman surveyed the Universal lot, there was an upside: The offices of the Orion executives and the offices of the directors, writers, and producers were all on the same floor, side by side. This egalitarian layout enabled me to create a free-flowing work environment that got the most out of everyone's creative energies.

I was somewhat hands-off in my management style of the L.A. office. I didn't want the layers between the creative executives and me to be visible or felt by my subordinates unless absolutely necessary, though obviously someone had to have the final say. My door was always open to anyone who needed me— literally. Often I would walk the halls and stick my head into meetings that my executives were having just to see how things were going. If I felt tension, I'd drop in for a few minutes and try to help ease out the rough spots. If I felt things were on track, I might introduce myself to the visitor and then slip away. This approach has been compared to the way Jim Burrows directed television. He would say "Okay, go" and then turn around and listen to what was happening without actually getting in the actors' faces.

My basic philosophy was: *Whatever it takes to get the job done*. Frequently I deferred to the younger guys in my department, the same way Arthur, Bob, and Eric had deferred to me when I started at United Artists in 1974. If a filmmaker preferred talking to a particular executive rather than dealing with me directly, that was fine. This was the same approach Eric used with me. At lunchtime, I often had food delivered for the staff, and we'd sit around the conference table talking about projects.

Frequently we'd invite actors, directors, and writers to join us
for a sandwich. If we were stuck on a casting decision or debating which way to go on a project, I'd sometimes get Eric, Bill,
and Arthur on the speaker phone to hear their opinions. At other
studios, production executives didn't have this informal access
to the heads of the company on a daily basis. This made the
opportunity unique for them and put them on a more rapid
learning curve.

I knew that the best way to earn the respect of my staff was to
treat them the same way I would like to be treated and respect
what *they* were doing. The only way to do this was to give them a
chance to play in the big leagues, then let them take credit for
their successes and understand their failures. The last thing I
wanted was a place where everyone—including me—was running around covering his or her ass. I wanted my staff to care
about the movies they were making and learn to voice their opinions rather than to play politics. Even though we were working
on tight production and marketing budgets, I didn't want our
hallways to be polluted with the fear of failure and the backstabbing that pervaded most other studios.

Ideally, you want people with commercial taste in material
and a Rolodex full of agents and filmmakers who are dying to
pass along their best scripts. You need people with conviction
and enthusiasm. In a practical sense, you need people to supplement what you do. I wanted a staff who could deal with filmmakers gently but also with the firm conviction of what the studio
needed done, and without imposing themselves on the creative
process. After all, they were studio executives, *not* filmmakers.
When I set about picking my staff of production executives at
Orion, the first criterion was to find people who had relationships with directors and writers outside of those who regularly
worked with the studios. Bob Sherman had left at the end of
1981 to slow down the pace of his life, so I needed a new head of
production. For this critical job, I hired Barbara Boyle, who traveled in entirely different social and business circles than I.

Barbara lived up the street from me, and she had become one
of the regulars at social events at my house. After leaving her law
practice, she went to work for Roger Corman. Corman was

something of a one-man farm team for a number of directors who eventually rose to prominence after doing their first films for him and his New World Pictures: Marty Scorsese made *Boxcar Bertha*, Francis Coppola made *Dementia 13*, and Jonathan Demme made *Caged Heat*. Barbara brought Francis Doel with her from Corman to work as story editor, and together they began to focus on the kind of emerging talent that Orion needed to remain vital.

More than once, this Cormanesque sensibility made my partners in New York question our sanity in the L.A. office. Ultimately, it led to our replacing her with two young executives, Rob Fried and Jon Sheinberg. A change in direction often requires new blood.

▧

Kevin Costner was probably most representative of the core philosophy we had for filmmakers who worked at Orion: Find someone who is talented. Put them in movies. Invest in their dreams. And let them fly.

▧

When Kevin Costner first came to our attention, he had an aw-shucks charm and he treated Hollywood as if it were a pick-up basketball game. Although he had a laid-back attitude about the movie business on the surface and he wasn't an obvious climber, he knew how to forge relationships that would help him get where he wanted to go.

I decided to find him a movie after I first saw him in *Fandango*, the story of five college guys on a road trip across the Texas Badlands, directed by his buddy Kevin Reynolds. We offered him a script for an offbeat futuristic comedy called *Cherry 2000*, which he liked, but he had already committed to star in *Silverado* for Larry Kasdan. Kasdan was making amends for cutting Costner out of *The Big Chill*: Costner had played the dead friend in *The Big Chill* in a flashback scene, but Kasdan felt he was too wholesome for the audience to believe that he committed suicide. Nevertheless, thrilled that Orion liked his work, Costner had his agent call us and ask if we would have lunch with him.

I arranged for lunch to be brought in to my office for Kevin, Barbara Boyle, and me. Kevin showed up in jeans, cowboy boots, and a mellow attitude that made him instantly likeable. He had the charm and good looks of a modern-day Gary Cooper. As we were talking and getting to know each other, I ran down the list of films that Orion was making for which Kevin might have been right. He was familiar with most of the scripts but not terribly interested in any of the roles, so I asked him what he wanted to do. His answer was a project called "Finished With Engines."

Barbara started to tell him that we read it and weren't planning to make the film, when I interrupted. "That's a perfect role for you," I said. "Let's do it."

My instinct was that Kevin Costner could carry just about any reasonably budgeted film, because he was cut from movie-star cloth. He was the type of actor we needed to get close to.

"Finished With Engines," which was based on a 1948 film called *The Big Clock*, had been put in turnaround by Warner Bros. After Costner left, we called the producers, Mace Neufeld and Laura Ziskin, to tie up the rights. We made Kevin's deal and hired Roger Donaldson, who had made *The Bounty* for us, to direct. The title was changed to *No Way Out*.

Before the film started shooting, I had lunch again with Kevin at my office. By this point, he had landed a big part in Brian De Palma's *The Untouchables*: he was to play Eliot Ness to Robert De Niro's Al Capone. Sean Connery had a supporting role in the film. But as nonchalant as Kevin was, he seemed as though he was planning for something bigger.

"You know," I said to him over lunch, "I have this sense that I'm sitting here with someone who is going to become a great big star. You're going to want to direct your own movies, produce your own movies, and you're going to end up leaving your wife and going through the whole Hollywood movie-star cycle."

"Nah, not me," he said. "That's not what I want. I love my family and I just want to be an actor, not a big star."

Most stars want to be known as actors, not movie stars, but they recognize that stars earn the big money.

The combination of *The Untouchables* and *No Way Out* transformed Kevin into a star almost overnight. Eric made a smart marketing decision to hold *No Way Out* until after *The Untouchables* was released. We hadn't seen *The Untouchables*, but the size of the film and its cast guaranteed that Paramount would give the film a wide release and a strong publicity push. Costner became the hot, new actor on the scene, and *No Way Out* became a hit. It wasn't a monster hit, but Costner got a lot of ink.

Shortly after that, Costner called Eric and asked for a favor: Ron Shelton had written an off-beat comedy about minor-league baseball that he was directing with Kevin in the lead. They were planning to shoot in two weeks, but Fox had just pulled the plug. Would Orion take a hard-and-quick look at *Bull Durham*?

To Eric's credit, he never followed the Hollywood mentality of caring what others thought of projects. The fact that five other studios didn't want a script meant nothing to him. He knew what he liked, others be damned. On occasion he helped pull me out of the Hollywood rut and see the merits of projects that everyone was talking down. Eric liked *Bull Durham* and gave his okay. I, too, liked the script but was a bit afraid of doing a baseball movie, because they rarely do well overseas. The characters were distinct and wonderfully drawn, and the dialogue captured the pathos of minor-league baseball. Most important, the characters drove the story rather than the other way around. It turned out to be one of our better films.

Bull Durham was the film that showed that Kevin Costner would have career longevity. It showed that he was a star who respected good writing and was willing to let others take the showy parts—and even, to some degree, outshine him.

Kevin is the star of *Bull Durham*, but what made the movie memorable and gave it depth were the supporting performances of Susan Sarandon as the groupie who beds one of the small town's minor-league players each season and Tim Robbins as the cocky, nerve-racked pitcher. What Kevin does is similar to the way that Tom Cruise carries movies like *Rain Man* and *Jerry Maguire* while Dustin Hoffman and Cuba Gooding, Jr., take home the Oscars for the flashier parts. It takes a star to be that generous.

My insight into Kevin came during casting: Susan Sarandon insisted on meeting with Ron and Kevin for the role. At the time, she lived in Italy and wasn't on the A-list for leading ladies. Kevin and Ron had someone else in mind for the part, but this didn't deter Susan. With that unfailing belief in themselves that actors must have, she insisted on flying to Los Angeles at her expense. Normally, when a studio is casting a film, they fly actors in for auditions. However, since no one wanted her, there was no reason to fly her halfway around the world. So Susan took the risk and Susan reaped the reward.

She came straight from the airport to the Orion offices to meet with Eric and me and blew us all away with her interpretation of Annie. From there, she met with Ron and Kevin. Ron still had some reservations about her, but Kevin felt she was perfect. I had to give Kevin and Ron credit for not slamming the door in her face because they felt she wasn't right for the part, and the same happened with Tim Robbins.

None of us at Orion thought that Tim was right for the part. As written, the role called for someone funny, and there was nothing overtly funny in Tim. In fact, there wasn't much on his résumé at all. But when he met with Ron and Kevin, they saw something special in him. In the finished film, one of the funniest scenes is when Susan tries to arouse Tim by reading poetry, while he lies in bed, supine and slack-jawed, wondering if he is going to have sex with her or not.

▦

In the two years after *Bull Durham,* Costner's career really took off. Next came *Field of Dreams,* a Universal film that Tom Hanks had turned down. *Field of Dreams* was a huge hit at the box office and ended up with an Oscar nomination for Best Picture. Kevin was beginning to taste the big time. He became one of the hottest actors in Hollywood at a time when salaries were jumping by leaps and bounds and the media was clawing for a leading man with a wholesome image. There were plenty of rogues on Wall Street and in professional sports to go around.

Soon, he decided it was time to direct.

Kevin was indeed smart enough to become a filmmaker on his own terms. For his first project, he chose an unlikely script written by his friend, Michael Blake, which he had followed for years through another friend, his producing partner Jim Wilson. The three had met in 1981 when Wilson was directing *Stacey's Knights*, a gambling movie set in Reno, which Blake had written. Kevin had taken the afternoon off from his full-time job as a stagehand at Raleigh Studios, and auditioned for the lead in *Stacey's Knights*. After the film, he and Jim formed a production company and rented office space at Raleigh. For years, Wilson and Costner followed the progress of Blake's novel about the adventures of Lt. John J. Dunbar on the American frontier in 1863. When Blake completed the novel, he wrote an adaptation, and Wilson, as producer, and Costner, as producer, director, and star, set about bringing it to the screen.

Control was a big issue for Kevin. He insisted on retaining the foreign rights and raising the money for them outside of the domestic distribution deal, which was what Francis Coppola had done to retain final cut on *Apocalypse Now*. To raise half of the budget through foreign presales, Kevin hired Jake Eberts, who had a hand in putting together such films as *Chariots of Fire, Gandhi*, and *The Killing Fields*. Jake was nothing if not persistent. It took him three years to get the rights to *Dances With Wolves*, as they bounced from Nelson Entertainment, a company run by Barry Spikings, who had backed *The Deer Hunter*, to Island Entertainment, another company that backed films through foreign presales, to Lakeshore Entertainment. Finally, Jake got his turn and started selling the foreign rights, country by country.

Although Kevin was coming off a string of hits, he had never directed a film, and on the surface, *Dances With Wolves* was a blatantly uncommercial project. Movies about Indians in general were supposedly taboo, but this one had subtitles and portrayed the Indians as heroes and the U.S. cavalry as barbarians. Westerns had once been a Hollywood staple, but they, too, had become taboo—not that people didn't like them, but current filmmakers couldn't do them right. My theory was that once the myth of the West had been debunked, the myth on which the Western had been built was no longer viable.

I have always believed that if you have a great story to tell— one that can move people to laughter or to tears—you can do it against a white wall. They say you're also not supposed to do movies about insane asylums or boxers who don't win the big fight, but my partners and I had some success with those. So after taking a hard look at the script and at the co-financing deal that Jake proposed, we agreed to put up half of the $18 million budget for the film. While the number seemed big, Kevin was thinking epic. He was also deferring almost all of his directing, acting, and producing salary to keep costs down.

When the film was finished shooting, the Hollywood naysay- ers came out in full force and dubbed the film "Kevin's Gate," a not-so-thinly-veiled reference to Michael Cimino's *Heaven's Gate*. A joke going around was that there were three places the gossip- mongers would die to be a fly on the wall: the Monday morning meeting at CAA, the men's room at Morton's on Monday night, and the editing room of *Dances With Wolves*. Every studio in town except Orion had turned it down, and every executive seemed to be certain he had made the right call.

But when the film opened in October 1989 to some of the best reviews an Orion film had ever had, the only one laughing was Kevin Costner. Even at a running time of three hours, the film began to make money so fast that we paid Kevin his defer- ment after the first month of the film's release. It was clear *Dances With Wolves* was going to be a hit. What those executives hadn't counted on was that the country was experiencing a self- reflection of our national values and the movie was tapping into an examination of how we treated the Native American Indians. Of course, no one predicted it would gross more than $180 mil- lion in the United States, an additional $250 million overseas, and win seven Oscars.

Due in part to the success of *Dances With Wolves*, Kevin became one of those stars the media must either celebrate or cas- tigate, with no middle ground. I remember being in Hawaii in 1995 when a journalist tracked me down to ask about *Water- world*, which was then the most expensive movie ever made. "Do you think this is the end of Costner's career if the film doesn't open?" the reporter asked me. "No," I said. "I'm sure Costner's career will survive just fine. He has talent, and that keeps you in business."

My lunchtime prophecy about Costner's career became a proverb. He ended up becoming a big movie star, winning a Best Director Oscar, divorcing his childhood sweetheart, and producing almost every movie he acts in. Maintaining your equilibrium in this town is hard when you're successful. Movie stars have access to such a grab bag of goodies that it's almost impossible for them to walk away from it. For me, there are very few highs better than taking a chance on a rising star and seeing your hunch pay off. I miss those days when Kevin would stop by my office back when *No Way Out* was in pre-production, and ask me what a stockbroker does.

I guess he knows now.

■

How does a boutique store survive in the age of shopping malls?

■

By the late eighties, studio executives needed big movies to survive, and audiences were increasingly willing to settle for the familiar over the challenging, which caused the industry to be afflicted with an epidemic of sequelitis. Studio executives all over town seemed to be married to the rule "Never use anything once that you can use twice." Audiences also seemed to like the idea of seeing the same characters again. Many of the top executives had come from television (or from the Paramount high-concept school). In television, the mentality is to find a series that works and stick with it; sequels are the film equivalent of a TV series. The audiences, too, were trained television viewers, more than willing to accept the same simplicity on the big screen.

So before the eighties were finished, there were two sequels to *Star Wars*, two sequels to *Raiders of the Lost Ark*, two Rambo sequels, and sequels to movies like *Beverly Hills Cop*, *Ghostbusters*, *Lethal Weapon*, and *The Karate Kid*. There was even a sequel to *Fletch*. Sequels were such a big part of moviemaking that Universal confidently shot two sequels to *Back to the Future* at the same time—and released them a year apart! When Dawn Steel was hired to run Columbia in the wake of David Puttnam's disastrous tenure, her main mission was to put together the sequel to *Ghostbusters*. New Line Cinema built its entire company on the original *Nightmare on Elm Street* and its four sequels, all of which were released in the eighties. And who could forget *Halloween*'s six sequels, all released in the eighties.

When Orion did business that way, it usually didn't work. Filmmakers generally wanted more money for sequels, so the films cost more to make. While there is a built-in audience, unless you add new elements, sequels tend to gross less at the box office. Traditionally, they do about two-thirds of the original. We made two sequels to *Robocop*, released in 1990 and 1991 respectively. We spent more on them and got a lot less in return. In retrospect, to make those sequels work, we would have had to do what Warner Bros. did with the *Batman* franchise in the nineties: hire a big star like Jack Nicholson or Arnold Schwarzenegger to be Robocop's nemesis.

We simply didn't think of it and probably wouldn't have spent the money anyway. We walked like a major, talked like a major, but we didn't have major film company resources—which didn't keep us from competing with the majors. What it did do was sharpen our resolve to try to make good films and avoid exploitative ones even though it created crises of self-doubt when we hit a string of failures.

▬

Of all the studios in the eighties, only Disney and Orion had discernible, quantifiable operating philosophies: Disney, run by Eisner and Katzenberg, was intensely script oriented. Directors and stars were secondary to the Disney philosophy. The studio would find a concept-oriented comedy and then cast recognizable faces who weren't big-name stars, particularly television actors who wanted to break into movies and movie actors whose careers were on the rebound. They also concentrated on reviving animation by creating new movies and re-releasing old ones. They kept their budgets low by controlling the filmmaking process from inside the executive suite, rather than giving the director total creative freedom. They cut their risk even more by using off-balance-sheet financing in the form of Silver Screen Partners, a series of four limited partnerships that put up much of the money for Disney's films during the eighties. This resulted in a string of hits that included *Down and Out in Beverly Hills, Stakeout, Big Business, Outrageous Fortune,* and *Three Men and a Baby.* Even the exceptions in terms of control, like Marty Scorsese's *The Color of Money,* starring Tom Cruise and Paul Newman, remained fairly close to the model. Two of those were remakes of French films, *Three Men and a Baby* and *Down and Out in Beverly Hills,* and one, *The Color of Money,* was a retelling of *The Hustler.* This strategy took an also-ran studio and made it the industry leader.

At Orion, we focused on directors. We backed directors we believed in over and over, even after they had failures. If we believed a director was talented, we wouldn't cut him or her loose after a failure. I taught my staff to find filmmakers and stay with them so that we could compete for talent against studios who flew their filmmakers around in private jets and sent them off to the company compound in Acapulco for R-and-R. We had to find talent on the way up and stick with them—and hope they would stick with us out of loyalty.

To a degree, it worked. Orion became a place for filmmakers with distinct and sometimes quirky visions, at the same time a continuation of United Artists and a throwback to Columbia and RKO in the thirties. Back then, Paramount was known for its romantic movies, Warner Bros. for its complex melodramas, United Artists for its broad, artistically minded productions, and MGM for its star-driven fare. But Columbia and RKO were places that took chances on the idiosyncratic visions of directors because these companies lacked any of the haughty pretensions of the other studios.

Orion films as a whole often questioned mainstream beliefs and were more inclined to explore unconventional subject matter and characters, which made directors, writers, and actors treat Orion like their home. We probably started or furthered more interesting careers than any other studio in the eighties, not just of Kevin Costner, Arnold Schwarzenegger, Jonathan

Demme, and Oliver Stone, but also of Susan Seidelman, Andy Davis, Danny DeVito, Jodie Foster, David Mamet, Dennis Hopper, Paul Verhoeven, Sean Penn, Madonna, and Barry Sonnenfeld. The talent felt comfortable in our offices because they knew we would never try to tamper with their vision, and most of them kept coming back, film after film.

▬

In the eighties, Creative Artists Agency rose to prominence and changed the way business was done. Besides advising talent, CAA served as an advisor on two of the biggest deals Hollywood ever saw: Sony's purchase of Columbia Pictures and Matsushita's acquisition of MCA/Universal. The agency was led by Michael Ovitz.

▬

I was at United Artists when Michael Ovitz first called me.

I had told a former client of mine, Trish Van Devere (who was married to George C. Scott), not to sign with the newly formed Creative Artists Agency, which had approached her. I advised her that if she wanted to be in television, CAA was fine. Ovitz and his original partners, Ron Meyer, Bill Haber, Rowland Perkins, and Mike Rosenfeld, had broken away from William Morris, where they had a strong background in television packaging. However, she wanted to be in the movies, and CAA was not the best place.

When I took the call, the voice said to me, "My name is Mike Ovitz. I don't know you, but I intend to be your best friend. I want to come and see you." I asked when. "Now," he said.

Fifteen minutes later, he appeared at my door, dressed in a banker's dark suit, with a crisp white shirt and a red tie, the uniform he insisted all CAA wore. He was well groomed, with closely cut hair and polished shoes. He was not overly aggressive, though he was visibly ambitious. The conversation was very low key and businesslike. I was impressed by him and we became friends.

Soon, I started inviting him to screenings at my house, where he met Dustin Hoffman and a list of other actors whom he eventually signed on his own. Slowly I realized that he was very good at what he did and that his agency was going to be the powerhouse of the future. I had no qualms about recommending him to people, and I did so often. When Robert Redford asked my opinion, I told him unequivocally CAA without hesitation. They were the agency of now. I did the same when my attorney, Gary Hendler, asked me where his new client Sean Connery should go for representation.

Ovitz started to change the way agents did business. He insisted his agents travel in groups. He felt there was strength in numbers and it showed unity in a business that had none. By the mideighties, Ovitz held sway over Hollywood more so than the way Freddie Fields and David Begelman had when they were at the height of their powers running CMA in the seventies when I was an agent there, but not quite the way Lew Wasserman did at MCA in the forties and fifties. Ovitz would become the doorkeeper for many big movie packages. From the mid-eighties through the late nineties, CAA controlled the flow of talent and, therefore, films from Hollywood to the screen. But CAA became more than a talent agency. Ovitz used his influence to reach into all areas of entertainment, from sports and music to the selling of movie studios. Ovitz even convinced Coca-Cola to hire CAA to redesign its image.

Ovitz did all of this at a time when the media was increasing its coverage of Hollywood. *Premiere* and *Entertainment Weekly* started doing lists of the 100 most powerful people in Hollywood. Ovitz was firmly entrenched at number one. In article after article, he wore the title "the most powerful man in Hollywood," a label assigned to him because of the agency's deep client roster and the way he used his status to manipulate deals. No horse trading was necessary; at times he simply bullied people to see things his way. Although ruling by fear is common in Hollywood, it never works in the long run, and I don't like the effect it has on people.

Ovitz encouraged his agents to trade on his profile to sign clients. It was common for a junior agent at CAA to call a young director and say, "I talked to Mike Ovitz this morning, and he told me I had to sign you because he sees great things in your future"— and it was highly effective. Ovitz and his CAA agents were able to get fast results, which underscored their omnipotence. We developed *Dirty Rotten Scoundrels* with CAA client Herb Ross for a year, but when the script was finished, Herb couldn't commit. Since CAA represented the stars, Michael Caine and Steve Martin, we sent the script to them to find us a new director. They gave it to client Frank Oz, and literally that weekend Frank was on his way to the south of France to direct the movie.

No other agency could move their clients around like that, and it became tough to make a movie without CAA somehow involved.

CAA brought talent packaging to a new level, which worked both to the benefit and the detriment of the clients. For example, on *Legal Eagles*, CAA packaged director Ivan Reitman with Robert Redford, Daryl Hannah, and Debra Winger—and nearly lost them all as clients when the movie came out and was universally panned. Films like this were made because the package was there, not because they were worthy of making. But on *Rain Man*, Ovitz kept the package of Tom Cruise and Dustin Hoffman intact through four director changes and got the film made at a studio that had since fallen apart. The secret was that Ovitz represented the screenwriters and the four directors, Steven Spielberg, Marty Brest, Sydney Pollack, and Barry Levinson, who ultimately directed the film and won the Academy Award.

But by the late eighties, the Ovitz-led CAA culture became oppressive. A scathing letter written by screenwriter Joe Eszterhas to Ovitz about Ovitz's alleged strong-arm tactics was faxed all over town. In the letter, Eszterhas, one of the highest-paid screenwriters, recounted what Ovitz had told him when the screenwriter informed the *über*-agent that he was leaving CAA for ICM. According to Eszterhas, Ovitz threatened that CAA's "foot soldiers, who go up and down Wilshire Boulevard each day, will blow your brains out." That night at dinner, Eszterhas alleged that another CAA agent told him that Ovitz would "put him in the fucking ground."

Ovitz quickly denied Eszterhas's charges, but the story, true or not, embodied the culture of fear that Ovitz created with his employees and clients and reflected the sentiments of many people in the movie business. Ovitz had too much power and he used it to push people around. What else could you expect from a guy who handed out copies of Sun Tzu's *The Art of War* as a primer on how to be an agent? All I knew was that I didn't want my management style to resemble this in any way.

Over time, as his power increased exponentially, I found Ovitz to be the kind of person who would never give you a straight answer, which is one reason the two of us never developed a true personal relationship. He became like so many people who attain power in the media age—arrogant. I could never figure out who the real Mike Ovitz was. He wore too many masks. I remember going to see him at his office when his number two, Ron Meyer, left CAA to run Universal after Seagrams bought the company. Ovitz had been negotiating running Universal as a job for himself. I asked Ovitz if he was upset that Meyer was going to Universal. "Not at all," Ovitz said dismissively. "I'm going to continue being an agent and run the agency, and we are going to do well." Two weeks later, Ovitz was named president of the Walt Disney Company, a disastrous tenure that lasted ten months and earned him a reported $90 million contract settlement. If you are constantly maneuvering yourself between two people, somebody is going to hate you. Ovitz got away with it because people thought he had his hand on some kind of nuclear launch button. The moment the fear disappeared, he became fair game for everyone who resented his methods.

At one time people thought Mike Ovitz knew everything. He convinced all of his agents that he was a demigod who could do no wrong. When it finally turned out that Mike didn't know everything, the town turned on him—but it was much his own doing.

▬

Orion was forced to be creative in choosing our talent because we couldn't afford CAA's packages, which were invariably overpriced. Rather than pouting about it, we improvised and made a leading man out of a sixty-plus-year-old, washed-up stand-up comedian: Rodney Dangerfield. We tapped into the world of pop music for singers who wanted to act: Madonna. We let playwrights direct films: David Mamet. And we worked with some of the more lovable rogues of the business: Dennis Hopper, Nick Nolte, and Francis Coppola.

For us, strong creative personalities were the only way our movies could get noticed. We also weren't afraid to do things that were different.

■

Based on the success of Susan Seidelman's first film, *Smithereens*, we picked up *Desperately Seeking Susan*, which was in turnaround from Warner Bros. Susan was a bohemian commercial director with no track record. Ellen Barkin was set to star with Rosanna Arquette in *Desperately Seeking Susan*, but Ellen couldn't get out of a commitment at Warner. Susan decided to hold a casting call for more than two hundred actresses in New York to find the right "Susan." The character was written as an old soul who happens to be charmingly promiscuous. After a tireless auditioning process, Susan settled on a little-known pop singer who lived in her neighborhood in the East Village and went by the stage name Madonna. She had never been in a film.

Barbara Boyle, my head of production who was supervising *Desperately Seeking Susan*, told Susan that Madonna would have to shoot an audition tape to be shown to my partners and me before her casting would be approved. At the time, Madonna was known among teenagers, but she hadn't broken out to stardom yet. She had one album in record stores that wasn't selling very well. Neither Barbara nor I had heard of her, but Barbara's fifteen-year-old son had a poster of her taped to his bedroom wall—a good sign in respect to attracting a teenage audience. Before the audition tape was made, Susan encouraged Barbara to meet Madonna face-to-face.

One afternoon, Madonna appeared in Barbara's office wearing a second-hand miniskirt over thick leggings, rhinestone boots, and plastic bracelets on her wrists. Madonna instantly sank to her knees, stretched out her arms, bowed dramatically, and purred to Barbara in her sexiest voice, "I'll do anything to get this role."

"I'm married and I'm straight," Barbara responded.

"Well, Barbara," Madonna retorted, "you should try everything at least once."

At Orion, sometimes it seemed as if we did.

≡

If each studio had formed a team to play rough touch football, Orion would have won hands down. Our lineup of intimidating talent included David Mamet, who got his break as a film director from us. Mamet had an original, idiosyncratic voice in both his scripts and his plays. His dialogue on the page was electric and menacing, and it read with the immediacy of street talk. His body of work as a playwright—*Sexual Perversity in Chicago* (which became the film *About Last Night . . .*), *American Buffalo*, and *Glengarry Glen Ross*—was reason enough for us to give him a shot at directing a sleight-of-hand mystery he had written called *House of Games*.

Our first meeting took all of ten minutes, and we made the deal in eleven words of low-level Mamet-speak. He showed up at my office, and I offered him a Cuban cigar (which I always told the press were Swiss because they came via Switzerland). He cut the end and lit it.

"So," I said, clenching my own cigar, "you want to direct a movie?"

Mamet nodded.

"Fine, let's do it," I told him.

Eleven words and off he went to Panavision to rent the necessary camera equipment.

When Mamet was finished with his first cut of the film, he and his producer, Michael Hausman, showed up at the Orion offices one afternoon, unannounced. They walked through my office door pushing a dolly cart with cans of film on it. When the cart reached my desk, Hausman stacked the film cans on my desk while Mamet grabbed a couple of Cubans from my humidor. "Here's your movie," Mamet said, as he and Hausman lit up and headed out the door.

That was delivery, Mamet style.

Mamet is a brilliant scenarist, but he needed some help shaving down the movie in the editing room. He was a playwright by trade, and in the theater the writer's word is sacrosanct and untouchable. As a first-time film director, he had to learn how to pace his movies. You can make or break a movie in the editing room, particularly one like *House of Games* whose plot hinges on a succession of small, subtle subplots. My theory in the editing room has always been: *Be honest without being hostile.* The more straightforward you can be with a director, the more he will respond to your suggestions. This was true in Mamet's case, and he ultimately crafted *House of Games* into a tight and eerie thriller, which I would place in my top-100 category.

▨

Orion was also the studio that enabled Dennis Hopper to turn his career around. I had known Dennis in the late sixties, when he often lived on the edge and let partying get the best of him. But when we started our working relationship with him at Orion, Dennis had left behind his *Easy Rider* days. Clean and sober, he almost always showed up at the office in a coat and tie. Nevertheless, he played the drunken Dennis of old in *Hoosiers* for us. It was a gem of a movie about an Indiana high-school basketball team written by Angelo Pizzo and directed by David Anspaugh, two college roommates. Dennis got his first Oscar nomination for Best Supporting Actor in the film.

Dennis then went to work for us as a director, first on *Colors*, a story about L.A. gangs that starred Robert Duvall and Sean Penn, and then on *Hot Spot*, a film noir with Don Johnson and Virginia Madsen. Dennis has one of the most wonderful visual senses of composition as a filmmaker and is very good with actors. He also has a wonderful eye for art. In fact, his modern art collection is one of the finest in Los Angeles. He did a terrific job on *Colors*, with Duvall as a veteran cop and Penn as his tempestuous partner. Their beat was the gang-infested ghettos of L.A., where life was about as precious as toilet water. It was the kind of picture on which Orion was willing to take a chance.

At the time I put it into production, the gang wars in South Central L.A. were a staple on the evening news. Dennis swears the script was originally set in Chicago and he moved it to L.A. to make it more topical. When Dennis informed me of the change of venue, he says that I asked if there were gangs in L.A. That's a tall tale, but I don't mind playing the role of the slick studio executive so Dennis could have a laugh at my expense. Dennis, Sean, and I spent a considerable amount of time at Dennis's house in Venice near the beach editing the film. It was an interesting process to have three sets of eyes from such different backgrounds and perspectives all working together.

By the time *Colors* was released, protestors were lining up outside our Century City and New York offices. The Guardian Angels sent toilet seats covered in something that looked like blood, to imply that Orion was making money with shit and blood.

This was the third Orion release that Sean Penn had done, after *The Falcon and the Snowman* and *At Close Range.* Along with a few other young actors, including Charlie Sheen, Sean had an office in our building. Sean was intense, serious, and dedicated to his work. He wasn't much of a conversationalist and idle chitchat was anathema to him. He focused on the matter at hand and regarded any small talk as a waste of time. Some mornings I'd come in and wonder if he had slept in his office after a night on the town with the guys. But that was Sean in the late eighties. This was the beginning of a relationship between the two of us that has developed into a friendship of mutual respect. Watching his sense of how a film should unfold in the editing room on *Colors,* I could see the early makings of a director. In my mind, Sean was always the best young actor of his generation, and it was only a matter of time before he became a very good director, though he remains an unswerving artist with no appetite for commerce or compromise.

Sean and Orion seemed to be trying to find themselves at the same time. He got into his share of scuffles in the media throughout the eighties, and Orion certainly had its share of problems. One of the things I came to respect about Sean—when I wasn't pulling my hair out over it—was his ability to fight for what he believed in. He often went about things the wrong way (and he often still does), but he has the courage of his convictions. He will stand up for what he believes in and put it all on the line at a moment's notice.

I have often defended Sean when I thought he handled things poorly, but I have never regretted it. In a certain way, Sean has become like another son to me.

Perhaps the wildest of Orion's wild bunch was put together for *Farewell to the King*: a rogues' gallery of unforgettable tough guys under one roof. There was big John Milius, a bear of a man whose passion for guns and military rhetoric is legendary in Hollywood; the raffish, rugged, and hard-living Nick Nolte; and *The Godfather* producer Al Ruddy all working on a film based on a novel I had been introduced to in my agency days.

Ruddy, who had just gone into partnership with André Morgan, is like a producer from central casting: tall with short, gray hair, he talks in a deep, throaty voice (probably from all those cigarettes he smokes) that makes Hollywood clichés like "Producers never lie, baby" and "Love ya, man" sound like sincere declarations from his heart. Al made his name as producer of *The Godfather* (for which he won an Academy Award), and his stories from that film rival any that have ever been printed. My favorite was the day that Paramount chief Frank Yablans called him and told him that some guys in the "olive oil" business needed to read the script, or shooting in Manhattan might be a "problem." Not wanting to sleep with the fishes, Al told Yablans to send them over.

Al kept the script in a safe deposit box in his office, so when the three guys in black trenchcoats showed up, he unlocked the safe and handed the script to the group's leader. The guy opened it to the first page and started to read. Five minutes later, he still hadn't turned the page. Al started to get nervous when the guy finally spoke. "What is this EXT here?" the guy said, pointing to the first word on the page. Al explained that EXT denotes an exterior, or outdoors shot, as opposed to interior, or indoors. The guy nodded. Seven minutes later, the guy was still on the first page. Finally, he looked up at Al and asked, "What's this ECU mean?" With a straight face, Al explained, "That's extreme close-up, when the camera zooms in on the actor's face." The guy closed the script, threw it to one of his colleagues, and said, "Here, you read it." As the guy headed out the door, he turned to Al and said, "I trust you. You're going to do good for the family."

Ruddy had actually given John Milius his first job in the early seventies. I was representing John at the time, and I called Al and told him if he gave John a job, I'd owe him one. So Al drove over to John's one-bedroom apartment to talk about doing a contemporary version of *Red River* entitled *The Texan*. As always, when producers hired John, they had to pay him and give him a gift of gratitude. Now it's always a shotgun for his collection, which has become quite valuable. Back then, they had to baby-sit his mangy dog.

John's dog was legendary. I'll never forget the day John came over to my house in his brand-new, fully loaded car with his dog in the backseat. John wanted to put the dog in my house while we went to dinner, but I wouldn't let him, so he cracked the windows and left the salivating beast in the car. When we returned from dinner, John opened the car door to let the dog out. The brand-new leather interior was in shreds. The beast had chewed up every last inch of it.

So after the deal with Al was made with, Al picked up John's dog and took the dog to his house in Beverly Hills. The dog raced through the house, out the backdoor, and jumped the fence. Al spent the next four hours chasing the dog through Beverly Hills.

We paired these two guys with Nick Nolte, who had been cast as the film's lead, a deserter during World War II who becomes shipwrecked in Borneo and forms a tribe of native headhunters. Nick has always been one of the more rugged actors in Hollywood. Emotions rise to the surface with him faster than water boils on a hot stove. He made three movies for Orion, *Under Fire, Farewell to the King,* and *Everybody Wins*. During those years, he lived hard, worked hard, and played hard, like a character from a Dashiell Hammett novel. A typical day for him was the afternoon when he walked into my office in the mideighties looking like a mugging trying to find a place to happen. His clothes were torn, his eyes were slits, and a smoldering cigarette was dangling from his fingers. He smelled like a party that had gone on too long.

"Nick," I said, as he stood half-alive in front of my desk, "you're on a slow train to destruction."

He grunted something that I couldn't make out.

"On second thought," I continued, "you might be on a fast train to destruction and I don't want any part of it. You're going to wind up killing yourself and I don't want anyone dying in my office so get out."

He took a drag on his cigarette and plopped down on the couch.

"If you don't get out, I'm going to leave you sitting in here all alone," I declared.

Nick shrugged his shoulders, pulled himself to his feet, and lumbered out.

A couple years later, he wandered into my office. He was medium straight. I couldn't smell any booze, but he still looked like shit.

"You know, Nick, nothing's changed," I told him. "But here's what we're going to do today. Instead of me lecturing you about how terribly you're living your life, I'm gonna take you out and buy you some clothes with my own money."

I walked him three blocks to the Century City mall and into a clothing store owned by a friend of mine. "Fit him for some clean clothes and a pair of shoes and send him back over to my office," I said to my friend.

"Who is he?" my friend asked.

"Just a bum I picked up on skid row."

As for Nick these days, well, the more things change the more they stay the same. When his company had a production deal with me in 1995 and 1996, he would often show up at the office wearing pajamas and an overcoat. Now the only thing he drinks is fresh squeezed juice. He's a heck of an actor and he's quite a character. I recently read a magazine profile where Nick took a blood sample from a journalist and then spun it in a centrifuge to check the guy's iron levels. Pure Nick.

Predictably, there wasn't a dull moment on *Farewell to the King*. During pre-production, John was having his house remodeled. They had roughed out the upstairs bathroom and laid a plywood subfloor. One evening, John walked into the bathroom to wash his face, and he fell through the subfloor. One of his legs got caught on a support beam, leaving him hanging upside down. The next day, he showed up at the pre-production offices in a wheelchair. He had escaped with a broken foot. "Nothing is going to stop me from doing this film," he declared.

Unfortunately, many things stopped *Farewell to the King* from being successful.

There were endless arguments between Al and John, and between John and us, over the cutting of the film. John ended up being mad at me for years, but we've become close friends again. In the end, the film just didn't play. Perhaps audiences weren't ready to see a white soldier become the king of an indigenous tribe in Borneo. It was one of a group of daring Orion movies that didn't make money but, in retrospect, is a movie we are all very proud to have been a part of. John's only regret was that Al and I didn't travel to Borneo to watch him shoot. As Milius told me not long ago: "Watching you guys in your Armani rough wear get lost in the jungle would have made it all worthwhile."

No one has a more volatile and checkered history in Hollywood than Robert Evans, who brought us a project that he picturesquely described as "gangsters, music, and pussy."

The film was *The Cotton Club*, and it told the intriguing story of a musician at the famous 1920s Harlem speakeasy who falls in love with the girlfriend of Dutch Schultz and a black dancer who falls for a chorus girl. It was the kind of world Evans thought he would have flourished in had he been born fifty years earlier. Even with all Evans's legendary shenanigans, we had no idea what we were getting ourselves into on *The Cotton Club*. While we weren't virgins to problematic films, nothing would have prepared us for this situation. What was to be Evans's directorial debut with a tidy $12 million budget ended up as a $47 million Francis Coppola epic, awash in lawsuits and red ink.

Oh yeah, there was a real life murder, too.

Though Evans had a production deal at Paramount, they wanted nothing to do with *The Cotton Club*. Evans had had a terrific run as head of production at Paramount: *The Godfather*, *Love Story*, *Rosemary's Baby*, and *The Odd Couple* were all made on his watch. When he moved into his producer's deal, Evans again hit pay dirt with *Chinatown*. But in the late seventies, Evans had hit a cold streak with films like *Players* and *Black Sunday*. His personal life had fallen off even further. At the time Evans began shopping *The Cotton Club* around, he had just gotten out from under a highly publicized drug arrest.

But, in his mind, *The Cotton Club* was to be his comeback. Not only would he produce, Robert Evans would make his directorial debut. He had optioned the property himself for $350,000 and raised $2 million in development money from Adnan Khashoggi, who had made billions as an arms dealer. Evans had hired *The Godfather* novelist and co-screenwriter Mario Puzo to write the script. But three years after he started, Evans had a script but no cast and no production financing. He had tried and failed to cast first Al Pacino and then Sylvester Stallone in one lead and Richard Pryor in the other. Finally, with financing from Las Vegas hoteliers Ed and Fred Doumani, he signed Richard Gere and Gregory Hines to play the leads. As collateral, Evans put up his house. Of course, Evans's spin on the situation was that he wanted more control of the film so he decided not to do it at Paramount, which would have had full control of the film.

When Evans came to see me to talk about *The Cotton Club*, he was still planning to direct the film. Our initial discomfort with doing anything with Evans was mollified by the fact that we needed movies. The original proposal that Evans made to us called for a $20 million budget, up from the original $12 million reported in the press. He had made a deal with the Producers Sales Organization for $8 million in guarantees for the foreign rights, and Orion had agreed to put up $10 million for the prints and advertising budget once the film was completed. Orion would get its money back in first position. I call this a "proposal" because it soon became apparent that Evans had no idea how much the film would cost—and even less of an idea where he would get the additional money. His strategy appeared to be to get the film in production and worry about where the rest of the money was coming from later.

By March 1983, Evans was deep in pre-production, but he still didn't have a script that was ready to shoot. For help, Evans hired Francis Coppola to rewrite the script. Coppola needed the money, so much so that he was willing to ignore his strained past with Evans. The checkered history of Francis Coppola and Robert Evans brings to mind a classic—and absolutely true— Hollywood aphorism: "I'm never going to speak to that guy again . . . until I need him." Each had claimed credit for the ultimate success of *The Godfather*: Coppola held that he had co-written and directed the masterpiece in spite of interference from Evans, then head of production at Paramount, while Evans insisted that he had saved the film from the scrap heap by closely supervising Coppola and then recutting the film himself. My money is on Coppola's version of the story.

By the time Coppola began rewriting Puzo's *Cotton Club* script, everyone was losing faith in Evans as the director—including Evans. While Coppola continued rewriting, Evans continued to spend money getting ready to begin filming. The elaborate sets, costumes, and period adjustments that needed to be made required money, and Evans was quickly running out. It was becoming clear to him that the money he would receive from the Producers Sales Organization and from Orion upon completion of the film would be woefully inadequate to make the film. He went looking for more money and what he found was more trouble: In a bizarre twist, a murder became associated with the film.

Though no one is certain exactly what happened, at this point Evans made a deal with ex–variety show producer Roy Radin, who apparently agreed to finance *The Cotton Club* and three other Evans productions. The introduction had been made by a woman named Elaine Jacobs (aka Karen Jacobs-Greenberger), a customer of Evans's limo service, but the deal turned out to be a lousy one for Evans. He soon discovered that Radin would receive his money off the top, as well as have control of the projects Evans wanted to do. After Evans made the deal, Jacobs and Radin reportedly began to discuss her finder's fee. She wanted a percentage; he countered with a $50,000 flat fee. According to a *New York* magazine article, the two met in a limousine to work out a deal. Radin had hired Desmond Wilson, the former *Sanford and Son* star, to tail them, but the limo soon lost Wilson. Days later, Ray Radin's body was found in a ravine with a bullet through his head. Because Evans had made such a rotten deal, he became a murder suspect. Authorities said that they believed Radin's murder was the result of a financial deal gone bad. Though Evans was never charged, it was hardly the kind of publicity the film needed. The whole thing was starting to unfold like an unintentional black comedy.

It was becoming increasingly evident that the only way the picture would get made was if Coppola stepped in to direct it.

According to Evans, Gere was also pushing for Coppola to direct. In hindsight, it appears that Evans was simply desperate to get the movie into production and, in doing so, he ended up eliminating himself from the movie. When he had to go back to the Doumani brothers for more money, the only way he could keep the funding going was by telling them that Coppola was taking over as director. We dodged a bullet.

While we had gone through hell and back with Coppola on *Apocalypse Now*, we were willing to work with him again for one simple reason: he was one of the most talented filmmakers alive. Our financial exposure was also capped this time.

By all accounts, *The Cotton Club* shoot was a chaotic one: Coppola fired Evans's cinematographer of choice, John Alonzo, whose $160,000 contract had to be paid off, because Coppola wanted to choose his own crew and not one that Evans had hired. Richard Gere didn't show up the first day because he was upset over Evans's broken promises regarding scheduling. This little disagreement initially cost the film $1.5 million, as Gere's salary had to be doubled. (It was later paid out of Evans's gross points.) Novelist William Kennedy was hired to rewrite parts of the script that Coppola wasn't happy with. He phoned his final scene in to Coppola from a phone booth. For once, Coppola had none of his own money on the line, and, accordingly, he was not about to be pushed into an orderly production schedule.

As the movie began consuming $1.2 million a week—roughly $300 a minute—the Doumanis hired a Lebanese B-movie producer named Sylvio Tabet to press Coppola. Tabet had no idea how to rein Coppola in, so he simply followed Francis around the set, shaking his "worry beads" to bring the production luck. Next, they hired as producer a man named Joey Cusumano, whose only experience in the movie business was attending them. To quote his succinct bio, as described in the August 1983 issue of *Life* magazine, in a story on the U.S. government's crackdown on organized crime: "Joseph Cusumano, 47, reputed mobster." Finally, six weeks into production, the Doumanis failed to make the weekly payroll, which caused the unions to shut down the film. Coppola, too, balked at coming to work because he wasn't being paid.

At this point, Orion refused to advance any cash to the film. Reports of the problems came back to us from Barrie Osborne, the line producer we had assigned to watch the film. Barrie was also worried about the constant flow of black limousines pulling up to the location: if another person involved with this film got into a limo and ended up being found with a bullet through his head, we might have a *real* public relations nightmare on our hands. As much as Orion needed *"The Godfather* with Music" for our 1984 Christmas release schedule, we couldn't afford to pour more money in and risk $40 million, or even $30 million of our own money on this film. From our point of view, if the film wasn't delivered, we didn't have to pay. However, we were forced to change our position when the Doumanis ran out of money. Our only demand was that Evans stay out of this picture entirely. The Doumanis agreed, but that didn't end the lawsuits.

Once shooting was finished and the film was being edited (at a total cost of nearly $47 million, or about eight times the cost of *The Godfather*) and tested (to relatively high marks in Chicago, followed by an Italian dinner arranged by Joey Cusumano), Evans sued to be reinstated. In a dramatic performance, Evans took the witness stand and broke down crying. His career, he told the court, was over if he wasn't allowed to work on *The Cotton Club*. He won the case but lost the war. Soon enough, the Doumanis paid Evans $500,000 in cash and returned the title to his house so he would get lost once and for all. As part of the deal, Evans retained sole producer credit, which would be of value only if the film won the Academy Award.

The press was, predictably, all over this unfolding drama. Everyone was wondering the same thing: Is the picture any good? If it were a masterpiece along the lines of *The Godfather* or *Apocalypse Now*, bad publicity would turn into good publicity. But if the film were terrible, the *Heaven's Gate* syndrome of negative press piling on would take hold. The result was a middle-of-the-road film, both creatively and commercially, long on spectacle and longer on plot. The problems could be traced back to the script, which was never sufficiently finished. Accordingly, the reviews were mixed. Half of the major film critics liked the film, half didn't.

For Orion, the situation came down to how much money to spend on an iffy proposition. We had $10 million in the film (the amount advanced to the Doumanis), and we were in first position to get our money back. As they did with almost every other picture, Eric and Arthur played the release conservatively. *The Cotton Club* opened to respectable business on opening weekend. As it expanded to more theaters the following weekend, it placed second at the box office behind the megahit *Beverly Hills Cop*. Even though the film was doing well, increased spending would probably have resulted only in diminishing returns for us. As filmmaker friendly as we were, the Robert Evans promise of "gangsters, music, pussy" tested our limits, particularly those of Bill Bernstein, who spent an inordinate amount of time on the project.

In the end, the gangsters turned out to be real, the music couldn't save the film, and there wasn't enough of the other to fill the theaters.

▣

Robert Evans violated the cardinal rule of doing business in Hollywood on The Cotton Club: *Never put up your own money.*

This rule was written for passionate artists and not studio executives, but clearly, Orion was different. Because the four partners had started the company ourselves, we were more invested in its fate than the average studio executive might have been at, say, Columbia, which was owned by Coca-Cola.

I violated the rule, too: To keep Orion from being taken over in 1985, I had to put up basically everything I owned (and some things I didn't) as collateral on a bank loan.

▣

The trouble began when we discovered that Warburg Pincus, the investment banking firm that helped us take over Filmways, was trying to sell their 20 percent interest (which they had diluted over time from the original 53 percent by selling shares) to Mario Kassar and Andy Vajna of Carolco, the *Rambo* producers. Arthur found out what was happening through a New York attorney and immediately confronted his friend Lionel Pincus, who told Arthur that he was upset that Orion wasn't "living up to his expectations."

Pincus then drew a line in the sand, telling Arthur that if he didn't want Carolco to own one-fifth of his company, Orion needed to buy Warburg Pincus out themselves. The price was $30 million and Pincus gave us ten days, or Kassar and Vajna would be sitting across the table from us at the next board of directors meeting.

The four of us collectively didn't happen to have $30 million lying around, so we went to Viacom. At the time, Viacom was run by Terry Elks; Sumner Redstone hadn't yet entered the picture. Elks was fine with a partnership that didn't involve Viacom controlling Orion. What he wanted most was Orion's films to exhibit on the Viacom owned Showtime, as well as through its overseas distribution channels, so he and Arthur were able to quickly hammer out an agreement in principle. While this was all fine and dandy, Viacom was a public company and it had to go through formal channels before cutting a $30 million check. Since it couldn't be done within the ten-day window imposed by Warburg Pincus, we each had to sign promissory notes for $7.5 million.

That was about five times my net worth.

Even more than the money, I saw the vulnerability of our dream being washed away. We had formed Orion to get out from under the iron hand of Transamerica, and we had left a much less oppressive situation at Warner Bros. to ensure we had total freedom. The feeling that we could be saddled with Vajna and Kassar as partners on ten-days' notice was chilling. Personally, I didn't have any problems with them; professionally, I wanted to choose my own partners. Thankfully, the Viacom deal closed and the notes were retired.

It wasn't long until we were fighting for our freedom again.

In 1987, about a year after Viacom had rescued us, Elks tried to take Viacom private in a leveraged buyout and hired junk bond king Michael Milken to do the financing. One of the smaller Viacom shareholders, the shrewd Sumner Redstone, decided he didn't like the price or the fact that it was being financed with junk bonds, so he put in motion a hostile takeover. The test of wills was ultimately won by Redstone, which wasn't surprising. Redstone once saved his own life in a hotel fire by hanging from a window ledge until firefighters could reach him. Redstone promptly dumped Elks. Now, instead of the friendly Elks-led Viacom, Orion was 20 percent owned by the Redstone-run Viacom.

Within a year, Redstone began buying up Orion stock, increasing Viacom's ownership stake to more than 25 percent, with no end in sight. These kinds of takeovers are so commonplace today that nobody thinks twice about them. For one thing, there are no longer any owner-managers running studios. At Orion, we were founders, senior management, major stock-option holders, and board members. Today studio executives are highly paid employees who have no ownership stake or deep personal ties to the company. As it became more and more clear that Viacom's intentions were not friendly, memories of Transamerica started haunting all of us, especially Arthur.

For help, Arthur turned to the richest man in America, his old friend John Kluge. At the time, Kluge's estimated net worth of $6 billion ranked him first on the annual *Forbes* list of the wealthiest Americans. Because Kluge's holdings were in meat-packing and cellular phone companies, Arthur started by putting Kluge and his top lieutenant, Stuart Subotnick, on our board of directors so they could learn about the company. Shortly after this, Arthur asked John to start a creeping tender offer and begin buying stock on the open market to head off Redstone, which he was finally able to do.

Years later, Redstone told me that he had no intention of taking over Orion. Whatever his goals, if that's true, it piles on even more irony.

We all felt that Kluge was a white knight of the highest order. He was wealthy enough not to be out shopping the company and, more important, he was a close friend of Arthur's. I had learned long ago that one of the distinguishing characteristics of Arthur's friendships was that the ties ran deep.

Unfortunately, they didn't run deep enough in this case.

■

Looking back, the three $100-million-plus grossing movies we had at Orion were genre-breakers, and all were turned down by every other studio that considered them.

The first was Platoon. *The second was* Dances With Wolves. *And the third was a little horror film about a man who ate people's livers with a side of fava beans and washed it down with a fine Chianti.*

▬

Very few people in Hollywood believed that Thomas Harris's grisly novel *The Silence of the Lambs* could be made into a general-audience movie, but I disagreed. The story had moments of true tenderness and was a nail-biter, and there were two fantastic roles: the female FBI agent and the serial killer. I called Eric and Arthur and told them we should buy the rights. Expenditures required the collective nod of all the partners. At this point, we were also trying to guard every penny, so when they heard it would cost $250,000 for the book and another $250,000 for an adaptation, they vetoed the project. I was convinced this one was well worth the fight, so I set about making the project more attractive.

Gene Hackman, who had done *Hoosiers* for us and was in the middle of shooting *The Package*, was interested in playing Hannibal Lecter and directing the movie. Bob Sherman, our head of production from the Orion at Warners days, was slated to produce. I told Gene's agent, Fred Specktor, that we would split the $500,000 in development costs with Hackman, who agreed. This little bit of risk-reduction brought my partners around, so a deal was made where Orion would put up $250,000 for the book and Hackman would put up another $250,000 when the time came. Ted Tally was hired to write the adaptation in November 1987. Though Ted had no produced credits, I knew his work well because he had worked on an adaptation for British director Lindsay Anderson, a former client of mine. Ted's as-yet-unmade script *White Palace* (later made into a film with Susan Sarandon and James Spader) was also well known around town at the time, and it was what convinced Gene to hire him.

While Ted was working with Gene and Bob on converting the story line from long form to short form, our legal department went to work on getting the rights to the name "Hannibal Lecter" from Dino De Laurentiis. Dino had made a movie called *Manhunter*, based on Harris's first Lecter book, *Red Dragon*. Because of that, Dino owned the sequel rights to the Lecter character, which meant we couldn't use the name without his permission. However, nothing stopped us from making a movie about an FBI agent named Clarice Starling (who wasn't in *Red Dragon*) pursuing a serial killer named Strang, the substitute name that Ted used for Lecter. We finally made the deal with Dino to license the Lecter name for *The Silence of the Lambs* for nothing, but Dino would get his glory out of Lecter years later when he exercised his first right of refusal to buy Harris's next Lecter book, *Hannibal*, which became a $165 million hit in the U.S. alone.

When Ted finished the script, Gene read it and had second thoughts about the violence in the book. The violence didn't bother us because we had always seen the film as a daring suspense thriller, so we offered to buy Gene out. In fact, the script was so sharp and riveting that we felt we could attract a first-class director. We agreed to let Gene off the hook for the $250,000, but he had to give up all credits, fees, and profit points in the film. Bob Sherman was paid a fee for his time.

I sent the script exclusively to Jonathan Demme without even telling Arthur and Eric. Jonathan got his start making films for Roger Corman, but then he garnered critical acclaim for the eccentric *Melvin and Howard*. Jonathan had made two interesting and somewhat offbeat films for Orion: *Something Wild* and *Married to the Mob*. He was a multifaceted director who had an affinity for odd people and places, and he was a master of delivering the unexpected. I also knew he could craft a thriller, which he had done with a film called *Last Embrace* for us at United Artists. Though he was clearly smart and talented, he was too original and idiosyncratic to be on any studio's A-list for thrillers. No one could seem to pin down exactly what it was he did so well, which is what made him such a great director. Jonathan was perfect for *Silence*.

I also knew that Jonathan was something of a critic's darling, which ensured that the film would likely get good reviews, essential for a movie with violent content. His reputation for originality also ensured that quality actors would want to work with him. If *The Silence of the Lambs* was going to be more than a film about a man who ate people for enjoyment, casting would be critical.

At the time, Jonathan was getting ready to do another picture for us that I hated but which my partners liked. It was such a piece of shit that I've blocked out the title. I saw *Silence* as a way of wedging myself between Jonathan and this mistake in the making. It took some convincing for him to read the script because it was classified as a horror film, but after he did, Jonathan saw the film was radically unconventional. It had a female protagonist with great psychological depth and asked the audience to live in her mind. He did, however, like the frightening aspects. "Every director wants to make a movie that scares the audience half to death," he said.

After Jonathan agreed to direct *Silence* and began fine-tuning the script with Ted Tally, the next step was casting. This part of the process always involves a delicate choreography between the studio and the filmmaker. You want to impress your ideas on the director, but at the same time, he or she has to come to casting decisions by themselves. If the director is forced to take a certain lead actor, he will spend the entire film complaining about how much better it would have been if he had gotten his first choice. The key is making your first choice his first choice. In this case, it came down to a little bit of horse trading.

Jonathan originally sent the script to Michelle Pfeiffer, with whom he had worked on *Married to the Mob*. Repulsed by the violence, she turned down the part of Clarice Starling. Meanwhile, Jodie Foster was pursuing the part. Her instinct for a good role is remarkable. She had just won the Best Actress Oscar for her riveting performance in *The Accused*—a role for which she was forced to audition and do a screen test. I thought Jodie's onscreen appeal and her intelligence made her perfect for the part, so I called Jonathan and lobbied for her. He hemmed and hawed, but agreed to fly from New York to L.A. and meet with her. After two lunches with Jodie, Jonathan liked her, but he wasn't completely convinced she could hear the lambs singing.

Of course, we needed a Hannibal Lecter, too. Jonathan wanted Anthony Hopkins based on his performance as Treeves in *The Elephant Man*, but I wasn't sure about him. My choice was Robert Duvall (who wanted the role) because he is such a versatile actor. Jonathan met with Duvall and felt he was too much on the nose for the part. He had gone to London and met with Anthony Hopkins, whom he felt could play the opposite of what the audience expected and therefore be all the more terrifying. It was time to push for a compromise.

"Let Duvall play the FBI boss," Demme said to me after his meeting with Duvall.

"Tell you what," I told him. "I'll make you a deal: I'll take Anthony Hopkins if you take Jodie Foster."

He paused. Jonathan was smart enough to know that he would probably get his way anyway, but at some level he was trusting in Orion as we were in him. "It's a deal," he finally said.

And with that, the way was paved for one of the most memorable tandems in recent film history. Of course, both won acting Oscars, and the movie became the first film since *One Flew Over the Cuckoo's Nest* (and before that *It Happened One Night*) to win all five major Oscars. One thing was certain: Jonathan was exactly right about Anthony Hopkins. He was on screen for only twenty-two minutes, but because you could feel Lecter's presence even when you couldn't see him, Anthony Hopkins's Hannibal Lecter loomed in every frame of the movie.

▤

The Silence of the Lambs became one of the great success stories of my career. The film was released on Valentine's Day in 1991, during the Gulf War, and it went on to gross more than $100 million in the United States and spawn a sequel that has earned twice that amount. But by the time *The Silence of the Lambs* swept the Academy Awards in the spring of 1992, I had already left Orion to become chairman of TriStar Pictures, where I had put into production *Silence*'s biggest Oscar competitor, *Bugsy*.

By the time the money started flowing in from both *Dances With Wolves* and *The Silence of the Lambs*, two of our highest-grossing films, the studio was dead.

One of the most unique, successful, and frustrating executive partnerships in Hollywood history was finished. Even Billy Crystal, to whom we gave a big acting break in *Throw Momma from the Train*, was cracking jokes at the Academy Awards: he called Orion the "studio in a coma." This stung us all pretty hard.

Orion had been thrown from the Hollywood train.

11 *Hollywood's Medicis*

Most of the time, the bottom line on the personal dynamics within a studio is that when the movies are working, everyone is happy, and when the movies don't work, everything falls apart because everyone is looking for someone to blame.

When Louis B. Mayer came west in 1918, eight out of ten movies made in the world were shot in Hollywood. The reason Los Angeles became home to the movie business was that the warm and consistent weather allowed you to shoot year round. The early industry pioneers were also mostly Jews, who were largely excluded from the WASPish, eastern social hierarchy. The social structure in Los Angeles in the early years of the century had yet to be formed, so it was relatively easy for the new movie moguls to become prominent society figures. You could enter the entertainment world with a blank slate if you knew others who could get you in, or if you could work your way in. As the prim, East Coast attitudes gave way to the unrestrained, exuberant style associated with the Warners and Zanucks, the door opened wider and wider for young, hungry guys like me to become successful in the movie business.

The day-to-day workings of the movie business have always been governed by a brash (and often changing) aristocracy that is based in Los Angeles. The big bosses may be mythical figures like Steve Ross who live in New York where the conglomerate is based, but most of the people who run the show are on the West Coast.

If you look at where the Orion partners ended up, it's something of a reflection of how the establishment works in Los Angeles: Arthur essentially retired, Eric formed a short-lived partnership with Barry Spikings and is now working out of Connecticut trying to put together movies with financing from Austria and Holland, and Bill Bernstein became an executive at Paramount. Due in part to the fact that I had become a Hollywood insider, I received an offer from Steve Ross to start a production company at Warner Bros., which I turned down to become chairman of TriStar Pictures.

Arthur, Eric, and Bob Benjamin (who was alive at the time) preferred New York to Los Angeles, so much so that when we made the break from United Artists in 1978, they turned down an offer from Steve Ross for all of us to run Warner Bros. They simply would not move to Los Angeles. At the time, Ted Ashley and Frank Wells were going to step down from the top two jobs at the studio, and the idea was for Arthur, Eric, Bob, Bill Bernstein, and me to step into the Warner's executive suite. From a purely practical standpoint, since the studio is based in Burbank, all of us would have needed to live in Los Angeles, not just me.

Years later I learned that Steve Ross had asked Arthur to become co-chairman with him of Warner Communications, the parent company of Warner Bros. This would have given Arthur the profile he truly deserved, but Arthur rejected the offer. He told his secretary, Charlotte Ermoian, that he was too loyal to leave his partners.

While loyalty was the defining characteristic of our partnership, we were all individualists, strong willed in our beliefs and confident in our opinions. To this day, Eric Pleskow thinks that I should have stayed at Orion until the bitter end, and he faults me for jumping ship when my partners were sinking with the boat. I had worked with the same partners for sixteen years, more than two-thirds of my professional life. I don't agree with him.

▦

"Hollywood is like being nowhere and talking to nobody about nothing."

—MICHELANGELO ANTONIONI

▦

While I was one of four equal partners, I had become the public face of Orion in Hollywood, to the point that one of Garry Trudeau's motley characters in the *Doonesbury* strip pitched me a movie idea over the phone. Despite my heightened profile in Los Angeles, I often felt, sitting in my Century City office while Arthur, Eric, and Bill worked like a close-knit family in New York, like an exile from the Orion nucleus. My partners' general view of Los Angeles as a cultural wasteland only heightened the tensions and misunderstandings between the two offices. Los Angeles may be culturally vapid, but it's where movies are made. If you want to be in the movie business, you need to understand what's happening in L.A. As a studio executive, you also need to understand *why* it's happening.

In *Adventures in the Screen Trade*, William Goldman's best piece of advice to anyone who wants to be in the movie business is simple: *Move to Los Angeles*. He's talking about novices, but it applies to seasoned pros as well. Although Eric rented an apartment in Santa Monica in the mideighties and would come to our L.A. office occasionally, he did so begrudgingly. He used to tell people, particularly reporters, that he came to town only "as needed, like taking medication." However, I think he enjoyed the trips, particularly when we were doing well.

When Eric, Arthur, and/or Bill were in town, I would sit down with them and fill them in on the chain of events on project after project. These meetings were the rare instances in which my partners and I conducted business face-to-face. We dealt with each other almost entirely over the phone.

As this arrangement continued year after year, I slowly soured on the idea of a movie studio being based in New York. Many of the advantages that this set-up brought with it were more relevant in the seventies: proximity to Wall Street, access to a more vibrant culture, a delay in the decision-making process that often resulted in clearer thinking. Increased competition in the industry and changing economics mandated that decisions be made more and more quickly, while spiraling budgets made decisions and talent deals more complicated. More important, I learned that you can't go through the decision-making process by summary. You have to live through each step along the way to fully understand what each bit of information means. I constantly felt that I was merely briefing my partners about developments and not having a dialogue with them about what needed to be done. No matter how many times a day I spoke to them on the phone, they couldn't fully grasp the nuances of the events, simply because they weren't in L.A. experiencing them.

This feeling of isolation was compounded when Pierre Lescure, the chairman of Canal Plus, later told me that Arthur and Eric had met with him in 1989 about the French television company buying Orion. Bill, too, was excluded. In time, I also learned that Ted Turner made a formal play for Orion. I often wondered what else I wasn't told in those years at Orion. Whether or not things were hidden from me before that, nonetheless, nothing was the same after that. Years earlier, my partners had kept me well informed about the Sumner Redstone–John Kluge battle; indeed, I had gotten to know both men fairly well. Now, at the most critical juncture of Orion, I was kept in the dark. It began to feel as if they were controlling my destiny by manufacturing a one-way street of information: I was telling them everything that happened in L.A., but they weren't telling me everything that was going on in New York. I had placed my explicit—and implicit—trust in them to the point that I had given Eric many powers of attorney to act for me. As the gap between us widened, I tried to get everyone in a room to hash things out. It never happened.

Ultimately this led me to leave Orion when the company was in the midst of crisis, something I never would have done in the early and middle years of our partnership.

■

By 1989, the four of us had all become sick of one another.

The company wasn't doing well, so everything was an issue, and the lines of communication continued to deteriorate. I'll never forget, for example, how Arthur had sent Bill Bernstein to Los Angeles for a period of months that year without even consulting me about the temporary move. It appeared that they had lost faith in me and were pushing for Bill to take my place. I felt I had earned the respect of the creative community in Hollywood, and I was trading on it to further Orion in every way possible.

Transamerica loved seeing its name below the fabled United Artists logo, but in the end they didn't fully understand the responsibility that went along with that.

We named Orion after the five-star constellation that lights up the wintry skies, though we later discovered that Orion is an eight-star constellation. Nevertheless, if you see a movie on TV with this logo before it, you know it will be different.

After I ran TriStar for four years, the company was offered to the three stars who formed their owned company, Steven Spielberg, Jeffrey Katzenberg, and David Geffen, but they turned it down and came up with their own name, DreamWorks.

To create a memorable logo for Phoenix with a show of independent strength, I wanted to combine the gong in the old J. Arthur Rank logo with the match strike from *Lawrence of Arabia*.

Desperately seeking a photographer. At Orion, financially we lived hand-to-mouth, and creatively we stuck with a core group of directors and even took a chance on letting an up-and-coming pop singer star in one of our films. Director Susan Seidelman (left), who made three films for us, gave Madonna her first film role, and the two made me a materially happy executive with *Desperately Seeking Susan*. (COLLECTION OF THE AUTHOR)

Celebrating *Platoon*'s victory on Oscar night with a cake at La Scala on March 30, 1987. From left to right: Oliver Stone, producer Arnold Kopelson, Tom Berenger, me, Willem Dafoe, Arthur Krim, and Hemdale's John Daly, without whom the script might still be on the shelf. Notice *Hoosiers* listed on the cake; it was also cofinanced by Hemdale. (COLLECTION OF THE AUTHOR)

The caption reads: "The first order of the day! Let's find another movie, Mike, and let's make it together. I'm for you, man!"—Kevin Costner. Orion greenlighted *No Way Out* because we thought Kevin Costner was going to be a star. About that, we were proven right. (COLLECTION OF THE AUTHOR)

The creative team behind *Mississippi Burning* (from left to right): director Alan Parker, producer Fred Zollo, cinematographer Peter Biziou. I thought this was the best film released by a studio in 1989. Coretta Scott King didn't agree; however, she didn't see the film. (COLLECTION OF THE AUTHOR)

Some of TriStar's stars celebrating ten nominations for *Bugsy* and five nominations for *The Fisher King* at the Bel-Air Country Club in 1991. Left to right: (back row) Jeff Bridges, TriStar executive Steve Randall, TriStar's overjoyed chairman, *Bugsy* director Barry Levinson, Annette Bening; (front row) *Fisher King* director Terry Gilliam; Warren Beatty; and Robin Williams, wearing a sport coat that tells you how much fun he is and using his tie to show how much he loves these parties. (COLLECTION OF THE AUTHOR)

jodie foster / anthony hopkins / scott glenn

the silence of the lambs

from the terrifying best seller

a jonathan demme picture / jodie foster / anthony hopkins / scott glenn / the silence of the lambs / ted tevine / music by howard shore / production designer kristi zea / director of photography tak fujimoto / edited by craig mckay, a.c.e. / executive producer gary goetzman / based upon the novel by thomas harris / screenplay by ted tally / R ———— produced by kenneth utt edward saxon ron bozman / directed by jonathan demme ————— ORION

It was a film about a man who ate people for a living that became a genre breaker and only the third film ever to win the big five awards at the Oscars, thanks to an incomparable creative team led by director Jonathan Demme, Anthony Hopkins, and Jodie Foster. (COURTESY MGM/UA)

Sony chairman Akio Morita watches as Steven Spielberg and I get in the stocks on the set of *Hook*, which I greenlit at TriStar. Maybe Morita's smiling because everyone told him the over-budget film would lose money and it ended up making a $50 million profit. (PHOTO © PETER C. BORSARI)

Our first film at Phoenix Pictures had a little more controversy than we expected when feminist Gloria Steinem took the film to task for supposedly glorifying a pornographer. I think it was one of the most distinctly American stories ever told, as well as the best film of 1996. (THE PEOPLE VS. LARRY FLYNT ©1996 COLUMBIA PICTURES INDUSTRIES, INC. ALL RIGHTS RESERVED. COURTESY OF COLUMBIA PICTURES)

The lovable rogue Woody Harrelson holding me up for more money in the Australian outback in 1997 during filming of Terry Malick's *The Thin Red Line*. (THE THIN RED LINE ©1998 TWENTIETH CENTURY FOX FILM CORPORATION)

Becoming President for a minute. One of the perks of my friendship with Bill Clinton was that he invited me and my wife, Irena, to spend the night at the White House—despite the fact that I wasn't a soft-money donor. (COLLECTION OF THE AUTHOR)

Proud parents Michael and Dora Medavoy flank their son holding the Cannes Film Festival's Lifetime Producer's award in 1998 with their son's beautiful wife, Irena, making the night even brighter. (PHOTO © BERTRAND RINDOFF PETROFF)

Throughout 1989, silly things increasingly became major issues. On a Monday morning after a trip I made to New York in September, I didn't arrive in the office in L.A. until 11 A.M. When Arthur found out I was tardy, he was furious. He called me and treated me like a mail room clerk who punched a clock. I told him I had arrived in L.A. late the night before and gotten a slow start that morning. That was a lie. In fact, I went to Washington on Sunday night to visit friends, caught the first plane back on Monday morning, and went straight to the office. But I was a partner, and it was ridiculous of him to care where I was. It was equally ridiculous of me to lie to him about something so trivial. This was the extent to which the relationship had degenerated. Over the years Arthur took out most of his frustrations on Eric and Bill and very seldom railed at me. But throughout 1989, he displayed frustration with just about everything I did. He had lost confidence in me.

The final straw came during a breakfast Arthur and I had together on December 22 in Los Angeles. While he had once left the production deals to me, Arthur was now looking at them under a microscope. "Jessica Lange is not a star," Arthur snapped. "Why are we making a deal with her?" While Arthur might have been right about Jessica Lange not selling tickets, I was making a deal for her to do *Blue Sky*, which wound up winning her the Academy Award for Best Actress. Then, when he asked me the status of several of our films and I detailed what was happening, he barked that I had answers for everything, but meanwhile nothing was getting done. On the one hand he dwelled on the company's dwindling cash situation, yet on the other hand he faulted me for not bringing in any big-talent packages, which required cash.

At this moment, I decided that for the good of all concerned I was better off leaving Orion.

Looking back, there was no single issue that triggered my decision, rather it was a series of events that unfolded throughout 1989. The real problem had nothing to do with any one deal: The real problem for all of us was that the movies weren't performing and I was as responsible as anyone.

To whatever degree I might have been abandoning my partners in their time of need, I remained loyal to them in other ways, specifically when John Kluge made a strange overture to me in the fall of 1989 that I dismissed out of hand.

I was visiting Kluge at his horse farm in Virginia when he told me that one of the reasons he was holding on to Orion despite the fact that he was losing millions on paper was because of me. "You're the future of the company," he told me. "Arthur and Eric are getting older." Instinctively, I cut him off and told him the same thing that I had told Jack Beckett on my final day at United Artists and Steve Ross in the final days of Orion's deal at Warner Bros.: "I'm at Orion because of Arthur and Eric, and I don't want to take the conversation to the place where I think you're headed. My loyalty is to them and if you take any power away from them, I'll quit. If you decide to do something with the company, that's going to be on your own nickel."

This was the second time that what I considered a coup attempt had been brought to me. In 1986 a frustrated Ernst Goldschmidt banded together Orion's CFO Mel Woods, video president Larry Hilford, and TV head Jamie Kellner, and then tried to enlist me. Ernst wanted to wrestle control of the company from Arthur and revamp Orion's strategy. I declined, and Ernst's plan eventually fell apart.

Leaving was one thing, but taking over for them was something that I wouldn't even think about. They had been loyal to me despite my flaws, and I intended to remain as loyal to them as I could be.

▦

1989: A good year for Cabernet Sauvignon, but a bad year for Orion.

▦

While we never lost our shirt on one movie, Orion's entire 1989 slate underperformed to such a degree that it put us in the throes of tremendous financial pressure. That year Orion released thirteen films. Collectively, they grossed less than $65 million domestically, with only two passing the $10 million mark. Following Arthur's philosophy of always protecting the downside, we were also making films to satisfy the output of our Showtime pay cable deal and our international video deal with Columbia Pictures, both of which demanded twelve to sixteen films a year. Arthur wanted films that cost in the $8 million range because he figured these would, at the very least, break even. The pressure on me to find such films was intense, mostly because picking films this way never works. Most of the films made in this period were designed not to lose too much money, like *Heart of Dixie*, which starred Treat Williams and Ally Sheedy; *Lost Angels*, with Donald Sutherland; and *UHF*, with Weird "Al Yankovic." But as they failed theatrically, the ancillary revenue shrank. Regardless of their relatively small budgets, they were still losing money. We were hoping for one winner, but none came.

Arthur's admonition to all of us was always "Stay in the game." But we needed to do more than protect the downside; we needed an upside strategy, and we didn't really have one. To make matters worse, Eric spent much of the year in which these films were put together in the hospital. The chemistry that the four of us had formed over the years was shaken, and it showed in the results.

While the figures were bad, not all of the films were rush jobs. The better films made that year were the kind of smaller, quality studio projects that had been the foundation of our existence at United Artists and Orion, but people just didn't want to see them in the numbers we needed to recoup our money. Milos Forman made *Valmont*, a thoughtful version of the Choderlos de Laclos novel *Les Liaisons Dangereuses*, but it was beaten to the screen by nine months by the sleeker *Dangerous Liaisons*. While our version had the medium profile of Colin Firth, Meg Tilly, and an unknown Annette Bening in the leads, *Dangerous Liaisons* starred John Malkovich, Michelle Pfeiffer, and Glenn Close. By the time *Valmont* was released, it was old news.

Coming off *The Big Easy* we thought Dennis Quaid could become the next Kevin Costner. Since we couldn't afford Tom Cruise or Harrison Ford, we were constantly trying to catch stars on the way up. We rolled the dice in a fairly big way on Quaid as Jerry Lee Lewis in *Great Balls of Fire!*, but the film didn't take at the box office. We had discarded a script written by Terry Malick as too dark, but the truth is that the story of a man marrying his thirteen-year-old cousin was inherently dark. We probably should have stuck with the Malick script or not made the movie at all.

In what seemed like some sort of perverse irony given what had happened when we were at Warner, one of the two films that grossed more than $10 million was Woody Allen's *Crimes and Misdemeanors*.

Imagine, Woody Allen was our breadwinner.

Even on some of our very best films we couldn't catch a break. For my money, *Mississippi Burning*, released in December 1988, was the best film of the year. *Mississippi Burning* is an example of a film where you are fighting an uphill battle from the day it starts production until the day it leaves the theaters. Going in, the film was commercially chancy because of its political content, but we stuck our necks out for it because we believed in the script and the talent involved. When I think about the embodiment of suspenseful, interesting filmmaking, this film immediately comes to mind. Chris Gerolmo's tightly written script was perfectly directed by Alan Parker, and the performances by Gene Hackman and Willem Dafoe, playing two Yankee FBI agents who came to a redneck Mississippi town to investigate the disappearance of three civil rights workers, didn't have a false moment. There was also the surprise performance of Frances McDormand, who, in just her third feature film, was unforgettable as a repressed Southern housewife. Though the film opened to good reviews, I had expected it to open to great reviews. Then came an unwarranted protest that completely sidetracked the film and undercut our efforts to promote it.

Coretta Scott King, Martin Luther King's widow, attacked the film publicly—without having even seen it. I was floored when I heard what had happened. Mrs. King attacked it on the basis that there weren't enough blacks in the movie and that their story was told from the point of view of the white law-enforcement officials. But that was the film's story. It wasn't a documentary about segregation in the South; it was a drama about two FBI agents trying to solve a racially motivated crime set against the backdrop of the Civil Rights movement. I thought the film was moving, truthful, and accurate. We tried to defend the movie without attacking King, but I don't think we ever recovered from her attack. The film ultimately earned seven Oscar nominations, including Best Picture, Best Director, Best Actor (Hackman), and Best Supporting Actress (McDormand), but lost the major awards to *Rain Man*, which, while an excellent film, was not, in my opinion, as powerful a story as *Mississippi Burning*. In fact, we had made our version of *Rain Man* a year earlier. Directed by Robert Young and starring Tom Hulce and Ray Liotta, it was a wonderful film called *Dominick and Eugene* that got lost in the multiplex shuffle the same way that *The Great Santini* had.

Industrywide, 1989 was a year when bigger was becoming better to audiences and the familiar brand-name sold tickets. The monster hit was *Batman*, which collected more than $250 million at the domestic box office alone. The other big $100-million-plus blockbusters included three sequels—*Lethal Weapon 2*, *Back to the Future Part II*, and *Indiana Jones and the Last Crusade*—and one high-concept sleeper hit, *Look Who's Talking*. Orion's films were *Great Balls of Fire!*, *Valmont*, *Crimes and Misdemeanors*, *Farewell to the King*, and *Bill & Ted's Excellent Adventure*. We let *Twins* slip through the cracks in script form before Arnold Schwarzenegger and Danny DeVito were attached. We also passed on a few very potentially interesting, probably risky, projects such as David Lynch's *Wild at Heart*, which made a big splash at the Cannes Film Festival but died commercially.

By and large our line-up was idiosyncratic films against high-wire action films and high-concept films, psychological portraits of different cultures versus comic book reality.

Commercially, we got our doors blown off.

▩

How could a company that was powered by the collective experience and intellect of its near-legendary partners fail to meet the challenges the industry presented in the last years of the eighties?

▩

Although my opinion is not shared by Eric Pleskow, one of the reasons for Orion's demise was our tight publicity and marketing budgets. Orion spent less money marketing its films during the eighties than other studios did, and this made us less competitive at all levels, particularly in regard to big-name talent and high-profile projects. While we offered more creative freedom, history shows that we didn't spend to open movies. Our publicity department was small and not very effective. Films like *The Terminator, No Way Out, Dirty Rotten Scoundrels,* and *Hoosiers* were terrific films that could have done better at the box office had we spent more on marketing or gotten more publicity. Ultimately all the autonomy in the world doesn't mean a thing to a director if the public doesn't know that the film exists. At Orion, we were never able to maximize exposure.

Miramax, a company that came of age in the eighties, has done with movie marketing what we couldn't do at Orion: They have found a way on some films to spend less on marketing and get results through a soft manipulation of the public. They start with a good movie like *The Crying Game, Shakespeare in Love,* or *The Cider House Rules* and build awareness through the media. They convince people that the movie is a small gem that needs to be sought out from the mass of multiplex fare. It's the opposite of plastering the *Batman* logo on every available billboard, but since both the media and the public are tired of being beaten over the head by brash and loud movie ad campaigns, it can be very effective. I admire that technique, every time they pull it off.

Miramax has also become frighteningly adept at marketing Oscar films, earning Best Picture nominations nine of ten years running from 1991 to 2000. Much of this is due to Harvey Weinstein. While filmmakers often complain about Harvey's heavy-handedness, they continue to make films for him because of his fighting spirit. They know that if Harvey gets behind their film with all his might, the picture has an excellent chance of finding an audience and possibly even winning an Oscar.

Because Orion had very few campaigns that worked perfectly and were economic (such as the one for *Platoon*), the four of us argued and debated about how much we needed to spend on marketing to be competitive with the other studios. The position of Arthur and Eric—Eric almost always had the same position as Arthur on everything—was that we spent less because we *had* less, but they always maintained that we were competitive. The evidence indicated otherwise, and it was often used against us by our competitors.

This problem first surfaced in 1982 when Mario Kassar and Andy Vajna complained about *First Blood*, and it began to snowball on *The Terminator*, when Gale Hurd and Jim Cameron felt we skimped on the marketing campaign, the trade ad, and that all-important bottle of vintage champagne. But it was really apparent on a handful of films that unquestionably should have done better at the box office, notably *No Way Out*, *Something Wild*, *Bull Durham*, *Robocop*, and *Dirty Rotten Scoundrels*, which is as smart and funny a comedy as you'll ever find. None of these films grossed more than $60 million. In fact, Orion's first $100 million film after *Platoon* was more of a pop-culture fluke than a marketing coup: *Dances With Wolves*.

As with almost everything institutional at Orion, geography was destiny. In 1984 Arthur and Eric moved the marketing department from Los Angeles to New York, which turned out to be a major mistake—marketing wasn't even in the same building with the corporate offices in New York. This was done as a cost-cutting measure. As a result of the move, the marketing and publicity executives were constantly flying to L.A. to talk to the talent and the press and to meet with my production department. It took only a few box-office flops before human nature took over and an unnecessary rivalry emerged between marketing and production. On films that didn't perform, we got into situations where each side was blaming the other long distance: we blamed them for not selling a film correctly, and they blamed us for making a film that was unsaleable. If we had both been under the same roof, we might have eliminated the us-versus-them mentality. But no one alone can be blamed for the failures because the reasons are always complex.

The truth is that none of the partners was particularly adept at marketing. Because of this we should have included the marketing people earlier in the process without giving them any authority in terms of greenlighting films, but when to bring the marketing department in on the process is always a tricky call. At TriStar, I learned that trying to decide whether a film can be marketed before it is made sometimes spells trouble. I passed on *A River Runs Through It* at TriStar because my marketing department told me that they couldn't sell a movie about fly-fishing. Robert Redford directed a beautiful and moving film, and it ended up being a moneymaker. In that instance, I fell victim to the mentality of making movies by committee. What I should have done was greenlight the movie and told them, or helped them to figure out, how to sell it. If the film works and the concept is popular, you can always get people to come and see it. If the film doesn't work because the concept or the execution is flawed, your marketing campaign will be able to take you only so far—which isn't that different from any other business. It's as simple as that.

The most expensive aspect of any campaign is television, and the high cost of advertising on television has become the reason many smaller films don't get made. While Eric realized we had to spend some money on opening weekend, he hated second-week television buys. On movie after movie, Eric, supported by Arthur and Bill (who kept a close watch on the purse strings), refused to spend money on television after opening weekend. His theory was that if the movie had done well in the first three days, then word of mouth would take over, and if it wasn't performing, second-week television ads amounted to throwing good money after bad. On the rare occasion that Eric wanted to buy second-week television, we would have to buy it at the last minute and pay top dollar. We also did not do upfront buys (buying ads in advance in bulk), which would have made the second week cheaper.

This tight-fisted approach drove Charles Glenn, our head of marketing, absolutely bananas. Charles had come from Paramount in the Robert Evans era, where he worked on the campaigns for *The Godfather* and *Love Story*. Those were two of the first wide-release, holiday movies. They were launched on more than one thousand screens at a time when five hundred was a lot, and Paramount spent accordingly. At Orion, Charles had to design campaigns that were inexpensive and ultra-creative. To promote *Robocop*, Charles had actors dress in the Robocop suit in nine major cities and walk up and down the streets. Newspapers and TV stations ran pictures of the Robocop, giving us free advertising, which, as part of a news story, is more valuable than paid ads. At Orion, this was considered radical and gimmicky. Maybe it should have been closer to the norm.

But Arthur Krim and Eric Pleskow leaned conservative on all fronts. This type of conservatism worked in the sixties and seventies when edgier movies were in demand. But in the eighties, the times were changing, and they were uncomfortable about changing with them. To be fair, they were always watching the bottom line, too. But their old-line thinking hurt Orion's chances. Orion was in a position where we had to *create* movie stars because we couldn't *afford* movie stars. Then having created them, sell them to the public. When Arthur saw the first poster for *The Terminator* with the tag line ARNOLD SCHWARZENEGGER IS THE TERMINATOR covering half of the poster, he thought the oversized letters made the campaign borderline B-movie. "Too bad it's not Clint Eastwood," he said. Arthur had nothing against Arnold, but his nature was to gravitate toward the familiar, to make the safe bet.

▬

This is a business that eats its elders instead of its young.

▬

The movie business changed on Arthur Krim and while he saw the changes going on, he depended on others to keep him abreast and to convince him what to do, which caused things to fall through the cracks. For most of his career, Arthur displayed extraordinary prescience in seeing the changes in the business and putting them to work for United Artists and Orion. But he missed out on the significance of the home-video boom, which was created when a major technological advance combined with a viewing habit change in the public. On one level, he was playing it safe by selling off video rights and protecting Orion's downside, but on another level, he let a major revenue source get away in the early years of Orion. When home video exploded, it became a cash cow for most studios—but not for Orion. The company's conservative approach and limited funding caused us to wait too long to create our own video division.

Then, once the division was formed, Arthur rejected the idea of taking the video division public to raise money that could have been used to fund Orion.

Despite the fact that video was an obvious goldmine by the early eighties, we didn't form Orion Home Entertainment Corporation until December 1985, and it wasn't until 1987 that we shipped our first titles, because the video rights to all the movies we had in production had already been presold. Larry Hilford, a capable executive who had run CBS/Fox Video, was hired to run the division, but millions of dollars had already floated out the window. Millions more floated out the window when Arthur wouldn't support Larry's plan to take the division public. Due to the fact that home video was so hot, it's possible that Orion could have raised $100 million by spinning off the home-video division.

When we formed Orion, we had presold the video rights to all the films we produced to Vestron Video domestically and to RCA/Columbia internationally. While these deals gave us steady advances for each film we delivered (and therefore cut our risk), we were only getting a fraction of what each picture was worth.

Vestron's chairman, a man named Austin Furst, was one of the first to understand the video boom. In 1980 Furst was an executive at Time, Inc. One day, he looked at the huge library of films the company had made in connection with *Life* magazine, long before Time and Warner Bros. merged. He convinced the company to let him license the video rights to the films, and he then began distributing them on video through his new company, Vestron Video. While this established him as a video distributor, Orion made him a multimillionaire. Vestron earned enough money distributing the Orion library from 1982 to 1987 to begin producing and distributing their own films theatrically.

Vestron was one of several companies the home-video boom allowed to move into the theatrical arena, though it didn't survive. Vestron scored big with *Dirty Dancing*, which was the highest-grossing independent film released at the time, but a string of forgettable movies like *Satisfaction* with Justine Bateman flopped and put the company out of business.

New Line Cinema was another company that was transformed by the revenue stream from the home-video market, and it was successful in using that money to build itself into mini–major studio. The video profits from the *Nightmare on Elm Street* series alone enabled New Line to bankroll bigger movies and to produce enough hits to cover the misses. Without video, it's doubtful that New Line would have ever become the player it is today.

Had Orion formed a video division earlier—or had it taken the video division public to raise much-needed production cash in the late eighties, it might still be a player.

▦

For Orion, the line between success and failure was a thin and subjective one. After I left Orion in February 1990 to become chairman of TriStar Pictures, I followed the progress of the studio, because I was partly responsible for the successes and partly responsible for the failures. No one wanted it to succeed more than I—except them.

Dances With Wolves *opened that fall and ended up grossing $180 million in the United States, by far Orion's biggest hit. In spring 1991, just as* The Silence of the Lambs *was about to cross the $100 million mark,* Dances With Wolves *won the Oscar for Best Picture. But Orion was on a downward spiral that couldn't be stopped.*

▦

Going into the first six months of 1990, Orion's films continued to lose money. Three films for which Orion had high hopes were all flops: *Cadillac Man,* with Robin Williams and Tim Robbins; *State of Grace,* with Sean Penn and Ed Harris; and Arthur Miller's script for *Everybody Wins,* with Karel Reisz directing Nick Nolte and Debra Winger. By summer 1990, the theatrical drought had virtually drained the company's bank accounts. Then, disaster hit like a tornado coming after a flood: the banks stopped lending money to Orion to back individual films.

Orion had always financed its films with off-balance-sheet loans. When a film was ready to go, the producers would take Orion's promise to pay for the completed film together with an insurance policy (in the event of a catastrophe like the lead actor dying) and a completion bond (in case the film went wildly over budget) to the bank and borrow the money to fund production. When the producer delivered the film, Orion paid off the bank. This allowed Orion not to tap into its primary bank credit line for individual films. However, Orion's box-office results were weak, and the credit markets in general were tightening up. Junk bond defaults and the failure of several savings and loans caused the banks to stop lending money for individual films. Another small detail didn't escape the bankers: the 80 percent owner of Orion was the richest man in America—why wasn't he putting up the money? For financing, Orion now had to tap into its primary credit line, which set the company up for a do-or-die situation. The company had to fund the films out of its existing—and diminishing—coffers.

By the fall of 1990, things had reached the breaking point, so Arthur Krim called John Kluge and asked him to pump some money into the company to keep it afloat, and Kluge responded with $25 million. Because Orion's primary credit lines were exhausted, this money was used to make delivery payments on several films, including *Mermaids*, starring Cher and Winona Ryder. A month later, Arthur called again and Kluge put up an additional $25 million. Again, Orion was unable to borrow money on its primary credit line and there wasn't enough cash flow from receivables to cover expenses. The next time Arthur called for a cash infusion, Kluge not only refused, he began to look for an exit strategy.

Among others, Kluge talked to Marvin Davis about buying Orion. By then, Davis had sold his interest in 20th Century Fox to Rupert Murdoch. All hope of a sale to Davis ended when the investment banker whom Davis had hired to evaluate the company basically declared that Orion was on its way out of business and wasn't worth anything. After reviewing the investment banker's report, Kluge declared Orion dead and demanded that the studio stop spending money. Draconian measures followed.

Kluge ordered Orion to sell off the five films in production, including *The Addams Family, Robocop 3,* and *Bill & Ted's Bogus Journey,* the equivalent of hanging a going-out-of-business sign on the door. Everyone in Hollywood now knew that the owner didn't support the management's business plan.

Even though Orion had put $38 million into *The Addams Family* and despite the fact it was going over budget, Paramount head Frank Mancuso saw the film's potential. The terms were simple: Orion sold all right, title, and interest in the film and all its sequels for what it had spent on it to date. *The Addams Family* became a $115 million hit in the United States and spawned a successful sequel that took in another $100 million–plus worldwide. Like so many times since the formation of Orion, another directing career was also started. *The Addams Family* was cinematographer Barry Sonnenfeld's first film; Barry has since gone on to direct *Get Shorty* and *Men in Black,* and is now one of the highest-paid directors in Hollywood.

After the forced sale of *The Addams Family,* things began to get dark. In spring 1991, shortly after *The Silence of the Lambs* was climbing toward the $100 million mark, John Kluge asked Arthur Krim to step aside and allow Kluge's people, led by Stuart Subotnick, to take control of Orion. Arthur had no choice.

Looking back, I now realize how hard it must have been for Arthur to swallow his pride and to keep asking Kluge for money. The more established you are, the more proud you become and the less you want to be the asker. I know how demeaning it must have felt for Arthur, as I too have been put in that situation in recent years.

And so, as gracefully and as quietly as he had walked into the movie business, Arthur walked out. His retirement was the end of one of the most sweeping and successful executive careers in movie history, and one of the most unheralded. Even among thieves, he always acted like a prince. If my career comes even close to his, I will die happy. What troubles me is that most young people in the movie business don't know who Arthur Krim was. But the lesson here is: *Don't do something to be remembered; it is the things you do that are remembered.*

Years from now probably no one will remember me, but they will remember *One Flew Over the Cuckoo's Nest* and *The Silence of the Lambs.*

Whatever our failings were at Orion, Arthur was the one who had chosen Kluge as a partner, and Kluge was the one who finally pulled the plug. For all the wisdom and foresight Arthur had, he was bad at choosing his white knights. Arthur had chosen to make the deal with Transamerica chairman Jack Beckett. He had made Orion's deal to go to Warner Bros. with Steve Ross. He had also brought in Lionel Pincus's company to arrange the financing for Orion to take over Filmways, a relationship that ended with Warburg Pincus nearly selling Arthur out to Mario Kassar and Andy Vajna behind Arthur's back. Over his career, Arthur had chosen all of his partners, and he ended up slighted by them, because all of them thought the movie business was about return on investment and none of them wanted to play for the long term. Had they all stuck with him, they would have reaped the rewards.

To this day, Eric's theory is that Arthur Krim was a healthy man until John Kluge stripped him of his pride by taking Orion away from him. Shortly after Arthur stepped down, he went into the hospital for bypass surgery and never recovered. Eric thinks he died of a broken heart. "Arthur Krim was killed by John Kluge," Eric told my co-writer in the fall of 1999. However, Arthur never personally expressed any animus toward Kluge to me.

Orion is dead now. There is no company called Orion Pictures, just a collection of titles that is part of the MGM/UA library. For all practical purposes, United Artists is nothing but a shell now, too. One of the greatest ironies is that Kirk Kerkorian now controls both the UA and Orion libraries. In 1997 MGM bought the film holdings of Kluge's Metromedia, which included Orion, for $578 million. The net return to Kluge was a couple of hundred million dollars, not bad for a bankrupt headache. I read this as vindication of Orion as a valuable company. Unfortunately, none of the principals who built the company will see the financial fruits of it.

It pains me to think that more than two hundred of the movies that I was a part of are owned by somebody else. All I have are video cassette copies. My partners and I built Orion into an eighth movie studio and nearly made it fly. In both phases of Orion, we all had aspirations of becoming another United Artists, but we didn't have the money or the depth of organization at a time when the business was rapidly changing. We didn't have an adequate marketing strategy or a foreign distribution apparatus, and we didn't have our own video division until it was too late. And we didn't change fast enough with the times.

The line between success and failure is very thin. Did we fail? I suppose, to some degree, we did. Orion ended not with a bang but with a whimper: on December 11, 1991, Orion officially filed for Chapter 11 reorganization and declared bankruptcy. You can't call bankruptcy success, and each of us bears some responsibility.

But, at the same time, Orion succeeded. Not only did Kluge sell the company to Kirk Kerkorian and make a quarter-of-a-billion-dollars profit, Orion left an indelible mark on the creative community.

▦

Part of Orion's lasting impact comes from the work of its Orion Classics division. Formed in April 1983 by Donna Gigliotti, Michael Barker, and Tom Bernard, Orion Classics was a natural complement to Orion's overall philosophy of acquiring films and not tinkering with their production. Like Orion, the classics division was defined by the executives who ran it. Donna—who first approached Orion through Ernst Goldschmidt—Michael, and Tom had learned all the old United Artists philosophy firsthand while working in the New York office at United Artists Classics in the early eighties. When Donna left Orion Classics in 1989 to go start a company with Marty Scorsese and Steven Spielberg, Marcie Bloom, a publicist for many of the classics division's films, became the third partner.

Our classics division focused on acquiring foreign films to release in the United States, and the partners at Orion Classics were as knowledgeable about buying and releasing these films as anyone in the world. When it came to deciding on whether or not to buy a film, the final decision required at least two of the three partners to vote yes, which was again very similar to the way we ran the main division of Orion. However, Orion's main division was totally hands-off and had no control over the classics division. They were allocated a certain (and small) amount of money to buy and market films each year, and as long as they stayed within their budget, the money was spent at their sole discretion. Over the years, they would remain profitable and distinguish themselves with such films as *Cyrano de Bergerac* with Gérard Depardieu, Agnieszka Holland's *Europa Europa*, *Babette's Feast*, Louis Malle's *Au Revoir les Enfants*, and the groundbreaking Chinese-language film *Raise the Red Lantern*. In nine years, Orion Classics added nearly two hundred titles to the Orion library, an incredible value at a very low cost, and it helped expose American audiences to different cultures.

Orion Classics also became a prototype for the art house companies of the nineties, such as Miramax Films (in its pre-Disney years), October Films (which has been folded into USA Films), and Fine Line Features. Interestingly, Donna Gigliotti worked at Miramax for a few years and became president of USA Films.

When Orion Classics was formed, no other studio had a classics or specialty division. Today every studio owns a piece of one.

Is the Orion legacy lost? At some level, all legacies are lost. Once Louis B. Mayer was gone, he was gone. He left an imprint on the sands of time, but his legacy is not relevant in the least to MGM today. His legacy is all the careers that he put in motion with the movies he made, and the same can be said of Orion.

At Orion, we provided the foundation for many careers: Jonathan Demme owes the furthering of his career to Orion, as does Jim Cameron. Andy Davis was fired from two movies, but we picked him up at Orion. We gave Ron Shelton his first greenlight. We put Rodney Dangerfield in the movie business, and we made the movie that made Arnold Schwarzenegger a household name. We stepped up and bought *Platoon* when no one wanted it, and we picked up and masterfully handled *Amadeus*. *State of Grace*, which I put in motion from a *New York Times Magazine* story about the Irish mob, hit the theaters with a dull thud, but it was where Sean Penn and Robin Wright met. We helped actors Kevin Costner, Jodie Foster, and Danny DeVito become directors, and we brought Dennis Hopper back behind the camera after a seventeen-year break.

Culturally, we started trends that affect the movies being made to this day. *The Addams Family* initiated the idea that studios could recycle old, kitschy TV series into blockbuster movies. Director Barry Sonnenfeld updated the characters' sensibilities, added special effects (such as Hand), and wove some nineties' attitudes into the story. As soon as studios and filmmakers saw how to do it, they dusted off their old series and began turning them into films as fast as they could. Warner hit pay dirt with *Batman, Maverick, Dennis the Menace,* and *The Fugitive* (which I had tried to get going at Orion in the early eighties). Universal had hits with *The Flintstones* and *Casper*. Paramount scored with two films based on *The Brady Bunch* and two based on *Mission Impossible,* while Fox had a winner with *The Beverly Hillbillies*.

Someone once called Arthur, Bob, Eric, Bill, and me "gentlemen filmmakers." When I think back on the Orion days, I am reminded of what Woody Allen once said: "There are people who call my agent to propose the same deal I have at Orion—just with more money. But you can sleep nights if you have a deal with Arthur Krim. It would be a sorry thing if there weren't a company like this."

12 *All the Money in the World*

The movie business has never cared where the money comes from. People in Hollywood just want the freedom to make their films and have them aggressively marketed. But Hollywood is a very high-profile place, and entertainment is our country's biggest export. When Sony purchased Columbia Pictures, and the sister studio TriStar Pictures, which I was hired to run, I found myself in the middle of a political and cultural maelstrom.

JAPAN INVADES HOLLYWOOD blared the *Newsweek* cover headline next to a picture of the famed Columbia Pictures lady wrapped in a kimono. The magazine's international edition went even further: JAPAN BUYS HOLLYWOOD.

The cause of this shrill rhetoric was Sony's purchase of Columbia Pictures Entertainment, which included Columbia Pictures and TriStar Pictures, in November 1989. The acquisition hit a raw nerve. Columbia was, after all, the studio where Frank Capra enshrined the virtues of small-town Americana with films like *It Happened One Night, Mr. Deeds Goes to Town*, and *Mr. Smith Goes to Washington*. Sony's move was seen by some as nothing less than an assault on American culture.

Around the time Sony bought Columbia Pictures from Coca-Cola, different groups of Japanese investors purchased Rockefeller Center, the Bel-Air Hotel, and the famed Pebble Beach golf course. The Japanese economy was on fire, and Japan was investing enormous amounts of money in everything American because the yen was strong against the dollar. Endless magazine and newspaper articles were published about how Japan would soon surpass America as the world's top economic power and what would become of America's heritage if the Japanese kept buying up our institutions. Many Americans expressed shock and even outrage that the Japanese were ravenously buying up our national treasures, yet few acknowledged the basic truth that there can't be a buyer without a seller.

Sony wasn't the first Japanese electronics company to take an interest in Hollywood, though at the time it was the company with the highest profile. In fact, Sony had gotten into the entertainment business when it bought CBS Records in 1987, with far less scrutiny. JVC, the electronics giant, invested $100 million in producer Larry Gordon's company, Largo Entertainment, and scores of smaller production companies were backed by Japanese companies like television giant NHK. But when Sony announced it was buying Columbia, the American media had their knives sharpened and ready to carve up the Japanese like sashimi. They seemed to feel it was their solemn duty based on a *Newsweek* poll that found that 43 percent of Americans disapproved of Sony buying Columbia, compared to only 19 percent who approved.

From the outset of the Sony deal, the media focused on the personalities, the price, and the premium that Sony had paid for the services of Peter Guber and Jon Peters to run the studio. The numbers were, in a word, eye-popping. Coverage of Sony's acquisition of Columbia spread from the business section and the entertainment pages to the gossip columns and political broadsheets. To buy Columbia, Sony paid $3.4 billion, plus another $1.6 billion of assumed debt; to bring in Guber and Peters, Sony spent $200 million for their company, which was 40 percent above the company's market value, and gave them lavish compensation packages. The fact that Sony paid such a high price made the culture police doubly suspicious. But even with billions of dollars flying around, the media focus was on the two producers Sony picked to lead their new Hollywood adventure, Peter Guber and Jon Peters. One of the witty lines tossed around summed it up: Peter Guber could sell sushi to the Japanese.

It wasn't long before I became part of that adventure.

≡

In February 1990, just as I was about to leave Orion, I got a call from Peter Guber, who had already started his job as chairman of Columbia Pictures Entertainment. He asked if he could come over to my house and talk to me. Peter showed up wearing his trademark outfit: a dark Armani suit, suede shoes, and a T-shirt. His hair was tied back in a tight ponytail, which he did to hide a growing bald spot, and he walked with his customary swagger, leading with his hips like John Travolta strolling through Brooklyn in *Saturday Night Fever*. Peter acted as though he owned the town and, for all practical purposes, at that moment he did.

Guber and Peters had each collected $55 million from the sale of their production company to Sony. Then there were their Sony employment contracts. Each would earn an annual salary of $2.7 million, plus an equal share of a $50 million bonus pool that would be created at the end of five years, plus 8.08 percent of any increase in Sony's overall value over those five years. Call me anal for listing that decimal point, but when the numbers get into the billions, eight-tenths of a percent can buy you a nice beach house. Eight is also is a lucky number to the Japanese.

Sony was also forced to make a settlement with Warner Bros. before the studio would let Peter and Jon out of their producing contract, which the two had allegedly breached by accepting the Sony position. The press gleefully reported that Sony had been fleeced, and people around town joked that the deal was revenge for Pearl Harbor. Variety estimated that the settlement had cost Sony more than $1 billion, which was the number that Warner's chairman Steve Ross said he was suing for. The *Los Angeles Times, Forbes,* and *Vanity Fair* also chided Sony for overpaying for the services of Guber and Peters, "a hairdresser and his ponytailed partner," as *Vanity Fair* flippantly referred to them. This made for good copy but it wasn't entirely correct.

To drop the suit, Steve Ross asked for half of Sony's share of CBS's record mail-order business and the cable distribution rights to Columbia's library. He also wanted to swap the 35 percent of the Burbank Studios lot that Columbia owned for the Culver City lot that Warner owned from its purchase of Lorimar.

The lot, which was once owned by MGM, had fallen into disrepair and needed millions of dollars in renovations. The truth is that Sony had wanted to bring Warner Bros. music product into the Columbia House record company for years. For Sony, a fifty-fifty partnership with Warners that gave them access to Warner's artists was worth more than owning all of Columbia House on their own. The deal was also great leverage against competition because it kept Warner from doing a similar deal with PolyGram. As for the studio back-lot trade, Culver City was much more desirable for Columbia because it would no longer have to share facilities with Warner in Burbank. It was also on the west side of town where most of the creative community lived. While Warner might have made out better financially, Sony didn't exactly get screwed, though no one would deny that Guber and Peters were expensive.

No two people were more representative of "Hollywood" in the second half of the eighties than Guber and Peters. The two producers were fearless showmen at a time when showmanship dominated the movie business. They were masters of self-promotion at a time when media coverage of the industry was exploding, and they were geniuses at selling themselves and their movies at a time when marketing was becoming more important than moviemaking. Costs were rising out of control and the window of time allowed for a film to succeed had narrowed dramatically. In Hollywood, as on Wall Street, the stakes were high and the harder and faster you played the game, the more attention you received—and nobody received more than Guber and Peters when they tore up their contract with Warner Bros. and convinced Sony to buy their fledgling public production company for $200 million.

Timing was everything. Coming off the one-two punch of *Rain Man* and *Batman*, Guber and Peters were Hollywood's Golden Boys. *Batman* was exactly the kind of film that studios wanted to be making in the late eighties: a fast-paced, quick-cutting action film with sequel potential, merchandise licensing, and fast-food tie-ins. The film has grossed more than a half billion dollars worldwide. What Guber and Peters were best at doing was highlighting their success and covering up their failures. Certain producers earn their reputations on the basis of their work and others are able to get noticed because of their personality, which is true in most industries but truer still in Hollywood. Not unusually, they took the credit for films on which they served only as executive producers, notably *Flashdance*, which was found by Lynda Obst and produced by Jerry Bruckheimer and Don Simpson; *The Color Purple*, on which they were banned from the set; and *Rain Man*, which won the Best Picture Oscar for its producer, Mark Johnson, and for director Barry Levinson. The famous post-Oscar photo taken of Peter holding Jon and Jon holding the Oscar was just another marketing tool; they had hijacked screenwriter Ron Bass's statue for the photo. But their résumés in that same period of time also included a string of misses such as *Clue, The Legend of Billie Jean, Head Office, Missing Link,* and *The Clan of the Cave Bear*. You never heard them tell war stories about those films.

When Peter and I sat down in my living room, he rested his foot on the edge of my coffee table and came right to the point. "I'd like you to come to work with us, but I don't want to get in a legal situation if you have a contract with Orion," he said. (He knew from where he spoke: Guber and Peters were sued for walking out on their contract with Warner.) Then I asked him if he was talking about Columbia or its sister studio, TriStar Pictures. He told me TriStar, adding that he already had someone in mind for Columbia. Little did I know that it wasn't Frank Price, who got the job initially, it was Mark Canton. Guber was simply waiting for Canton's contract to expire at Warner, so he could reunite the boys' club that I had helped create when Orion was based at Warners.

I later learned that there were no plans for me to be part of their clique.

I pressed Peter on how he saw his role: Would it be that of a Steve Ross, a visionary entrepreneur who left the running of his studio to the executives, or would it be that of a Terry Semel, who was a hands-on production executive? Guber assured me that he would leave the production, marketing, and distribution of the films to his studio chiefs. He had big dreams to move the studio into the future, and it would take all his efforts to bring them to fruition. What he needed, he explained, was someone he could trust to pick the pictures.

This was an incredible opportunity for me to make movies without the kind of budget restrictions I had at Orion. I would have an annual budget of $500 million (the same as Columbia's) to make and market my slate of films, and roughly $50 million a year for development. Considering Orion had started in 1982 with a total of $50 million, this was a staggering amount of money. In 1990 the average cost of a studio film was roughly $26 million to produce and another $12 million to market, meaning that I was expected to make about twelve to fifteen movies a year. Three to five movies would come from a deal that TriStar had to distribute Carolco's films. As chairman, I would have unilateral authority to develop and greenlight movies, as well as oversee production, marketing, distribution, and all other areas of TriStar's motion picture unit. Even the personalities seemed to line up. I would be working under Peter, a longtime friend for whom I had an immense amount of respect, while Jon would supervise Columbia. Given how successful Peter and Jon had been in the eighties, I thought I could learn something from them, particularly about marketing big films.

After getting clearance to leave Orion before my contract expired, I formally accepted the job. Almost immediately, the passive-aggressive nature of Peter Guber began to show itself. As my TriStar contract was being hammered out, Peter called and told me that I couldn't be officially hired without Jon Peters approving it since Jon was technically a co-chairman. "He's my partner, so he has to okay it," Peter said. Reading nothing into Peter's actions, I went to Jon's to have dinner and kiss the brass ring, as it were.

As I drove up the windy streets of Bel Air to Jon's house to be validated for my new job, I kept asking myself the same questions that many in town were asking: Why is Peter Guber still in business with Jon Peters? What qualifies Jon Peters to run a studio besides the fact that he is Peter Guber's partner? I didn't know the answer, but in the coming years I would certainly find out.

When I arrived Jon was pleasant and bouncing off the walls as usual, but his unrestrained energy leaves no dull moments in a conversation. Like the proverbial kid in the candy store, he dragged me from room to room in his house, showing me his

Remington sculptures and his koi pond. When the two of us finally sat down to dinner, he talked about how he and Peter were going to renovate the Columbia back lot and turn the studio into a Shangri-La where everyone would want to work. His business plan seemed relatively simple: we've got our own studio now, we'll make movies and it'll be great. As for the matter at hand—my employment—Jon told me that he had never forgotten how I put him on *Caddyshack* back in the late seventies and how excited he was to have our relationship come full circle. He added that it was his idea to bring me in, and he was happy that everything was going to work out.

Shortly after I had verbally accepted the job from Guber (but before my lawyer had ironed out my new contract), Steve Ross called me and asked me to join the Warner Bros. family as a producer. Steve had just lost his top producing team of Guber and Peters and was getting ready to sue them for breaching their contract with Warner Bros. and sue Sony for enticing them to do it. "I'll make whatever deal you want," Ross told me. "Name the numbers. I know this isn't the best way to negotiate, but I'll fly in and we'll work out a deal." He also said that it was a mistake going to work for Guber and Peters because regardless of their promises, they would never live up to them.

I toyed with the idea for a few seconds. A rich producing deal was something a lot of producers would have died for—especially at Warner—but I knew I couldn't do it. Besides the fact that money has never been the guiding factor in my career, I had given my word to Guber and it was too late to go back on it. Furthermore, I really wanted to run a properly financed studio more than I wanted to be a producer working for one. I figured I could always do that, but I might not have the opportunity to run a studio again. I called Steve and told him that I had given my word.

"But their word is not worth anything," Steve reiterated. "You're going into a situation in which you may keep your word but they never will." Steve Ross's words were prophetic.

▦

When I assumed the job of TriStar chairman in March 1990, I was well aware that I had been hired into a contentious culture.

The press was focused on every move at the studio and Sony was immediately on the defensive, but I had confidence in the people with whom I would be working. Most of the heat was felt by Mickey Schulhof, the president of Sony Software and vice chairman of Sony USA, who was based in New York. Alan Levine was named president of Columbia Pictures Entertainment, the parent of Columbia and TriStar, and I considered him a levelheaded businessman who could serve as a buffer to some of the crazy business ideas I was hearing from Guber and Peters. I also counted Alan as a friend. Back in my UA days, Alan and I used to play tennis regularly, and over the years Alan's law partners, Gary Hendler first and later Barry Hirsch, had represented me. Also, Alan had represented Peter Guber since 1972, so if anything came between Peter and me, Alan could be an effective mediator.

Ultimately the fact that a Japanese company owned TriStar was a nonissue. The Japanese owners had little impact on how I ran TriStar. The Sony executives were virtually invisible in the decision-making process, and there were no defined cultural or philosophical boundaries in which we were forced to operate. So here I was, the son of Russian Jews born in China, raised in Chile, sworn in as an American citizen in 1963, making movies for a Japanese-owned company in the United States.

In my years at Sony, the only project on which Japanese cultural concerns played a role was a film about sumo wrestling called *Hell Camp*, and these weren't the concerns of our owner. Milos Forman, the director of *Hell Camp*, had always been a stickler for authenticity, so he traveled to Japan to research the sumo culture. However, when the head of the sumo's top organization disliked the script, Milos's access to the inner world of the sport was cut off. In Japan, sumo wrestling is a sacred ritual, and they weren't about to let a movie company into this church. It was the equivalent of asking the Amish to install electricity in their homes so the cameras could film them at night. When the Sumo Federation turned Milos down, Peter Guber asked the Sony corporate brass in Japan to help. However, they probably saw this as something of a double standard: they had promised not to interfere in our culture, so they thought we shouldn't ask them to interfere in theirs. Guber then hired Henry Kissinger to mediate with the Sumo Federation, but this proved to be harder than opening China. Japanese culture was very conservative, and no one was going to change it over a movie project. When Kissinger failed to reach a détente, we abandoned the project.

By the time Columbia Pictures Entertainment had been renamed Sony Pictures Entertainment in August of 1991 (at Guber's suggestion), the media was no longer interested in the Japanese angle of the story. The new story line in the press was the excess of Peter Guber and the lasting excess of Jon Peters, who had left his job in May 1991 with a reported $20 million severance package before any of the new regime's movies had been released.

Guber and Peters had started out by spending enormous amounts on spec screenplays such as *Radio Flyer* (which became an expensive miss), *Fire Down Below* (made years later at Warner Bros.), *Cold As Ice* (still on ice), and *Spiderman* (now at Columbia with Peters as producer). Guber and Peters felt that they needed to get some high-profile projects immediately to revive the studio and to re-establish its vibrancy. The studio was moribund when they took over because Columbia's owner, Coca-Cola, had been polishing the studio for sale. The recent films had not been particularly dazzling.

One film, *Bloodhounds of Broadway*, was released across the country with an entire reel missing. Amazingly, nobody had noticed.

By the time Guber renamed the studio, the $100-million-plus overhaul of the Culver City studios was well underway and would become—for better and for worse—the enduring symbol of the Guber-Peters regime. The lot had fallen into disrepair and was in need of a good scrubbing. Guber and Peters wanted to turn the lot into the premiere studio lot in the film industry, so they hired Anton Furst, the production designer of *Batman*, to oversee the renovations. They wanted to create a campus for the top creative people in the business. Unquestionably, the lot was restored to a luster that would have made Harry and Jack Cohn hold their breath in awe—and one that made everyone else gasp: we were all working behind period antique desks, walking on teak wood floors, and smelling freshly cut flowers every day.

≡

I expected a lot from myself from the day I started at TriStar. It was the culmination of sixteen years of hard work as a studio executive. I felt that I was a professional and now had all the money and staff that was missing from Orion. I could invest in the type of big-budget, event-driven movies that the marketplace demanded, and I would have enough money to support these films with aggressive marketing campaigns. No longer would things like second-weekend television buys take up a day of meetings, nor would internal fights end in a quick retreat because I was sure I would never win. In short, I could compete with the other major studios on a level playing field. Furthermore, for the first time in my career, I would have a chance to fly solo, to pursue my own distinctive vision of how films should be made, one that wasn't dependent on a show of hands from four partners. It would be the ultimate test of my creative mettle. At no point in my career had I ever felt so liberated or so challenged.

Although contractually I reported to Guber and Peters on "all creative matters" and to Levine on "all operational/business decisions," I was given complete authority over TriStar personnel, as well as its development of all projects. For the most part I would also have control over production decisions. As a practical matter, there was also a greenlighting approval process for other films, in which Guber, Peters, Levine, and I all discussed the pros and cons of films I wanted to put into production. This was something I welcomed because I felt it was important for them to know what I was doing and why I was doing it so there wouldn't be any major surprises. At Orion, I had learned that when the lines of communication were open, things ran more smoothly, and problems were solved in a rational manner. At TriStar I didn't anticipate any roadblocks because I was working with my friend Peter Guber, who had promised me complete autonomy.

My contract also stated that if either Guber or Peters left the company, I would be allowed to make a certain number of pictures per year at certain budget levels at my sole discretion. The number of films would increase with each year I worked at Tri-Star. For example, in the first year it was two films with budget caps of $20 million, and in the fourth year, it was four films with budget caps of $23 million. The idea was to give me even more freedom if management layers were added. Finally, there was a provision that stated that I did not have to release any film I didn't feel comfortable with.

In terms of compensation, my annual base salary was $1 million a year, plus at least a $250,000 annual bonus. Further bonuses were to be awarded at the discretion of the board of directors, as well as slightly more than 6 percent of the profit pool that was allotted to Guber in his contract. The perks ranged from a large interest-free loan that Columbia retired a portion of each year to the building of a screening room at my home (which I was required to repurchase when I left TriStar). While this is a lot of money, remember that Guber and Peters were making more than three times this amount—not counting the premium Sony had paid for their company—and most of the other senior studio executives in the business, such as Sid Sheinberg and Tom Pollack at Universal and Bob Daly and Terry Semel at Warner, received millions in stock options because they worked for public conglomerates. Consider also that the two previous heads of production at Columbia and TriStar, Dawn Steel and Jeff Sagansky respectively, had each earned about $7 million when Sony bought Columbia from Coca-Cola.

This was more money than I had ever been paid, but for me getting rich wasn't really the goal—making good movies was. If I could do that, everything else would take care of itself in due course.

▰

The unusually large development budget at TriStar allowed my staff and me to take chances on unique and ambitious ideas. Perhaps the most intriguing one that didn't come to fruition was the deal I made to bring David Lean out of retirement to make Joseph Conrad's *Nostromo*. Unfortunately, Lean was very ill and he died before the film ever had a chance of getting made.

For the first time in my career, I could compete financially with any studio for any filmmaker, so I set out to establish a first-class family of filmmakers. One of the hottest filmmakers in town was Danny DeVito, so I made a five-year production deal with his production company, Jersey Films, which was run by Michael Shamberg and Stacy Sher. I had previously made a deal with Shamberg at Orion and later suggested Shamberg to Danny's agent, Fred Specktor, as a possible partner for Danny. My personal history aside, this was a deal that any studio would have made: Danny was a one-two-three punch with acting, directing, and producing, and he was at the top of his game. Since we gave him his directing break at Orion with *Throw Momma from the Train*, he had directed (and played a small part in) *The War of the Roses*, a dark, satirical look at marriage starring Michael Douglas and Kathleen Turner, and he was in pre-production on *Hoffa*, with Jack Nicholson playing the legendary Teamster's boss. He had also been cast as the Penguin in *Batman Returns*.

Besides the fact that he could make movies for us, this was also the kind of deal that set the tone for the kind of studio I wanted to run. He was a high-profile, well-liked figure with whom other actors and directors enjoyed working. Building a team of production deals is something like an NFL team's signing free agents in the off season. You need some real stars to be the leaders and the attention-getters so others will follow, and that was my plan for Danny and his company.

I signed several other actor-production deals. As was traditionally the case with most actor deals, we were paying for access to the stars and not necessarily for the projects that we were developing. Partly, I wanted to announce that TriStar was open for business, and, partly, I wanted to make deals with actors I wanted in our films. In the first year, I brought in Denzel Washington (who would star in *Philadelphia*), Dennis Quaid and his partner Kathleen Summers (who brought in the Quaid film *Wilder Napalm*), Richard Gere (who would star in *Mr. Jones*), Robert De Niro (who would produce *Thunderheart*), and Dustin Hoffman (who would star in *Hook*). Later I made a housekeeping deal with Robin Williams (who would also star in *Hook*) and his wife–producing partner Marsha. From that deal came *Jumanji*, which was made after I left.

One of the stranger aspects of my new situation was that TriStar had an existing deal to distribute Carolco's films, which led to *Terminator 2: Judgment Day* being released on my watch.

Carolco continued to be run by Mario Kassar and Andy Vajna, who had been the co-heads of the company when Orion distributed the first *Terminator* movie. (Mario eventually bought Andy out.) Although they had been unhappy with Orion's handling of the first *Terminator* film, this was no time to hold a grudge. They had a huge film on their hands, and we had the money to mount a full-blown marketing campaign. In fact, Carolco virtually put the entire company on the line: the film's budget crested at about $100 million, the highest ever at the time. Jim Cameron took the special effects to a new level, and Arnold was back—as he had promised in the first film—and better than ever.

This time no one was disappointed: *Terminator 2* ended up grossing more than $200 million in the United States and finished 1991 as the highest-grossing film of the year.

While I didn't have control over the making of Carolco's films, I did have some input into the release of their films, because the TriStar marketing department, run by Buffy Shutt and Kathy Jones, reported to me. I planned to give them as much creative leeway as possible because I had a lot of faith in their abilities. Carolco provided TriStar with anywhere from two to four films a year. The basic arrangement was that Carolco would bankroll the production and TriStar would pay 10 percent of the film's budget for domestic theatrical and video. The two companies would then split the marketing costs. In exchange, TriStar received a distribution fee. On occasion, TriStar would also purchase some foreign territories to the Carolco films.

Having Carolco's films helped fill out TriStar's slate, much the way that Chartoff-Winkler did at UA and Hemdale did at Orion. It was my feeling that from a business standpoint film companies are first and foremost distribution outlets, followed closely by library-title holders. As budgets were rising faster than ever before, I liked the idea of having two producers with big appetites for star-driven movies assume most of the risk on a few event movies each year. When I arrived at TriStar, the company was losing money on the deal, but after Carolco delivered *Total Recall, Basic Instinct, Terminator 2,* and *Cliffhanger,* Sony's numbers rocketed into the black. This also meant that I wouldn't be pressured into making risky, tent-pole films because they were willing to make them for me. In the end, TriStar made the most money of all the participants in the Carolco deal.

When Carolco delivered a film like *Total Recall*—which grossed more than $119 million in the United States and a worldwide total of $352 million, making it the number six film of 1990—TriStar reaped a decent reward. But when they delivered a flop like *Air America*, TriStar was mostly protected against deep losses. TriStar earned $56 million in pure profit from *T2*, but we lost about $10 million on *Air America*, the most costly failure Carolco delivered. The deal ultimately put far more pressure on Carolco than it did on TriStar because Carolco was almost always exposed for the big money with no safety net. In the end, TriStar earned more than $150 million in pure profit from the life of the deal, which ran from 1985 to 1996. Just like Orion, through a series of presales and foreign deals, Carolco gave away too much of its upside.

Understandably and unfortunately, Carolco is no longer in business.

More and more throughout the nineties, as studios looked to limit their risk in times of increasing costs, deals like the Carolco-TriStar venture became an important part of the studios' supply lines. Today almost every big-budget studio film has at least one other equity partner besides the primary studio backing it, and in 1999 Universal chairman Edgar Bronfman insisted on having co-financing for every single film. Paramount, too, adopted a similar strategy, which has paved the way for M.B.A.'s to run studios. While these deals take pressure off the studios, they have hurt the quality of films. Instead of trusting the instinct of one person, developed over time, studios make the films that have the best deal, with an eye on the films' marketing potential, based on the marketing department's assessment.

There's an old saying: Nobody ever goes to their local theater to see the latest deal.

They go to be entertained.

■

Hudson Hawk was a disaster in the making from my first day at TriStar.

Shortly after I arrived, I took one look at the film and told Guber that I wanted to back out of it. Guber put me in a tricky spot. He told me that it was my decision, but he emphasized that the studio had already spent $12 million and had made costly pay-or-play commitments with Bruce Willis and producer Joel Silver, meaning that if the plug was pulled we still had to pay them their full fees. This would be taken from TriStar's development budget. The film was a caper comedy co-written by Willis, who also wrote the title song, directed by Michael Lehmann, who had done the small but cult hit *Heathers*. From that little credit crawl alone, you can see three classic problems: (1) the star is the co-writer, (2) the producer is more powerful than the director, and (3) the director had never done a big film.

This was the kind of picture on which a producer like Joel Silver, who has made numerous hit action movies such as *Lethal Weapon*, *Die Hard*, and, most recently, *The Matrix*, gets a job because he has been successful in the past. Joel was the quintessential eighties producer. He wore oversized Hawaiian shirts and he was a wonderful salesman at a time when Hollywood placed a startling premium on salesmanship. He had all the right words and he exuded enthusiasm in spades, both of which he used to his advantage. Everyone wants to talk to someone who they think knows something.

Within the first three weeks of shooting, the film was over budget, so I flew to Rome to see what could be done. As soon as I saw the first dailies, I was certain *Hudson Hawk* would be, to use the popular Hollywood euphemism, "a total fucking disaster." While there was no way to stop the train wreck, I was hoping there was a way to minimize the damage. The performances were uneven. While it is admittedly hard to tell in dailies what is funny and what isn't, everyone in this film seemed to be "acting funny" but no one *was* funny. I sat down with Joel and Bruce Willis to see what could be done about the cost overruns and what I felt was the lack of a coherent story. "Maybe you have a movie in mind but I gotta tell you, I don't see it," I bluntly told them. Neither of them, however, seemed terribly concerned. They thought they were right and I was being an alarmist, or that I simply didn't know what I was looking at. The only thing I could do was whisper to the director that this would be his neck and not theirs if the film failed.

He didn't think that was funny, but what could he have done anyway?

Joel felt that as long as they stuck to the fail-safe formula of using the "whammo chart," the film would be fine. This technique supposedly came from Joel's former partner, Larry Gordon, who supposedly got it from an Egyptian who worked for the low-budget king Sam Arkoff at AIP. Basically, it involves having an action sequence every ten to twelve minutes to wake the audience up. The technique worked particularly well in the late eighties when audiences' attention spans shrunk, and Joel had used it successfully on films like *Predator, Die Hard,* and *Lethal Weapon.* Regardless, I don't think anything could have saved *Hudson Hawk.* It was labeled a disaster the minute it hit theaters.

The evening after my story conference with Joel and Bruce, I had a wonderful Italian dinner with Joel at the Piazza Navona, the kind that makes you happy to be alive and fortunate enough to be able to enjoy. Afterward, we were walking on the Via Condotti and I turned to Joel and asked him, "Joel, what do you want out of life? What makes you happy?" And he stopped walking, looked around at the splendor, and said, "You know what I want? I want . . ." His voice trailed off and he paused for fifteen seconds before finishing the sentence. ". . . Everything." I thought to myself, *Of course, why did I even ask? I was right in the center of Hollywood-a-go-go.*

13 _Captain Hook and Bugsy Siegel Take Over My Life_

In the early nineties, having access to big money to make event movies was more essential to the moviemaking process than ever before. American and foreign audiences alike demanded more thrills per minute. Filmmaking was reaching new highs in terms of technology and budgets—and new lows in terms of storytelling.

The primary audience had become teenagers and young adults who had been raised on television and schooled by MTV. They liked their stories simple and action-packed. Sequels were still the order of the day, but now they were viable only if they transmogrified into that hydra-headed revenue source: the franchise. While James Bond had started it all, the Indiana Jones series was a huge moneymaker for Paramount, and Batman minted money for Warner Bros. with all of its merchandising tie-ins.

With the arrival of Total Recall _in 1990, each event film upped the ante on the quality of special effects. It was not enough to have high-wire stunts and lots of explosions. The laws of physics had to be abrogated and new worlds brought into existence._

If you could bring about all of these feats, you had an event movie—and if you could get Steven Spielberg to direct it, then you really had something.

When a new studio head takes over, he or she typically has a reflexive response to dump all the scripts in development and begin anew because they all have the smell of someone else's aftershave. Before I even moved into my office at TriStar, I began sifting through TriStar's moldy development inventory, reading scripts, books, and treatments to see if there was anything there that was makable. There were a few, and one of the best was an action-adventure script titled "Captain Hook."

I had always loved the idea of doing a movie based on Peter Pan. There is something irresistible about creating a fantasy world for characters that you have known since your earliest memories. When I was an agent in the early seventies, I was asked to put together a version of Peter Pan with Michelangelo Antonioni (who had just finished *Zabriskie Point*) directing Mia Farrow as Peter Pan. Since I was the only one at my agency who knew Antonioni, Mia thought that I should make the introductions. On the designated evening, I picked up Mia, who, at the time, was a flower child, and we drove over to the Beverly Wilshire hotel to meet with Antonioni. When we walked into his room, Mia raced over to him and fell to her knees. "Maestro," she pleaded, "I would really like you to direct me as Peter Pan." Antonioni had a nervous tick in his neck that made his head bounce back and forth. As his head bobbed uneasily, he got a deadly serious look on his face and said to Mia, "My dear Mia, Peter Pan was a boy."

The idea died right there.

As I read "Captain Hook," which was written by Jim Hart and Nick Castle, I felt that the times were right for a modern-day retelling of the Peter Pan story. The late eighties had been a materialistic time that resulted in much soul searching about what was truly important to our country. We needed to simplify our lives and to return to our moral and ethical roots. In this version, Peter Pan rejected who he had become—a modern day Wall Street yuppie with all its sour connotations—confronted his old nemesis Captain Hook, and recaptured his childlike spirit. The trick was how to do this and make it entertaining without seeming like a heavy-handed morality play.

By page 30, I was convinced that Dustin Hoffman should play Captain Hook. This would set the tone of making a serious version of a fairy tale. So as one of my first official acts as TriStar chairman, I sent the script to Dustin with an enthusiastic note. A few days later, Dustin's agent called me and turned down the project. "There is too much violence in this movie," he said, adding flatly: "Dustin isn't interested." Before I could get into a protracted dialogue, the agent had jumped onto another call.

I decided not to give up that easily. I have a dictum about getting talent for a movie that I try to follow if I believe in something strongly and it is at all possible: *Go directly to the source.* So I flew to New York and had breakfast with Dustin. I told him I had a terrific project for him; it was the Peter Pan story with him as Captain Hook. I conveniently left out the part about his representative passing on the project. He sounded genuinely intrigued and asked me to send him the script, which I did.

Three days later, I was back in L.A. driving through the San Fernando Valley returning from lunch. My car phone rang; my assistant had Dustin on the line.

"You're absolutely right; this is terrific," Dustin said. "Let's do it." He paused. "Who should we get to direct?"

"I'd like Spielberg to do it," I said. "He's perfect. The movie is about somebody recapturing his childhood. Who can do it better than Steven?" Spielberg had told *Time* in 1985: "I have always felt like Peter Pan. I still feel like him. It has been very hard for me to grow up."

"If you can get him, fantastic," Dustin said. "I doubt that you will, he was supposed to do *Rain Man* and he pulled out."

Operating on the philosophy that there are no rules in the movie business, or rather that you make up the rules as you go along, I set about getting Spielberg to direct "Captain Hook." I sent him the script and started to dream of the possibilities.

By 1990 Spielberg was the filmmaker every studio executive in Hollywood most wanted to work with. The eighties had been his decade. More than anyone in the entertainment industry, Spielberg possessed a preternatural sense of the stories and themes that moviegoers around the world wanted to see. He directed and produced the kinds of films that brought everyone to the theater again and again. His run in the eighties started in 1981 with *Raiders of the Lost Ark*, which spawned two hit sequels that he also directed. He shattered all box-office records in 1982 with *E.T.: The Extra-Terrestrial*, which brought in nearly $400 million in the United States alone and was, until *Titanic*, the highest-grossing film of all time. He had also made *The Color Purple*, which collected eleven Academy Award nominations. He had two commercial missteps, the underrated *Empire of the Sun* and *Always*, but five for seven isn't bad. On top of his directorial efforts, through his production company, Amblin Entertainment, Steven had overseen *Gremlins*, *Poltergeist*, *Back to the Future* (and its two sequels), *The Goonies*, and *Who Framed Roger Rabbit*, all of which were megahits or hits.

While getting Spielberg was like a baseball team's signing Babe Ruth, it was a delicate proposition because he had made almost all of his films for Universal. His production company, Amblin, had been based there since it was formed in the early seventies. Steve Ross had managed to use his considerable powers of persuasion to bring Spielberg to Warner Bros. for two films. For me, there was also a little bit of history to overcome since I had abandoned Spielberg as a client in the seventies when he refused to take my advice and break his contract with Universal. On the long list of filmmakers I had worked with in my career, the most glaring omission was Steven Spielberg. The closest I had come was at Orion, when I tried to convince my partners to do *Raiders of the Lost Ark*. Unfortunately, the deal was too risky for a small company like Orion. At TriStar, I had the money. Because Spielberg could make whatever movie he wanted wherever he wanted, I felt that the best way to woo him was the soft sell.

While I believed that I had the perfect material with "Captain Hook," my real ace was Dustin Hoffman, with whom Spielberg had planned to work on *Rain Man*. Spielberg had dropped out of the film five months into pre-production to turn his attention to *Indiana Jones and the Last Crusade*. I figured if he had any regrets about the films he didn't make, that had to be one of them. He had once said that he had a "stomachache" because he hadn't worked with Dustin Hoffman. I also figured that Dustin was the type of actor that Spielberg would be drawn to at that stage of his career: Dustin had just won his second Oscar for *Rain Man*, while Steven had missed out on an award for *The Color Purple*. Realistically, these were probably very small points, but when you are putting together a movie, you look for any ray of hope you can find.

A few days after I sent the script to Spielberg, he called and told me he thought it was excellent. I reiterated that I had Dustin Hoffman as Captain Hook and told him that Robin Williams could and probably would play Peter Pan. With his limitless kinetic energy and eternal youthfulness, Robin was ideal to play Peter Pan. Although he had not yet committed, I was willing to risk that he, too, would see that he was born to play the role. I also figured I could get Robin because I knew that Dustin and Robin wanted to work together, and I was fairly certain that Robin would play the role if Spielberg was directing. Who wouldn't? Steven said that he would have Kathleen Kennedy, his producer, read it and get back to me in four or five days.

This was my chance. Landing a Spielberg movie would set the tone for my entire slate at TriStar, and I knew I was close. Peter Pan might be his mythical alter ego, but this wasn't going to be enough. My next call was to Dustin. "Here's your chance, Dustin," I told him. "Call Steven and tell him you're delighted he's doing the movie."

Dustin was skeptical about Spielberg committing. He repeated that Spielberg had signed to direct *Rain Man* and then backed out at the last minute. "He's going to do it to me all over again," Dustin moaned.

"I'm telling you, Dustin, he's going to do this movie," I interrupted. "Call him."

After Dustin and Steven spent some time together walking on the beach and talking about how they saw the film, Spielberg committed to direct. His team at Amblin—Kathy Kennedy, Frank Marshall, and Gerald Molen—signed on to produce the film. By this time, I had called Robin Williams and brought him up to speed on his next movie. As expected, the prospect of working with Spielberg and Hoffman brought Robin aboard. The all-star cast was complete when Julia Roberts, coming off the success of *Pretty Woman* and *Sleeping with the Enemy*, was cast as Tinkerbell.

I felt this was the kind of film that could appeal to kids and adults alike. While Peter Pan was primarily a youth story, our film version would be a retelling of the fable with a modern twist. To entice the teenagers, we would have Robin Williams as Peter Pan flying through the air and a seven-inch Julia Roberts as Tinkerbell. These production values, as well as Dustin Hoffman playing a dead-on Captain Hook, were what hip was all about.

In my mind, *Hook* would be *the* event movie of 1991.

▬

As I saw it, my job on a star-heavy film like *Hook* was to limit the studio's risk as best as possible while still giving the director the resources to make the film. I don't tell filmmakers how to make their films, least of all Steven Spielberg. I knew that the sets and the special effects would be costly. Star prices were already starting to climb rapidly, so the talent deals would be even more costly. Even though the film could easily earn the gross national product of a small country, there was no sense spending money so flagrantly that Sony would never see a profit.

To establish a reasonable budget, we structured a deal that made Robin, Dustin, and Steven our partners in the film. Since all three were high-profile CAA clients, the deal was struck with Michael Ovitz. Their gross deals totaled 40 percent of the first-dollar money that TriStar would receive from box-office receipts, but paying them their full fees up front would have been prohibitive. This exceeded what was believed to be the largest previous back-end deal, the 35 percent given to Arnold Schwarzenegger and Danny DeVito by Universal for *Twins*. The first budget drawn up for *Hook* was an unrealistic $25 million. It then increased to $35 million. By the time we started building sets, the budget was revised upward to $52.5 million, which turned out to be unreasonably low given the scope of the film and the time restraints.

There were two other deals that had to be made before the film could go forward. Since Nick Castle had been signed to direct the film before I came to TriStar, an arrangement had to be made to accommodate him. Of course, I had set the chain of events in motion by sending the script to Spielberg; I wanted to be fair to Castle and so did Steven, who rightly did not want to be responsible for putting Castle out of a directing job. We agreed to assume the responsibility and pay Castle his full fee (roughly $850,000), give him another project of his choosing, and allow him to share story credit with Jim Hart. (Hart also ended up with shared screenplay credit with Malia Scotch Marmo, who was brought on by Dustin Hoffman to rewrite much of his dialogue.) Arrangements also had to be made with Jerry Weintraub and Dodi Fayed, who had acquired certain rights to the Peter Pan story when it fell into the public domain, and with the Children's Hospital in London, which controlled the rights held by the J. M. Barrie estate.

A carefree, charming, and warm guy, Dodi was the son of Mohamed Al Fayed, a billionaire best known as the owner of Harrods department store and the Ritz hotel in Paris. Dodi had a reputation as a playboy who lived the high life, and he loved the allure of Hollywood. At Orion he had worked on the film *F/X*, but he could be a bit erratic and a bit lazy at times. One time when a group of us planned a trip to Egypt, Dodi volunteered to fly us over on his private jet. We were surprised, but we happily accepted. On the morning of our departure, Dodi called and told us the plane was running late. A few hours later he called again; the plane had landed in L.A. but it was being repaired. Finally, as darkness was beginning to set in, someone called the airport, and it turned out there was no plane. Instead of waiting for Dodi to call again, we all headed to the airport and flew commercial.

On *Hook*, Dodi was very accommodating. In exchange for his rights, Dodi agreed to take an executive producer credit on the film and a production deal at TriStar so he could develop some other projects to produce. (He and Weintraub also received $1.7 million.) His father would occasionally speak to me about watching over Dodi. Each time I would explain to him that I didn't have time to follow Dodi around and motivate him; I had a studio to run. My advice was always to let Dodi stand on his own two feet, which, in my opinion, he was quite capable of doing without the push and pull of his powerful father.

After the Castle and Fayed issues were settled, I began to focus on the film's budget, which continued to climb from the

$52.5 million figure we had set. At this point the main issue I faced was that we were operating on a crash schedule. Filming needed to begin by March of 1991 at the latest in order to have the picture in theaters by Christmas. While many movies go over budget because of problems that occur during shooting, shortening the pre-production schedule on a big film while the script is being rewritten is a sure way to increase costs. Before the cameras rolled, the budget was revised upward to $60 million, still a reasonable number for this type of high-profile event film at that time.

The biggest challenge in terms of the production was the building of the sets. John Napier, who was responsible for the Broadway sets of *Cats*, *Les Misérables*, and *Starlight Express*, was hired to supervise the construction on Neverland. *Hook* needed a treehouse the size of a New York loft for the Lost Boys house, an entire pirate town, and a separate area to shoot Tinkerbell flying against a blue screen. (The blue screen unit alone had thirty-eight crew members.) But the wonder of production design to behold was the eighty-foot version of the Jolly Roger and the lagoons and docks surrounding it. The elaborate black-and-gold pirate ship was built on Soundstage 27, where Oz was constructed for Dorothy to walk through in 1939 when the studio was home to MGM. When the ship was finished, it became something of a tourist attraction for celebrities; everyone wanted to step into the world of Peter Pan. My feeling was, why not show it? Warren Beatty, Barbra Streisand, Michael Jackson, David Hockney, and Queen Noor of Jordan all came to the lot for a tour of Neverland. The studio even held its 1991 Christmas party on the *Hook* set.

▬

"AQABA! AQABA!" cried Peter Guber at the top of his lungs. It was the middle of the Christmas Party and he was standing on the bow of the Jolly Roger, using the battle cry from *Lawrence of Arabia* to fire up the staff. Few people understood what he was talking about, but it was clear to all that Peter Guber couldn't have been happier about *Hook*, the type of film he could dine out on from Beverly Hills to Tokyo.

One Saturday morning, Guber hosted a brunch on the Jolly Roger for Sony chairman Akio Morita and invited Steven Spielberg, Dustin Hoffman, Robin Williams, and Julia Roberts—but not me. I didn't have a clue why he excluded me. Once filming reached the midway point and the budget began to snowball, Guber began complaining behind my back about the film's cost, and this began to strain my relationship with him. I was beginning to discover that Peter wasn't the type of person I could have a reasonable conversation with because he avoided any type of conflict.

He knew that there was very little I could do about the budget. Both Steven and Kathy Kennedy were apologetic about the costs, and I tried to be understanding, but it seemed nothing could be done to contain them, especially since the scope of the film kept growing. When it became clear that it would be tough for us to make any money on the film, with the escalating budget and the talent's gross-profit deals, we went back to the talent and renegotiated their contracts. They would now receive 40 percent of the first $50 million (or $20 million) that TriStar collected, TriStar would receive the next $70 million, and they would receive 40 percent thereafter.

By the time the film was finished, it ended up costing $84 million.

While I never believed the movie should be made at any price, it was clear to everyone that this was a flagship movie for the studio. If it worked, it would be a franchise that could have sequels, spin-offs, and even a Saturday-morning cartoon series. During production, we were so confident in the film's potential that we turned down an offer from Universal to buy the sets and use them in a ride on the Universal Studios Tour as a promotional tie-in. We all felt that *Hook* was a valuable asset to the company, and we didn't want to give any part of it away. Sony wanted the film to demonstrate how synergy would work within the company.

Personally, I was in turmoil over the escalating budget, but there was no one I could share my thoughts with. I didn't want to be tagged a spendthrift by the media or the Sony management, but I could hardly plead with the filmmakers to help save my neck. This was one of those situations where the studio head stood to be the biggest loser of them all because if the film didn't work, someone was going to suffer the consequences. It wasn't going to be Peter; it wasn't going to be Steven Spielberg; it *was* going to be me.

I was taking steps to make sure there was added value. During this time, I also made a deal with Spielberg to develop *The Mask of Zorro* at TriStar, which gave Sony one Spielberg film in production and another on the drawing board. Originally, Spielberg was going to direct *Zorro*—though it turned out that he only produced it. Sony ended up making a lot of money on *Zorro*.

I was laying the groundwork to break Steven away from Universal and bring him to Sony to direct and produce films. The first step was to give him an office on the lot to make him feel that he was welcome there when he was not in production. I invited Kathy Kennedy over one day, and we looked at potential spaces for an Amblin outpost at Sony. Ultimately, Guber refused to give Spielberg an office because Spielberg wouldn't commit to making films at Sony.

I believe that Guber's rebuff of my efforts to bring in Spielberg ranks among his biggest mistakes at Sony. I sat down with Guber and tried to convince him it was about the relationship, not the real estate. We were wasting money in many other pursuits with no visible payoff, yet the payoff from this could be huge. Never mind that Guber's wife had a production deal and an office on the lot and so did Jon Peters's ex-wife, and no one realistically expected them to produce any movies. What was one more free office? We were talking about the most successful commercial filmmaker in the history of the movie business.

I became so frustrated that at one point I asked Guber if he wanted to be Steve Ross, the visionary leader of the entire company, or the head of the studio who makes the day-to-day decisions I was supposed to be making. Ross didn't have a formal deal with Spielberg, but he constantly wined and dined him in hopes of future business. Because Ross formed a very tight relationship with Spielberg, Warner Bros. ended up being second in line for projects from Spielberg's company. This led to them securing Spielberg for *The Color Purple,* as well as the Amblin productions

The Goonies, Gremlins, and *Innerspace*. What I found out in time was that Peter Guber didn't want to be head of production because that meant taking the blame, and he wasn't capable of being a visionary like Steve Ross. What he wanted to be, I later found out, was a producer.

Interestingly, the producer rarely gets blamed for a failure. Only the star, the director, and the studio head do.

▬

Hook opened on December 11, 1991—the same day that Orion filed for bankruptcy protection—and it went on to gross $119 million in the United States and $180 million overseas. But because so much was expected of a Steven Spielberg film, the media continually portrayed *Hook* as a failure, which it wasn't. While *Hook* appealed to a wide range of moviegoers, the film was released in a tough marketplace. Receipts were already off more than 4 percent from the previous year and 6 percent from 1989— despite the fact that ticket prices had increased. The summer box office had fallen off 25 percent from 1990, finishing at its lowest level since 1971. There was also tough competition from *Beauty and the Beast,* Disney's animated film, which played to adults and children like a modern-day fable, exactly what we wanted to do with *Hook*.

Beauty and the Beast came out strong with a premiere at the newly refurbished El Capitan in Hollywood, and the film seemed to cut across demographic and even cultural barriers. Women found the lead character Belle something of a nineties feminist, and *New York Times* theater critic Frank Rich went so far as to proclaim the film's score the best Broadway musical of the year—even though the story hadn't gone to Broadway (yet). The film ended up being a double threat: it grossed more than $145 million domestically, and it became the first animated film ever to be nominated for Best Picture. But while the positive glow around *Beauty and the Beast* detracted from *Hook,* the fact remains that *Hook* was a misunderstood hit.

Every time *Hook* comes up in a conversation, I get defensive. When all revenues were counted, including the $10 million received from the sale of the television rights, and all the gross profits were paid out to Dustin, Robin, and Steven, the picture ended up with a profit of more than $50 million, and it's still making money because of its perennial value in video, and TV. Because the budget climbed, we changed the talents' deals and put a "hiatus" on the gross participants, which allowed the film to be very profitable. There's always someone else who then counters that it didn't measure up to its potential (that is, as a Spielberg film). While that may be true, when someone hands a company a check for $50 million, the response should be "Thank you" and not "Where's the rest?"

Hook might not have been *E.T.* or *Jurassic Park*, but it wasn't *1941* or *Always* either.

In retrospect, there are things that could have been done differently: If we had more time for pre-production and editing, we could have brought the budget under control. Guber believed that we needed another, younger name on the marquee so Julia Roberts was cast as Tinkerbell, but things didn't go well for her. Shortly after filming began, she ended up in the hospital with a severe fever. She then called off her wedding and took a short vacation in Ireland. When she returned to film her part, she spent most of her time suspended in a harness against the blue screen reading her lines. Even Steven has said publicly that their collaboration was not a pleasurable one.

The making of *Hook* offers an ideal glimpse into the studio head's ultimate dilemma: *What do you do when a film is way over budget and your hands are completely tied?* When the director is the most successful filmmaker in the history of the movie business—as well as a former client and friend—and the cast is filled with Hollywood's highest-paid actors? When the sets are so fantastic that they have actually become a private tour attraction for some of the world's luminaries. *What do you do?*

You put your fate in the hands of the gods.

Besides, *Hook* wasn't the only star-driven film I was working on at the time.

In late 1990, Jeffrey Katzenberg, who was then chairman of the Walt Disney Studios, wrote a widely circulated, twenty-eight-page memo about the state of the movie business, much of which focused on Disney's experience working with Warren Beatty on Dick Tracy. Katzenberg concluded that Disney had spent too much time, effort, and money on Dick Tracy to justify the results, and he placed the blame directly on the demands of Beatty, the film's director, producer, and star. In the end, Disney had spent $47 million to make Dick Tracy—and a shocking $54 million to market the film— and ended up with a domestic box-office gross of just over $100 million.

The memo quickly became part of Hollywood executive lore. Katzenberg wrote it while he was on vacation in Hawaii during the 1990 Christmas holidays. Apparently, it started to rain and Katzenberg was starved for activities, so he began writing a mission statement on how to return Disney to the profitability it had enjoyed in the mideighties with their flimsy comedies. In fact, the memo closely resembled one written by Michael Eisner when Eisner was Katzenberg's boss at Paramount. Eisner employed basketball terminology while Katzenberg settled for baseball metaphors. Eisner bemoaned Paramount's making of the Beatty film Reds, while Katzenberg focused on the Beatty film Dick Tracy.

Katzenberg's basic theory (as was Eisner's before) was that making and marketing blockbusters is a dangerous business and that the best way to succeed is to go for singles and doubles at the box office and let the home runs come as a bonus. In retrospect, there was a lot that was right in that memo. Studios need tent-pole movies—movies that make enough money to support the other films—to take chances on smaller films. But at the same time, studios need to make sure they have midlevel successes to sustain them so that they are not trying to hit a home run every time. Those films are generally lower-budgeted genre films aimed at a specific audience demographic such as teenagers, young men, couples, or even families.

As for Warren Beatty, Katzenberg concluded that if the filmmaker showed up with another $40 million film, Disney should "soberly conclude that it's not a project we should choose to get involved in." In fact, Beatty had been developing such a project for eight years, and I made it at TriStar.

I hadn't read the memo.

Life according to Warren Beatty is different from life according to anyone else in the movie business. Somehow, he is able to make his own rules and then persuade others to follow them. He is alternately difficult and charming, demanding for his cause yet sympathetic toward yours, and he never gives less than his entire being to the project. He got me initiated into his working ways by stopping by my house on a Sunday afternoon to give me a lecture that was part cautionary tale, part pep talk.

"Look at you," he said to me at one of our first meetings after I greenlighted *Bugsy.* "You've got to get in shape and you've got to start dressing better." He motioned up and down his body, which was swathed in a black suit with an elegant, thin cashmere sweater under it and finished off with a pair of suede lace-ups. "I'm going to take up a lot of your time, and I'm going to push you on this film harder than you have ever been pushed." He made good on his word; he was all over me from the first day of preproduction to the day the film left the theaters. Given that Warren had acted in only three films since 1978 (*Reds, Ishtar,* and *Dick Tracy*), he was certainly well rested enough to work me and my marketing staff over.

I got to know Warren during the Gary Hart campaign, and for all Warren's apparent eccentricities, I gained an immense amount of respect for him. He carved out a place in the movie business that is completely unique. While he never enjoyed the commercial success of Robert Redford, won the acting Oscars like Dustin Hoffman and Robert De Niro, or became a cult figure like Jack Nicholson, Warren has managed to keep himself at the top of the Hollywood pecking order for thirty years. His career and his life are as interesting and as varied as any leading man's in Hollywood.

The brother of Shirley MacLaine, Warren became an instant star after his first film, *Splendor in the Grass,* which co-starred Natalie Wood and was directed by Elia Kazan. He proved himself a skillful producer and a charismatic leading man on *Bonnie and Clyde,* and he won an Oscar for Best Director with *Reds.* For a short time, he even hired the venerable *New Yorker* film critic Pauline Kael to develop scripts for him. Politically, he was always very devoted to liberal causes, and he put aside large parts of his career to work on them. Professionally, he was Teflon, shaking off the disaster *Ishtar* and never dropping off the A-list. Along the way, he became legendary for seducing all of his leading ladies, from Natalie Wood to Julie Christie to Diane Keaton to Madonna. As an agent, I had dealings with Warren on *Shampoo* because I represented the director, Hal Ashby, and on *The Fortune* because I represented the writer, Carole Eastman. At UA and Orion, I had always been interested in making a film with him, but his long gestation period between films and our lack of resources had prevented it from happening. From the first time I read *Bugsy*, I realized that a gangster biopicture was risky, but I felt that it was the ideal material for him, and it was a film that I wanted to make.

Bugsy was the story of Benjamin "Bugsy" Siegel, the 1940s gangster who built the Flamingo Hotel in Las Vegas and was responsible for setting the town on its way to becoming the gambling mecca of the world. The film was loosely based on the novel *We Only Kill Each Other: The Life and Bad Times of Bugsy Siegel*, by Dean Jennings. James Toback, a self-professed wildman writer who was a friend of Warren's and a former client of mine, worked with Warren on the script for a number of years. As with most projects, Warren seemed to toy interminably with the material until the light fantastic hit him. In this case, it hit him when Barry Levinson agreed to direct.

Warren had a choice of doing *Bugsy* for Columbia, which was being run by Frank Price, or for TriStar. After I prevailed upon Warren to do the film with me, I let Columbia have *A Few Good Men*, a project that was in the works when I arrived at TriStar. *A Few Good Men* was a military courtroom drama based on the Broadway play by Aaron Sorkin, and it had been optioned and set up at TriStar by veteran producer David Brown. When I heard that Rob Reiner was interested in directing the film version, I went to New York and saw the play. I agreed to proceed with Reiner directing, provided that it be made at TriStar, even though Reiner's production company, Castle Rock Entertainment, had a deal with Columbia.

Frank Price really wanted *Bugsy*. He was under a lot of pressure at the time, and there were rumors swirling that he was going to be let go. I didn't like the way Frank was being treated, so after it was clear that Warren was going to do *Bugsy* for me, I told Guber that Frank could have *A Few Good Men*. It seemed like a natural fit and an amicable—and dare I say charitable—way of doing things. Besides, with *Bugsy* and *Hook* going, I had the momentum and Frank didn't. After all, Columbia and TriStar were corporate teammates; we were supposed to compete against Warner Bros., Universal, Paramount, and Fox, not against each other.

Little did I know that Frank Price's tenure was doomed anyway, that Mark Canton would replace him and take credit for *A Few Good Men* when it became a $100 million hit and received a Best Picture nomination, and that I would need every last chit to keep my job.

▦

Bugsy changed Warren's life and, in the end, it probably changed mine a little bit, too, though not as dramatically. During the casting of the film, Barry and Warren met with several actresses, including Michelle Pfeiffer, to play the part of his moll, Virginia Hill, but the one who caught Warren's eye (and never let it go) was Annette Bening, who was best known for her role in *The Grifters*, which had earned her an Academy Award nomination. Warren might have been a career bachelor who had a reputation for having relationships with his leading ladies, but this situation quickly proved to be different. He fell in love with Annette. One day, he called and asked me what I thought of her for the part. "Are you kidding, she's great," I told him. "As a matter of fact, that's the girl you should marry."

The fascinating thing about Warren is that he has a way of prying information out of you and not reciprocating. He usually starts the conversation with "What's new?" and then you find yourself telling him the most intimate secrets about your life; when you walk away, you realize that he hasn't told you anything about his. Initially, Warren was predictably coy about his relationship with Annette, but we were on to him long before he knew. Reports came back from the set that the two were having an affair. Good for him, I thought, at least I was right about something.

As an actor producing a movie he was starring in, Warren had an interesting way of mixing the business of producing with the artistry of acting. He was intimately involved in all the producing decisions before the film began. He helped cast the film, hire the production crew, choose the locations, and work out budgetary issues. He even personally hired the caterer. However, the day shooting began, he turned into an actor, concentrated on playing his part, and let Levinson's partner, Mark Johnson, handle all the producing details. Then, the day the film wrapped, he became the producer again, putting daily and sometimes even hourly pressure on the studio to do right by his film.

As we were structuring the marketing campaign, Warren called me constantly over the smallest things. If a story about holiday movies appeared in the trades or the *Los Angeles Times* and *Bugsy* was not prominently displayed as an important entry, Warren would call me and read me the riot act. Once during a meeting at my house with my marketing team, Warren called and asked me if I had read an article in *Weekly Variety* that mentioned *Bugsy* several times. When I told him I hadn't had a chance yet, he shot back: "How can you be in the business? You are lazy." There were also positive aspects to this. Marketing was an area that I hadn't been intimately involved in at Orion so I did have a lot to learn. Warren's attention to detail and care for his work was an example all filmmakers should follow . . . perhaps with less crankiness.

The marketing campaign on *Bugsy* was difficult. There were three distinct and opinionated voices on every decision: the studio; Warren, and Barry and Mark Johnson. Warren obsessed over every detail. He spent hours trying to figure out which quotes from the reviews to use and in which order they should be listed. Every photograph, every still, and every trailer had to be perfect, or Warren would order it redone—no matter the cost. In terms of fastidiousness, Barry was no slouch either. He pushed for the trailer and TV spots to be edited and re-edited until they conveyed just the right mood. Even when everyone was in sync, the dialogue still took a long time to complete.

Selling the movie to the public was an uphill battle. Warren at the time wasn't the kind of star like Harrison Ford or Mel Gibson who could automatically open a movie to successful numbers at the box office just on the strength of their names. His films had to be sold with a clearly focused marketing strategy. Furthermore, *Bugsy* was an old-time gangster picture at a time when that genre was out of favor. Robert Benton's *Billy Bathgate*, for example, which starred Dustin Hoffman, had been a costly failure for Disney. Personally, I felt that *Bugsy* was more reminiscent of *The Great Gatsby* than *Bonnie and Clyde*. In the same way that Gatsby believed indelibly in the green light, Bugsy Siegel was portrayed more as a dreamer than he was a criminal or a lover. And just like Gatsby will never be able to have Daisy, Bugsy fears the same about Virginia, which is why he accuses her of two-timing him.

We decided that positioning the film more as a romance than as a gangster film would keep us away from that ghetto, hence the tagline GLAMOUR WAS THE DISGUISE. After I saw the picture, I was certain that the reviews would be good. Though my staff wasn't entirely convinced, I knew we had to run a review-based campaign, one that built from the critical acclaim. If we got the critics, we would be in the race for the year-end awards, which would also help position the film as one to be taken seriously commercially.

Sure enough, *Bugsy* did open to glowing reviews. The Los Angeles Film Critics association awarded it Best Picture, Best Director, and Best Screenplay, and the National Board of Review, a critics organization, voted Warren Best Actor. The film was also nominated for the Golden Globe for Best Picture (Drama). Nevertheless, the picture opened fairly lukewarm over the crucial first weekend. For whatever reason, despite all the good reviews, people didn't want to see the film in large numbers. Maybe we could never convince people that it was a Gatsbyesque tale that transcended its genre.

The persistent pressure that Warren exerted on studios' marketing departments was well documented, and *Bugsy* would be no exception. It started in 1967 on *Bonnie and Clyde*, which he made for Warner Bros. The film opened to fantastic reviews and mediocre business, and it closed after an unspectacular theatrical run. But when *Time* magazine put the film on its cover and hailed it as a watershed event in cinema, Warren saw this as a tremendous opportunity and acted on it. Using his considerable powers of persuasion, he pressured Warner Bros. to rerelease the film based on the continuing critical mass, which was unheard of in the sixties. Warner caved in and the film reopened on the day it received ten Oscar nominations. This was the origin of Warren's clout as a producer, which he continues to wield on his movies to this day.

One week after *Bugsy* opened, I left town for a holiday cruise with some friends on the Nile River. When the film continued to do poorly in its second weekend, Warren began calling Guber two, three, even five times a day to complain that the film wasn't doing well and I wasn't around to work on the situation. It reached the point where Warren even called an emergency marketing meeting at his house on Christmas morning. Buffy Shutt, Kathy Jones, and Ed Russell all gathered to go over the new images Warren wanted to use on the poster, but that didn't help the box office either. A slow burn began in Guber that lasted for the rest of the time I ran TriStar. Though Guber never confronted me over the issue, he undoubtedly felt that I should have been fielding the complaints from Warren, not him. After all, he was vacationing in Aspen.

I heard every complaint in the book: Jim Toback, the screenwriter, was telling people the film was booked into B theaters because *Hook* was playing in all the A theaters, which was as ridiculous as it was untrue. I'm not sure what else I could have done for *Bugsy,* short of standing on the street corner in Westwood and begging people to see the film, or dragging them up to the box-office window with a gun to their head and making them buy a ticket. But that wasn't good enough for Warren. Barry and Warren had delivered a very good movie, but we all knew it would be a tough sell. The ad campaign, which Warren had been involved with right down to the font size of the letters on the poster, was in place when the movie opened. TriStar spent around $25 million in the weeks surrounding the film's opening, which was above the norm. As it turned out, our checkbook was anything but closed at that point.

In late January, *Bugsy* won the Golden Globe for Best Picture in the drama category, beating out *The Silence of the Lambs.*

While the Golden Globes are given by a rag-tag bunch of foreign journalists living in L.A., the winner of the Best Drama award had gone on to win the Academy Award for Best Picture the previous eight years running. Shortly after the Globes win, the film received ten Academy Award nominations, including Best Picture, Best Director, Best Actor for Warren, and Best Supporting Actor for both Ben Kingsley and Harvey Keitel. *Bugsy* was now the frontrunner for the Oscar.

Because of this—and to satisfy ourselves that we had done everything possible—we began pouring more money into the film's advertising campaign. By the time the Oscars rolled around, we had spent an additional $25 million in marketing on *Bugsy*, very little, if any, of which boosted box-office receipts. It only served to keep the film in theaters longer. Whatever bump it received helped Warren and the filmmakers because they were getting a piece of the gross receipts from the first dollar taken in by the studio.

Katzenberg's memo, which I had read by this time, seemed to be coming to life. To quote him: "The number of hours [*Dick Tracy*] required, the amount of anxiety it generated, and the amount of dollars that needed to be expended were disproportionate to the amount of success achieved."

I now had more to lose than anyone on *Bugsy*.

On Oscar night, my allegiances were torn. Two pictures that I had been deeply involved in were competing against one another for Best Picture. I was sitting with the *Bugsy* contingent of Sony executives. The film had been such a fight, and winning the Academy Award might have vindicated me in some way in both Peter Guber's and Warren's eyes. But it was a big-studio film with a lot of the money in the world behind it. *The Silence of the Lambs*, on the other hand, was something that very few people believed could be made into a quality film at the book stage. Not only had Jonathan Demme done a terrific job, but Orion had released the film at a time when the company was in dire straits.

The underdog in me wanted to celebrate the Orion way one more time.

There was no certainty either picture would win, as the other three Best Picture nominees, *The Prince of Tides*, *JFK*, and *Beauty and the Beast,* were highly competitive. Early in the evening, *Bugsy* collected the awards for Best Costume Design and Best Art Direction, but once *Silence* won for Best Actor and Actress, I knew it would win the ultimate prize. The crowning irony came when I was thanked by Jonathan Demme when he won the Best Director award for *The Silence of the Lambs.* I had been widely criticized by Warren for not doing the job on behalf of *Bugsy,* and the director of the picture that beat *Bugsy* was thanking me in front of a billion people. I sat there thinking back to the days when some people in Hollywood thought I was crazy pushing for Demme to direct *The Silence of the Lambs.*

I've always tried to live in the moment, letting the highs elate me and the lows wash over me, while continually trying to maintain some sort of emotional equilibrium. I've found that you don't want to hold on to an Oscar win any longer than you hold on to a box-office defeat. But having both happen in the same night in such unusual circumstances left me feeling numb. To paraphrase the famous Kipling quote that adorns the entrance to the Wimbledon Centre Court, I had met with triumph and disaster and treated those two imposters the same.

■

Bugsy and *Hook* were watershed events in my tenure as chairman of TriStar Pictures, though for different reasons. *Hook* had done well, but not well enough at the box office (and, more important, in the press) to give me any breathing room, and, in hindsight, *Bugsy* had ruptured my relationship with Guber beyond repair. Though it drove a wedge between Guber and me, we never sat down and had a conversation about those two films. Guber never told me to my face that he was disappointed in any way with either of those two films, or the decisions I had made on them. As a matter of fact, there was never a substantive, face-to-face discussion with Guber about *anything* work related in four years.

Bugsy cost $43 million to make and it ended up losing nearly $30 million—just about the amount of money we spent on the second round of advertising. We would have done fine with the money if we hadn't spent $50 million chasing a gross that we couldn't possibly achieve and an Oscar that we didn't get. From Warren's point of view, he wanted TriStar to get results even if it meant spending itself to death because, after all, he had first-dollar gross profits. Between Warren on the one hand and Barry Levinson and Mark Johnson on the other hand, the filmmakers had 30 percent of the gross from dollar one. Besides, Warren—like all filmmakers—thought that with better marketing the film would have done better.

To this day, my conscience is clean on both films. If Steven Spielberg came to me to make an event film like *Hook* and I had the financing, I would do it again in a heartbeat. And if Warren Beatty came to me with another drama the caliber of *Bugsy* and I had the resources, I would make that, too. The fact is, if you don't make pictures like *Hook* and *Bugsy* when you have the resources, then you shouldn't be running a movie studio. Films like that are why major studios exist: to take chances on artists and to make films that will endure. Making teenage comedies doesn't improve the value of your library, though that may be the easy short-term solution; the hard road is better in the long run. What's the use of a studio with worldwide tentacles building a library of B movies?

I don't ever regret having made *Bugsy*, because I am proud of the film; I only regret the fact that I had to go through a public crucifixion over the movie, one that would shadow me for the rest of my time at TriStar.

14 *The Fish Stinks at the Head*

Another old Hollywood aphorism, which is in turn a Japanese proverb, holds that the fish stinks at the head.

At United Artists and Orion, the gentlemanly way we conducted business was shaped by Arthur Krim and Bob Benjamin and flowed down through the company.

At Warner Bros., the philosophy of largesse in all things began with Steve Ross and extended to the way studio heads Bob Daly and Terry Semel treated stars and budgets.

Disney's ever watchful eye over every detail of a film was a directive issued by Michael Eisner and capably carried out by Jeffrey Katzenberg.

Fox chairman Barry Diller's production executives were nicknamed "Killer Dillers" for their loyalty to the boss's cause.

But nowhere did the fish stink more at the head than at Sony Pictures Entertainment.

There were two cultures operating on the newly refurbished Sony lot over the four years that I worked there: In the Thalberg Building, located at the southeast corner of the lot, which housed Columbia as well as Guber and Sony's other senior executives, there was constant action. Everyone was in perpetual motion. You almost had to duck from the verbal bullets flying out of their offices: "Get me legal!" "Get me Ovitz!" "Where's my script coverage!" If Guber was hyperkinetic, then Mark Canton, who was hired as chairman of Columbia Pictures in fall of 1991, was Guber on steroids. He was constantly backslapping someone or dropping names of stars he had wined and dined the previous night. "You see that hat?" Mark once asked when I walked into his office. "Jack Nicholson gave it to me."

Canton was hired to replace Frank Price as chairman of Columbia Pictures after Frank's ouster, which seemed to be in the works for a while. Besides being responsible for a few films that didn't work, Frank had other problems: Guber had apparently promised his job to Canton when Canton's Warner contract ran out. However, when Warner Bros. unexpectedly released Canton from his contract, Guber had to make good on his promise. Basically, Canton wanted to run Columbia, not TriStar, and he refused to report to Frank Price—so that was the end of Frank Price.

Canton's production executives, who included Barry Josephson, were much the same. In the summer of 1993, the *Last Action Hero* failed at the same time there were newspaper stories reporting that Barry Josephson's office number at Sony was in the black book of the alleged Hollywood madam Heidi Fleiss, who had recently been arrested. Michael Nathanson, Canton's president of production, took the unusual step of issuing a preemptive denial through his lawyer that he had any involvement in the alleged call-girl ring. Whatever went on in the Thalberg Building, the walls were getting more of an earful than they did in the days when United Artists had its offices there.

Canton arrived around the time that his and Guber's final collaboration at Warner Bros., *The Bonfire of the Vanities,* was released. This was exactly the kind of project that suited both of them. Based on a literate, best-selling novel by Mr. Zeitgeist himself, Tom Wolfe, the film was littered with stars like Tom Hanks, Bruce Willis, and Melanie Griffith, and everyone was paying attention to it. When Guber got his hands on the rights to the book, he called it "the devil's candy." Though Guber left before production began, Canton was there when the film was finished. He walked out of the first screening of the film and declared it was the best film the studio had made. Of course, *The Bonfire of the Vanities* was one of the biggest bombs, commercially and artistically, ever released. Never mind this, though. Canton and

Guber had been partners on the film, and there were rumors flying from the minute Canton walked in the door that he was going to become the head of both Columbia and TriStar, thereby pushing me out of a job.

In the newly christened TriStar Building, situated at the northwest corner of the lot, I tried to carry out the daily business in a very measured manner. There was no yelling or screaming in the decision-making process. Compared to the guys on the other side of the lot, we were boring copy for the press. When an entertainment business reporter from the *Financial Times* in London came to the lot to do a story on Sony in the spring of 1993, I was asked to give him a tour and an extensive interview. No one at Columbia seemed particularly interested. Peter Wilkes, the studio's head publicist, joked that I was the only production executive on the lot who read the *Financial Times*.

When I came on board at TriStar, I didn't make any immediate changes to the key personnel who remained from the pre-Sony days. I decided the existing production executives—Alan Riche, an agent I had known from CMA and was very fond of, Chris Lee, and Steve Randall—would all be equal until I got a sense of who did what and who was most effective. On paper, Randall had seniority and probably should have been head of the division, but I wasn't ready to make that call yet. The marketing division led by Buffy Shutt and Kathy Jones, publicity head Ed Russell, and distribution head Bill Soady also remained in place. From Orion, I brought along my projectionist, Jim Cushman; my post-production supervisor, Sol Lomita; and Jonathan Darby, an Oxford grad who was one of the sharpest executives who ever worked for me.

The way I hired Jonathan at Orion can serve as a lesson for anyone looking for a job in the movie business: I first met Jonathan when he was a Fulbright scholar trying to get into the production side of the movie business. As a test, I gave him the script for *The Silence of the Lambs* to read and critique. The following day he showed up with dark circles under his eyes. It turned out that he had read the script and found nothing to comment on, so he went to the book store at 11 P.M. to buy the novel, hoping to find some failing in the script. After reading the novel, he realized that nothing could be done to make the script better. Usually, people come in and say something like, "It's a little weak in the second act." When you ask them for specifics, they say something like, "It just doesn't seem to go anywhere." When I asked Jonathan about *Silence*, he said that he couldn't find anything wrong with it and told me to make it.

Since I had come to the same conclusion, I hired him on the spot.

Unfortunately, many of my TriStar team's accomplishments were overshadowed by the faster, racier culture at Columbia. In the summer of 1993, the constant criticism of *Last Action Hero* trumped the success of our films *Cliffhanger* and *Sleepless in Seattle*. On the one hand, it was nice not to be watched, but on the other, there was a feeling of isolation. The fact that we were so far from the epicenter of power also made my staff feel like orphans on occasion. This feeling was underscored by the fact that people around town often used "Sony" and "Columbia" interchangeably and regarded TriStar as a division of Columbia when, in fact, Columbia and TriStar were siblings and Sony was the parent.

Part of the problem between the opposite corners of the lot was due to the uncommunicative relationship that had developed between Guber and me, and part of it was due to the efforts of Columbia people in the Thalberg Building to position themselves in the media and with the rest of the town, many of whom were hoping that whole operation would implode. They wanted everyone to know that Columbia was the primary studio and TriStar was the poor sibling that was going to be put under Columbia's jurisdiction at any minute. Peter Guber was the leader of this schadenfreude culture, and he revealed his true colors to me early on.

Shortly after I started at TriStar, Guber asked me to call Mickey Schulhof and tell him that I thought the studio could be capably run by him and Levine. He further wanted me to tell Schulhof that Columbia was better off with Levine than with Peters, who he didn't think was needed. While I didn't disagree, I wasn't the one who had insisted that Peters be the co-chairman. It was quite clear that Guber was trying to dump his longtime partner, and he wanted me to help with the dirty work while his hands remained clean. By this time, I was beginning to understand why Guber had needed Peters: Jon Peters was the dark side of Peter Guber. Stranger still, after I talked to Schulhof, Guber told me from then on never to talk directly to the Sony brass. "They are my account," he said.

The bizarre twist to the situation was that Guber and Peters were in therapy together at the time, presumably pouring their hearts out to the shrink about how they could make their "relationship" work. To Peters's face, Guber was putting on airs of trying to work out whatever differences they had, but behind his back, he was trying to cut his legs off. Over the course of my time at TriStar, it became evident that Guber was doing the same thing to me. If it had been pitched in the early nineties as a movie, this backstabbing, undermining, and posturing would have been described as a cross between *Falcon Crest* and *Macbeth*.

In Hollywood, Cassiuses and Brutuses are more prevalent than Caesars.

Much of the intrigue revolved around whether or not Canton was going to become the head of a combined Columbia-TriStar, which many people presumed would push me out of a job. From the day Canton arrived, I was dogged by the rumor that I was on my way out the door. Guber apparently saw nothing wrong with the company running this way because he did nothing to quash the rumors. Funny enough, I had given Canton his first job as an office boy at United Artists, and my friend Bob Sherman, while working for me at Orion in the early eighties, had helped Canton get his job with Jon Peters.

When these rumors were at their height, I challenged Canton to a friendly game of tennis. For fun, of course. The executive battlefield of choice in Hollywood is either the tennis court or the golf course. Undoubtedly feeling spry and youthful, he accepted my challenge. Since movie executives are gamblers by nature, we agreed to wager $100 on the outcome. Around 10 A.M. on Saturday morning, Canton arrived at my house on Coldwater Canyon with his coach and Chevy Chase in tow. He was suited up in starched white Fila from head to toe and carrying a half-dozen rackets and one of those large duffel bags that the pros bring on court at Wimbledon. He needed a lot more than his sheath of rackets and moral support from his coach.

Quickly, handily, and easily, I won. His excuse: he didn't have sufficient time to warm up before the match.

Mark Canton never paid the hundred-dollar bet either.

▤

Why I passed on Pulp Fiction . . .

▤

While I seemingly had all the money in the world to make movies, after putting together my 1991 slate, I found myself getting cautious about greenlighting movies. There were several projects that we had spent a small fortune developing, but they just weren't coming together. The deal we had made with DeVito's Jersey Films company, for instance, was draining money and not resulting in any movies. Jersey went through money like it was water, and the TriStar horse never got to drink at the trough. The other problem with the deal was that Danny was being tied up with *Hoffa* and then as the Penguin in *Batman Returns* for the better part of two years. Over the life of the deal, Jersey spent more than $7 million developing projects and millions more on overhead. Only two projects came to fruition— *Matilda* and *Sunset Park*— both long after I left.

Under the Jersey deal, I agreed to invest $125,000 for a script based on an idea pitched to me by Quentin Tarantino, whose first film *Reservoir Dogs* had caused a stir in the movie business. There was a mutual respect: I liked Tarantino's perpetual energy and his rat-tat-tat, one-film-allusion-a-minute way of talking, and he loved several of my better failures, such as *Breathless*. But when he turned in the script for *Pulp Fiction* after working on it for two years, I felt that in a growing climate of antiviolence in the country, it was unredeemably violent. Quentin described the violence as cartoonish, but I didn't see it that way. I had heard this before from Sam Peckinpah and times had changed.

Violence has always been a part of movies, but I felt that *Pulp Fiction* had gone beyond the pale. Furthermore, I had reached a point in my life where my conscience wouldn't allow me to do a film with such violence. Quentin told me that the now-famous scene where a dopey criminal gets his brains blown out and splattered all over the inside car windows would be mordantly funny and not disgusting.

He was right. Both audiences and critics laughed.

When you are young, you are more apt to push the envelope. The older we get, we all begin to realize that there is indeed some connection between violence in films and how people act in real life. We also realize that we will be judged on the kinds of films we have made. The truth is, I might not have done a film like *Taxi Driver* either at that point in my life, but I was willing to do it when I was younger.

Ultimately, I passed on *Pulp Fiction,* mainly because of the violence, which turned out to be a mistake for the company, but it's a mistake every other studio in town also made—until Miramax finally picked it up.

While Peter Guber was a secretive meddler by nature, he began interfering with the running of TriStar after the Japanese owners rebuffed his attempts to become the next Steve Ross. When Guber and Jon Peters took the reins of the studio, they prepared a master plan dubbed "Map One." This document, which I was never allowed to see, contained Jon's plan to build "Sonyland," a theme park in the mold of Disneyland, in Oxnard where Sony owned a two-thousand-acre lemon orchard, as well as a super channel for Europe. The Japanese shook their heads and said, "Make us a few Batmans and we'll talk." So Guber set out to do that in a way that usurped what I was hired to do.

When Guber began poking around TriStar, some of his decisions were downright puzzling to me. For example, TriStar had a project called *Sommersby,* a remake of *The Return of Martin Guerre.* We thought about putting the project in turnaround, but when we discovered that Jon Amiel was attached to direct with Richard Gere and Jodie Foster playing the leads, we understandably decided to move ahead. Somehow, Terry Semel got Guber to sell it to Warner against my will. The fact is, *Sommersby* was a profitable movie that he inexplicably gave away.

Guber was also questioning my decisions behind my back. When I confronted him about this, he would deny it in such a circuitous way that I felt as though I was walking through a maze. I later learned that he complained to Alan Levine about my hiring Michael Apted to direct *Thunderheart*. Released in April 1992, the film was about a murder on a Sioux reservation, and it starred Val Kilmer and was produced by Robert De Niro and his partner, Jane Rosenthal. Both De Niro and I thought Apted was the right guy for the job. Apparently, Guber was dissatisfied with Apted's work on *Gorillas in the Mist*, a film on which Guber and Peters served as executive producers. I thought the film was fine and I'm not sure what more Apted could have done with it. When *Thunderheart* came out and wasn't a hit, Guber gloated to Levine, "I told you so." For whatever reason, Guber never expressed his sentiments to my face. In truth, the film is one of those that ultimately will not lose money.

In retrospect, I realized that Guber never totally trusted me. In May 1991, before *Hook* or *Bugsy* was released, Guber had my contract altered to give him more authority over me. Peters had been pushed out of the co-chairman's seat that month, triggering the contractual provision that allowed me to make a certain number of films each year at my sole discretion. However, exactly twenty-two days after Peters left, I was presented with an amendment that stated that only if Guber was terminated would I have that right. The document also stated that on all business matters I would report to both Levine and Jon Dolgen, who had been brought over from Fox to work in business affairs at my suggestion. At the time, I was juggling enough egos without worrying about my own, so I signed it. Besides, I always figured that if I made enough good films, they wouldn't get rid of me. I was wrong about that.

The rules were being changed in the middle of the game, and there was nothing I could do about it except resign, which made no sense.

One of the things that Peter always held over me was that he let me make *Hook* and I doubled the budget. Given the complicated task at hand, there was little that we could do about it. The sets were elaborate and crowded with extras, which doubled the amount of time Spielberg needed to set up his shots. If Spielberg hadn't increased the budget to $84 million, then the picture would be $100 million in the black. However, the truth is, we just might have decided to do an $80-million Steven Spielberg action-fantasy movie with Dustin Hoffman, Robin Williams, and Julia Roberts.

My 1992 results were poor because I couldn't find pictures that I wanted to make, and I was preoccupied trying to get *Hook* and *Bugsy* finished throughout 1991. That year, TriStar released only eight films. Output was a problem because Sony had pre-paid slots for as many as forty movies a year with U.S. and German pay television, but the studio couldn't deliver enough movies. Part of this was my fault: I couldn't turn out pictures just to build inventory. I always tried to treat films as artistic endeavors, not widgets. When a studio head starts second-guessing himself too much, the situation can become paralyzing. It's similar to a boxer being afraid to get his nose broken in the ring. The minute the fear creeps in, he isn't half the fighter he was.

My general reluctance in pulling the trigger was that I didn't see a reason to make movies that I thought would not make money. My philosophy has always been to make sure that I am not embarrassed by my choices. When possible, I always choose the high road because nothing is worse than a film with bad reviews and bad results. Undoubtedly, there are some people who would have made as many movies as possible just to compete with the year-end grosses of the other studios. We later learned that this is what Jeffrey Katzenberg was doing at Disney—because his bonus compensation was tied to the *total gross of all the studio's films,* and not the profits.

I also reasoned that Carolco was delivering three promising films for 1992: There was the steamy thriller *Basic Instinct,* with Michael Douglas and Sharon Stone; the Jean-Claude Van Damme action film *Universal Soldier*; and Richard Attenborough's *Chaplin.* I expected these films to pick up the slack at the box office and, in the case of *Basic Instinct,* I was right—only after we insisted on an R rating and not an NC-17. The film became a cultural hot button and grossed more than $300 million worldwide, leaving TriStar with a profit of nearly $21 million domestically and another $10 million foreign.

When *Basic Instinct* was released, we ran into a public relations headache. GLAAD (the Gay and Lesbian Alliance Against Defamation), the gay media watchdog, had tried to disrupt filming in San Francisco, and picketed theaters showing the movie. They were upset at the portrayal of the lesbian girlfriend of Sharon Stone's character as a crazed killer. Public protests of film content was a dilemma I had seen before (on such films as *Colors*), but in the age of political correctness the situation was magnified. But as tough as *Basic Instinct* was from a public relations point of view, it was nothing compared to the mess we found ourselves in with my old friend Woody Allen in the summer of 1992, just months before the release of *Husbands and Wives*.

▬

I brought Woody Allen to TriStar for several reasons, mostly because I admired his work and felt that he would give me some peace of mind. After Orion plunged into bankruptcy, Woody Allen needed a place to make movies. Since TriStar had the resources, I was more than happy to sign Woody to a three-picture deal. He was one of America's most respected, talented, and private filmmakers. There had always been a public relations value to being in business with Woody Allen. All of his films were, at the very least, interesting. I also figured he would give me one film a year with no headaches. He was the safe director in New York who was uncontroversial, made his tart comedies, and stayed out of the Hollywood arena. Woody at TriStar seemed like a nice antidote to the glitzy, corporate world of Sony Pictures.

Woody's first picture for TriStar was *Husbands and Wives*, a film about weak men married to manipulative women who use sex and children as a way of keeping their husbands in place. The story was told in a documentary-like fashion. Because the first reel is shot with a hand-held camera to show the chaos of a domestic argument, some theater owners had to post signs to tell the audience that there was nothing wrong with the projector, the dizzying effect was caused by the director. But the cinematography of *Husbands and Wives* was not nearly as dizzying as what happened on August 14, 1992, the day that Woody Allen was accused of being a child molester and his private life became front-page news in the New York tabloids. Had there ever been this much interest in one of his films, the movie would have grossed $200 million.

The sordid details of this tabloid epic were that Woody was having an affair with Soon Yi Previn, the adopted adult daughter of his longtime companion, Mia Farrow. Worse, the world soon learned, Mia had found naked pictures of Soon Yi taken by Woody. The stakes were raised considerably when Mia filed charges in Connecticut, where she lived, accusing Woody of sexually molesting their young daughter, Dylan. So instead of a quaint filmmaker who kept to himself, I had brought Sony a guy who was being beaten up in the press worse than Guber or Peters ever were.

To top it off, there were eerie parallels in *Husbands and Wives* to the private tour that the public was getting of Woody Allen's personal life. In the film, Woody and Mia are husband and wife. He plays a college professor who becomes attracted to one of his students. He is manipulated by his wife, used by his friend, and he ends up alone, with only himself to blame for his predicament. It wasn't long before bootlegged copies of the unreleased film began selling for $200 on the street in New York.

I was distraught for everyone that something like this could happen to such a private and reserved friend. Woody never sought publicity; in fact, he practically refused to give interviews for his films. He didn't even attend the Academy Awards when he was nominated, which was nearly every year. My feelings aside, from TriStar's point of view there were two central problems: The first was what to do about releasing *Husband and Wives*, which we had scheduled for Christmastime. To say the least, it would be very difficult to mount a press campaign for the film. The second issue was that TriStar had a pay-or-play deal with Woody for two additional films. I sat down with Guber, Alan Levine, and Jon Dolgen, who served as president of the studio's operations, to talk out our options. By now, this was the committee I had to face for all major decisions.

Dolgen, who had been so helpful in making the deal, wanted to get TriStar out of the deal as fast as he could. Levine was worried about the film in the can, and Guber, as usual, was deferring to everyone else. Personally, I felt we had an obligation to Woody and we should fulfill it, especially since Woody hadn't been charged with any crimes. Frankly, I liked and trusted Woody and didn't believe he was ever capable of molesting a young child. Furthermore, I have always felt that people's personal lives were their own business. However, his personal problems had become my professional problems, so it was clear that we had to talk to him. There was no way I could duck this one.

Since I had the long-term relationship with him, I would obviously have to be there. Given that Guber was chronically nonconfrontational, he certainly wasn't going to have any part of the situation. We couldn't very well send Dolgen, whose biting sense of humor had a way of embarrassing people in the best of situations, so Alan Levine and I took a twenty-four-hour trip to New York to see Woody and to discuss the film's release with him.

After a long flight during which Alan outlined the various scenarios to me and I nervously expressed my dislike for all of them, we arrived in New York and met with Woody in his screening room on Park Avenue. I had been there many times before in the days at UA and Orion, and the feeling had always been one of excitement. I would almost always be there to see the final cut of Woody's new film. This was the place where I had seen Woody's career unfold; now I felt as though I was here to watch it unravel.

Woody looked as if he was in a trance. He had been beaten up daily in the *New York Post* and the *New York Daily News*, and it seemed painfully obvious that the entire situation was weighing heavily on him. Alan and Woody sat down in the back of the theater in oversize chairs facing each other. I chose to pace. I just couldn't sit down; I was literally jumping out of my skin. I walked up and down the aisles, stopping occasionally to sit on the back of a seat and try to focus on the conversation. We were about to release a movie that we had spent $15 million on, and the allegations against him and the circus-atmosphere tabloid coverage they were receiving could kill the film and his career. We needed a plan.

In a highly clinical manner and without revealing any emotion one way or another, Alan looked Woody in the eye and asked him what had happened. Alan calmly explained that we needed to know certain information to determine when we could release the film. Woody nodded his head. Despite having stayed completely outside of the Hollywood system for the past thirty years, Woody understood how things worked inside a corporation.

For about a half hour, Woody openly and honestly explained that his relationship with Soon Yi had been going on for quite some time. They were both adults he pointed out, and he was in love with her. He detailed the tensions between him and Mia over the kids, and he surmised that discovering his affair with Soon Yi had led Mia to bring the child molestation charges against him. He insisted that those charges were false. When Woody was finished talking, he slouched in his chair. It was the kind of conversation Woody had never had with two studio executives.

"So what's going to happen in the Connecticut court?" Alan asked, referring to the investigation that was taking place due to Mia's allegations.

When Woody explained that the first in a series of decisions would be handed down after the first of the year, both Alan and I realized that we had to move up the release of the film. If the film came out in October, it would be out of the theaters by the time the Connecticut judge handed down a ruling.

Alan looked to me to deliver the news, and I told Woody that we would probably want to move up the release of the film. He seemed relieved and said that would be fine. Alan then asked him when he was going to start his next film, *Manhattan Murder Mystery*, which was supposed to co-star Mia. Woody said he was prepping the film to start in the next few weeks and that he planned to replace Mia with Diane Keaton.

"Can you be funny?" Alan asked him.

"Yeah, sure," Woody deadpanned.

Husbands and Wives opened on 865 screens—the most for any of Woody's previous films—with little promotion amid the swirling controversy and did mediocre business. Women, Woody's once faithful audience, no longer trusted him, and this showed at the box office, as the film finished with a domestic gross of $10 million. But Hollywood shook off Woody's troubles, and in February 1993, *Husbands and Wives* received two Oscar nominations, one for Judy Davis for Best Supporting Actress and one for Woody for Best Original Screenplay. After a six-month investigation, Woody was cleared of all of the molestation charges. Mia was replaced by Diane Keaton in *Manhattan Murder Mystery*, which opened in August and did poorly, grossing just over $11 million in the United States. By this time, Woody had teamed up with producer Jean Doumanian, who raised financing for his next several films, so TriStar making the third film under his deal was a moot point.

In the end, I was sad that I didn't get to make another film with Woody. Besides the fact that I like Woody and his films, it goes against my sense of honor not to finish an agreement, but I was happy for Woody that he had a new source of financing already lined up. I returned to being a booster rather than a backer of his films.

▬

If the movies are working, then no one gives a damn about how much you're spending. During Jeffrey Katzenberg's run at Disney, he started an entire film division, Hollywood Pictures, to placate an executive situation: Ricardo Mestres needed a place to work when David Hoberman was promoted to head Touchstone Pictures. When Katzenberg made that decision, Disney's movies were minting money, the company's stock was going through the roof, and releasing fifty movies a year seemed like a good idea. The same was true of the glory years of Bob Daly and Terry Semel at Warner Bros. When they were making hits like the Lethal Weapons *and the* Batmans, *they were applauded for making rich deals with talent.*

But when the movies stop working, the relationships become damaged. There is very little grace period, if any, for an executive to recover from the losses and to regain his footing. The stakes are too high.

▬

Perhaps my biggest mistake at TriStar was letting Columbia have *A Few Good Men*. In hindsight, the idea that I did this to facilitate teamwork on the lot resonates like a bad joke, particularly since I had such a bad run in 1992 and even more so because I was deliberately functioning as a team player among some of the most predatory and ruthlessly self-serving executives in Hollywood history. In this atmosphere, credit was given only because you had a hit film that no one else could call their own, not because you were being a nice guy.

A Few Good Men, a TriStar project that I had given to Columbia to help Frank Price when Warren Beatty decided to let me and not Columbia back *Bugsy*, became an example of the dysfunction between the two Sony labels. The budget on *A Few Good Men* became top heavy once the film was cast with Tom Cruise, Demi Moore, and Jack Nicholson. Columbia ended up financing the entire film. In the end, the film turned into a windfall, grossing more than $100 million and earning an Academy Award nomination for Best Picture. But by the time the film was released in 1992, Frank was long gone and Mark Canton had come aboard and, in true Hollywood style, adopted the film as his own.

From the day Canton came on board, everything changed.

▬

In my first two years at TriStar, the process for greenlighting films was relatively collegial and straightforward. I would decide how to spend the development money and then when a picture was ready to be put into production, I would outline the specifics at one of the periodic meetings held with Peter Guber, Alan Levine, Ken Lemberger (who was TriStar's head of business affairs), and, later, Jon Dolgen. Even when Jon Peters was serving as co-chairman at Sony, he never attended the meetings; in fact, I seldom saw him on the lot at all. Apparently, he liked to work from home, which is strange for the co-chairman of a movie studio (except for the fact that we are talking about Jon Peters). While everyone would pitch in their opinions during the meetings, the final decision usually rested with me. After all, I had been hired to run the studio.

The process began to go haywire when Guber started soliciting each department's opinion on every film and then throwing that into the mixture. Guber couldn't make decisions on his own and wanted some plausible deniability if a film didn't work. He would ask the domestic distribution, foreign distribution, marketing, and even home-video departments what they thought of the various scripts. I considered this strategy to be lethal. Besides, it's impossible to argue with a committee.

Nobody knows for certain what will work and what won't. Trying to have a platoon of people measure a film based on numbers is a fool's errand. At least at Orion, the discussions among the partners focused on the material, the cast, the filmmaker, and whether we should make one film rather than another. You can't base your decisions on last week's box-office chart. The final decision should be about following your instincts as to what you think will work and trusting the filmmaker to make that a reality. The decision comes down to your gut, and the film comes down to the love and passion of those who make it. When you start a business, you have to be passionate about the product and then make money on it, rather than set out to make money and then try to be passionate about the product. In the movie business, as with everything in life, there is no certainty that the future will repeat the past. Every new film is an adventure, and when a studio is making the decision to go along for the ride, somebody's intuition needs to be followed. That's the person who is responsible for greenlighting the picture.

This new system for greenlighting movies changed the rules of the game yet again. My feeling was that there is no point is giving someone greenlight ability and then putting in ways of stopping them.

Dolgen, for one, had the remarkable ability of being able to see movies as budget numbers on a page, rather than artistic endeavors with numbers attached to them—which was exactly what he had been hired to do. This was fine when Dolgen challenged whether or not a picture should be made for $30 million or $25 million, but it became surreal when he declared that *Philadelphia* shouldn't be made for $26 million because the lead actor has blotches on his face for much of the movie.

"We don't want to make an AIDS movie, we want to make a courtroom drama," Dolgen said.

How could I even answer that question? Had he read the script?

I saw *Philadelphia* as a modern-day story of prejudice. It was a poignant story about a man's fight for his life and his self-respect wrapped in a courtroom drama. This was at a time when AIDS had entered the national debate, but movie studios still had refused to make a mainstream film involving the subject. As I saw it, Dolgen's job wasn't to challenge what was in the script, it was to worry about how the numbers added up, but a studio head can only take these positions when he is hitting home runs at the box office. Otherwise, he will be constantly second-guessed about all aspects of his films.

Admittedly, I let the situation get the best of me. I gave up on films I should have fought for, namely *A River Runs Through It* and *Quiz Show.* I grew tired of constantly trying to justify myself and hearing about all the conversations that Guber was having with my marketing team behind my back. Even when he met with them and me together, he was constantly under-cutting my authority. I resented not being trusted, and I began to feel that life was too short to figure out how to manipulate the greenlighting process at Sony. There were times I should have stood up for my beliefs, pinned Guber to the wall, and made him face me, but it wasn't in me. The more the opportunity to reinvent a studio slipped away, the more worn down I became.

Ultimately, this debilitating situation cost me my relationship with Robert Redford.

■

Friendships are a funny thing in Hollywood. Everyone talks about what good friends they are with everyone else. In truth, most people in the entertainment industry have many acquaintances and few friends, at least in the way I define friendship. In a movie script, you can create a fifteen-year friendship in fifteen minutes, but in real life it takes fifteen years.

Movie stars are a special case because everyone wants to have them as friends—or let the perception around town be that they

*are friends with the stars—but few truly do because stars are hard
to be friends with. Throughout my career, I have always prided
myself on the quality of my relationships, rather than use them as
business tools.*

Then came the confusing case of Robert Redford . . .

My relationship with Robert Redford, which dates back to the
early seventies, was a classic example of a friendship devoid of
development deals and go pictures. Over the years, Bob and I
developed a friendship rooted in what I thought was mutual
respect, not one predicated on what he could do for me or what I
could do for him. In fact, we never worked together. But what I
learned about Bob is that he is difficult to be friends with
because ultimately a friendship must be all on his terms.

I learned a few things about myself, too.

Bob has always been one of the smartest and most private
movie stars, which was one of the things I admired most about
him. He never let himself be swept up in the publicity juggernaut or allowed the press to lay bare the details of his private
life. He would speak on causes near and dear to him like the
environment but never in a way that seemed heavy-handed. As
much as if not more than any other high-profile actor, he has
lived his life without making public adjustments because of the
media. He married once, and he and his ex-wife have three wonderful children.

I got to know Redford around the time I helped package *The
Sting*. From the first day I met Bob I found him soft-spoken,
funny, and easy to be around. Through this early professional
relationship, we developed a casual friendship. He too had a
wide variety of interests, and it wasn't uncommon for us to play
tennis and then sit around discussing the environment, global
warming, and the preservation of national parks. He invited me
to become a founding member of the board of directors of the
Sundance Institute. Taken from his character's name in *Butch
Cassidy and the Sundance Kid*, the institute was located in the
idyllic Wasatch Mountains, near Salt Lake City. The original idea
was to create an incubator for ideas for independent filmmaking,

and the man behind Sundance was Sterling Van Wagenen, whose cousin was married to Redford.

As Sterling remembers the story, Bob sent him to me to jump-start a combination indie film makers workshop (Redford's idea) and an indie film festival (Sterling's baby that Bob had agreed to support). I told Sterling that if he put the full idea in writing, I would raise $5,000 from each studio, starting with Orion, where I worked at the time. When Sterling received the six checks, he paid off a debt from the 1978 United States Film Festival, which he had originally asked Redford to help cover, and opened a bank account in the name of the Sundance Institute. What I remember best is cautioning Bob that if the idea failed, he would take the blame and not the rest of us. This elicited a facetious "Thanks a lot, Mike."

Once Sundance was established, Bob offered several plots of land in the Wasatch Mountains to his friends in Hollywood to buy and build vacation homes. Unfortunately, I wasn't in the position to be investing in land in Utah at the time. Nevertheless, for years I spent every Christmas at Sundance as his guest in one of the cabins on the expansive Sundance property. During those cold winter nights, Bob and I often sat up and talked for hours about politics and movies, though the conversation never got too personal.

The only time after *The Sting* that we even came close to doing business was in the late eighties and we talked about forming a production partnership together. Bob had a small production company called Wildwood. Through it he had optioned the rights to *All the President's Men*. His idea was to expand the company and make more films that he could oversee but didn't have to star in or direct. For advice, I turned to my lawyer, Gary Hendler, who also happened to represent Redford. I told Gary my fear was that if Redford and I became partners and at some point became angry or disappointed with one another, it might destroy our friendship and that was more important to me. Gary looked at me and said, "Never wait for Robert Redford on the sunny side of the creek. You'll die of sunstroke."

The first bump in our relationship came on *A River Runs Through It,* the third film that Redford directed, following *Ordinary People* and *The Milagro Bean Field War.* The project was originally owned by Carolco, and under the deal between TriStar and Carolco, TriStar was obligated to put up 10 percent of the $15 million budget when the finished film was delivered. However, during pre-production Carolco ran into cash-flow problems, leaving Redford's production company stuck with the bills for all the pre-production expenses. For help, Redford got in touch with Jake Eberts, the producer-financier who put *Dances With Wolves* together and who helped finance *Driving Miss Daisy,* two Academy Award Best Pictures.

Jake had always been a fan of the project, so he agreed to take over the funding of pre-production while Carolco put together the production financing, which it did through a series of presales and bank loans. However, when the film was in post-production, Carolco asked Jake to take the entire film off its hands. Carolco was trying to refinance its bank loans and didn't want the film on its books. Through his European sources, Jake raised $15 million and bought Carolco out entirely. Carolco then left it up to Jake to deal with TriStar, which had the right to buy the domestic rights for $1.5 million. At this stage, Jake came to me with the project. Since it was no longer officially a Carolco film, TriStar was under no obligation to put any money into it. As complicated as the making of *A River Runs Through It* was, my decision was equally difficult.

Since this was strictly a distribution deal, I asked my marketing team for their thoughts on the film. That was when they declared a movie about fly-fishing was probably unsalable. At the time, the film's cast—Craig Sheffer, Tom Skerritt, and Brad Pitt—had little to no discernable box-office appeal. They had been cast the old-fashioned way: because the director thought they were the best actors for their parts. Clearly, Redford's instincts were right. Pitt had done only two movies of note. The first one, *Johnny Suede,* had disappeared without a trace, and the second was *Thelma & Louise,* in which Pitt's performance in the small part of a hustler had left an indelible mark. Still, he wasn't known, so he received just $75,000 for *A River Runs Through It.*

Even though the marketing department was down on the idea,

I probably would have still picked up the film had my relationship with Guber not been so strained. The film required an investment of only $1.5 million plus another $10 million or so in marketing costs. But I knew that the first thing Guber would ask me was what marketing thought, and I was fairly sure they had already passed along their opinions. Reluctantly, I passed on the film.

The crowning irony came when Jake screened the finished film for all the studios and Mark Canton bought the film for Columbia to distribute. Sony ended up with the movie, and I ended up with Redford angry at me for not coming to his rescue. I later found out that Canton had problems convincing Guber and Dolgen to let him buy the film, which was now priced at $8 million for domestic rights, but to his credit, he took the chance and deserved the reward. When I had the chance to get in on Redford's next film, everything got even worse.

▓

Quiz Show was a chancy project commercially from the beginning, based on the Faustian tale of Charles Van Doren and the rigged fifties game show *Twenty-One*, a *Who Wants to Be a Millionaire* for its time. The subject matter was of personal interest to me because I had watched the show as a teenager shortly after I arrived in the United States, and I remember being fairly decent at answering the questions. For someone who wasn't intimately familiar with American culture, I found the show to be a learning tool. My confidence in historical trivia was so high that I wrote to Groucho Marx's game show *You Bet Your Life* and asked to be a contestant. The show sent back a postcard and told me I was preapproved, which scared the daylights out of me. First of all, I was living in Long Beach and didn't have a car, so I had no idea how I would get to the studio. Then I became anxious just picturing myself on TV. What if I got stage fright and clamed up? All my friends would certainly be watching and sharing a good laugh at my expense. Three weeks passed before I mustered the courage to reply. Thankfully, the show was canceled, ending my dilemma.

While *Quiz Show* had been submitted to me several times in both book and script form over the years, it wasn't until Barry Levinson and his producing partner, Mark Johnson, came to me at TriStar and asked to develop a new script that I said yes. If anyone could put the story in perspective, it was Barry. He had the ability to create tension out of sedentary scenes, which this material would require. We commissioned a former *Washington Post* movie critic named Paul Attanasio, and he did a terrific job with the largely cerebral story line. Then Barry asked me what I thought of Redford directing instead of him. Having missed an opportunity on *A River Runs Through It*, I was more than willing to do it, and I told Barry that short of him directing, I thought Redford directing was a fantastic idea.

However, when Guber read the script, he, Dolgen, and Levine absolutely refused to make the movie. Not commercial was their verdict. Since my relationship with Guber was deteriorating and my job was on thin ice, I folded. Fighting for quality material had been my trademark in my years at UA and Orion, but my will had been sapped by the back-biting culture at Sony. Everyone seemed to be feeling it. The whole place had become demoralized. At the time, someone inside Sony was using the press to let me know that my job was in jeopardy. I was in an awful situation. Even though I was still the chairman of the studio, I felt totally powerless.

Sitting down with Redford to talk about why TriStar wasn't going to make *Quiz Show* was one of the most awkward meetings of my life. The conversation was filled with long, silent pauses that had been foreign to our relationship before the problems with *A River Runs Through It*. I told him that we were not going to make the film, and there was nothing I could do to make it happen. I wouldn't be surprised if Redford lost all respect for me professionally. What kind of studio head couldn't make his own decisions? In retrospect, I should have told Bob about my situation with Guber. As a friend, he might have understood. At the very least, he would have better understood why I couldn't get the movie made. But I didn't. I took the cowardly way out. Confessing to anyone, even myself, that I couldn't somehow get the movies done that I wanted would have been an admission of failure.

Ultimately, from a financial standpoint, Guber, Levine, and Dolgen were right. The film wound up losing money for Disney, despite the fact that it received stellar reviews and five Academy Award nominations, including Best Picture and Best Director. I was a fan of the finished film, and I wish I had been part of it because of my personal interest in the subject matter. It is also a pretty good film to have in a studio library. As for my relationship with Redford, who knows what would have happened had I been able to push the film through at TriStar. Perhaps other grievances would have surfaced that would have strained our friendship.

The next time I saw Redford was a year later at the Sundance Film Festival when I attended a filmmaker's workshop that he hosted. I hadn't talked to him since the *Quiz Show* situation. At the end of his presentation, I approached the dais to say hello.

"What are *you* doing here?" Redford asked, putting just enough emphasis on the "you" to make me feel like a trespasser.

"What does that mean?" I asked somewhat defensively.

"Well," he asked again, *"what* are you doing here?" This time the emphasis was on the "what," as if a former studio executive who was now starting his own company had no business being at Sundance.

We were interrupted by the people milling around, so we never finished the conversation. Whatever he meant, I was really sorry that it had come to this. Clearly, there were still some lingering wounds over *A River Runs Through It* and *Quiz Show*. When I got back to Los Angeles, I wrote him a long letter and told him that I always felt that we were friends *despite* the business and not because of it, and I closed by telling him that if he didn't want me at Sundance, I wouldn't ever go again.

Redford never responded to the letter, and I haven't been back since.

15   *Hollywood, D.C.*

The one continuously positive aspect of my life during my years at TriStar was my interest in politics and foreign affairs. I learned my lesson from the Hart campaign about investing too much of my time and becoming distracted from my studio work, though I continued to follow Arthur Krim's lead and kept up with Democratic politics.

I disapproved of many of the Reagan and Bush policies, and I felt that the country had become complacent about critical social, economic, and environmental issues. I have always felt that there is a role for government in people's lives, particularly helping those in need.

More than ever, we needed an agent of change, and I felt certain that change could come with Bill Clinton.

first met Bill Clinton in 1988 when he was the governor of Arkansas. Clinton was one of the leaders of the self-styled new Democratic movement, which sought to move the party to the center and away from the staunch liberalism that many voters had rejected during the Reagan years. They sought to maintain the ideals of the New Deal and the Great Society while being more fiscally conservative, stronger on foreign policy, and tougher on government spending. The central theme that Clinton adopted was restoring hope to the middle class. What I liked most about Clinton was his openness to new ideas, his charisma, his powerful intellect, and his ability to talk to anyone. Except for a few native Arkansans like Harry and Linda Bloodworth-

Thomason, Gil Gerard, and Mary Steenburgen, I was one of the first people in Hollywood to get behind Bill Clinton.

Long before Clinton was even on the national radar screen as a presidential candidate, I set up a dinner for him to meet some of the entertainment community at Bud and Cynthia Yorkin's house. At the time Clinton was head of the Democratic Leadership Council and the presidency was a distant dream. Because few people even knew who Clinton was, everyone who attended was an idea-oriented political activist, like Warren Beatty and Sydney Pollack. Not everyone that night was convinced, but I kept pushing. Later, I introduced Clinton to Dawn Steel and her husband, Chuck Roven, and they hosted the first presidential fund-raiser for him at their house.

My house was under construction at the time so the dinner couldn't be held there, but Clinton stayed with me that night. It was the first of a few nights we stayed up into the wee hours of the morning talking.

Clinton and I kept in touch, and in September 1991, about a month before Clinton announced that he was running for president, he called me and told me he was coming out to L.A. He wanted to meet with me and some of his other supporters to discuss his run for the White House. It was clear to him that we would be able to help bring money and glamour to the campaign, both of which are crucial to political success in our media-centric age. The support of Hollywood was an important building block in the early stages of his candidacy.

Even after he announced his candidacy, Clinton was anything but an easy sell to Hollywood. After Jimmy Carter, confidence in Southern governors was pretty low in general in the Democratic Party, and the country had just watched George Bush "win" the Gulf War. Bush's approval rating was so high that most people in Hollywood, even many politically active veterans, thought that a second term for him was a certainty. Besides, Clinton also had to deal with a slew of Democrats in the primary, notably Paul Tsongas and Bob Kerry. Hollywood loves backing a winner, and it wasn't sure that Bill Clinton could be a winner. Until the entertainment industry had some evidence that he could win, they were going to keep their checkbooks closed.

While I wasn't that heavily involved in the nuts and bolts of the Clinton organization, I was often making calls on his behalf, asking people to donate $1,000 for a meet-and-greet. Since Michael Ovitz had shown interest in politics during the Hart campaign, I called and asked him to become a supporter. At the time, Clinton wasn't the front-runner, so Ovitz declined. When I first approached Peter Guber about supporting Clinton, he, like most people, wasn't interested.

Besides, Guber told me, he was a life-long Republican.

But by the time the presidential election rolled around in November 1992, Clinton had more Hollywood supporters than he knew what to do with. Among them were Ovitz and Guber, who by that time was barely speaking to me. In his typical, underhanded way, Guber tried to send a signal that I was on the outs by not including me in his group that flew on the Sony corporate jet to Little Rock on election night. Instead I wound up going with Lew Wasserman. Given that Lew's ties to the Democratic Party reached back to the days of Arthur Krim's, I was proud to be in his company.

With the election in hand, several of Clinton's supporters gathered in a ballroom at the Excelsior Hotel for a party at the end of the night. Around 2 A.M., I gave up waiting for Clinton and started walking back to my hotel. After I had walked a block or so, I looked up and saw Clinton and his entourage headed straight for me. When our paths crossed, Clinton put his arm around me. "Come on, Mike," he said, hugging me. "Let's go celebrate."

Escorted by the Secret Service, we entered through the hotel's kitchen. As Clinton stopped to shake hands with every cook in the place, I was thrust forward with his family through a door and wound up on a makeshift stage, standing next to a large sheet cake with the presidential seal on it, looking out on a crowd of one hundred or so people behind a rope line. Two of the first people I spotted were Peter Guber and his wife, Lynda. As Bill and Hillary Clinton bounded onto the stage, I waved to them.

After the cake cutting, I brought Clinton down from the dais, closer to the rope line. I sidled the president-elect up next to my boss and said, "Bill, you remember my friend Peter Guber, don't you?"

History, which in Hollywood consists of a series of rumors mixed with innuendo and gossip, has recorded this unique fact about my career: I was the only studio executive whose job was saved by a presidential election. The moment came in December 1992, when I was honored as the Motion Picture Pioneer of the Year. The dinner featured tributes from a long list of movie stars, including Robin Williams, Tom Hanks, Tom Cruise, Jeff Bridges, Denzel Washington, Arnold Schwarzenegger, Sylvester Stallone, and Meg Ryan, as well as Senators Ted Kennedy and Chris Dodd, and Motion Picture Association of America head Jack Valenti.

Peter Guber attended the dinner and, I later learned, stewed for hours ahead of time about what to say about me to the crowd. He settled on a few impersonal lines laced with double entendre, which, knowing him, was probably just the tone he wanted to strike. But no one much remembers what Peter Guber said because he was greatly overshadowed by a flattering testimonial to me from the president-elect himself.

"Mike has been a friend of mine for many years," Clinton began in his taped tribute, "and he seems to be an even better friend now, not because I won the election but because so early in this election cycle he came out and endorsed me. He told me he would support me in the beginning and he did through thick and thin." Clinton continued by saying that I had always given good advice and constructive criticism throughout the campaign and that the road to the presidency had brought us closer together than ever before. He concluded by addressing me directly. "One of the things I have become very, very grateful for is the great gift of your friendship."

Whether Clinton's tribute bought me more time at TriStar is something that only Guber can answer, but it did lead to the rumors and media stories that I would be joining the Clinton administration. I have never been interested in being in politics because I don't have those kinds of personal ambitions or needs. My involvement stems from the fact that I care about my adopted country and its people. So while I didn't end up as the U.S. Ambassador to Iceland, I felt as though I was now in the Hollywood version of Iceland.

No president has connected to Hollywood and artists in general the way Bill Clinton did, so I wasn't surprised when filmmakers, actors, executives, and musicians continued to support him in the wake of the Monica Lewinsky scandal. After all, he had the ability to stand in front of a Hollywood crowd at a $25,000 per couple fund-raiser, address the issue of violence in movies, and not be called a hypocrite. Personally, I was disappointed that he was not forthcoming about the Lewinsky affair, and shocked that he would risk his political career by giving his enemies so much ammunition to discredit him.

So what do I think of Bill Clinton today? I continue to be his friend, and I think he was a terrific president. What he did with Monica Lewinsky—every aspect of it—was embarrassing to his party, his country, his family, and, most of all, himself. Clearly, he tarnished his place in history. Looking back, I am glad I wasn't more intimately involved as a friend or a supporter because watching that happen to someone who cares so deeply about this country and its people was hard enough to handle without being in his inner circle.

Haynes Johnson recently wrote a book titled *The Best of Times: America in the Clinton Years* that perfectly captures our culture in those eight years, but it was Robin Toner's review of the book in *The New York Times Book Review* that summed up those years of the lowest common denominator. "The Clinton scandal was the last cultural bonfire of the 1990s," she wrote. "Looking back, even now, is like trying to reconstruct a vast drunken brawl. The question is the same: 'What were we thinking?' "

*Breaking Bread with Them
What Wronged You*

---

*All studio executives are sitting in rented chairs,
and the day always comes when the landlord shows
up with an eviction notice. While this can never be
a pleasant experience, only in a culture like the one
on the Sony lot could I have had a year like I did in
1993 and been on the street in January 1994
because of something that happened in December
1991.*

*In a way, it was déjà vu all over again from my
Orion days: I was forced out right about the time
the movies started working.*

Peter Guber often said that producers peddling their scripts
were just dogs with bones in their mouth that they couldn't let go
of. It turns out that Guber had plenty of things he couldn't let go
of and one of them was *Bugsy*. The funny thing was that he was
less upset at the movie's performance than he was with Warren
Beatty's unhappiness with the studio's job—or so it seemed.

After a year of not being able to find movies to make, I refo-
cused my efforts and some of the risks I was taking were beginning to pay off. In 1993 TriStar released three big financial winners: *Cliffhanger, Sleepless in Seattle,* and *Philadelphia.* These far
outweighed the misses like *So I Married an Ax Murderer* and
Wilder Napalm. But little did I know Guber was still stewing over
the phone calls he got from Beatty complaining about the performance of *Bugsy* over the Christmas holidays in 1991. So while I

was putting together a trio of the biggest hits to come out of Sony in 1993, Guber was plotting how to get rid of me without having to face me alone.

The situation was so twisted that the fact that I was making hit films didn't really matter. It was already over, and everyone knew it.

■

The nineties were becoming so much about hype that movies weren't really about anything. My feeling was that studio executives were causing this and not the audiences. Something in me was crying out: *Audiences still like classic movies, whether they were love stories, action films, or great human dramas.* Refocusing on these basics delivered results.

By far the biggest hit I made at TriStar was *Sleepless in Seattle*, which I was inspired to do after seeing the French film *And Now My Love*, though by no means was the film a sure thing when it went into production. The script, written by Jeffrey Arch, and then rewritten first by Larry Atlas, then by David Ward, and finally by Nora Ephron, was a story about a widower and a girl he meets on a radio call-in show. It defied the modern tenet of romantic comedies, which was that the couple has to kiss (or preferably have sex) in the first thirty minutes. In *Sleepless in Seattle*, the couple didn't even meet until an hour and a half into the film. After a steady diet of films where the couple meets in the first scene and jumps into bed together in the second scene, I felt that audiences would warm to the old-fashioned, 1940s sweetness of a film like this. Of course, this relied heavily on who played the couple.

Most studio executives live by the general rule that you are only as good as your last movie, but my instincts told me that this wasn't the case with the pairing of Tom Hanks and Meg Ryan. The last film the two had appeared in was the bomb *Joe Versus the Volcano*, so people thought I was crazy wanting to pair the two of them again. My feeling was that Tom and Meg weren't the problem with that film, the concept was. Even Nora Ephron, who directed *Sleepless in Seattle*, questioned the casting of Hanks at first. She felt he wasn't quite right for the part, and Hanks, too, had some initial concerns. But finally Nora warmed to the idea. She was a risk, too, since her last film hadn't worked, but I felt that she could rewrite it and direct it, so I went with her.

The ends more than justified the means on *Sleepless in Seattle*. The film was a sleeper summer hit, bringing in more than $127 million at the domestic box office. The film finished 1993 as the fifth highest-grossing movie of the year, behind *Jurassic Park, Mrs. Doubtfire, The Fugitive,* and *The Firm*. Because of its modest $25 million budget, *Sleepless in Seattle* remains one of Sony's most profitable films of the nineties. More important, it showed that the forties style of romantic comedy could work in a culture that Hollywood declared craved more overtly sexually driven films like *Fatal Attraction, Basic Instinct,* and *Disclosure*. Nora Ephron proved this again when she paired Tom Hanks and Meg Ryan in *You've Got Mail,* her 1998 updating of Ernst Lubitsch's 1940's *The Shop Around the Corner*.

Cliffhanger was a bigger risk financially. The film was directed by Renny Harlin (who had done *Die Hard 2*) and starred Sylvester Stallone. At the time, Stallone's marketability had fallen because of the failure of two comedies, *Stop! Or My Mom Will Shoot* and *Oscar,* and Carolco was beginning to have financial problems of its own. I liked the project, and my gut told me that a suspenseful action film centering on the simple idea of man versus mountain with Stallone in the lead could find a wide audience, not unlike my feelings at Orion when we did *First Blood*. Also, Stallone's appeal in the foreign market in the action genre was time-tested. Carolco was strapped for cash, so they came to us to up our investment, which ended up saving Carolco by giving the company more time to refinance its credit agreements. We invested $35 million of the $65 million budget plus the domestic marketing costs. *Cliffhanger,* which was released in May 1993, turned out to be one of the biggest hits during my tenure, grossing $84 million in the United States and returning Sony more than $35 million in pure profit after the overseas receipts came in. The film also revitalized Stallone's career and allowed Carolco to stay alive for two more years.

But, as was typical of my time at Sony, there was no time to take a bow. While the loud, fast culture that Guber and Canton had fostered in the Thalberg Building was coming back to haunt them, it was overshadowing my success. *Cliffhanger* opened in May 1993 and *Sleepless in Seattle* opened a month later, giving me back-to-back hits. Despite the fact that *Sleepless in Seattle* was on its way to becoming the sleeper hit of the summer, the film was released a week after Columbia put out the costly special-effects film *Last Action Hero,* and the media was focused on how fast *Last Action Hero* was sinking at the box office.

Here were the numbers: *Last Action Hero* grossed $15.3 million over its first weekend; the following weekend it dropped 47 percent to just $8 million while *Sleepless in Seattle* opened to $17.4 million that weekend.

If I had been half the self-promoter Peter Guber was, I probably could have gotten the media to write story after story about how well Mike Medavoy's films were doing that summer. But so many people deserved credit for *Cliffhanger* and *Sleepless in Seattle* that I would have sounded like an ass standing up and taking credit. The *Cliffhanger* deal between Carolco and TriStar was put together by Ken Lemberger, and the film was made—on a mountaintop, no less—by Renny Harlin and his crew. The fact that I helped bring Tom Hanks and Meg Ryan together again wouldn't have meant much if Nora Ephron hadn't delivered such a good film and the marketing staff hadn't done such a good job selling it.

We capped our year at TriStar by releasing *Philadelphia,* surely one of the proudest moments for any Hollywood studio. *Philadelphia* was much more like an Orion project than a TriStar one, which was why getting it made in the Sony environment was such a tense process. Indeed, Marc Platt had put the project in motion at Orion after I had left; and when he joined me at TriStar in early 1992, he helped bring it over. Marc deserves much of the credit for getting the film made. Under director Jonathan Demme's supervision, screenwriter Ron Nyswaner went through three or four drafts before we even picked it up. The film's story was challenging in every way: a homosexual lawyer sues his firm when they fire him after he contracts AIDS.

Philadelphia is easily one of my favorite films. I cried when I saw it screened for the first time, something I never do.

I knew all along the film would be a triumph. The casting of Denzel Washington as the homophobic lawyer was an inspired choice by Demme, and his performance drove the film. And for an actor like Tom Hanks to take on such a role at that time and play it with all his heart was courageous. Films like *Philadelphia* make all the anguish that comes with working in the movie business worthwhile. Jonathan Demme's brilliant and sensitive direction proved that he is one of the best working directors. Here was a man whose films included *Melvin and Howard*, *Something Wild*, *Married to the Mob*, *The Silence of the Lambs*, and now *Philadelphia*.

Measure TriStar films against Mark Canton's first slate at Columbia. Released the same year, 1993, besides *Last Action Hero*, were two of the most expensive bombs of the year at any studio—*I'll Do Anything* and *Geronimo*. Ignoring the quality of those landmark films, let's look at the bottom line: *Last Action Hero* cost nearly $87 million to make and another $30 million to market, but it grossed only $50 million in the United States. When foreign revenues were counted, *Variety* pegged the loss at $26 million. *Geronimo*, which Mark Canton's brother, Neil, brought to him and produced, ended up at least $35 million in the red. *I'll Do Anything*, a Jim Brooks film shot as a musical, ended up losing roughly $40 million.

But this sea of red ink didn't seem to matter. By this time, it wasn't about the films. It was, as I learned the hard way, every man for himself.

▬

Napoleon Bonaparte's observation of "what is history but a fable agreed upon" was obviously *describing the six-year reign of Peter Guber as chairman of Sony Pictures Entertainment, four years of which I worked as chairman of TriStar Pictures under him.*

▬

In January 1991, as I was getting ready to celebrate my fiftieth birthday, I received an urgent call from Peter Guber. He told me that I was needed on Soundstage 7 immediately about the budget overruns on *Hook*. It was so urgent, he said, that he would pick me up at my office and brief me on the way. But when I walked onto the soundstage, three hundred people yelled "Surprise!" I was mortified. I hate surprise parties, and I'm not particularly good with large crowds.

Peter and Jon had secretly arranged a lavish party and made me the guest of honor. An orchestra played in front of a set built to look like the glittering L.A. skyline. There were art deco chandeliers hanging from the ceiling and the champagne flowed like water. The guests included Warren Beatty, Barbra Streisand, Richard Gere, Gene Hackman, Sylvester Stallone, Sally Field, newlyweds Jane Fonda and Ted Turner, Jeffrey Katzenberg, Gregory Peck, Al Ruddy, and Saul Zaentz.

While most of the people were my friends, I was uneasy at the thought of the party. Yes, the gesture was magnanimous. But it was clear that the party doubled as a kick-off event for the Guber-Peters regime. The underlying point was that if Guber and Peters lavished such a party on one of their studio heads, then imagine what it would be like to work on a film at Sony. Of course, the press had a field day, reporting that the party cost $80,000 and possibly ten times that much!

≡

While my working relationship with Peter Guber didn't turn out the way I expected, there is no denying that I learned some tricks of moviemaking from him, particularly about marketing films. Guber was a very skilled marketer, which partly explains why he was so successful in the late eighties. He understood how to cut through the clutter and make audiences pay attention to his films. He had started in the seventies with the film *The Deep*. Peter smartly positioned the film as the next *Jaws* and came up with the famous poster of Jacqueline Bisset in a wet T-shirt.

Guber's forte was creating a gripping trailer. He had an interesting method: Every good trailer had certain signposts. The sound level was critical: it had to be louder than the other trailers being shown. The trailer needed to start with a bang to grab moviegoers' attention as they searched for their seats or television viewers as they contemplated channel surfing. He also insisted that the trailer end with a cliffhanger or a joke.

In an odd way, Peter sold himself the same way. He grabbed people's attention from the first moment you saw him, he kept things short so your attention wouldn't waver, and he always left on a high note. More than anyone else in my generation in Hollywood, Peter had an uncanny instinct on how to sell himself to anyone. In a classic show of bravura, Guber was once asked if he was surprised that Sony wanted to hire him to be the CEO of Columbia. Guber responded: "I had the credentials, I was twenty-five years in the business, produced the greatest films in the last ten years in Hollywood, five times for Best Picture, fifty other Academy Award nominations, had been at Columbia for six years, had been CEO of PolyGram for six years, produced music and television shows, had four degrees, all these degrees. Why wouldn't I be a candidate!"

One of the many ironies was that Guber loved to host lavish corporate retreats that were designed to bring everyone closer together. At the first retreat, Guber, Jon Dolgen, Alan Levine, Frank Price, a few television and marketing executives, and I took the Sony jet to Guber's ranch in Aspen. The stated overall purpose in the three-leaf binder we received (along with T-shirts and hats with MANDALAY, the name of Guber's ranch, embossed on them) was: "To take advantage of the collective intelligence of this team to move the company forward." One of the specific objectives included: create a bonding—one company, unified. There was also a written outline for the guidelines for executive interaction at the company. A few gems that practically redefine irony: "Tell each other the truth"; "no hidden agendas"; "take a nonjudgmental, nondefensive, sympathetic, appreciative tone toward each other"; and "be sensitive to others' core issues and proceed with extra care as you approach these." Guber hired a facilitator to teach classes on corporate bonding and to help us solve internal conflicts and generally open the lines of communication. Another retreat for about thirty of the company's executives was held in Sedona, Arizona. Everyone was flown to lunch on a mountaintop; presumably, the tranquility would help ease the tensions. On the surface, these were good ideas. They were a way to get the entire management team together and discuss the problems at the studio. However, Guber himself could have solved more problems by being more open and honest with everyone.

Partly in an attempt to deal with Guber's working style and partly because I felt changes were needed, I made two key executive changes at the beginning of 1992. I hired Marc Platt, who had stayed behind at Orion when I left, to be president of TriStar, and I brought on Stacey Snider as president of production. Marc was the devil that I knew, and I needed someone who knew my taste in material and my method for putting together movies and handling talent.

Stacey Snider came over from the Guber-Peters Entertainment Company, which, for some reason, had been kept active after Sony bought it to secure the services of Guber and Peters. Perhaps Guber wanted the company to stay active in case he decided to return to producing—which, it turns out, is what he wanted to do from the day he took the Sony job. Finally, after Peters left and started his own company, GPEC closed its doors and folded its projects into Columbia. When the news broke that Stacey was coming over to TriStar as a production executive, several people cautioned me that she was extremely political and would simply function as Guber's mole. Not only had she worked for Guber, she had roomed with Mark Canton's wife, Wendy Finerman, in college. By that time, I was happy not to have to talk to Guber directly. If there was a perception in Hollywood that she was some sort of shadow head of TriStar, then that was the price I would have to pay for not having to deal with Guber.

When I first approached Stacey, she turned me down. I don't know why, but eventually, she agreed to take the job only if I hired Platt, which was my plan all along. As for the gossip about my power being usurped, I figured I was secure enough with myself that if I did the right thing then Stacey would relay what I was doing to Guber along with my reasoning. In other words, if I could make her an ally, she would handle Guber for me. This would save me the wear and tear of talking to Guber and then hearing what he really thought from others. As it turned out, it backfired on me. I never knew where she stood, and ultimately, she couldn't cope with Guber either.

One of the greatest ironies to working under Guber is that he never seemed to enjoy his job as chairman of Sony Pictures. At the ShowEast theater-owners convention in Atlantic City, New

Jersey, in the fall of 1992, Guber confided to me that he wanted to be a producer again. He was constantly plotting his deal by soliciting advice from all the various branches of the company. I remember him asking an executive in the video division what the ultimate deal would be for a producer. In hindsight, it is clear that after Sony rebuffed his more grandiose ideas, he set his sights on masterminding the perfect production deal for himself.

When Guber renegotiated his employment contract with Sony in September 1994, he had an entire addendum added about Sony funding his production company if he left the chairman's job. This provision was so detailed that it was clear he planned to return to producing. It spelled out how many films he could make and at what budget level he could make them. He would be able to cherry-pick projects from either Columbia or TriStar and funnel them through his company, which would be named Mandalay (after his Aspen ranch). The deal turned out to be so one-sided that Guber was forced to redo it after everyone discovered what had been done.

▬

By the end of 1993, the whole town knew that Guber was going to push me out. Never mind that *Sleepless in Seattle* and *Cliffhanger* had been hits or that *Philadelphia* had opened over the Christmas holidays to strong business and considerable Oscar buzz, I was far out of favor with Guber and had been for a long time. The worst part about it was that there was no one I could really talk to. I got along well with Ken Lemberger, who was handling TriStar's business affairs, and with company president Alan Levine, and I trusted both of them. But the conversation I needed to have was with the guy who brought me in, my old friend Peter Guber. That was all but impossible because we were barely on speaking terms.

The end finally came when I was standing in a New Jersey shopping mall in early 1994 watching a group of post-grunge-era teenagers file into a test screening of *Johnny Mnemonic*, a film starring Keanu Reeves that TriStar was releasing in 1995. I was in the middle of a phone conversation with Jon Dolgen, who was relaying some subtle message from Guber. Midway through the conversation, I cut him off.

"Jon, I'm really tired of this. Please, who do I have to fuck to get off this train?"

I'm sure the feeling was mutual at that point.

▨

Executive executions are public in Hollywood.
Appeals based on facts are never heard.

▨

When studio heads lose their jobs, their photographs are splashed across the front page of *Variety* and *The Hollywood Reporter*. At the studio commissaries and the regular lunch spots like The Grill in Beverly Hills, agents, producers, lawyers, and executives all talk about the fact that so-and-so got canned. Then they try to assess what it means to them. In my case, *Variety* followed the conflict closely as it unfolded, and after I finally was asked to resign on Friday, January 7, 1994, both the *Los Angeles Times* and the *New York Times* ran front-page stories in their business sections and had follow-up stories on my situation a few days later. Easily, the most biting irony of all, which the press pointed out, was that my movies were making money.

Philadelphia had opened wide to a strong $12 million. Besides the fact that it stands as one of the proudest films ever made by a major studio, it was also the highest-grossing film of 1994 released by a Sony Pictures company, finishing up with $76 million in domestic box-office receipts. Two films that I developed and Stacey and Marc brought to fruition after I left also became Sony's two highest-grossing movies in 1995, when *Legends of the Fall*, a film that I dragged out of development hell, did $66 million, and the Christmas release *Jumanji* did $54 million that year and ended up with a total gross of just over $100 million.

In short, the films made under my TriStar regime were Sony's highest-grossing films in 1993, 1994, and 1995. In return, I was replaced and my contract was settled out. There were also several movies that went into development during my time at

TriStar but didn't get made until after I left. A project I bought for producer Laura Ziskin called "Old Friends" that was going to be directed by Penny Marshall was eventually directed by Jim Brooks and released in 1997 under the title *As Good As It Gets*. The film was a box-office hit, and it won Jack Nicholson his third Academy Award and Helen Hunt her first. That same year, *Donnie Brasco*, which I developed and tried to package with Tom Cruise and Al Pacino, was made. *The Mask of Zorro*, which came through the relationship with Spielberg during the making of *Hook*, was made in 1998 and became a big hit. The one that slipped through the cracks was Dr. Seuss's *Oh, the Places You'll Go*, which we bought for Roland Joffé. It stalled over an argument about whether to do it as traditional animation or computer animation and was never made. It was another lost opportunity in a sea of them.

Further, I had been largely responsible for the formation of Sony Pictures Classics. In December 1991, when I heard that John Kluge wouldn't let Eric Pleskow authorize a $1 million payment that the classics division owed for *Howards End*, I called the three partners at Orion Classics, Michael Barker, Tom Bernard, and Marcie Bloom, and asked them if they wanted to come to Sony and form a classics division there. I talked to Guber and he gave the idea the greenlight. The three formed Sony Pictures Classics and, as their first film, picked up *Howards End*. They mapped out a brilliant marketing campaign, and it picked up nine Oscar nominations and earned $26 million at the box office. To this day, Sony Pictures Classics continues to be a successful stand-alone division at Sony under the same leadership, their most recent triumph being *Crouching Tiger, Hidden Dragon*, which won four Oscars and stands as the highest-grossing foreign film ever in the United States.

Looking back, I would hold up my record at TriStar against any studio heads over the last decade. Sure, I had some costly misses—notably *Another You*, a comedy that reunited Gene Wilder and Richard Pryor, and *Mr. Jones*, a drama with Richard Gere and Lena Olin—but what studio head doesn't? If there is a disappointment it's that I wasn't able to get to a place where I could go beyond the day-to-day operations and work on a more

visionary level. My method has always been to give my subordinates the ability to enter the process and help them make decisions for themselves. The idea of having to take such a degree of
oppression every single day with very few people you can really
talk to is difficult. In that regard, TriStar was the opposite of the
United Artists and Orion situations. Whether I liked it or not,
there was always somebody at UA or Orion to have an honest,
productive conversation with. While Arthur Krim and Eric
Pleskow were often pessimistic about things, at least I could con-
front them with my ideas and problems and talk through the situation.

More so than anything else, my time at TriStar underscored
the fact that a good friendship and a good professional relationship are nearly impossible to balance. You can know someone
for fifteen years in one context, as I did Guber, but when your
relationship is tested in a different context, the result can surprise you. The line between social friends and business friends in
the entertainment industry is a very fine one for most people. I
thought I knew the difference between my friends and my
acquaintances, but in a few cases it turned out I was wrong.

The only time Guber and I ever really talked about what
happened was after the fact. He kept trying to underscore that I
should be thankful because I made nearly $20 million total
from my employment at TriStar and that was more than I had
ever made. When I left he had also offered me a production
deal, which I wouldn't have taken if I never worked on another
movie again.

What Guber could never grasp was that what I cared about
most was being *respected* for the work I did. That was all that
mattered. The rest was B.S. After that one conversation, we
agreed to disagree, and now we are trying to put this period
behind us. In a small community like Hollywood, you are
inevitably going to run into each other. The choices are to look
away and let the anger bubble inside, or to deal with it in a
grown-up way by redefining the relationship.

So when Guber called me in the early summer of 2000 and
asked me to have dinner, I accepted. We met in Brentwood at the
Italian restaurant Toscana, an informal neighborhood bistro.

What became apparent in the years after we worked together is that Guber doesn't have a lot of friends. During our dinner, the days at Sony never came up. If we had had an in-depth conversation, it wouldn't have helped. Whenever Guber is pinned down, he resorts to his trademark speech patterns—pausing and nervously repeating himself with regularity, because he has nothing to say. We talked about surface issues, like our new projects and where we thought the Internet was headed. It was clear that we were never going to revisit the past.

In some ways, it was all very Hollywood. Breaking bread with them what wronged you is as common as air-kissing in the movie business.

▤

With time has come perspective for me, and the one thing I hold on to when I reflect on my years at TriStar is that we are never exactly who we think we are.

We are somewhere between what other people think we are and what we think we are.

▤

Over the past forty years, press interest in Hollywood has grown immeasurably. Sitting down to review the mountain of press coverage or talking to people about the years I spent at Sony, the most often used word to characterize the Guber era at Sony is "excess." Journalists Nancy Griffin and Kim Masters wrote an entire book titled *Hit and Run: How Jon Peters and Peter Guber Took Sony for a Ride in Hollywood* to chronicle the journey of Guber and Peters at Sony. It's true that Guber and Peters were spending money that wasn't theirs as fast as they could. Their feeling was that if you spend big, you will eventually get a *Batman*. But you know right from the subtitle that this is a gotcha book. Peters's name comes first even though the previous company was called Guber-Peters Entertainment Company and Jon worked at Sony for only fifteen months while Guber was chairman for five years. Jon is a hot button for controversy. He makes for better copy.

While the facts might be subject to interpretation, you at

least have to start with them. Among my biggest complaints was that the authors got my birthday wrong. *Hit and Run* repeatedly interpreted several situations using the wrong facts. They gave TriStar credit for releasing *In the Line of Fire* under my watch; it was a Columbia movie done under Mark Canton. On the surface, those are small details, but the authors use *In the Line of Fire* to make the point that Columbia, under Frank Price, couldn't release any movies that made money.

The authors talked about the overly rich deals that the Guber regime was making, such as the one with Jim Brooks. They reported it as a $100 million deal; in fact, it was $40 million. The book also says that Columbia outbid Fox and Universal by $20 million for Brooks. While this may be so, the salient fact that needed to be ferreted out was that Columbia wasn't the highest bidder. Like the Spielberg situation on *Hook*, the Brooks deal was made at a time when everyone wanted to work with him. Brooks was coming off *The Simpsons*, and he had recently made a deal with ABC for the network to fund three shows with twenty-two-episode (full season) guarantees. Prior to Columbia, Brooks had a deal at 20th Century Fox, but there was tension because Brooks had made a deal at ABC and Fox chairman Barry Diller had wanted him to make all of his TV shows for the Fox Network.

Hit and Run told the story in a fast-and-loose tone that made for better reading, proven by the book's appearance on the best-seller list. Much of the interest was due to the fact that in November 1994, Sony announced it was taking a $3.2 billion write-off in the second quarter due to losses associated with Sony Pictures Entertainment. This occurred just two weeks after Guber officially resigned as chairman of Sony Pictures. While Guber and Peters parachuted out with a rumored $300 million between them, the story quickly became that Guber, with the help of Peters, burned up the $3.2 billion. Because I ran TriStar for four of those years, I, too, was tagged with part of that loss.

However, if you actually sit down and do the math, the story isn't that juicy.

From Wall Street to Sunset Boulevard, it was generally believed that Sony got fleeced when it bought Columbia Pictures Entertainment; whether they did or not will be open for debate until they decide to sell the studio. But when Sony finally admitted that it had overpaid, the media largely ignored this and pinned the loss on the Guber-Peters regime. That's what you call "changing the angle of the story."

There were three elements to the $3.2 billion write-down: excessive good will on the books from the purchase price; reserves for ongoing litigation with HBO that Sony inherited; and the operating losses from the studio. There was $2.7 billion alone from the inflated purchase price, including such things as lawyers' and bankers' fees. That number was sitting there from day one. Sony had overpaid for the studio and five years later it was determined that the amount of good will was too great to be written down over forty years so it had to be written off.

So if you take $3.2 billion and subtract $2.7 billion, we're at $500 million. $300 million of that figure was money that was set aside at the time of the purchase for ongoing litigation with HBO that Sony assumed by buying Columbia. The balance of $200 million was losses directly attributed to Guber's tenure at Sony. A small part of this was from what is called "garbage clean-up." When a new management team moves in, they clean house. Production deals they no longer want are paid off. Pay-or-play commitments to talent on films that the new management team doesn't want to make are satisfied and then written off. There was also a charge for closing some movie theaters. The balance, which is some number between $100 million and $200 million, was the actual loss for movies and television programming. While that's not nearly as good a story as Guber and the rest of us running through billions of dollars, that is the truth. But the apocryphal story of Guber losing the money has become cemented in Hollywood lore.

The truth is that Guber did a lot of good things at Sony. He restarted the engine of a studio that had been dormant, and he painted the lot for the first time in twenty years and made it the most attractive place to work in town. Of course, this is like giving Mussolini credit for getting the trains to run on time. If anything, his style of management squandered the opportunity to deliver on the promise of a re-energized studio that could have become a great studio where the business and art of making movies could co-exist. That is the real shame of the Peter Guber era at Sony. It was a lost opportunity and one of the last of its kind.

≡

One aspect of my years at TriStar reminds me of the explorer who climbed Mount Everest and upon reaching the summit discovered that all that was there was snow and ice. I took this to heart as I began to think about what I wanted to do next.

I had never made the kind of big money that Guber or most other studio heads did. By the midnineties, the Warner's co-chairmen, Bob Daly and Terry Semel, were said to be making $50 million a year and eventually left with a payout of about $250 million and a Gulfstream jet each. When Matsushita bought MCA/Universal, Sid Sheinberg collected $113 million for his stock, signed a contract for $8.6 million a year, and received a $21 million cash signing bonus. In the coming years, severance packages kept increasing: Michael Ovitz collected $90 million after being ousted from Walt Disney after just one year. Despite the fact that Guber tried to sell me on the fact that I had made out well, I needed a job—and I wanted one, too.

I had interest from Fox in making a production deal, but I didn't want to become a studio producer. Several people called with unsolicited advice. Some advised me to become involved in international relations, others thought I should go into politics. Mike Ovitz told me to take a year off and think about what I wanted to do. That was easy for him to say because he had pocketed tens of millions from helping broker Sony's purchase of Columbia and Matsushita's buyout of Universal, and he had a place to go to work every day.

Anyway, I'm not built that way. My parents taught me to get up in the morning and go out and accomplish something. They had been forced to start over three times in their lives in three different countries, once in Shanghai, again in Chile, and finally in the United States. There are very few people who can do that and maintain their equilibrium. Certainly, I could handle starting over in the cocoon of Hollywood.

My father always used to say to me, "You need a profession that you can fall back on." In fact, each time my father moved during his life, he would always start out in the car business because it was universal. He didn't need to know the language to work on cars. When we moved from Chile to Long Beach, he got a job working the night shift at the General Motors plant; he would eventually work his way up to the management of Isuzu (USA). When I left TriStar, I finally realized that I do have a profession: I know how to make movies. There is always going to be room for someone who knows how to make good movies.

That was what I wanted to do when I was seven years old and that's what I decided to continue doing.

17 *A Phoenix Rises*

In a matter of days after I left Sony in January 1994, God greeted the Los Angeles area with an earthquake that measured 6.8 on the Richter scale and shook the mountains, valleys, and beaches to their core. Glassware crashed to the floor, television sets went flying, houses were destroyed, and entire apartment buildings collapsed. Even those who escaped with minimal damage to their personal property were forced to alter their lives for months as the city put itself back together.

This cataclysmic event seemed to send off after-shocks across the movie business that lasted all year, including for myself.

The earthquake was also upsetting.

For the first time in my career, I was without a job. Regardless of my severance package from TriStar, being unemployed for the first time in more than thirty years produced conflicting emotions. On the one hand, there was the prospect of doing great things in the next chapter of my career, but on the other hand, the fear loomed that I wouldn't be able to do anything at all. Some people in the movie business talked about me as if I were dead, while others went out of their way to be nice to me—either because they genuinely liked me or just in case I landed somewhere that they could make their next film. My producer and agent friends continued to send me scripts to help me jump-start my new company, but now they were giving me free "options" on the projects until I got going.

Even the film courier offered to deliver for free. For my part, I tried to focus on what I wanted to do and to ignore the noise.

To paraphrase one of my favorite quotes, a poem by the Italian poet Montale that I keep in my office as a constant reminder, I was experienced enough to see that the desire to huddle in groups, escape thought, and talk about others was a sign of desperation and despair.

Personally, it was a difficult time, as I was reassessing where I was in the business. After my experience at TriStar, I began questioning my talent and my ability to read people—all people. How could I have been so wrong at something I was so good at? Was the lesson of *Hook* that my philosophy of not interfering with a filmmaker was dated? What could I have done to reverse the tide with Guber after *Bugsy*? Was I missing part of the big picture? I knew I should have stood up and fought for *Quiz Show,* but wasn't there some way I could have handled the situation with Robert Redford better? As always, the business was growing younger every day. Was I part of a dated old guard whose days were numbered? Did people still want to make movies with me? Or was the cruelty to others that I had witnessed so often about to hit me?

While these questions followed me like a Shakespearean ghost, I was determined to keep making movies as long as I could—and certainly not when others told me to stop. I also realized that I would never tire of getting my hands on a great script, finding the right director and cast to bring the project to life, and putting together the deal that turns a film—which, at its core, is an art form—into a viable business. The only thing I was burned out on was corporate politics. I was entering my first solo entrepreneurial phase, which is something most people do at the beginning of their careers rather than the end. The turbulent nature of the business gave me more of an adventure than I bargained for. I wanted to build a relatively small company that had the freedom to make the kinds of quality movies that were largely missing from the marketplace. This would prove to be quite a challenge in the wake of the metaphorical earthquake that the movie business was going through.

Larry Gelbart once said, "In half a century, we've gone from Citizen Kane *to candy cane. That's what comes from playing it safe."*

■

By 1994 studio films had, for the most part, become a mishmash of special effects, gutter humor, over-the-top action sequences, and more explosions than there are in the solar system. I've always preferred wit and reality to toilet talk and banality. There was also more studio interference than ever before in the film-making process, partly because costs were spiraling out of control. There were more bodies at these studios than ever before, yielding millions of different opinions and often paralyzing the decision-making. In the seventies, the studios had basically left filmmakers alone, and they had delivered a diverse and varied array of great films. But in the eighties, freedom had given way to heavy-handedness. Now, in the nineties, the average studio movie had thirty people doing story notes, twenty people playing producer (and taking screen credit for it, too), and focus groups composed of disaffected Gen-Xers causing entire films to be re-edited into cookie-cutter models.

Marketing was controlling the decision-making process to the point that it had become the reason films were made. If studios thought they could sell it, they gave a film the greenlight. If studios were high on a project but unsure of how to market it, they would do whatever it took to make a salable film: insert an actor just to have a "name," change the genre, make it a male buddy film instead of a love story. A studio executive's gut was no longer his guide; his marketing research report was. I'm not against market research, but the fact is that it relies so heavily on what has happened in the past. You are always looking in the rearview mirror, always checking to see what worked in the past, and always justifying why it worked. The problem with this thinking is that it doesn't allow for films that don't fit the mold.

One Flew Over the Cuckoo's Nest, Rocky, Amadeus, and *Dances With Wolves* would have never been made had we based our decision on market research.

At the box office, 1994 had turned out to be the year of half-wits and gimps. *Forrest Gump*, a movie project that had been knocking around the studios for years about a half-wit adventurer with a heart of gold, became the fourth-highest-grossing film of all time and eventually won the Academy Award for Best Picture. Violence turned mainstream cool when Quentin Tarantino's *Pulp Fiction* became all the rage, grossing more than $100 million, earning several Oscar nominations, and bringing John Travolta's career back. It was also a year when a comic actor named Jim Carrey, heretofore known as the only white guy on the Fox sitcom *In Living Color,* dominated the box office with three hit films in the gutter-humor genre: *Ace Ventura: Pet Detective* in February, *The Mask* in August, and *Dumb & Dumber* at Christmastime.

The movie business was also consolidating. A year-long battle for Paramount Pictures between Barry Diller's QVC and Sumner Redstone's Viacom ended with Viacom winning—for about $3 billion more than it wanted to pay. Both Castle Rock and New Line Cinema were purchased by Ted Turner's Turner Broadcasting. Awash in cash, New Line set out to become a major by paying a record $4 million for *The Long Kiss Goodnight,* a spec script by Shane Black, which was made into a mediocre movie that lost money. But perhaps the biggest ripple effect came not from consolidation but from the tragic death of Walt Disney president Frank Wells, who was killed in April in a helicopter crash.

Wells's death set off a chain of events that dramatically rearranged the power structure of Hollywood in ways that are still being felt to this day. When Michael Eisner refused to promote Jeffrey Katzenberg, who ran the company's film operations, into Wells's job, Katzenberg left the company to team up with Steven Spielberg and David Geffen. In the fall of 1994, just as I was raising money to start my own company, the three formed a new company that was eventually named DreamWorks, which they promised would become the first full-fledged Hollywood studio built from the ground up since United Artists was formed in 1919. They should have called me—I could have told them how difficult it was.

Before anyone had any inkling there would be a DreamWorks, I called Steven to tell him what I was doing and to feel him out about joining forces. I doubted that Steven would join me in my new venture, but what I didn't know was that Katzenberg and Geffen were onto a similar plan.

Had Katzenberg gotten the job he wanted at Disney, things might have turned out differently. . . .

The formation of DreamWorks was greeted with great fanfare. Initially, when Spielberg, Katzenberg, and Geffen were casting about for a studio to distribute their movies, Alan Levine told me he had offered them TriStar. (This was shortly after I left.) Levine's basic idea was that they were three stars, so the name fit. His proposal was simple: in return for their services and the rights to distribute their films, Sony would provide them all the financing they needed and give them the keys to the Culver Studios lot (where Sony's television operation was housed) as a home base—the same lot that housed the office that Guber refused to give Spielberg when I asked. They turned Levine down. While the final chapter on DreamWorks is a long way from being written, it is likely they will be absorbed by a major studio at some point, thereby continuing the consolidation trend.

▬

I recently had a dream. I was getting ready to receive an award and Arthur Krim called me. "This isn't just another Hollywood beauty contest, is it?" Arthur asked.

Putting together a new production company that can finance movies is no pretty matter.

▬

My new company was eventually named Phoenix Pictures, not for the Phoenix rising from the ashes but because it is a strong-looking symbol. Phoenix had also been the name of my wife Irena's company, and I hoped that would bring me luck. I set out to create an on-screen logo that would be memorable by using the gong in the J. Arthur Rank logo as a guide and the match strike from *Lawrence of Arabia* as an inspiration, and then I called Jerry Goldsmith to record the logo music. Phoenix was born.

Control was a key issue for me. I wanted to have the final word on all creative decisions. Throughout my career I have always looked for colleagues, partners, and subordinates who complement my strengths and fill in the gaps of my weaknesses. To make things run more smoothly, I wanted to find two types of people to help me: one to handle the business end and one to be the emissary on the entrepreneurial front. Even before I left Tri-Star, I knew that I wanted my partners to be Arnie Messer, a lawyer who had worked as a senior business executive at Columbia, and Peter Hoffman, a former Carolco executive with strong overseas relationships. When I approached them, they both agreed to join me. Peter was one of the primary architects of the initial structure for Phoenix and the man who came up with the insurance company–backed financing that allowed us to finance our first five films. This deal was the first of its kind and it involved borrowing money from a bank to fund a film and then buying an insurance policy to insure against any potential loss. Peter left shortly after the company was formed because some of our major investors were uncomfortable with having him as a partner, and he took a nice size payout for his work.

My goal for Phoenix was to return to the days of United Artists, when filmmakers were given a modest amount of money to realize their visions. I wanted to make the kind of director-driven movies I had been a part of at United Artists and Orion. I envisioned a return to the roots of the five approvals, where once the script, cast, director, budget, and producer were agreed upon, the filmmakers would go off and make their movie with minimal interference. I didn't want to repeat the past; I wanted to rekindle it. If possible, Phoenix would make its own signature films that would stand apart from those made by other companies. I wanted to avoid replicating what I did previously. In fact, I had never liked making sequels, although I knew that the needs of the business force you to make them. They are a staple of the business and the only near-sure thing.

There were several ways we could get our new venture off the ground: The first was to buy an existing library, or to take over a company that had a library. Immediately after Arnie and Peter agreed to partner with me, we wrote a letter to John Kluge and his partner, Stuart Subotnick, and set forth a proposal to either join Orion and reactivate it using Kluge's financial capabilities, raise new production and development funding, or take over the company's distribution arm for our own films.

Before meeting with Kluge, Arnie and I went to see Arthur Krim at his apartment in New York. Arthur had recently been in the hospital and still looked very frail. We had a pleasant meeting, during which we discussed the business and reminisced about some old times. His training as a lawyer prevented him from revealing anything that might be too personal about Kluge or how to deal with him. But mostly, I wanted to thank him for all that he had given me and let him know that I wanted to carry on the great tradition of UA and Orion as best I could. At the end of the meeting, he wished me the best in my new venture, and I wished him well. His last words to me were, "The body can't but the mind is still there." He paused. "Do call me if it all comes together." It was the last time I saw Arthur. He died shortly thereafter.

Armed with these various scenarios of how Kluge could become involved, Arnie and I met with Kluge's partner, Stuart Subotnick, in New York to discuss a deal. Subotnick was like a poker player who never betrays any emotions, which made him a tough guy to warm up to. We went through the various scenarios, outlining our operating philosophy as well as our financial ideas, but once the price of the library came up, he seemed to lose interest. It turns out that he and Kluge were already looking at selling, so I decided to try to find a buyer who would take it off his hands and let me and my partners run the company.

I arranged a breakfast meeting to introduce Kluge to Larry Tisch, who owned CBS. My idea was to have Tisch buy Orion from Kluge and spin it off as a separate company. Both men got along fine, and we had a perfectly pleasant breakfast at the Metromedia offices in New York. However, before I finished my first cup of coffee, I realized that I was sitting there with two sellers and no buyers. The fact was that Tisch probably wanted to sell CBS just as much as Kluge wanted to unload Orion. At least I didn't have to buy breakfast.

Arnie, Peter, and I decided the best thing to do was to go out and raise the money on our own. Over the years, I had come across dozens of people who professed to be interested in investing in the movie business. After all, despite being one of the most difficult businesses in the world, it is one of the most exciting.

There were scions of wealthy families, princes with an entire country's economy as their bank, and just generally rich guys who like the idea of being part of the movie business. We put together a road show (not unlike the modern-day ones that high-tech companies do for their IPOs) to raise $100 million in equity financing, which would allow us to leverage close to $1 billion through various loans, but we quickly discovered in our travels that many of these people we were meeting, by and large, were just colorful characters with little money to invest who just wanted to sniff around show biz, or meet starlets.

One night in Singapore, Arnie, my wife, our bankers from Normura Securities International, and I had dinner with two English expatriates working as investment bankers in Hong Kong. They had written extensively about the return of Hong Kong to China in 1999, and they were better conversationalists than most people who wanted to be in the movie business. As diverse as their philosophical meanderings on the subject of what would happen to Hong Kong were, they were absolutely united on where the best Chinese restaurant in Singapore was. Once we got to the restaurant, the two experts also agreed the lobster sashimi appetizer was one of the greatest dishes of all time. But when this succulent gourmet feast arrived, my wife went to take a piece of lobster and the crustacean started to move. It was still alive. Our second dish was tamer but no less frightening: live shrimp drowned in burning alcohol.

Then there was a Middle Eastern businessman who professed to be one-stop shopping for our financing. He was the client of Nomura Securities International's London office, which was helping us raise money. However, this fellow proved to be terribly elusive. When they finally pinned him down, we flew to Belgium to meet with him. My first impression: this multimillionaire was wearing $25 shoes. After treating us to a lavish three-hour lunch, he pulled me aside. "I don't want to deal with any of these bankers," he told me. "I'll just write you the check for seventy-five million dollars and we'll keep the deal between us." Stunned, I asked him, "Right here at lunch? Before dessert?"

After I explained to him that either he or we had to pay the bankers a finder's fee at the very least, he agreed but confided in me that he didn't trust his bankers. By the time we got back to London to work out the deal with the bankers, it turned out that the guy was a total fraud. Not only did he not have any money, he was traveling under a false passport. Nomura, which had not done its due diligence, had spent $100,000 courting this purported multimillionaire and had nothing but a bad real-estate deal and a couple of lunch receipts to show for it.

However, London turned out to be good for us. It was there that we met James Lee, who became the catalyst for putting together much of Phoenix. James had the kind of varied background that was uncommon to people who made careers in the movie business. While working as a strategy consultant in the seventies, he helped reorganize the National Health Service in England and aided the Catholic Archdiocese of Malta with its financial planning. His film credentials were also solid. James had been involved with Goldcrest Films during its heyday in the eighties when the company backed such films as *Chariots of Fire*, *Gandhi*, and *The Killing Fields*. James agreed to become a consultant, for which he was later given an equity stake in Phoenix. His most important contribution was introducing me to an extraordinary Canadian businessman who was interested in learning about the movie business, Gerry Schwartz.

Gerry's company, Onex, based in Toronto, was a multibillion-dollar company that owned everything from an airline-food supply company to a chain of bookstores (and has since taken control of Loews Cineplex Entertainment Corporation, a movie-theater chain). While he was interested in making a modest investment in the movie business, Gerry didn't just want to write a check with lots of zeros on it and hope for the best; he genuinely wanted to learn something about how the movie business worked. He learned about each business he invested in. As we got to know each other, it was clear to me that I could learn a lot from him. The one promise I made to him was that I would always keep him in the loop. Without his investment and his support, Phoenix would never have existed. The relationship with Gerry proved to be spectacular because he was loyal, honest, and smart.

Initially, Phoenix raised $62 million in equity financing, and we later added another $12 million, all of which we were able to leverage into roughly $600 million in production financing. Besides Onex, our equity partners included a Canadian investment firm named Altamira; Showtime, a division of Viacom; the British media conglomerate Pearson; and Sony Pictures. The French TV giant Canal Plus and the Japanese electronics company Pioneer signed on as distribution partners. At the time, we also had interest from Paramount to be an investor and/or our distributor, but I later heard that Jon Dolgen, who had moved to Paramount to oversee its film operations, never felt sure that we could raise the money. Thankfully, he was wrong.

The basic structure was that each partner would put up a certain percentage of the budget for each film we did. Sony would distribute the films theatrically and on home video worldwide, with the exception of Japan, which we kept for ourselves. We took advantage of the influx of foreign television money and made a deal with Canal Plus for European television rights. The Sony deal, which was made by Alan Levine and Ken Lemberger, called for Sony to take a distribution fee on each picture. In an unusual step to these types of deals, we also didn't take any producer's fees on the films. The financing structure of Phoenix allowed us to unilaterally greenlight any film under $30 million; above that required each equity partner to increase its investment. The premise behind these deals was for Phoenix to own the copyright to the films so we could build our own library over time. Holding the copyright became my primary focus, since we could never have afforded to distribute our own films.

■

I wanted to keep Phoenix relatively small and contained, with overhead under $5 million a year. After we made the deal with Sony, we took over the three-story Frankovich Building directly across the street from the Sony lot. We hired a staff of about twenty people to handle development and business affairs, and to oversee production and publicity. Over time, I made development deals with a few production companies, including Sean Penn's Clyde Is Hungry Films and Nick Nolte's Kingsgate Films, and gave them offices on the first floor. Arnie and I took offices on the third floor at the east end of the building. Fittingly, not only did the ghost of Rocky roam the halls, as the building had been built by Bob Chartoff and Irwin Winkler, my office faced south toward the Sony lot, giving me a perfect view of the Thalberg Building.

Sony's and our initial plan called for us to focus on movies in the $25 million to $30 million range, but before the ink was dry on the contract, the business began changing in a way that made this unworkable: leading actors' salaries virtually doubled. The influx of money from the foreign markets in the early nineties began pushing the salaries of a select group of actors to unheard-of levels. Invariably, hefty raises for stars come from independents who are setting up films by preselling them abroad. In the seventies, Dino De Laurentiis did business this way, and in the eighties Mario Kassar and Andy Vajna of Carolco took it to a new level by paying Arnold Schwarzenegger $10 million for *Total Recall* and Michael Douglas $12 million for *Basic Instinct*. As big as these numbers were, there were bigger paydays to come.

The pay scale for movie stars was thrown completely out of whack in early 1996 when Mark Canton, who was still running Columbia TriStar, agreed to pay Jim Carrey $20 million to star in the black comedy entitled *The Cable Guy* because Canton was desperate for a summer movie. Due to his string of recent hits, Carrey's price was already at $10 million, but this was a huge jump because it leapfrogged Carrey over every major star in the business and triggered a chain reaction. Stars who had consistently turned in $100 million hits over the years, such as Arnold Schwarzenegger, Tom Cruise, Tom Hanks, Mel Gibson, and Bruce Willis, all made the case that they were worth at least as much as Carrey, if not more. Next, the agents began to reason that if those guys were worth $20 million, then Kurt Russell, who had had five of his last seven movies open at number one, was worth at least half as much. And if Kurt Russell was worth $10 million, then Alec Baldwin had to be worth $5 million, and so on. At the same time the lawyers began demanding greater perks. Because studios were forced to spend so much for a film's stars, they began cutting the prices of the character actors. The movie-star price war was on.

The agents and lawyers have a cover for the raises. Their first line of defense is always: "Don't pay it. It's your choice." If that doesn't work they tell you: "If I can't get the client his money, he will leave us and go with someone who can." Both of these are bogus because someone else will pay it. If actors are making the decision based only on the dollars, they are not serving themselves well. Maybe an actor wants to do it just for the money, but that is short-sighted on his or her part and is not the way actors do their best work. The fact is that the agents and lawyers have done as much—if not more—to drive up actors' prices to unreasonable levels, and this has hurt the quality of movies and the kinds of movies that get made.

Sadly, what you seldom find anymore is an actor (or his agent) saying, "What's the best deal I can get and still be in your movie?" People don't work on that basis, and I think it hurts everybody, including the audience. Many good projects don't get done because of this.

By 1996 this salary escalation priced the midlevel movie out of the market. You couldn't afford the stars proven to open movies like Arnold or the Toms in a $30 million movie, and there was no guarantee that paying a midlevel star $10 million would open your movie. So it became a fool's errand to spend $30 million plus another $20 million for marketing on a film that you weren't sure could score a big opening weekend. Every picture now had to "open" or it was headed for the video graveyard. To make money and limit risk, we needed to shift our focus to genre films or simply make the big-event movies that had the possibility of filling theaters on opening weekend.

Over time, Phoenix has altered its focus to conform to the marketplace, which led to our making the teenploitation film *Urban Legend* and its sequel, as well as the event film *The 6th Day*.

Sony also became a very different place by the time we released our first film in November 1996. On orders from Tokyo, Alan Levine fired Mark Canton that year, and when Sony wouldn't let Levine hire who he wanted, Levine himself was forced to resign. John Calley, who had returned from a twelve-year hiatus to help bring MGM/UA back by renewing the Bond franchise, was hired as chairman of Sony Pictures.

We now had someone overseeing our deal who hadn't made the deal. Calley told me that he felt awkward about the possibility that we would disagree on projects. I felt that those discussions were part of the creative process and I welcomed his politely sarcastic opinions, but he clearly felt uneasy about the situation.

If we were successful, no one would be happier than John Calley (except me, of course). If we failed, well, then it wasn't John Calley's deal.

▤

Ramping up: Phoenix's first two projects are the high-profile films Milos Forman's The People vs. Larry Flynt *and Barbra Streisand's* The Mirror Has Two Faces.

▤

During the first year, Phoenix put roughly fifteen projects in development, but our first two films, *The People vs. Larry Flynt* and *The Mirror Has Two Faces,* came from Sony's inventory. Both films had already been greenlit by Sony, and they asked us if we wanted to start Phoenix off by investing in them. We agreed to assume the cost of both films and oversee their production and marketing. This would allow Phoenix to jump off the starting line with two first-class films. Both films were financed through the insurance deal and later sold back to Sony. From a creative standpoint, the two films were naturals for me because I would be working with two old friends, Milos Forman and Barbra Streisand, two people I could trust to spend money responsibly and make decent films. While I ended up feeling that Barbra's film was too expensive and Milos's was too risky, they were still bets I was willing to make.

The People vs. Larry Flynt suggested just how hard it would be to put out interesting, provocative, and entertaining studio-sized films at a time when audiences craved *Ace Ventura* and political correctness was the buzz phrase sweeping the country. This was a distinctly American film that told the story of a bottom feeder who succeeded in a rough industry and ended up—inadvertently—becoming the Constitution's champion. In many ways, it represented the ultimate virtue of our democracy: even a reprehensible human being can become a hero of certain proportions. What made the film all the more interesting was that it took an immigrant director, Milos Forman, to see through the cluttered life of our most notorious pornographer and be able to show how a cold-eyed hustler could become an exemplar of an American ideal. The producer was none other than Oliver Stone, whose idea it was to go after Milos.

One of the things I wanted to do at Phoenix was to work again with certain filmmakers whose paths I had crossed in my career, and Milos was at the top of the list. However, my first reaction to *Larry Flynt* was that the subject matter was difficult because he was such an unsympathetic character. But I only had to remember what Milos did with *One Flew Over the Cuckoo's Nest* to convince myself that he could deliver an entertaining film.

Over the years, Milos and I found that we shared a lot: we both grew up outside of the United States, and we both owed much of our success to being able to live and work in a land of opportunity. Most people born and raised in this country take this for granted or regard it as a cliché, but it was very real for both of us. Because of our family histories, Milos and I both have a larger view of the world than many people in the movie business. Although my family escaped Russia before the Jewish persecution that occurred during World War II, Milos was not as lucky: He saw both of his parents taken to a concentration camp. That he never saw them again gave him a particular appreciation for the preciousness of life, liberty, and the pursuit of happiness. It's no wonder that he lives every day to its fullest or that he is not adverse to having a beer and a fine cigar for breakfast.

I've always thought there was an interesting comparison to be made between Milos and Roman Polanski, whose parents were also taken from him to concentration camps; Roman's mother died in Auschwitz. Milos has an almost starry-eyed outlook on life in the United States, while Roman seems to regard it as something of a trap. Much of this difference between the two comes from the contrast in their own personal constitutions and their experiences in America. When Roman fled the United States in 1978 after being charged with seducing a fourteen-year-old girl, he had a very different vision of America. First, he lost his wife Sharon Tate to Charlie Manson's gang; then he felt wronged by our court system when he was accused of pedophilia. As his years of exile continued to mount, Roman seemed to have lost faith in what America stands for, while Milos continued to embrace it. This may have a lot to do with why Roman makes dark films like *The Ninth Gate* while Milos works to turn stories like that of Andy Kaufman into films.

Milos made a powerful and tightly constructed film with *The People vs. Larry Flynt,* and it was wildly controversial from the day it was released. The film featured terrific performances and achieved a level of verisimilitude that was haunting. Woody Harrelson brought Flynt's demons to the surface and portrayed him as someone slightly too self-destructive to be heroic. Courtney Love floored critics with her devilishly kittenlike turn as stripper Althea Leasure, and Edward Norton showed his versatility as an actor playing Flynt's bookish lawyer. I thought the film stood an excellent chance of winning several Academy Awards, but I underestimated the impact its critics would have.

Here was an engaging film, one that I thought dramatized the basic and inherent contradiction in a society where freedom of speech is so highly valued. I thought it outlined the battle for the First Amendment in the most interesting terms. This was the conflict that Milos found intriguing and fundamental to our country's value system.

But *The People vs. Larry Flynt* was savagely attacked by Gloria Steinem and the National Organization for Women, who proclaimed the film misogynistic. They accused the filmmakers of trying to make a hero out of the pornographer whose *Hustler* magazine had showed brutal images of women. This was something of a one-sided debate in which they declared they were right, we were wrong, and there was no middle ground for artistic interpretation. A conservative group called Media Action Alliance joined the fight and started a postcard-writing campaign, promising to boycott all future films made by Milos and producers Oliver Stone and Janet Yang. To me, it seemed that their cries for censoring the filmmakers reeked of McCarthyism.

Even though I had been through similar situations in the past when Coretta Scott King attacked *Mississippi Burning* and GLAAD picketed *Basic Instinct,* I underestimated the damage these attacks would do to the film both in and out of Hollywood—and particularly within the studio that we so desperately needed to support it. Despite the fact that the film portrayed Larry Flynt as a guy who just wanted to get laid and make money and not someone who ever intended to be a freedom fighter for the First Amendment, the stigma that the film glorified a pornographer became permanently attached to it. The first blow came when Gloria Steinem lambasted the work in an op-ed piece in the *New York Times* on January 7, 1997, comparing Larry Flynt to a publisher of Ku Klux Klan books and a Nazi on the Internet.

Steinem's piece was published two weeks after the film opened, and it was reprinted ten days later in *Daily Variety* during the height of the Oscar campaign. The ad was taken out by an advocacy group called Public Citizen but it was paid for anonymously. We were on our way to spending $21 million marketing *Larry Flynt* and trying to build on its critical acclaim, but even as defenders surfaced we could never seem to overcome the attacks. In late February, the ACLU took out an ad praising Milos as a First Amendment advocate and a courageous and creative artist. Not every strong, independent-minded woman supported Steinem's position: I received a letter from Bonnie Bruckheimer, Bette Midler's partner in All Girl Productions, telling me that I should be extremely proud of the film. She wrote that she was no fan of Flynt's before or after seeing the film, but that she celebrated the liberties we share in this country.

For his part, Milos was puzzled and infuriated by the attacks and he fought back. At one point he told the *New York Times*: "When the Nazis and Communists first came in [to Czechoslovakia], they declared war on pornographers and perverts. Everyone applauded: Who wants perverts running through the streets? But then, suddenly, Jesus Christ was a pervert, Shakespeare was a pervert, Hemingway was a pervert. It always starts with pornographers to open the door a little, but then the door is opened wide for all kinds of persecution."

Sony just wanted it all to end. In particular, they wanted Milos to shut up so the controversy would go away. John Calley called me in Berlin, where the film won the Golden Bear at the Berlin Film Festival, and asked me to tell Milos to dial down his rhetoric. "You have to get him to stop because we can't win this fight," Calley pleaded. I argued that the fight would actually help the film—especially since the film was about free speech. When I passed Calley's message along, Milos was even more incensed than I. Both of us were appalled that a studio would not only refuse to defend a film that was rooted in the First Amendment, but would go so far as to ask the director not to speak out against the film's detractors. Milos was speaking for himself and not the studio. This was one of the many lessons I learned about not being able to re-create portions of the past in the current climate of the business: United Artists would have backed our filmmaker in the face of such nonsense, not begged him to throw in the towel so we didn't have to take the heat.

Of course, the film ended up losing in the short run. As much as any film, *The People vs. Larry Flynt* is truly one whose place in the history of cinema will be measured by time. The first round of the fight, however, came on our watch and cost us a solid run at the box office and Academy Award recognition. When the nominations were announced—only Milos Forman (for Best Director) and Woody Harrelson (for Best Actor)—Columbia was running away from the film so fast that you could hardly tell who the distributor was. When they refused to give Larry Flynt a ticket to the Oscars, Woody invited him because he felt it was the right thing to do. With all the violent and unredeemably trashy films that were in the marketplace, singling out an intelligently made film that didn't have any car chases, bloody beheadings, or even gratuitous nudity for that matter made little sense. Gloria Steinem and NOW, who even went to the point of showing up at the Academy Awards and picketing the film, simply made the wrong call.

▬

Despite the fact that Barbra Streisand is one of the great performers of her time, I have always felt there was a vulnerability about her that most people don't understand. Many people attack her for the wrong reasons. I have always been very protective of her. People misunderstand both her film work and her political activism. There is something tremendously humane about Barbra, which often gets mistaken as misplaced earnestness. She has always demanded to be accepted on her own terms, without compromise, and her fans have done just that.

Since the day I met her thirty years ago, Barbra was always a larger-than-life star in the public eye. Her fame transcends that of her peers in a way that makes her an easy target for critics. In her movies and her singing, she has been highly personal, which has proven dangerous as well. Being a smart and expressive artist often leaves one nowhere to hide. With *Yentl*, for example, she was willing to put her entire persona on the line to tell a story, which I found very admirable and brave. She is also not afraid to record a love song about her husband. She's always been there for me and I think I've always been there for her, so the friendship runs deep.

The Mirror Has Two Faces was the first project we had contemplated working on together since Jon Peters torpedoed Orion's involvement in *Yentl*. The film was about two Columbia University professors who fall in love. Barbra had been approached with the project when I was running TriStar, but I found the deal too expensive to make in the wake of all the money spent and the profits given away on *Hook* and *Bugsy*. We ended up about $1 million apart, but after I left she ended up making a deal with Mark Canton at Columbia.

At the time, she was angry that I wouldn't give her as much money as Canton would. She later asked me why, as her friend, I didn't make the deal. I explained to her that I thought friendship had to be separated from business. I knew how to do it and I expected others to as well. Unlike what happened with Redford, this didn't fracture my relationship with Barbra in the least. We are good friends to this day.

And, I ended up with *The Mirror Has Two Faces* anyway.

I agreed to pick up the film at Phoenix because I liked the idea and it had the kind of profile we needed to launch the company. Sony was pushing us to take the film, and I didn't want to start off on the wrong foot with our home studio. At that point, the budget, which was about $30 million, wasn't as big a concern because it was covered by the insurance deal that Peter had put together, a classic example of how decisions change based on the circumstances.

Largely because Barbra was the director and the producer, Phoenix didn't need to be heavily involved in the making of *The Mirror Has Two Faces*. The film had been greenlighted by Columbia, so much of the apparatus was in place. Barbra also knew what she wanted to do creatively, so it wasn't like we sat around and talked about a list of shots she needed to get for a particular scene. We did help finish the casting with Lauren Bacall playing her mother, which I thought was a nice touch. The film earned

Bacall an Academy Award nomination as well, and she should have won it, too.

We did get involved in the marketing of the film, which cost more than $23 million. *The Mirror Has Two Faces* was released just before Thanksgiving to take advantage of a time slot where there were no other strong female movies in theaters. It went up against *Ransom*, Ron Howard's film about a family whose son is kidnapped, and *Space Jam*, the Michael Jordan extravaganza, but it simply didn't do well enough at the box office. Awareness was high, but attendance was low.

The press attacked Barbra for being a perfectionist, and they attacked the film as a vanity project. As always, the criticism was unfair. Every decent director is a perfectionist, and the film was not a vanity project but a director's attempt to tell a story with passion for the subject matter she cared about. If you didn't like it, fine, but why resort to personal attacks?

▬

Phoenix had just gotten started and already we were finding out how tough things would be.

Arnie Messer and I had big arguments about whether we should have taken on *The People vs. Larry Flynt* and *The Mirror Has Two Faces*. His feeling was that we were spending too much money to launch our company, and ultimately he was proven right. Because we paid for the marketing, these first two films put us in a big hole. My feeling was that we couldn't claim to be a full-fledged production company if we didn't bet on Milos Forman and Barbra Streisand. The only reason Phoenix ended up not losing a significant amount of money is that we sold the films back to Sony and took a payout on what we would have earned from them over the next four or five years.

But "Don Quixote" was an even bigger cash drain. A script written by the late Waldo Salt (*Midnight Cowboy, Coming Home*), based on the classic novel by Cervantes, the film never got made. We poured $2 million into developing "Don Quixote" with director Fred Schepisi for Robin Williams and John Cleese to star in. Things went awry when we kept hiring writers to bring the project around to where Fred felt comfortable making it.

Unfortunately, as sometimes happens, the scripts kept getting worse.

During this time, I was being pushed by Robin's managers to make a pay-or-play deal with Robin—meaning that we would pay him his full salary even if we didn't make the film. He hadn't worked in a while and he wanted to start a film, which I fully understood. Finally, we held a reading with Robin and John, at which time it was clear to everyone that the latest script didn't work. Phoenix dropped out—$2 million poorer.

For a company that was not yet fully capitalized, that was a big hit.

Our next group of films was smaller in scope, but they were the kind of filmmaker-driven movies I wanted to make. I called Oliver Stone one day and asked him what he wanted to do next. We met at the Hamburger Hamlet, and he told me about a low-budget film noir he wanted to make. I jumped at the chance before even reading the script. The film was *U-Turn* (then titled "Stray Dogs"), a movie that I thought couldn't lose. It was budgeted at $15 million, and Stone assembled a great cast who all worked for near scale: Sean Penn (who replaced Bill Paxton at the last minute), Jennifer Lopez, Nick Nolte, Powers Boothe, Claire Danes, Billy Bob Thornton, Joaquin Phoenix, Jon Voight, and Liv Tyler. This was the only kind of low budget studio film you had a chance on: big names, small budget. What could be wrong?

Well, going in, I knew the film was dark. Sean played a small-time gambler, on his way to Las Vegas to pay off a debt, who becomes stranded in a dust-bowl Arizona town when his car breaks down. He gets mixed up with several of the locals, who are stranger than fiction, and things become truly bizarre. Creatively, there were things that hurt the film, particularly a gratuitously violent ending that wasn't in the original script. But I let Stone make the film he wanted. Then he also increased the budget from $15 million to $21 million, which added to its loss. But I think what hurt the film most was that some people found the film distasteful. Some even found it morally bankrupt. Without favorable notices from critics, these kinds of edgy films crash and burn. It did—though I felt that film was much better than the critics or the box office gave it credit for.

I also made *Apt Pupil*, with director Bryan Singer, who was coming off *The Usual Suspects*. Again, Bryan was the kind of director I wanted to back at Phoenix: He had a clear vision of what he wanted to do, and he could realize it on a reasonable budget. Adapted from a Stephen King novella, *Apt Pupil* was a dark film that told the story of a high school student who discovers that his neighbor is a Nazi war criminal. The film delves into how the nature of past evil doesn't die. Creatively, I was pleased with the result and I would do another film with Bryan in a minute.

But somehow, *Apt Pupil* didn't make money either, despite its low cost.

As a result, it was clear that we had to revamp the structure of the company and rely less on tricky financing deals. We either needed to put more money into our movies, which would greatly increase our risk on each film, or put less money in by making films on a "to hire basis," meaning we would develop the material and then bring it to a studio for them to fully finance. Ultimately, we were successful in doing this on two films, *The Thin Red Line* and *Vertical Limit*. But this also meant we would have to do some audience chasing. We needed to make films in the genres that were "working," which is not my preferred way of working. Trying to shoehorn a type of film before the audience has moved on to something else that is fresher is risky. If you are too late and make something that people feel they've already seen, you wind up looking foolish.

But the one thing I could never give up on was making quality films and backing directors I believed in. I decided to invest considerable resources in making a film by a director who hadn't made a film in nearly twenty years, but who was regarded as such a legend that virtually every actor in Hollywood wanted to work with him.

18 *The Thin Red Line*

In many ways, the fate of The Thin Red Line
reminds me of what happened to Raging Bull *when
it was released.* Raging Bull *didn't make money; in
fact, it lost money. Only when people looked back at
the eighties after the decade ended did they begin to
regard* Raging Bull *as one of the best films (if not
the best film) of the decade.* The Thin Red Line
*won't get its due until well into the new millen-
nium. Marty Scorsese, who directed* Raging Bull,
has already called The Thin Red Line *one of his
favorite films of the nineties.*

It was late September 1997 and I was standing on the bow of an
open-air boat of dubious craftsmanship in a winding river in the
Daintree Rainforest, deep in the Australian outback. Sean Penn
was at the helm and Woody Harrelson, the only other passenger,
was in the rear. The murky water was infested by crocodiles, and
judging by the way they were growling, snack time was rapidly
approaching. Even more frightening than the crocs were these
two wonderful crazies I was boating with. With no other human
being anywhere in the vicinity and no cellular phone service, it
was anybody's guess as to what would happen next.

Ever since Sean and Woody arrived in Australia to work on
The Thin Red Line, they had been involved in an escalating war of
pranks that reached funny but dangerous levels. What started
with an egg in the helmet and a snake at the door escalated into
an elaborate game of gotcha. Sean was the first to raise the
stakes: He and a friend posted fliers all over town late one night

advertising "Woody Harrelson Day." Locals were invited to gather at the town's center, where, they were told, Harrelson would sign autographs for $10 each. The saturation was so complete that radio stations began advertising the event and Harrelson was forced to show up, sign a few hundred autographs—explaining to everyone that they were free—and pose for pictures with every kid who lived in a forty-mile radius.

But this was grade-school stuff compared with Woody's retaliation. After Woody's part wrapped, he said his good-byes and headed back to Los Angeles. Or so everyone thought. In fact, he stayed in town and plotted his revenge.

Early one evening, Sean received an urgent phone call from Nick Nolte, who had just arrived for his six weeks of shooting. Nick told Sean he had been in a car accident and was at the police station. He explained that he was fine and that the police had arrested the guy he hit, who was wanted for outstanding warrants. All he needed was for Sean to vouch for him because he was a foreigner. As a formality, a doctor was coming to test his blood alcohol level.

This was all complete bullshit, but Nick is quite a storyteller.

The police station had a long hallway connecting the front waiting room with the offices. When Sean arrived, Nick was sitting in the front with two officers. Next to him was a burly, tattooed Aussie in handcuffs. The prisoner was complaining that if the cops didn't let him go to the bathroom, he would urinate on the floor. One of the officers uncuffed the guy and led him down the hallway to the bathroom. Minutes later, a scuffle broke out in the back and the second cop ran to help. Sean followed the cop down the hall, but just as he reached the back, shots rang out.

Sean whirled around and began frantically trying to escape, but all the windows and doors were locked. The cops returned to the front room and hit the floor. Behind them was the burly Aussie brandishing a .45 and yelling that he wanted to get out. Terrified, Sean hit the deck, too.

Suddenly, there was a knock on the door. The guy with the gun started yelling, "Who's that! Who's that!"

A cop explained it was just the doctor arriving for Nolte's

blood test. The guy told Sean to get up—they were getting out of here. "Don't shoot," Sean pleaded, as the guy seemed to take him hostage. "It's all right, man. Calm down."

When Sean opened the door, there stood Woody with a shit-eating grin and a camera. He snapped a picture of Sean Penn scared stiff. Woody couldn't wait to show everyone the picture—along with a videotape Woody had shot by hiding cameras throughout the police station.

That night, Woody, Sean, and a half dozen guys in the cast were hanging out on the beach. Woody was razzing Sean about his cowardly performance, which had been recorded by two hidden video cameras. Eventually, Sean mentioned a party he had heard about, and he and Woody headed off in a four-wheel drive with Sean at the wheel. Forty miles into the outback, Sean became agitated and told Woody they were lost. He pulled a U-turn and got stuck in the sand.

Sean told Woody to take the wheel while he pushed, but Woody protested that he was stronger so he would push. As Woody stepped out of the truck, Sean jammed it into four-wheel drive and literally left Woody in the dust, stranded in the rainforest, in the middle of the night, with no food, no water, and no way home except on foot. On his long walk back, Woody was eventually picked up by an extra who was on his way to work.

So there I stood on that bow of that boat, in the middle of nowhere, waiting for these guys to unleash the final gag in their battle, realizing they might kill me in the process. It was like the bridge scene in *Deliverance*—all that was missing was the banjo music. After swimming with proverbial Hollywood sharks for more than thirty years, getting eaten by a croc would have been a hell of a way to go out.

As much as any film in my career, *The Thin Red Line* was a film that required balancing egos, politicking, agenting, and a little luck to keep it all together. In many ways, it was something of a culmination of everything I had learned in my career up to that point. After getting *The Thin Red Line* in production, it would have been devastating not to see the finished product.

"John," I said to Sony Pictures Entertainment chairman John Cal-
ley, "this is why we're in the business, to make movies like this.
Every film is a risk. This is how you made your reputation."

   Calley paused at my challenge. "This film will cost more than
you have budgeted and will be too long. Besides, I'm in this busi-
ness to make money."

▬

When *The Thin Red Line* was first presented to me, the prospect
of making a movie with Terry Malick was very attractive. I had
always admired the inner calm that Terry projected, the quiet
and thoughtful resolve in every word he spoke, as if he actually
thought about what he was saying before he said it—a rarity in
Hollywood. Terry had always marched to the beat of his own
drum, one that I was never quite sure of, but it was one that I
always liked.

   Terry grew up in Waco, Texas, where he spent summers
working on oil wells and driving cement mixers. He then
attended Harvard, where he graduated Phi Beta Kappa and won
a Rhodes Scholarship to Oxford. When he was accepted into the
inaugural class at the American Film Institute in 1969, he was
teaching philosophy at Massachusetts Institute of Technology.
This unusual combination of backgrounds is part of what makes
Terry's work so compelling.

   As an agent, I represented Terry in the early seventies. I
signed him out of AFI, and he quickly made a name for himself
at the typewriter, working on several drafts of *Dirty Harry* and
rewriting the idiosyncratic Western *Pocket Money*, which starred
Paul Newman. But when *Deadhead Miles*, the first film he
received credit on, turned out so bad that Paramount didn't think
it was worth releasing, Terry decided he wanted to direct his next
film himself.

   With the backing of Ed Pressman, a fledgling producer who
was spending part of his family's toy fortune to break into the
business, and some oil money raised by his brother Chris in
Oklahoma, Terry managed to cobble together enough money to
begin shooting his own movie. *Badlands*, based on the killing
spree of Charles Starkweather and his fourteen-year-old girl-

friend, starred Martin Sheen and Sissy Spacek. It was guerrilla production at its finest, but it also had the attention to detail that makes Terry a superb director. For one sequence, leaves were glued on the trees to make it appear to be fall. Eventually, Terry ran out of money and called me for help.

I asked Terry if he had any old scripts lying around that I could sell. Like most writers, he did. I told him to sit tight for a few days.

Terry had become a fairly well-known writer among the younger, revolutionary filmmaking crowd in Hollywood, so I called a producer who was constantly asking about his work. I told the producer he could own a Terry Malick script if he wrote him a check for $50,000 that cleared the bank and agreed to pay Terry another $100,000 when the movie got made. However, I told the producer there wasn't time for him to read the script; I needed the money immediately. Slightly stupefied, the producer protested that he wasn't going to buy a script that he hadn't read. I explained to him that this was the only way he was going to get into the Terry Malick business because Steve McQueen wanted to pay Terry $300,000 to write a script, so why would Terry *need* him. Besides, I promised to help him get the script made if he bought it.

Terry got the check that afternoon.

Terry ultimately finished *Badlands* and the film was bought by John Calley, who was running Warner Bros. Calley had a reputation for loving filmmakers more than the film business, and he was a master at making himself seen like the patron saint of filmmakers and, in many ways, he was. *Badlands* was regarded as a highly original, distinctly American film, whose director had a cinematic voice as acute as that of Mark Twain. Film historian David Thomson called it the most assured American debut since Orson Welles's *Citizen Kane*. The film put Terry in the group of young directors to watch.

His next film, *Days of Heaven*, was very different in tone and substance. Set just before World War I, the hauntingly poetic film tells the story of an out-of-work drifter, played by Richard Gere, who travels to Texas with his younger sister (Linda Manz) and a woman he claims is his older sister (Brooke Adams). They find work as sharecroppers on a wheat plantation run by Sam

Shepard, where anger and loneliness collide as Shepard falls for Adams, who is in love with Gere. The film was shot and beautifully lit by the late cinematographer Néstor Almendros with magic hour light, and it played liked cinematic poetry. Years later, *Variety* hailed it as "one of the greatest cinematic achievements of the decade."

But after writing and directing two of the more stunning films of the decade, Terry dropped out of moviemaking. At the time, he looked to have a career every bit as promising as his contemporaries Marty Scorsese, John Milius, Paul Schrader, and Brian De Palma. In fact, Milius once suggested that Terry might be the most talented director of their generation—a generation that also included Spielberg and Coppola. During these years, Terry split his time between Paris, where his then-wife lived, and Austin, Texas, where he had gone to high school. He traveled extensively from the ancient caves of Nepal to the Swiss Alps. By the mideighties, when everyone in the movie business, from journalists to actors, was again craving the type of ferociously American signature films made in the seventies, people began wondering where Terry Malick was. All that seemed to be left were his two films, which played occasionally on a double bill at a revival house on Beverly Boulevard with lumpy seats and poor sound.

There were many theories as to why Terry didn't direct for so many years. Indeed there are entire magazine articles written on this very subject. Only Terry knows the real reason. John Travolta once claimed it was because Terry became distraught at the process of making movies when Travolta was unable to get out of his contract for *Welcome Back, Kotter* to star in *Days of Heaven*. Indeed, Travolta and Geneviève Bujold had been Terry's first choices for *Days of Heaven*. But Terry's brother Chris simply said that Terry was just doing other things that interested him more than directing movies. I never fully believed any of the theories, but I never asked Terry why he didn't make a film for so long because I figured that was his business. Besides, I don't think he would have told me anyway.

Terry adapted *The Thin Red Line* from a novel by James Jones that recounted the story of America's bloody defeat of the Japanese at Guadalcanal in 1942. Jones had also written *From Here to Eternity,* which was made into an Academy Award–winning movie, but *The Thin Red Line* was very different. The story follows the C-for-Charlie rifle company from their landing, through battles and personal turmoils and up to the departure of the members who survive. *The Thin Red Line* was a less romantic, more realistic examination of what the young men who were sent to war went through.

Although the book had been filmed before in a somewhat truncated form, two little-known, ambitious New York producers named Bobby Geisler and John Roberdeau decided to try and turn it into an epic. They purchased the rights to the novel in 1988 from Jones's widow, Gloria, and paid Terry to adapt the novel, hoping that he would one day direct it. Over the years they worked on other projects with him as well. When they came to see me about becoming involved in *The Thin Red Line* in January 1995, Geisler and Roberdeau were in dire straits financially. They asked me to option the script from them for $100,000 and become involved in putting the project together. They knew that Terry wasn't going to make a movie with just anyone after all these years, and they thought that I, as his former agent, could help push along his comeback as well as provide interim financing through my new company.

Twenty-five years had passed since I was Terry's agent, but on Terry's timeline that was like yesterday.

There were two issues for me: the money and Terry Malick. I had recently left TriStar but had not yet capitalized Phoenix Pictures. In short, I wasn't exactly looking for film projects to buy with my own money, though the prospect of Terry's directing again after fifteen years was immediately interesting. However, I was understandably skeptical. I had hired him to write *Great Balls of Fire!,* the Jerry Lee Lewis story, at Orion. He turned in an excellent script, though it focused more on the tragic aspects of Lewis's life than we wanted it to.

I knew that he would arrive at the decision to direct again on his own terms. Just because he had labored over a script on and off for seven years didn't mean he was going to commit it to film. No one could force Terry Malick back behind the camera. In fact, when I asked Terry point-blank if he would direct *The Thin Red Line*, he told me that he might want to return to filmmaking with a smaller project. The bottom line was, in my mind, he was strongly considering it but remained uncommitted.

Nevertheless, I didn't want to miss out on the chance to make a film with Terry because it was a chance to complete a circle. The producers, Geisler and Roberdeau, told me they needed the money soon, or they would have to shop the script elsewhere. Over the years I had been talking to Larry Lawrence and his fourth wife, Shelia, about the possibility of investing in movies. Larry was a distant cousin by marriage with whom I had become close during Gary Hart's campaign. The principal owner of the venerable Hotel del Coronado, Larry was one of Gary Hart's biggest financial backers.

Movies often get financed in bizarre ways that lead to trouble later, as I learned at Orion when we handled *The Cotton Club*, so this seemed like a relatively straightforward situation. Years later, Larry died while serving as U.S. Ambassador to Switzerland and ended up being buried at Arlington National Cemetery, but Shelia was later pressured into having his body disinterred when his World War II record turned out to be false.

Although Larry wasn't interested in getting involved personally, he thought it would be a good business venture for Shelia. She liked the glamorous aspects of the film business, so she agreed to invest $100,000 of "her money" in *The Thin Red Line*. I, in turn, loaned this money to Geisler and Roberdeau to keep them going in exchange for an option on the material, as well as two other projects they were working on. I agreed to give Shelia an associate producer credit and let her learn the business of moviemaking. However, after Larry died, this arrangement turned into a small headache: Shelia preferred corresponding through her lawyer. Ultimately, Shelia was repaid—with interest—and she retained her associate producer credit on the film.

Once Phoenix was formed, I rolled *The Thin Red Line* into our development inventory. With the exception of "Shanghai," a film set in the city where I was born at the time I was born, there was probably no other project that I wanted to get into production as much as *The Thin Red Line*. When word got out that Malick was recruiting for *The Thin Red Line*'s C-for-Charlie company, it seemed like every actor wanted to join. The film was shaping up as a throwback to the auteur days of the seventies, when actors wanted roles in films because they were good parts, not just good deals. It was exactly the kind of film I had envisioned Phoenix backing.

In the spring of 1995, Malick staged a reading of his script in progress at my house with Lukas Haas, Kevin Costner, Martin Sheen, Ethan Hawke, and Dermot Mulroney, among others. In the next several months, Ed Norton, Matthew McConaughey, Billy Baldwin, Ed Burns—even Leonardo DiCaprio, hot off *Titanic*—had flown to Austin to meet with Terry. By the time Terry was ready to decide on his final cast, he had also had serious conversations with Johnny Depp, Nicolas Cage, Brad Pitt, and Matt Dillon. I had even set up a call with Terry and Tom Hanks, who politely declined because, by that time, he was committed to *Saving Private Ryan*. Even with a who's-who sampling of the Screen Actors Guild ready to ship off with Terry, there would inevitably be rough waters ahead.

▬

By early March 1997, because we were ready to start filming, I needed a firm commitment from Sony, which had an option to invest and distribute the film. At this point, Phoenix had invested nearly $3 million in pre-production costs for the film.

Terry was scouting locations in Australia with his production designer, Jack Fisk, and his line producer, Grant Hill. Fisk was typical of the passion Terry inspired. He had been the production designer on *Badlands*, on which he met his wife, Sissy Spacek, and on *Days of Heaven*, and then became a director. Jack had lost touch with Terry during the eighties, but when he heard that *The Thin Red Line* was getting off the ground, he sent a fax to our office telling Terry, in short, that he would rather be a production designer on *The Thin Red Line* than direct a film of his own.

Sean Penn had been committed since the day he ran into Terry in a bar in the mideighties and told him, "Give me a dollar and tell me where to show up." Now he had vowed to recruit the rest of the cast himself if he had to. Terry and Nick Nolte had spent time at my house talking about the script, and it looked like Nick would take a part, too. John Travolta had repeatedly told Terry he would play whatever part Terry wanted him to.

Everything was coming together for Terry Malick to finally get behind the camera again, but it was up to me to get the financing together.

The film's $52 million budget would exceed Phoenix's $30 million trip-wire with Sony, so I needed the studio's consent to pull the trigger. It was clear that *The Thin Red Line* would not be a conventional movie. It was also clear from Terry's 190-page script (with obviously doctored margins to make it appear shorter than it really was) that it would not be a short one. It would need special care and handling in the marketing, so I wanted the studio behind it 100 percent. I didn't want a situation where Sony was forced to take a film they didn't want and, because of that, give it less than their best on the marketing front. I'd seen it happen too many times.

John Calley gave his final no, and although I didn't agree with him, I understood his decision. He didn't feel secure enough about that film. Nothing was more indicative of how the business was changing than Calley's decision: an executive once known around Hollywood as the great friend of the artist was now looking solely at the commercial aspects. It had been a long road for *The Thin Red Line*, but seldom does an artist like Terry Malick get a chance to make a big-budget film, and I wasn't going to let this rare opportunity slip away.

With Sony out for good, I had to find someone to finance the film relatively quickly. Terry needed to start shooting in a matter of months so he could finish before the Australian rainy season began in November. There was also the matter of finalizing the cast, which couldn't be done until all the financing was in place. I hadn't really shopped a movie package since my agenting days, but I thought I had a pretty good one to sell. I made some calls and Peter Chernin and Bill Mechanic at 20th Century Fox, riding high on the success of *Titanic*, immediately stepped up to take the movie.

Terry and Grant Hill returned from Australia and we met with Mechanic, Chernin, and Laura Ziskin, who was running Fox 2000, Fox's new adult-oriented film division. For someone who clearly didn't like being on display, Terry helped win Fox over. We discussed the logistics of the film and the budget. Grant Hill assured them that the film could be done for the amount we had budgeted, and Terry outlined some of his ideas for the movie. We also talked about the long list of actors, led by Penn, who were interested in being in the film.

Fox agreed to go ahead, provided that we cast at least five name actors for marketing purposes from a list of those who were interested and some they suggested. To keep the budget down, it was agreed that each star would be paid $50,000 per week to a maximum of $1 million. Of the actors, only Sean Penn would receive a back end. Because Fox was fully financing the film and paying for the marketing costs, Phoenix would not own the movie. We would serve as the producers and receive a fee for our efforts. This was the cost of getting the movie made and protecting our investment: the fact that Sony had opted out meant that *The Thin Red Line* wouldn't be part of our library.

Sean became the lynchpin for the other actors, a tribute to the high regard that others have for his work. As soon as Sean agreed to spend nine months working in the Australian jungle for $50,000 a week, it was okay for other actors to do the same. He called Harrison Ford, who declined, but Sean did help land Woody Harrelson and Nick Nolte. The push was on to get five stars who were ready, willing, and able to be in the film. Terry got back in touch with Matthew McConaughey and Brad Pitt to gauge their interest, and scripts went out to George Clooney, Bill Pullman, John Cusack, Robert De Niro, Robert Duvall, and Tom Cruise. In the end, Fox approved a list of actors from which five names had to be cast: Penn, Clooney, DiCaprio, Cusack, De Niro, Travolta, Pullman, Harrelson, Norton, Jason Patric, Viggo Mortensen, and Chris O'Donnell. Rick Hess, Phoenix's executive vice president of production, spent two months rounding up the actors.

Despite the fact that Terry was required to put five approved names in the film (Penn being the fifth), he was careful to cast unknowns in several of the major roles. Not only did he want fresh faces, but most of the soldiers who fought at Guadalcanal were also between eighteen and twenty-two years old. The final cast included more than enough names to satisfy Fox: Penn, Harrelson, Nolte, Cusack, Clooney, Pullman, and Travolta. (Clooney,

Pullman, and Travolta all had cameo parts.) Terry rounded out the cast with the solid up-and-coming actors Ben Chaplin, Elias Koteas, John C. Reilly, and Lukas Haas, and a group of unknowns in important roles, led by Adrien Brody, Jim Caviezel, and Dash Mihok. He had also promised to write a role for Gary Oldman, but once filming began, Terry realized that perhaps he had too many primary characters already.

By this time, I had also asked George Stevens, Jr., to take a break from his duties as producer of the Kennedy Center Honors and come aboard as executive producer. George had known Terry since he admitted him to the AFI in 1969, and the two had remained in touch over the years. Terry had asked that Bobby Geisler and John Roberdeau not be allowed on location. The situation between Terry and the producers was like a family falling out: The three had worked together for eight years on three projects, and for whatever reason, Terry wanted out from under them. My concern was for the movie, and since Terry was the director, he would be in charge of the set. Besides, even if Geisler and Roberdeau went to Australia, they wouldn't actually be producing the film, they would merely be looking out for Terry. George could handle Terry as well as they could. If Terry became gun-shy, George could give him a gentle nudge, though somehow I knew deep down that only Terry could control Terry.

This was the kind of moviemaking process that had produced so many path-making films in the seventies: you give a genius millions of dollars to go to the end of the earth in hopes that he will return with a masterpiece. Francis Coppola had managed to succeed with *Apocalypse Now*. Michael Cimino had failed with *Heaven's Gate* and ended up losing his career because of it.

We were hoping to remake a career on our set.

≡

"This is a film that must be made for an economical price. It will have to have a tight budget and a tight shooting schedule. There is nothing sure-fire about it from a commercial standpoint. It will make an outstanding film, there is no question about that, but there is also no question but what it is a financial gamble."
—Memo from Darryl F. Zanuck to Jean Renoir

≣

Production on *The Thin Red Line* began in June 1997 in the Daintree Rainforest just outside the tiny town of Port Douglas, in northern Australia. The journey to the location required a thirteen-hour flight from Los Angeles to Sydney and a three-hour connection to Cairns. From there, it was an hour drive up the coast to Port Douglas and another forty-five minutes inland to the location. The mountainous terrain was chosen because it closely resembled Guadalcanal, but the film's primary location, a mountain named Dancer, was so rough that trailers and production trucks could not make it up the hill. A base camp was set up on low ground and roads were carved out of the mountains for military vehicles to carry the cast, crew, and cameras up and down each day. Transporting the 250 actors and 200 crew members up the hill took two hours each morning and another two hours down at sunset. Grant Hill called the shoot logistically more difficult than *Titanic*, which he had worked on.

The production virtually took over the entire town of Port Douglas, a two-block strip of restaurants and knickknack shops best known as the embarking point for boat trips to the Great Barrier Reef. The younger cast members filled the smaller hotels and turned them into college dorms, while Penn and Harrelson rented houses so their families could visit. Malick rented a house with a basketball court and invited the actors over for pickup games every Sunday. The Community Women's Association building was converted into a makeshift movie theater. At the end of each day, the senior crew members would gather on metal folding chairs, beers in hand, and watch dailies. The standard uniform was outback shorts and work boots, and everyone was perpetually dirty. Malick himself did not attend dailies, though he often watched select footage on Sunday, the production's day off.

Because the film was a period piece, every set and prop had to be built. An entire airfield and seven World War II fighter planes were constructed in the flatlands about twenty minutes from Dancer mountain. More than two thousand uniforms were sewn to the exact specifications of those worn in Guadalcanal.

Principal photography lasted five months, and both the cast and crew were exhausted by the end. In all, there were more than sixty speaking parts and over two hundred extras, all of whom were dressed in full combat gear.

When I visited the location, it didn't take long to determine that Terry wasn't making a commercial movie. It also belied the description "art film." What Terry was making was best described as a "picture." He wasn't shooting the script; he was shooting the *essence* of the script. Often times, he would alter the way characters felt about scenes by filming the first half of a scene and then waiting to complete it until weeks later. I had been concerned that there were too many characters in the film, but Terry was always going to make the movie the way he wanted.

Terry shot for one hundred days in Australia, twenty-four days in Guadalcanal itself, and three days in the United States. Guadalcanal was not used exclusively because it could not accommodate a large production. Under tough conditions, Terry managed to finish only two days behind schedule and, more important, on budget. He shot a million feet of film and then took ten months to find the movie in the editing room.

The story Terry wanted to tell contained the same themes as Jones's novel, but it was different in many ways: One of Terry's central themes was the contrast between man at war in a nature that is at peace. He also wanted to look at the effect of the battle of Guadalcanal on the Melanesians who inhabited the island, gentle people whose lives were overturned by a war that didn't involve them. In doing this, Terry pared down the screen time of a few of the novel's main characters, particularly Corporal Fife, who was played by Adrien Brody. In the script, Fife was the central character. But by the time Terry arrived at his first cut, he had substantially downplayed his role and made the film more of an ensemble. In the process, he ended up cutting out Bill Pullman and Lukas Haas entirely.

When I saw Terry's first cut, which came in at just under four hours, I felt there was a problem with the film's clarity. He had made an impressionistic film, but he needed to shore up the narrative. He had been unwilling to combine minor roles and to focus on the premise of the two central characters, Fife and Witt (played by Jim Caviezel). To help the images flow, the decision was made to add a voice-over narration, so Terry culled together bits and pieces from the novelist Jones's writings and wrote the narration. Billy Bob Thornton, who wasn't in the film, recorded the narration, but Terry decided to go more impressionistic. He would use eight characters from the film to narrate. My concern, which I told Terry, was that he had to make sure the audience knew who was speaking. I also felt that a title card should have been added to start the film—a simple "Guadalcanal 1942"—but Terry was against this.

During the editing phase, Terry never saw the entire movie put together. "I work from the inside out," he told me. Again, this resulted in the disjointed feeling the audience came away with. There were aspects to working with Terry that were frustrating; nevertheless I stuck to my life-long philosophy of not tinkering. My feeling was that once you surrender yourself to the artist, you are at his mercy. If you try to force yourself into the process, you are, in effect, a fifth wheel. At one point, Terry promised me he would make a David Lean–style epic. In the end, he was simply not the kind of linear storyteller that Lean was.

▦

As I learned in my agency days, it's not what goes into a movie that's important, it's what comes out on the screen.

▦

On December 23, *The Thin Red Line* opened in New York and Los Angeles to reviews calling the film everything from the sacred to the profane. In the *New York Times,* Janet Maslin called it "intermittently brilliant," which I thought was a pithy assessment. In the *Los Angeles Times,* Kenneth Turan wrote that it was "an intimate, dream-time epic, an elliptical, episodic film, dependent on images and reveries, that treats war as the ultimate nightmare, the one you just cannot awaken from no matter how hard you try." But echoing what many said, Turan concluded that it "was a stubbornly personal film," while Maslin wrote that the film "shows why being a great film director and directing a great film are not one and the same."

All of this seemed to intrigue audiences. By January 4, the film had earned about $1 million in seven theaters, with an impressive $53,000 per screen average. (Often times, the best gauge of how a film in limited release is going to perform is the per-screen average.) The limited release strategy was working. Strangely, the film didn't receive any Golden Globe nominations from the mercurial Hollywood foreign press association, who probably didn't understand it. As planned, Fox expanded the film's release to twelve hundred theaters in mid-January.

But the film was dealt a near-fatal blow when *Saving Private Ryan*, which had opened in July and grossed nearly $200 million, was rereleased to bolster its Academy campaign and to push video sales. The move surprised me, but there was little we could do. It was hard enough selling the type of thoughtful film we had without having to go up against a Steven Spielberg film starring Tom Hanks, Ed Burns, and Matt Damon that covered similar subject matter.

There was a huge blast of sunlight when *The Thin Red Line* was nominated for seven Academy Awards, including Best Picture, making it the seventeenth film I had been involved with to be nominated for Best Picture. It was up against *Saving Private Ryan*, *Shakespeare in Love*, *Life Is Beautiful*, and *Elizabeth*. From the day the nominations were announced, the Academy Awards turned into a spending battle between *Saving Private Ryan*, which was a DreamWorks film, and *Shakespeare in Love*, which was a Miramax film. The battle was personal because, for the first time in the history of Miramax, Harvey Weinstein had taken a "produced by" credit (rather than his normal executive producer credit), meaning that he would personally get a trophy for his mantle if the film won.

In all the Oscar campaigns that I have been involved with in my career, dating back to *Rocky* in 1976, I had never seen anything like the one that pitted *Shakespeare in Love* against *Saving Private Ryan*. DreamWorks had struggled during its first four years, so it wanted to prove its worthiness as a creative force by winning an Academy Award. Miramax had won the prize with

The English Patient, but Harvey himself hadn't won. Both studios poured millions of dollars into their campaigns and then argued in the press about who was spending the most. I had never seen two studios so commercialize the process. The Academy Awards have long been used as a marketing tool by studios, but it seemed to me and to many others that each studio was trying to buy the Academy Award. The Award was being trivialized like never before.

For a while, I held out hope that there might be a backlash against both films, and we could sneak through and win, but we ended up being shut out. I thought Terry had a good chance to win the Oscar for Best Adapted Screenplay because the film was so daringly original, and that John Toll (who had two Oscars) might win for Best Cinematography for the film's imagery, but neither happened. For us, the fact that the film was recognized by so many craft branches of the Academy would have to be the triumph. On Oscar night, in what was considered the biggest upset since *Driving Miss Daisy* won over *Born on the Fourth of July*, *Shakespeare in Love* took home Best Picture, while Spielberg won Best Director. I knew how DreamWorks felt because I had watched *Apocalypse Now* lose to *Kramer vs. Kramer* and *Raging Bull* lose to *Ordinary People*. Still, I wasn't terribly surprised. After all, *Shakespeare in Love* is a film that celebrates actors, and the actors' branch of the Academy has by far the most members.

It was deeply satisfying to be sitting in the orchestra section rooting for a film that I had been intimately involved with. More than the other sixteen films that had been nominated for Best Picture, this one was especially personal. I felt we had made a film of great substance and quality. Instead of chasing a teenage audience or trying to blow people out of their seats, we had attempted to make a thought-provoking film. Over lunch after the film had run its course in theaters, Terry admitted to me that he might have had too many characters. Nevertheless, at its core, *The Thin Red Line* was the apotheosis of filmmaking. The long, laborious process of putting a film together suddenly seems worthwhile. It was a film whose result redeemed the pettiness that occurs on a daily basis in the movie business.

If you have this experience once a decade, then you are doing pretty well.

19 *Surviving in a Bloodbath*

The movie business is no longer about movies; it's about "content and distribution," "controlling rights," and "distribution fees."

The strange thing about the business today is that the new cost structure is undermining these basic principles. From a studio's point of view, movies are so expensive that studios are forced into split-rights deals just to get films made, which runs counter to what made them solid companies that have survived the test of time.

For a boutique production company like Phoenix Pictures, this climate means taking enormous risks to survive: one of mine was Arnold Schwarzenegger.

The movie business has become almost unrecognizable from my early days in the industry in the late sixties. Currently, eight companies—News Corporation, Walt Disney, AOL Time Warner, Viacom, Sony, Vivendi-Universal, General Electric, Bertelsmann—control nearly all of the movies, television shows, music, books, and magazines seen by wide audiences. Four of those companies are controlled by foreigners: Sony is Japanese, News Corp. is Australian, Vivendi is French, and Bertelsmann is German. The reach of the biggest three, AOL Time Warner, Disney, and Viacom, is staggering. All of the following companies operate under the corporate umbrella of AOL Time Warner: Warner Bros., New Line Cinema, the WB Network, CNN, Turner Broadcasting System (including TBS, TNT, and Turner Classic Movies), HBO, the Atlanta Braves baseball team, the Time Inc. magazine group (including *Time, People, Sports Illustrated,* and *Entertainment Weekly*), Time Warner Publishing, the Warner Music Group, Time Warner Cable, and America Online—delivering movies, television, magazines, books, and the Internet to millions of people of all ages.

Movies, as you can see, are one division within a company that has ties to every single conceivable media business, but that division is the basis from which all else springs, including often the reputation of the company.

This is one of the biggest sweeping changes I have seen over the last thirty-six years, and tracing how and why this has happened, and what the effect has been on movies, was one of the reasons I decided to write this book. As with Orion and now MGM/UA, it is very difficult to operate as a stand-alone movie company. This is particularly true in today's media world.

The first wave of conglomerate corporate parents rode into town when I was an agent in the late sixties and early seventies: Gulf + Western bought Paramount, Transamerica acquired United Artists, and Coca-Cola bought Columbia Pictures. But how different the business model was then! At that point, companies with unrelated businesses were buying movie studios to use their cash flow to prop up the balance sheet. Today, General Electric, which owns NBC, is the only major owner of a media company that doesn't have direct parallel entertainment interests in its other core businesses.

How has this trend of the movie studios becoming vertically integrated affected movies?

Tremendously.

Basically, the film business has become just another content business. Major studios no longer rely on movies to earn them money. In fact, the profit margin on movies at the major studios has dropped to 5 or 6 percent. This means that, on average, there is no real profit to be made by releasing films in theaters. Only in the case of a gargantuan hit like *Titanic* does a film's box-office performance directly impact the bottom line of its parent company. For the record, *Titanic* grossed a worldwide total of $1.8 billion—$600 million in the United States and $1.2 billion overseas—by far the all-time record. Instead, the media conglomerates make their money from movies by feeding the movies into the other businesses they own—like home video, cable television, satellite broadcasting, merchandising, and theme parks. Previously, the power of movies was that they were the convergence of an art form, a commodity on the marketplace, and a recollective memory of our times. Today, movies are titles in a library that can hopefully one day be used in new forms of media. Walt Disney, in particular, wants films that can create attractions for its theme park and merchandise that can be sold through its Disney stores. Broadway shows like *Beauty and the Beast* and *The Lion King* can be created and then turned into multicity road shows if they are successful in New York. In short, Disney is interested in movies that become brands that will survive the test of time. A "movie" is limited to playing on cable, DVD, or, someday, a multi-purpose platform on a TV-size screen, but a brand can produce toys, sequels, theme park rides, and interactive games.

≡

In today's box-office climate, movies take years to come to fruition and a Friday night to die.

Today things have become so cutthroat that if you are releasing a major film, you must have a solid opening weekend at the box office or you are staring failure in the face. On most studio films, everything relies on the opening weekend. Studios spend millions and millions of dollars to get that opening-weekend gross. The most effective way to reach a mass audience is through television advertising, which also happens to be the most expensive form of advertising. A prime-time ad on network television in 1999 ran between $150,000 and $500,000 and sometimes up to $1 million, depending on the show. To cut through the clutter of all the other films, you must show your movie trailer over and over again. This becomes frighteningly expensive, but studios spend because the opening-weekend box-office number, which is estimated by the studios themselves and then reported to Exhibitor Relations on Sunday morning, is more than just a cocktail party topic. It's life or death, determined in 36 hours.

How a film "opens" becomes the basis for whether or not a studio will continue supporting the film. Because the opening now drives all ancillary markets, most of the time it determines how well the film will ultimately do.

The system of tracking the public interest for a movie before it opens and after the first few days in the theaters is similar to exit polling in elections. When a movie opens on Friday night, the studios call the major theater chains and get estimates. These estimates in certain key theaters can be compared with research information about who is going to see the film. These awareness percentages indicate what percent of the moviegoing audience will see the movie. Armed with a few estimates and poll numbers, studios can make a reasonable guesstimate at how the movie is going to perform. By Sunday morning, the studio can predict the opening-weekend nationwide gross. Perhaps the most dangerous part of the process is that the studio can soon predict with some certainty how the movie will do the following weekend, as well as its final U.S. gross. At this point, the studio then decides whether to continue supporting the movie with advertising or to make cuts in both advertising spending and the number of theaters in which the film is playing.

The only real exception to this vicious cycle are smaller art films and limited-release films. In their case, the most important number is the per-screen average. A film that grosses $15 million on three thousand screens has a per-screen average of $5,000, which is an okay result. For a limited-release film that is playing on fewer than twenty screens and hoping to build word of mouth in suburbs and other cities, the per-screen average needs to be above $10,000 and closer to $20,000 for the film to have the potential to break out. This wasn't true in the early eighties. *Arthur* opened to $5 million and then added $5 million a week for nearly a year.

This cold game of numbers affects the kinds of films that are being made. Studios now make most films to get the biggest possible opening-weekend gross, and this has pushed quality to new lows. Most of these films don't have the depth to stand the test of time.

Competing in this climate is very difficult. It's no longer enough to make a quality film. That film has to be made at a workable cost and marketed within an inch of its life—and even then you need some luck to turn a profit. Consider that *The*

Insider, Michael Mann's gripping 1999 film about the tobacco whistle-blower Jeffrey Wigand and his battle to tell his story on *60 Minutes,* ended up losing $35 million. The film starred Al Pacino and Russell Crowe, received a phalanx of publicity and marketing dollars, earned seven Academy Award nominations, and lost a small fortune.

The question facing Phoenix and other smaller companies as the new millennium arrived has been, quite simply, how to compete in a changing environment without a big wallet.

▦

As the legendary UCLA basketball coach John Wooden once said, "Pride is a better motivator than fear."

▦

Phoenix ended up making money on *The Thin Red Line* because it became a fee-basis film when Sony forced us to sell the film to Fox. But after that, I knew we needed to make some movies that added cash to our bottom line. We needed to make an event movie that had a chance of turning a big profit. Inherently, there would be high risk, but there would also be the possibility of high reward. In such a competitive marketplace, smaller movies have become increasingly difficult to sell. At Phoenix, we had personally experienced this problem in the summer of 1999 with the film *Dick,* which was a wonderful, well-reviewed film, but a marketing—and financial—disaster.

Dick was a biting parody of Watergate written by Andrew Fleming and Sheryl Longin. The basic plot of the film was that two high school girls (played by Kirsten Dunst and Michelle Williams) become Nixon's dog walkers and end up at the center of the key events in the Watergate scandal. When I read the script, I thought it was hilarious and smart—*All the President's Men* meets *Clueless.* I thought that if we could position it as a smart and cool film, then teenagers would come and so would adults who lived through the crisis. At Andy Fleming's suggestion, I sent the script to Gale Anne Hurd, who had discovered Andy out of New York University film school and produced his first film for Fox, and she agreed to come aboard as producer. I hadn't worked with her since *The Terminator.*

We needed to create a hip phenomenon around *Dick*, and we didn't have the right plan to accomplish that. Instead, the marketing people at Sony went for the obvious audience, teenage girls who would be attracted to Kirsten and Michelle. The film was released in August, which was probably a mistake. The upside of our date—that teenagers are out of school in August—was trumped by the fact that summer is the most crowded season for movies. While girls twelve to twenty-five liked the movie, after the first weekend it was clear that adults with firsthand memories of Watergate were even more enthusiastic. The reviews were very good, and both the *New York Times* and the *Washington Post* ran feature stories on the film. John Dean called me to say that even he liked it. However, *Dick* got such a slow start that it never recovered.

The other picture we produced for the summer of 1999 was *Lake Placid.* As with *The Thin Red Line*, Sony did not want to support our efforts on the film, so I went to Fox for the financing. While I could have contractually forced Sony to make the film under the terms of our deal, I didn't want to be in the position of having Sony market a film that it didn't want. With the growing importance of marketing, this would have been suicide. The film, which ended up getting to $35 million domestically and twice that much abroad, will earn Fox a profit, and the rights will revert to our library after fifteen years.

What Phoenix needed was a hit.

My problem had become that I couldn't do as many movies as I wanted because our films weren't profitable enough.

The only way to ensure any level of freedom is to make hits.

We hadn't produced a film that turned a solid profit since *Urban Legend*, which earned us roughly $15 million of pure profit. It was clear to me that we needed to make a sequel. My idea was to advance the premise of the urban legend to what is real and what isn't real. Essentially, we would have a movie within a movie. I hired John Ottman, who had worked for Bryan Singer as a music supervisor and editor, to direct his first film.

My feeling was that Phoenix had to do some genre movies aimed at teenage audiences. Once the first *Urban Legend* became a hit, we would have been stupid not to make a sequel in such a tough marketplace. Would I have made the first one years ago? Probably not. Was I forced to? Probably. The problem was that this led to us trying another film aimed at teenage audiences, *Whatever It Takes*. The idea was Cyrano in high school, and while I liked the film and it didn't cost much, it was a mistake for us. Those films rely heavily on hitting the target market—as we learned on *Dick*—and we never came close on *Whatever It Takes*. Somehow, the title seemed appropriate for Phoenix.

▦

In the spring of 1999, I discovered that I needed to have a heart valve replacement. Nothing concentrates the mind faster than the prospect of death. While thousands have had successful open heart surgery, when it's your turn you can't help but look at your own mortality. For me, that meant the possibility of giving up my Saturday tennis game of doubles that I had played for twenty-five years.

At the time, I was also in the process of trying to put together what would become the biggest movie budget-wise of my career. Coincidentally, the movie star I wanted to play the lead had undergone a similar open heart procedure: Arnold Schwarzenegger.

▦

The 6th Day would be the first movie in my career on which I gave myself a producer's credit. I did it for two reasons: Arnold asked me to produce the film, thereby sharing the creative risk with him, and I wanted to be more actively involved in this particular film because the subject matter interested me. The central theme of the film is an issue that stares back at us from the front page of the newspaper on a continuous basis: human cloning. I felt that if we could make an intelligent film about a newsworthy topic, fill out the movie with a strong supporting cast, and deliver the type of action and plot twists that audiences demand, we would be able to break out in the marketplace.

In the film, Arnold plays Adam Gibson, a man who arrives at his house one night and discovers that he has been cloned. Someone who looks exactly like him is singing happy birthday to his daughter and kissing his wife. The film is set a few years in the future, so we created a new world for audiences to enter. There is a multinational science company called Replacement Industries, run by the sinister, profit-driven Michael Drucker (played by Tony Goldwyn), that has developed technology to clone animals and human organs. Despite the fact that the Supreme Court has ruled it illegal, they also clone entire human beings. In fact, the High Court has ruled that any clones discovered must be destroyed.

Adam's attempts to get his life back lead him into the inner sanctum of this company. To play the company's chief scientist, Dr. Griffin Weir, who is conflicted over the use of this amazing technology that he has discovered, we hired Robert Duvall, easily one of the finest character actors alive. To play the company's assassins, we cast Sarah Wynter, who had recently appeared on the gatefold cover of the annual *Vanity Fair* Hollywood issue, and the intense Michael Rapaport.

Even with a large budget, putting the film together was not easy. The original script, written by Cormac and Marianne Wibberley, set up the story and created a fascinating world, but my development executives at Phoenix and I felt that the script needed to be polished to step up the conflict. We hired John Sayles, one of the most highly regarded independent filmmakers of our time, who pays for the small, personal films he likes to do by taking writing assignments on big studio films. Often, as in the case of *Apollo 13*, he doesn't receive onscreen credit for his rewrite work, which also ended up being true in our case, mostly because we kept very little of what he put in the script.

Getting Arnold to fully commit required a combination of the hard and soft sell. He was coming off *End of Days*, a story about a battle against Satan on the eve of the millennium, which was not one of his best films commercially or creatively. The film grossed $48 million in the United States, which is poor for a Schwarzenegger movie, and $225 million overseas, which is about average for him. Arnold had also taken a lot of grief in the media about the film's violence, and he wanted his next film to be smarter and less violent. I felt that *The 6th Day* was both a better story and a more accessible one for audiences—and that it would be his best role since the Terminator.

Pairing one of the biggest stars in the world with a director is always a delicate matter. While the director is in charge from a practical standpoint, the star is the de facto boss. To direct we hired Roger Spottiswoode, who had made the political thriller *Under Fire* for me at Orion. Roger is a transplanted Brit with an active mind and a good eye for detail. His results over the years, including *Air America* with Mel Gibson, *Stop! Or My Mom Will Shoot* with Sylvester Stallone, and *Turner and Hooch* with Tom Hanks, were mixed, but in 1998 he had a smash hit with the Bond film *Tomorrow Never Dies*. In my mind, Roger could work with movie stars, he knew how to do comedy as well as action, and he was someone I could work with. We considered other directors along the way, but I felt Roger was the best fit with Arnold and the material, and Arnold agreed. I hired Jon Davison to be line producer, the person responsible for the day-to-day logistics. Jon had line produced both *Robocop* films at Orion, as well as *Starship Troopers*, and I trusted his ability to watch the bottom line and to keep the film rolling.

Before Arnold would sign on the dotted line, he wanted to be totally comfortable with the script, and I didn't blame him. To alleviate his concerns and finish ironing out some of ours, we hired a writer he suggested to do a polish. Andrew Marlowe, best known for *Air Force One*, received the tidy sum of $400,000 for this "production polish." While this sounds steep, some screenwriters get as much as $1 million for this type of work. Unfortunately, Andrew spent six weeks and didn't deliver what we needed, so *another* writer was brought in. Dan Petrie, Jr., had worked on virtually every genre of film, from *Beverly Hills Cop* to *The Big Easy* to *Toy Soldiers*, a film I greenlit at TriStar, which Dan also directed.

Not only did we give Dan free rein to change whatever he needed to make the story work, I got on a plane with him in mid-August, along with Arnie Messer and Arnold's agent, Robert Stein, to meet with Arnold at his vacation home in Sun Valley. I wanted everybody on the same page, literally and figuratively. The creative process had started back on May 3 when I first had lunch with Arnold to discuss the movie. It was now more than three months later, and we needed to get the film off the ground.

Arnold's wife, Maria Shriver, became very involved at this stage. She made notes on all drafts of the script and wrote up cue cards for the creative meetings. She saw her role as her husband's adviser and protector. In one meeting at Arnold's house, attended by Maria, Arnold, Robert Stein, and me, she was the only one who had any real problems with the material, so I began addressing my questions to her, as if she were the one who had to be fully sold on the material. In a way, she was. No matter how much money we paid Arnold, he wasn't going to do the movie unless both he and Maria felt comfortable with the script.

Most of the time, Maria's tough-love criticism was pointed and constructive. However, at one point, I remember begging Robert Stein for mercy. "Look," I said, "I've been through all these meetings with Arnold and now Maria. With Maria, there was a point where she was helpful on the script, but we've passed the point. We moved the movie from Toronto to Vancouver to accommodate him. He's got to decide if he's in or out." Finally, both Maria and, more important, Arnold, were in. From that point forward, Maria stepped aside and Arnold became both the star and the co-producer, and he gave his all to the film as I had hoped he would.

It all came together in one final conversation with Arnold. By this time, it was late September. The art department, led by art director Jim Bissell, had been hard at work in offices on the Sony lot developing the look of the film. Jon had scouted out and secured most of the primary locations in Vancouver. We were casting about for the other principal roles and preparing to start December 6.

The conversation began with Arnold expressing some last-minute doubts. "Arnold," I told him, "I only want to make the best movie. We all have the same interests. When we are finished filming, we'll cut the movie with you and if you're not satisfied, I'll let you preview your cut. If it gets a higher score, then that's what we'll go with. I'm not stupid."

There was a long pause on the other end of the line. It was either going to happen or fall apart in the next two minutes. As much as I knew Arnold wanted to do the movie, I knew there was a chance he might not. I could sense his doubts. His last true breakout hit in a film that he carried had been *True Lies* in 1994, before his heart valve surgery.

"Arnold, if this movie isn't ready to go on December 6, we won't go at all. But you've got to leave this decision to me because I'm the one with everything to lose."

"Okay, Mike," came the heavy Austrian voice on the other end of the line. "I'll leave it to you."

▰

The budget was also a big hurdle. Even with the whopping salary Arnold commands, I made up my mind that we needed to do the movie for a reasonable price. It had to come in well under the $105 million figure that was spent on *End of Days*. There were several ways to pick up value without compromising the production, such as shooting in Canada. As an incentive for Hollywood producers to shoot films in Canada, the Canadian government offers a generous tax-benefit package. Basically, the production receives an 11 percent refund on every dollar spent in Canada. This provision, combined with the strength of the U.S. dollar against the Canadian dollar, results in a 20 percent increase in the value of every dollar. This has resulted in what Hollywood unions call "runaway production." While I'm all for films being shot in the U.S., the fact is that we couldn't afford to shoot *The 6th Day* in Los Angeles.

The budget was set at $85 million. All of Phoenix's partners had to increase their share, so there was quite a bit of jockeying behind the scenes. I first enlisted the support of my own board of directors, particularly Gerry Schwartz, to give me some leverage for pushing everyone else to step up on what would easily be our biggest film to date. The most important commitment had to come from Sony, which needed to put up $56 million. The advertising budget of roughly $25 million would be advanced by Sony, and they would get that money back before we recouped our investment.

The back-and-forth I went through with John Calley and his second-in-command, Amy Pascal, was typical of my relationship with them. As I was trying to bring the movie together in the summer of 1999, I was getting mixed signals from both of them.

Calley questioned the script's readiness and said that it would be irresponsible to give it his okay without seeing a final script. Amy, at one point, offered her support when Arnold was wavering by saying that if Arnold didn't want to do it, then we should get somebody else. They, too, were under a great deal of pressure because the studio was running dead last among the majors in the box-office rankings due to a number of costly failures.

At the same time, we were also in a disagreement over *Vertical Limit*, an action film that was one of their Christmas releases. Phoenix had developed *Vertical Limit* and brought aboard the director, but we didn't have the money to back the film, so we let Sony make it. Sony then sold the pay-television rights to HBO, despite the fact that all our movies are required to go to Showtime. To smooth over the situation, I agreed to take Phoenix's name off the film and settle out for a producer's fee.

Finally, Sony formally picked up its option on *The 6th Day*. However, Sony and Phoenix ended up debating the letter of the law on the financing of future films this size. I realize now, looking back over our deal with Sony, that from the moment John Calley came in we were very much at arm's length from each other. The lesson here is that a deal only works when both parties need—and want—it to work.

Arnold, Roger, and I all agreed that no matter what needed to be changed or cut out of the script prior to shooting, we couldn't go over the $85 million figure. There were tense conversations about what had to be cut to keep us on budget. Whenever a sequence was dreamed up that would enhance the film creatively, something had to be taken out to satisfy the budget. We all agreed to keep Dan Petrie on during the shoot to polish dialogue and overcome rough spots that emerged. Roger and I agreed to each put up $100,000 out of our own pockets to pay Dan. At this point, adding anything to the budget meant going back to the bank and all the partners, which was totally impractical at best and a potential disaster at worst.

The shoot went fairly smoothly. I visited the set in Vancouver several times, certainly more than I had on any other film I've been involved with. While I had spent considerable amounts of time in the editing room trying to tighten movies such as *Wolfen* and *House of Games,* I had never concerned myself with so many intricate details of production. For the first time in my twenty-six years as a studio executive, I found myself talking minutiae with the director and then balancing it with what the line producer thought the cost would be. Never before had I spent time discussing whether a wide shot of the city should lead to a close-up of a building or whether we should just start with an establishing shot of the building. There was something liberating about being involved in so many details. Ultimately, however, I followed my nature of leaving the creative decisions up to the director.

When *The 6th Day* finished principal photography, we cut together a version and set up a test screening. As much as I hate relying on a group of people recruited from a shopping mall to evaluate one of my movies, we needed to see if audiences felt it worked. We tested the film in Orange County and the results were encouraging. However, it was clear that they wanted an ending that tied up the loose ends. The question now was whether or not to invest money in additional shooting.

This is a classic situation of the creative forces versus the suits. Typically, filmmakers always want more money to shoot extra scenes or to reshoot existing scenes to enhance the film, while executives are skeptical about putting any more money into the film. As I reviewed the options, I had to rely on my instinct.

We had a good ending in the script, but there was no way to know if it worked until we put it on film. This often happens. *Fatal Attraction* is one of the better-known examples. In the original film, the last shot was of the Glenn Close character under the bathwater with bubbles rising to the surface. The message: *She's not dead.* But after this tested poorly, the ending was changed to have the wife of the man she had an affair with shoot and kill her. My feeling on *The 6th Day* was that we had come this far, we needed to go all the way. Since we all thought there was a tighter, more satisfying ending, we needed to shoot it.

In this case, I was functioning both as a producer and as a studio executive. After all, my company's future was possibly at stake here. The additional $3 million or so needed for location shooting at the Santa Monica Airport and on a soundstage at Sony would come directly out of Phoenix's pocket. We wouldn't know until the film was released if we were getting our money's worth.

By the fall of 2000, the stakes were frighteningly high for Phoenix. In many ways, *The 6th Day* felt like a make-it-or-break-it film for us. If it didn't deliver at least the domestic and international grosses of Arnold's last film, *End of Days*, we might be forced to scale back our company. By the time the film was released, we would have roughly $40 million on the line. Some nights while the reshoots were in progress, I would lie awake, staring at the ceiling, wondering if the film would perform. So many things had to come together.

In late September, Phoenix got a little breathing room when *Urban Legend: Final Cut* opened at number one at the box office. As good as that result was, it would have been better had we not been blindsided by the rerelease of *The Exorcist*, the classic horror film directed by William Friedkin from William Peter Blatty's novel. Originally, *The Exorcist* was only going to play on fifty or so screens, but the studio decided that since the film was tracking well and every dollar that came in was profit, the film should go out on eight hundred screens. Sony never warned us about this. I couldn't believe that in 2000 we were competing against a film that had opened in 1973, when I was still an agent.

I also began sleeping a little more soundly after we finished the additional shooting on *The 6th Day*. Everyone involved agreed the ending worked better. When the film was recut, I showed the finished product to Arnold. "Before it was an eight, now it's ten," he declared. There was a lot riding on the film, but my confidence that it would deliver was growing.

Marketing would be critical, not to mention expensive. We eyed two possible opening dates, November 10 and November 17. On the 10th, we would be against the new Adam Sandler movie, and the following weekend we would be against Jim Carrey in *The Grinch*. Since our core audience was teenage boys, we opted to go head-to-head with *The Grinch*, which felt like more of a family movie. The 17th also had the advantage of being the Friday before Thanksgiving, which is the official beginning of the second-biggest moviegoing season of the year after summer. Under our contract, it was Sony's decision to set the opening, and I left the choice to Jeff Blake, the head of distribution.

Another important choice we made was to go for a PG-13 rating rather than an R. We figured this would significantly increase the number of teenagers (particularly boys) who could see it. While several R movies have grossed more than $100 million, the climate for R movies was poisonous. It was an election year and the culture police were out in force. In the fall, eight representatives from the studios had testified before the Senate Commerce Committee about their marketing practices. Any R movie released would have to be doubly careful. The last thing I needed were political problems.

Before the public could be sold on the film, the Sony marketing staff had to be sold. After a disconcerting meeting with Sony publicity executives, at which they listed all the magazines that didn't want to run stories about the new Schwarzenegger film, I decided to show them thirty minutes of the movie. I had to get them to realize this wasn't just some overwrought, shoot 'em up action film. This was a new Arnold. Yes, we had three superior action sequences, but they fed the story. So before the reshoots were finished and without telling my director, I started screening footage for the publicity and marketing people. With all I had been through with marketing people in my career, never was I more dependent on a group to sell a film than I was with *The 6th Day*.

They all liked what they saw and called to tell me so. Ed Russell, the longtime head of publicity who had worked for me at TriStar, told me that he was "jazzed." His superiors were also surprised that we had created such an interesting, intelligent piece of work. The question now was, could they sell it? I felt that we had done everything possible on the film and the finished product was first rate. Arnold was certainly going to do his part making the rounds of the talk shows. But what we found was that Arnold was a tougher sell because his previous film hadn't worked.

We decided to premiere the film at the Tokyo Film Festival on October 28, three weeks in advance of the U.S. opening. In the past, this would have been highly controversial and even questionable. Until the midnineties, the United States always came first. But since the foreign box-office figures have passed the domestic ones, studios are focusing more and more on the overseas potential of a film. The Tokyo Film Festival has become a publicity platform for the rest of the world, just as the Toronto Film Festival in September serves as a sending-off point for many fall releases in North America. In fact, *Titanic* debuted in Tokyo two months before its U.S. opening. In our case, Arnold's last two films had delivered big grosses overseas, so rather than being a risk, it was something of a safety net.

It turned out we would need every advantage we could get.

Crushed by *The Grinch*, *The 6th Day* opened to a lukewarm $13 million at the box office, and we weren't able to recover. The film was scoring lower in exit polls than it did at our test screening before the changes were made. I thought it was a better movie with the reshot scenes. The fact of the matter is that once you've made the movie, you can reshoot one, two, maybe three scenes, but you can't really change the movie that much. Once you have pushed the button, the die is cast.

The film ended up grossing more than $100 million theatrically worldwide, but that is not the kind of numbers we needed to turn a profit. Ultimately, we will break even on the film, but that's not the same thing as a moneymaker. It helped me realize that in this new climate, the most viable way to run a production company is as a supplier to *all* studios. Phoenix, whose deal with Sony ended in September 2001, would be better served to develop films and shop them to studios, rather than be tied to Sony exclusively.

Our first post-Sony film to go into production was the military thriller *Basic*, directed by John McTiernan and starring John Travolta and Samuel L. Jackson. Phoenix developed the script and put the package together, and we then went to Intermedia for the financing. Intermedia ended up making a deal with Sony to distribute the film domestically. (Small world, Hollywood.) We have also decided to develop and produce more television, which led to us set up *The Chris Isaak Show* at Showtime.

One of the things about Phoenix is that if the company fails, it will be because I chose the wrong movies. Even on the worst days, I kind of like that feeling.

In hindsight, I don't regret backing *The 6th Day*. The film was another example of things coming full circle for me. I was working as an active producer for the first time with a core group of people who had come in and out of my career: Arnold Schwarzenegger, Roger Spottiswoode, and Jon Davison. I knew there would be tough going at some point—there is on every movie—so I wanted to create a braintrust of people whom I had watched and admired over the years. I felt that they delivered a first-class product; I'm sorry that the public didn't think so.

Adolph Zukor once declared that "the public is never wrong." Mike Medavoy's corollary is: *Sometimes studio executives are.*

▬

The definition of success changes as you get older and more established. When I started out in the movie business, I wanted to be successful. This meant being involved with great movies, winning Oscars, making money, and being highly regarded in the film community.

Today success is more ethereal and more internal. It now means having people respect me, learning something new every time I undertake a new project, teaching others the way Arthur Krim, Bob Benjamin, and Eric Pleskow taught me, and being true to what I've learned over the course of my thirty-six-year journey. More than anything, it means staying true to my beliefs—win, lose, or draw.

My journey through the film business was founded in a need to understand human nature and, in that regard, it has been successful. As a young boy, I was always curious what was around the corner, across the street, and oceans away, and I have tried to maintain that curiosity throughout my life. The forces that shaped my beliefs in my younger years gave me a necessary resilience to the imperfect process that is filmmaking. Even in the times that I lost my sense of direction, I was able to maintain a sense of wonderment about what films provide. Seeing how films can bring people together is the reason that I never gave up.

As I look over our upcoming slate of movies at Phoenix, I am working to fulfill this criterion of success. We have developed more than $25 million worth of projects with directors like Milos Forman, Phil Kaufman, Paul Verhoeven, John Boorman, and Andy Davis. I want to bring these to fruition, both for myself and for others who will build their careers on these films. As I finish this book, I feel that these projects are some of the best I have worked on in a very long time.

≡

Personally, I now aspire to heights that are probably just out of reach. Often, I am reminded of an old quotation from William Fox, the founder of 20th Century Fox. Reflecting on his career, Fox said: "As I became established and expanded my business, and life was no longer a battle to survive, my thoughts changed . . . and I realized there was a great deal more in life than just making money. What concerned me far more was to make a name that would stand for the finest entertainment the world over."

I feel I have accomplished the first part. The second part is still very much a work in progress.

But you have to have something to get you out of bed in the morning.

EPILOGUE   *The Seventh Act Break*

> *"The past has been an obstacle and a burden; knowledge of the past is the safest and surest emancipation."*
>
> —LORD ACTON

The movie business now stands on the brink of technological and creative revolution unlike any it has seen in the past seventy-five years, which is one of the reasons I wanted to sit down and take a look back over what I have seen. Digitization, which is the conversion of images, sound, and text into computer-readable data, is poised to make studio libraries more valuable and to open up the medium to an unprecedented number of filmmakers by giving them less-expensive ways to make movies and greater access to audiences.

The film business has so little order that it tends to cherish what order there is, which accounts for why it can act like the proverbial dinosaur in the face of technological advancements. Initially, filmmakers and studios alike were suspicious of sound and color, but they soon became so enchanted by these enhancements that films were too bright and too loud. The same has happened with the advent of other media that exhibit film. Legend has it that when television arrived in the late forties, Jack Warner had TV sets banned from the Warner's lot. Studios rooted against the VCR because they were afraid it would cut into box office. This is how the studios initially regarded digital cinema and the Internet.

It's no secret that technological advances have been slower manifesting themselves in the film business than in most other

347

industries. As prices have dropped, sales of DVD players have quadrupled in the past two years. While the VCR crowd has welcomed DVD, theatrical films are still produced on the same film stock as they were a century ago, despite the fact that digital cinema is cheaper, easier, and more durable than celluloid. By contrast, the music industry has transitioned from vinyl to cassette tapes to CDs. Quality is better and profits are up. While music can also be downloaded easily from the Internet in an efficient and cheap way, film is still years away from perfecting Internet distribution.

Presently, the studios are focused on the here and now. Because movies are so expensive to produce and market, studios are forced into split-rights deals just to get films made. In the seventies, studios didn't want to give away any of the upside to their competitors. When Freddie Fields made a deal for Fox and Warner to co-finance and co-distribute *The Towering Inferno*, it was revolutionary. Now it's rare for a studio *not* to have a cofinancing or co-distribution arrangement on every film. Typically, one studio distributes the film in the United States and a second studio takes the rest of the world. Studios even take equity positions in competitors' films that they don't co-distribute: When *Almost Famous* was deemed too risky by DreamWorks, the studio sold half its interest in the film to Columbia.

While the parent companies that own the studios see this state of affairs as risk management, movies as a whole have become nearly a zero-sum game on corporate balance sheets, which could prove dangerous to the long-term values of these companies. Digital distribution will give studios a new outlet for their libraries, but it will also provide a burst of creativity that will accompany new technologies.

In each of the four decades I've been involved in film, realworld events that conspired to change the times also changed the motivations of filmmakers. The chaos of American society in the late sixties and seventies created an indelible mark on a generation of filmmakers, much the way the greed of the eighties affected how and why films were made in that decade. The complacency that took hold in the nineties informed a new wave of filmmakers who looked to the seventies for inspiration. But just when we started thinking that we would all get richer and live forever, our world was radically changed when the U.S. was attacked on our own soil by terrorists on September 11, 2001. Just as the counterculture of the seventies influenced filmmakers of that time, the fallout from the terrorist attacks over the coming years will no doubt inform the sensibilities of the next generation of filmmakers.

In short, both movies and the business of movies are about to be changed.

■

Reflecting on the evolution of the movie business, Arthur Krim once said, "There's always going to be another turn of the screwdriver." Because of the daily blizzard of meetings, script submissions, phone calls, lunches, and required-attendance events that is the life of a production chief, it was sometimes easy for me to miss the changes that were going on in the business as they were happening. Recently I sat down and mapped out what I call the act breaks of the movie business in an attempt to understand how we reached this point and where we might be going.

An act break in a script is a critical transition point. There are seven major act breaks in the movie business, and the first three occurred one on top of another. These act breaks can explain how and why certain companies have succeeded and others have failed over the past fifty years.

The first act break was put into motion in 1938 when the U.S. Department of Justice sued the eight major studios for anticompetitive practices. The case ended up in the Supreme Court, and in 1948, the High Court handed down a decision known as the "consent decree," which forced studios to sell off their theater chains. Previously, studios made the films and then exhibited them in their own theaters, creating a monopolistic environment. Theaters were forced to play shlocky films made by their parent company, and in a double whammy that all but shut out the independents, the theaters traded with one another for films.

Around this time, the studio system crumbled. This was the second act break, and it broke the studios' vice grip on talent. Under the studio system, the cigar-chomping moguls had final say over everything—and they never shared the profits. The studios' actor contracts allowed the moguls to put their actors in whatever movies they pleased; if the actor refused, he or she was suspended and forbidden from working anywhere else. But in 1945 Olivia de Havilland sued Warner Bros. over her restrictive contract and won. As a result, the studios were no longer able to suspend actors who refused to work for them, which allowed actors to work elsewhere whenever they chose to. Suddenly, there was a pool of talented people looking for someplace less restrictive to make movies. Arthur Krim and Bob Benjamin put this act break to work in their efforts to revitalize United Artists by opening their doors to actors who wanted to work in a place that not only welcomed talent, but shared the profits with them.

As the studios were busy trying to delay the mandated divorce between production and exhibition, and deal with actors fighting to get out of their contracts, the third act break was occurring right under their noses: television. Bad economic times combined with the advent of television in the early fifties caused people to stay home for their entertainment. Television replaced B movies. Theater admissions dropped rapidly, from 90 million moviegoers a week to 30 million. Film production sank from 600 films a year to 150. Despite the fact that the studios desperately needed a new source of revenue, they stubbornly ignored television until the early sixties. Even Darryl F. Zanuck, as smart as he was, wondered who would want to get their entertainment from a little black box when they could get it from that big, silvery screen. Zanuck obviously never realized that the TV screen would be almost as big as a movie screen—and even bigger than in some theaters these days.

The fourth act break, which hit in my agency years and played itself out while I was at United Artists, came with the three TV networks—ABC, NBC, and CBS—paying top dollar for feature films. Emerging in the late sixties when studios were awash in red ink, this act break was the single most important business transformation as the seventies unfolded, and it virtually saved the movie business. Television's appetite for product created a new and reliable revenue stream for movie studios that would increase exponentially in the eighties as pay cable became a reality with

HBO, Showtime, and later TBS and TNT. The advent of cable television caused a radical financial impact by giving its owners two sources of income: subscription and advertising revenue.

Orion Pictures might still be alive today had we seen the fifth act break coming: the home-video boom. This happened because a major technological advance changed the viewing habits of the public. The videocassette recorder, commonly known as the VCR, had first come out in 1975, but there were two competing machines, Sony's Betamax and Matsushita's VHS system. Intense competition between the two companies, combined with the high cost of the machines themselves and lack of prerecorded movies, stagnated the growth of VCR until the early eighties. By that time, Matsushita had licensed its technology to other makers. Consequently, VHS became the dominant format and prices fell. I'll always remember how Saul Zaentz insisted on retaining what were then called the "home use" rights to *One Flew Over the Cuckoo's Nest*. Because Saul had made his money in the music business and seen technology alter the face of recording, he had the foresight to know that movies would catch up. How right he was.

The true home-video boom took hold in the early eighties when studios began releasing their first-run movies and their libraries on video. In the early days, studios would price the movies between $80 and $120 a copy, netting the studio roughly $50 to $90 for each copy sold. The balance was kept by the video-store owner. Of course, the real money came from rentals. As video stores began to rent movies for anywhere from $2 to $5 each, watching movies at home became more affordable to people; as more people rented movies, video-store owners began buying more copies. The growth of home video was staggering. From 1980 to 1985, the number of VCRs manufactured and the number of movies available on tape roughly doubled each year. Amazingly, in 1986 studios grossed $2 billion from video sales compared to $1.6 billion from ticket sales. Today there is even more money to be made because video chains like Blockbuster are now paying studios a percentage of each rental on some titles.

The sixth act break came in the early nineties when the foreign market exploded. International revenue climbed from 50 percent of a studio's domestic take to 150 percent. For the first time ever, demand for American entertainment was growing faster outside the country than inside. Due to rising marketing and production costs in the United States, by the end of the nineties, the American theatrical market was approaching a zero-sum game for studios. Mining foreign territories became the only way for studios to make money on first-run feature films on a consistent basis. This explosion of the overseas market began when companies like Carolco raised large amounts of money to make films by preselling the overseas rights. Because overseas markets liked movie stars, Carolco and others began paying astronomical amounts to a select group of actors, which started the bidding up of movie stars' prices.

By the midnineties, foreign revenue was still pouring in, but most of it was coming from television. Companies like Canal Plus in France, Kirsch in Germany, Rupert Murdoch's BSkyB satellite broadcasting company, and Silvio Berlusconi's web of TV companies in Italy were paying enormous amounts for broadcast rights to American films. Libraries of films had been driving American TV stations for more than a decade. Remember, Ted Turner had bought MGM just to get control of the rights to its library for his domestic superstations. By the turn of the century, the buying power of foreign television companies became the key revenue driver in the movie business. In fact, it has reached the point today where the French television company Canal Plus has become so powerful that the man running it is also in charge of Universal.

The seventh and perhaps the most powerful act break of all is upon us now: digitization. The three main engines of this wave of change are digital technology, the Internet, and broadband delivery, and the ultimate goal is convergence, or the coming together of content, the place you receive the content, and how the content gets to you.

While there have been enhancements in the world of celluloid, film itself remains a nineteenth-century technology. Since film was born in 1895, sound and color have been added and special effects have risen to unimaginable levels. Computer-generated images have made it possible to alter reality. In *Forrest Gump,* for example, the filmmakers were able to insert Tom Hanks's character into various historical settings in an almost seamless fashion. When Oliver Reed died during the filming of *Gladiator,* the filmmakers took his face from previous shots and digitally placed it on his stand-in to finish his scenes. A Warner Bros. executive told me that in 2000 alone the studio spent $250 million on digital enhancements. Sound, too, has gone from mono to stereo to Dolby Surround Sound, which creates the effect of putting audiences in the middle of the film.

Previously, films were edited by literally cutting the film and pasting together the images the director wanted to use—hence the term "cutting room." Today most films are edited on television-screen-size machines called Avids. But in comparison to other communications media—the evolution from the telegraph to the telephone to the fax machine to the wireless telephone to e-mail—these are relatively baby steps. The truth is that the process of shooting film and projecting it at twenty-four frames per second is remarkably similar today to when D. W. Griffith's *The Birth of a Nation* became the first feature-length motion picture to play in America. However, digital cinema stands to modernize filmmaking because it is cheaper, easier, and more durable.

Traditional filmmaking is a laborious process. The camera must be loaded and then reloaded for each new sequence. The finished product requires multiple reels. Once a film is locked, prints must be made from a master copy, and then shipped to theaters around the world. But the biggest problem with film is that it physically deteriorates over time. Colors become washed out, and eventually the film stock itself disintegrates. While older films have been preserved by print restoration and recolorizing, this process is costly, and the film can never be returned to its original state.

In contrast, digital films are shot on digital video and can be edited on personal computers. Digital movies can be distributed via phone and cable lines or satellite transmission, so there is no need for shipping prints. In fact, because digital projectors do not

use film, prints are eliminated altogether. These projectors function like computers. Their memories store copies of the movies
that can be played with the touch of a button. Synergy, that long
forgotten buzzword of the eighties, also has a chance to be reborn
with digital cinema. The first digital film made by a studio was
Mike Figgis's *Time Code,* which was released in 2000; it was
backed by Sony, which also manufactures digital equipment.

Many people in the film business are starting to come around
to the idea that digital filmmaking will be the way of the future.
The cost savings is considerable. A Panavision film camera costs
more than $100,000, while a digital camera can be purchased for
as little as $1,000. A print of a film costs about $1,800 to make;
therefore, a major studio release requiring three thousand prints
costs the studio more than $5 million, not including transporta-
tion costs. Prints sometimes become scratched or damaged during use. Digital distribution would eliminate this because films
would simply be beamed to the theaters by satellite or transmit-
ted through cable lines, as well as preserving the current version
more effectively than celluloid.

Changing the current system of film distribution to digital
will be costly and difficult. The biggest problem is that very few
theaters are equipped to show digital films. The cost of converting the current projectors to a digital system is about $100,000
each, multiplied by thirty-four thousand movie screens in the
United States alone. It's an understatement of epic proportions
to say that theater chains don't have the money to reconfigure
themselves. In 2000, three major theater chains filed for bankruptcy protection and nearly every major chain posted losses.
This was a result of all the overbuilding done to accommodate
the era of the blockbuster, which required theaters to have multiple screens to show the "big" films on opening weekend. Movie
studios are reluctant to buy the new projection equipment
because they see exhibition as the exhibitor's business. But they
had better be receptive to the idea or theater owners may start
buying films directly from producers, thereby eliminating the
middleman distributor.

Presently there are problems with both the Internet and digital cinema. Filmmakers often complain that digital film does not

have the lush quality of celluloid. Often digital images are flat and bland, as opposed to the rich and multidimensional ones on 35-millimeter and 70-millimeter film. However, digital filmmaking has been used by feature filmmakers with good technical results on *An Ideal Husband* and *The Celebration,* and it is frequently used for documentaries. Wim Wenders, who used it for his documentary *Buena Vista Social Club,* has said that digital film made it easier for him to quickly adjust to different light conditions, thus enhancing the spontaneity of his film. When it comes to Internet viewing, filmmakers are also worried about the quality of the picture on a computer screen. Again, technology will go a long way to correct this.

The combination of digital filmmaking and Internet distribution is potentially potent. Costs are significantly lower and the potential audience that can be tapped for very little money increases astronomically. As these two compatible technologies evolve over the next couple of years, filmmaking will explode. It will begin to feel like the seventies when maverick filmmakers broke down the studios and demanded to be heard. More people will make and see films than at any time in our past. While many of these films will be terrible, there will be infinite variety, and creativity will be stimulated.

The final ingredient to the new technologies affecting the movie business will be broadband delivery—which is to say a method to transmit movies at warp speed across phone and cable lines. Speeding up delivery will ultimately help solve many of the quality problems as well. The confluence of these technologies will become the vanguard of filmmaking for the twenty-first century. More so than with any of the other act breaks, creativity will be enhanced by digitization, and the art form that is film will be able to scale new heights.

The movie business has a habit of appearing trapped in the present, ignorant of the past, and indifferent to the future. But as the world is being transformed by a technological revolution, this is no longer acceptable. In many ways, digital filmmaking, the Internet, and broadband delivery are as much about democratizing movies, building for the future, and creating something that will be here long after we are gone, as they are about making money. Indeed, I have deposited copies of all my films with the UCLA film archives.

Part of me fears that the communal feeling of sitting in a darkened room, watching a film, and having a shared experience with a group of complete strangers might suffer if the Internet becomes too important a distribution outlet for films. However, I take solace in the fact that the home-video boom didn't kill moviegoing. What people found was that they liked catching up at home on movies they had missed, but they also wanted the chance to get out of the house on Friday night or Sunday afternoon and see what wonders were in store for them on the big screen.

Currently the future of the movie business looks more exciting than ever before. The possibilities of movies are more limitless than at any time in my life. The dreams will be far bigger than those imagined and realized by an immigrant boy sitting in an adobe building in Chile picturing himself battling with Captain Hook, or even those of a studio head worrying about how to update Peter Pan's story for a new generation.

For confirmation, we need look only as far as the latest cinematic phenomenon, *Harry Potter and the Sorcerer's Stone*. The film is based on a book that sprung from the imagination of J. K. Rowling, a British woman on welfare. Not only could *Harry Potter* become one of the most valuable movie franchises of all time, it's also the kind of movie that can touch people of all ages and nationalities.

As long as we can ensure that the human touch and the sense of wonderment are not lost along the way, I can't wait to see what happens to the medium that I have given so much of my life to. People need movies to be entertained, to feel connected to one another, and, in short, to live.

I know because I am one of those people.

Acknowledgments

Over the course of thirty-six years, details are often forgotten, subtleties change shades, and unintentional revisionism takes hold. To add perspective and clarity the authors have relied on books, newspaper articles, magazine clips, notes, records, call logs, letters, and, particularly, the recall of those who were there. The authors gratefully acknowledge the following people for their recollections, stories, and insights: Bob Sherman, Saul Zaentz, Freddie Fields, David Picker, Frances Doel, Gale Anne Hurd, Barbara Boyle, Peter Dekom, Woody Allen, Donna Gigliotti, Oliver Stone, John Milius, Dan Rissner, Tony Bill, Arnie Messer, Tom Pollack, Jon Sheinberg, Bob Chartoff, Lynwood Spinks, Marc Norman, Brian Medavoy, Michael Medavoy, Dora Medavoy, John Daly, Donald Decker, Marcia Nasatir, Fred Roos, Jim Cushman, Rob Fried, Arnold Schwarzenegger, Marc Platt, Michael Barlow, Jonathan Darby, Alan Levine, Freddie Goldberg, Michael Barker, Tom Bernard, Jack Valenti, Gary Hart, Bobby Geisler, John Roberdeau, Peter Wilkes, David Permut, James Monaco, Jake Eberts, Larry Bernstein, Julia Phillips, Dennis Hopper, Ruth Vitale, Mark Johnson, Quinn Redeker, Charles Glenn, Richard Zanuck, Sterling Van Wagenen, Gary Foster, Diane Baker, Buffy Shutt, Kathy Jones, Al Ruddy, Ken Lemberger, Ernst Goldschmidt, Charlotte Ermoian, and, most of all, Eric Pleskow and Bill Bernstein, without whom none of it would have been possible. A special tip of the hat to the late Arthur Krim and the late Bob Benjamin is imperative.

During the two years the authors worked to prepare the manuscript, many others also contributed their time and energy. The authors wish to particularly thank the following: our agent,

Andrew Stuart, for his indefatigable support and editorial guidance; Paul Schnee for buying the book at the proposal stage; David Thwaites, Dan Butler, Brad Fischer, Will Taylor, Jeff Steele, Dennis Dalrymple, James Dicker and Lindsey Bayman for their administrative help; Maggie Schmidt for introducing the authors to each other; Maggie Murphy, Sean Penn, Jamie Young, Robert Graham, Art Leeds, Bob Rosen, and Ken Lipper for their thoughts on the manuscript; and Mitchell Ivers, Judith Curr, and their colleagues at Pocket Books for their efforts in putting out the hardcover; Amanda Patten and Atria Books for publishing the paperback edition; and Julie Nathanson for her work on the marketing of the book.

Index